The Limits of Reform

Russian Research Center Studies, 81

The Limits of Reform:
The Ministry of Internal Affairs in Imperial Russia, 1802-1881

Daniel T. Orlovsky

Harvard University Press
Cambridge, Massachusetts
and London, England
1981

Publication of this book has been aided by a grant
from the Andrew W. Mellon Foundation

Library of Congress Cataloging in Publication Data

Orlovsky, Daniel T   1947-
   The limits of reform.

   (Russian Research Center studies; 81)
   Bibliography: p.
   Includes index.
   1. Russia. Ministerstvo vnutrennikh del—
History. I. Title. II. Series: Harvard
University. Russian Research Center. Studies;
81.
JN6550.V5074   354.47063'09   80-18868
ISBN 0-674-53435-2

To my parents

Acknowledgments

It is with the greatest pleasure that I can now thank the individuals and institutions that have helped me to write this book. I owe much to Richard Pipes, who has been an unfailing source of encouragement and advice. Gregory Freeze, Edward Keenan, W. Bruce Lincoln, Brenda Meehan-Waters, Marc Raeff, and Theodore Taranovski read and commented upon various drafts of the manuscript. Whatever clarity it has attained is due in large measure to them. Richard Wortman served as a valuable sounding board for several of its arguments. I especially thank W. Bruce Lincoln for his early help extended to me as a young historian.

I shared a stimulating exchange of ideas over a three-year period with Walter Pintner, Don Karl Rowney, and our companions in the Russian bureaucracy study group. This joint effort was an unusual example of scholarly cooperation and communication. In the Soviet Union I received helpful advice from the late N. G. Sladkevich and from V. G. Chernukha, a leading historian of the Russian Reform Era.

R. Hal Williams, fellow historian and presently Dean of the College at Southern Methodist University, provided constant moral and material support for my work on this book; my colleagues in the SMU Department of History have also encouraged me.

The Russian Research Center of Harvard University provided intellectual sustenance and financial aid while I was a graduate student and has always extended a warm welcome when I have returned to Cambridge.

I acknowledge large debts to the International Research and Exchanges Board and the Fulbright-Hays Doctoral Dissertation and Faculty Research Abroad programs which made possible my extended research in the U.S.S.R. and Helsinki, Finland. I also acknowledge generous grants received from the American Council of Learned Societies and the National Endowment for the Humanities.

I thank the staffs of these libraries and archives for help beyond the ordinary or expected: at Harvard University, the Russian Research Center, Widener, and International Legal Studies libraries; the Slavic Collection of the University of Helsinki library; in the U.S.S.R., the Saltykov-Shchedrin and Lenin libraries, and the Central State Archive of the October Revolution in Moscow (TsGAOR). I owe an enormous debt to the professional staff of the Central State Historical Archive of the U.S.S.R. (TsGIA SSSR) in Leningrad, without whom the book could never have been written.

I thank the University of North Carolina Press for their kind permission to publish here in modified form my contribution to Walter M. Pintner and Don Karl Rowney, eds., *The Bureaucratization of Russian Society from the Seventeenth through the Twentieth Centuries* (Chapel Hill, 1980).

I am grateful to Kathleen Triplett for her patience and industry in making my barely legible draft into beautiful typescript, and for accomplishing it with unfailing good humor.

Last, I thank Alexander, Kate and Matthew, and Barbara for including my experiences as author among the events and pleasures of family life.

Contents

The Limits of Reform

Transliteration in this book follows, with a few exceptions, the Library of Congress system. Archival citations follow the form commonly used: F., *fond* (collection); op., *opis'* (inventory); d., *delo* (case, affair, file); l. or ll., *list* or *listy* (leaf or leaves); ob., *obratnaia* (verso). Dates conform to the old style or Julian calendar, which in the nineteenth century lagged twelve days behind that of the West.

Ministerial Power
in Prerevolutionary Russia

1

This study examines aspects of Russian institutional and political history from the creation of the ministries in 1802 through the reign of Alexander II (1855-1881). The major focus is upon one central government institution, the Ministry of Internal Affairs (MVD). That ministry is taken as a paradigm for asking questions about the nature of Russian autocracy as a system of government and about Russian political culture. The result may be termed an integrated approach to institutional history that attempts to go beneath the surface of political conflict to those institutional forces and structures which shaped, and were shaped by, political actors. This volume, then, is concerned with bureaucracy, a set of related social and political institutions. I examine the structure and personnel of a powerful government institution to determine how they interacted and influenced domestic policy and political conflict in late imperial Russia.

An integrated approach is particularly relevant for understanding the course of late imperial history, since bureaucratic institutions played such a dominant role in it and, indeed, in Russian politics over many centuries. In a sense, this is a study of how a traditional bureaucratic state met the problem of rapid historical change during the last half of the nineteenth century. It is the story of how new institutions are created within traditional political cultures, how they evolve while maintaining features of their predecessors, and how they fare in their dual roles as guardians of tradition and harbingers of innovation. I believe that the history of Russia's bureaucratic institutions contains keys to an understanding of the revolutionary upheavals during the first two decades of the twentieth century. The method is structural in that it looks for those deep patterns of institutional life that serve to define the limits of human action in specific historical and cultural contexts.

After the Crimean War, the Ministry of Internal Affairs was Russia's most powerful ministry of domestic administration and politics. The MVD played a leading role in the preparation and implementation of the 1861 emancipation of the proprietary serfs and the 1864 law that created the *zemstvo* organs of local self-government. By the mid-1860s the MVD directly controlled provincial and district administration and police, censorship, affairs of the nonorthodox religions, orthodox sects, public health and welfare, and a significant number of other economic and social matters. At the height of the Reform Era, the MVD was virtually a state within a state. Its regulatory powers and army of officials affected the lives of Russians and non-Russians of all social estates.

The minister of internal affairs, in part because of his proximity to the tsar, but largely because of the powerful institution at his command, was one of Russia's most influential government figures. The minister participated in the empire's highest policy-making and legislative councils. It is not surprising, then, that several of prerevolutionary Russia's most eminent statesmen, P. A. Valuev, M. T. Loris-Melikov, and P. A. Stolypin, used the MVD as a base in their attempts to unify the tsarist government and initiate reforms to adjust the autocracy to changing political, social, and economic conditions. It is also not surprising that the MVD, under a variety of second-rate, though influential, leaders, was instrumental in, and may be seen as a symbol of, the rapid demise of the Old Regime during the years leading to 1917. The Russian Revolution was largely the result of a deeply rooted institutional crisis. A primary task for historians today is to define the institutional weaknesses that encouraged the radical solutions of 1917.[1]

Even during the reign of Alexander II, reform was not the MVD's entire stock in trade. After the 1861 emancipation, the ministry became an ever more visible symbol of a static conservatism, and the hegemony within the Russian body politic of administrative and police authority became an ideology that at heart was ironically anti-institutional in its belief in the primacy of personal power over that of law. The student of the late imperial MVD must consider why its role changed so rapidly—from prime mover in the emancipation process and haven for progressive bureaucrats, to conservative supporter of autocracy and the landed gentry and uncompromising upholder of administrative power. Within the MVD hierarchy the rise of prominence of men such as A. E. Timashev, D. A. Tolstoi, V. K. von Plehve, and P. N. Durnovo, and of their ideas, must be accounted for.

The study of these problems reveals a close relationship between the fate of the MVD after the Crimean War and the fate of autocracy itself.

The striking legacy of unfinished state business and incomplete reforms that was passed on by the government of Alexander II to its successors testifies to the centrality of the Reform Era in the political history of late imperial Russia. Many of the policy questions examined by the tsarist government from 1905 to 1914, for example, were on the agenda of ministerial departments and legislative commissions during the 1860s and 1870s. These included such vital matters as the creation of a unified cabinet and a form of representation within the legislative process, provincial administrative reform, and the agrarian question. Yet, at that time the government (and the MVD) failed to act decisively. The ministerial system that looked so promising and productive during the early years of the post-Crimean War Reform Era proved unable to cope effectively with the issues it confronted later during the 1860s and 1870s.

The backlog of incomplete reforms and policies, structural weaknesses in government, and conservative statist ideology passed on to successor governments after 1881 had a profound influence on the course of Russian history. The successive crises of Russian autocracy during the late imperial period were in part caused by the inability of Russia's governing institutions to develop and implement policies that could ameliorate specific political and social problems. Here Russia lagged far behind European and, indeed, Asian regimes. The Russian government failed to solve the basic political problem, faced by contemporary governments, of how to harness social change and build political consensus by increasing the political participation of dominant social and economic groups. I have undertaken this study in the hope that the MVD's experience might clarify the political history of the reign of Alexander II, the implications of that reign for the autocracy after 1881, and the parallel experiences of what I term other "conservative renovating regimes" in Europe and Asia during the late nineteenth century.

In Russia the executive ministries were created by a series of laws in 1802 and 1810-11.[2] By mid-century they had become the principal organs of Russian government, a role they retained until the collapse of the Romanov dynasty in 1917. To Russians of all political persuasions, the ministries were synonymous with state power, bureaucratization, and centralization. The ministries and the principles of government they stood for were as symbolic of the Russian autocracy as the tsar himself. This was hardly surprising, since the ministries had statutory responsibility for regulating Russian political, social, economic, and even intellectual life. The men who held ministerial portfolios were among the most powerful of the empire. In addition to commanding their own bureaucratic structures, they participated in high policy- and law-making bodies and acted as the tsar's personal advisers, with the right of direct access and report.

Although no nineteenth-century Russian would dispute the importance of the ministries to the autocracy, not everyone judged them by the same standards. Opinions differed on the principles of government represented by the ministries, their effectiveness in meeting stated goals, and whether, in fact, they promoted the general welfare.

Basically, those who supported ministerial government within the ranks of the bureaucracy fell into two groups, each of which sought justification in Russian tradition. One group that had emerged very clearly by the eve of the Great Reform was "institutionalist" in its belief in the primacy of the empire's regular governing institutions and laws in the face of the traditional personal authority of the monarch.[3] The second group, also defenders of the ministries and, indeed, of the bureaucracy, was "traditionalist" in its deeply held belief that personal authority, which began with the tsar and flowed downward and outward through the institutional fabric of the society, was the ethical foundation, or the "spirit," of Russian statehood.[4] These men also supported the bureaucracy and the state principle, but they owed their first allegiance to the tsar's personal authority and, less overtly, to the traditional clannish and personalized forms of politics and power that emanated from earlier Muscovite political culture.[5]

Although these two groups would be seriously at odds during the reign of Alexander II and would contribute to the cleavage within the government that helped to paralyze the state at crucial moments of choice, their differences were muted and their common support of the ministries more visible during the first decades of ministerial government after 1802. Whether they believed in the primacy of personal authority or of institutions, supporters of the ministries, including ministerial officials and official historians, viewed them as a progressive force in Russian history and as a positive influence on Russian society.[6] During the early decades of the nineteenth century they saw in the ministries the triumph of monocratic forms of organization, the rationalization of functions and division of labor, and the organization of government institutions according to fixed and impersonal rules. Further, the ministries represented the enlightened organs of executive and police power that would lead an uncultured, almost primitive, agrarian society along the path of historical development. To defenders of a strong state, the ministries stood above class interests—as upholders of the general good.[7] When supporters criticized ministerial government, they desired to cure its operational weaknesses rather than alter its unique status in the Russian polity.

This view was expressed in the 1802 Manifesto creating the ministries, and it was repeated one hundred years later in the centennial history of the MVD.[8] According to the 1802 Manifesto, the supreme power's goals of national prosperity and well-being

could only be realized when the government has salutary means, not only to correct all overt manifestations of evil, but especially to eradicate the very roots of such evil, and to deter all causes that might give rise to the destruction of the general or private tranquility, to reveal and anticipate the needs of the people—and to prudently, zealously and actively assist the observance and affirmation of order necessary for all—and to increase the national wealth and the productivity that serve as the foundation for the power and might of the Empire.[9]

The ministries were the "means," and the manifesto emphasized the historical necessity of a well-ordered governing apparatus to the attainment of these ends: "The example of ancient and modern times confirms that the more adequate the means to satisfy the above and the more the rules of state administration are in accordance with these aims—the more harmonious, stable, and complete was the entire body politic and the more satisfied and fortunate was each of its members."[10]

The defenders of the ministries chose as their historical model the regulated, or well-ordered, police state of Peter the Great.[11] They viewed Peter's reforms as a break with Russia's past and the first attempt to create the "means" necessary for construction of an orderly and powerful secular empire. The 1802 Manifesto portrayed the ministries as the heirs of Petrine tradition and philosophy of government, while not taking any notice of the fact that Petrine government itself was an amalgam of Muscovite tradition and European forms and terminology.

Eminent critics of the ministries, who viewed them as forms foreign to Russian tradition, could be heard even at their creation in 1802. A notable example of this early criticism that viewed the ministries as contrary to eighteenth-century government principles (both Petrine and Catherinian) was the 1816 polemic of the Catherinian dignitary (*sanovnik*), Senator D. P. Troshchinskii. Troshchinskii saw the 1811 hierarchically organized ministries as a perversion of Alexander I's intentions. According to Troshchinskii, the monocratic principle was alien to Russian experience and tradition, and the ministries were based solely on the "abstract concepts of newly arisen philosophy."[12] Troshchinskii was one of the architects of the myth of "senatorial" or "collegial" government as the eighteenth-century constitution that conformed to Russian tradition and social realities.[13] Troshchinskii was defending the status of prominent eighteenth-century elite officials and courtiers in the face of a state and bureaucracy that had grown more powerful and freer of any social base. Although he accused the proponents of ministerial bureaucracy of subverting eighteenth-century tradition, his naivete about the history of executive organs, and particularly of the very colleges he praised, is striking.

As the nineteenth century wore on, the critical voices grew louder and louder.[14] As the autocracy's principal apparatus, the ministries represented bureaucratization and centralization. Commentators representing the political spectrum viewed ministerial government not only as alien to Russian tradition, but as arbitrary, inefficient, and hostile to the interests of the Russian people. Ministerial government in Russia was perceived to express perfectly the radical separation of state and society that had long been a fact of Russian life.

Within the government, criticism of the ministries early in the reign of Alexander II centered on promotion of a unified cabinetlike institution to improve the workings of executive power. It was precisely the independence of the ministries, as supported by the fact that each minister was subordinate only to the tsar rather than to commonly held policy objectives, that resulted in 1857 in the creation of a new unifying collegial organ for the executive branch, the Council of Ministers. This council was meant to function alongside the older Committee of Ministers which was created at the same time as the ministries. The council remained secret for four years and played a relatively minor role for the remaining twenty years of the reign. It epitomized the conflict between institutions and autocratic personal authority in prerevolutionary Russia. During the first two years of Alexander's reign, the impetus to create the council grew out of the widely held belief of such diverse writters and publicists as I. S. Aksakov, M. P. Pogodin, M. A. Dmitriev, M. P. Pozen, P. F. Dolgorukov, and N. A. Mel'gunov that it was necessary to end the fragmented, personalized nature of government authority. From within the bureaucracy, P. A. Valuev and N. A. Zherebtsov argued in a similar vein, the latter submitting to Alexander a memorandum titled "On the Organization of the Ministries and the Ministry of Finance in Particular." Following M. Speranskii's ideas and European models, Zherebtsov called for institutionalized collegiality and control of the ministries to cure Russia's crisis in executive power.[15]

In late 1857 Alexander commissioned P. N. Bludov to prepare a project for a Council of Ministers. Bludov and A. Sukovkin, the director of affairs of the Committee of Ministers, argued that Russia needed to nurture or institutionalize a "political tradition" of collegial discussion at the top level of ministerial government that would help create a unified "political system." Bludov and Sukovkin also recommended institutionalization of this collegiality within the executive branch in the new Council of Ministers to be chaired by the tsar. It was hoped that the council would eliminate the worst features of disconnectedness (*razobshchennost'*) among ministries and the uncontrollable, secretive, and highly personalized system of "most loyal" (*vsepoddanneishii*) reports that were perceived to be hindering articulation of effective government policy. The council, created to eliminate, or at least alleviate, the problems described, was more specifically mandated to discuss regularly important legislative projects, "most loyal" reports (except the highly secret), and all vital matters pertaining to economic, estate, and administrative reform.

In practice, however, the Council of Ministers cannot properly be said to have been institutionalized. Because the council was chaired by Alexander, the tsar's personal authority and traditional relationship to his ministers was bound to dominate. Further, the council met irregularly and considered insignificant matters. Symbolically, its existence was hidden so effectively from those outside the membership that both pre- and postrevolutionary historians made the mistake of believing it to have been created only in 1861, when the official decree announcing its existence was published.[16]

This secrecy, irregularity, and preoccupation with insignificant affairs despite the tsar's mandate for unity and his physical presence offer good evidence of the influence of personal power in both the self-image and actual workings of Russian autocracy. In his heart, Alexander II, much like his father, Nicholas I, and his son, Alexander III, was deeply hostile to any institutions that threatened to weaken the personal authority that was inextricably bound up with tsardom.

In late 1861 a group of high officials, this time with P. A. Valuev as spokesman, tried again to reform the executive branch in conjunction with simultaneous efforts to establish a form of representation in the provinces (the future zemstvos) and in the central government's legislative process. Alexander's response to Valuev's plan to reform the older Committee of Ministers exemplified the difficulties of institutional reform in late imperial Russia. Without admitting his own interest in preserving the very confusion in government that was to be remedied, Alexander blamed the ministers for unwillingness to bring the most important matters to either the already moribund Council of Ministers or to the Committee of Ministers. Alexander recognized the existence of ministerial sabotage, but was unwilling to sacrifice or temper his personal role in favor of institutional change. He declared that he would tolerate procedural reform only in the new Council of Ministers "in my presence" (*v moem prisutstvii*).[17] Thus he adamantly refused to permit creation of a cabinetlike organ to be chaired by someone other than the autocrat. The Council of Ministers was then "officially" created, a solution that in practice failed to unite the central government. The anti-institutional and personal had triumphed again, strengthening and helping to perpetuate the component of ministerial power that derived from the autocrat's power position.

Criticism continued during the late nineteenth and early twentieth centuries. By then, classic statements were made about how the ministries had become symbols of a type of government that was less and less tolerable to educated Russians. In 1906, S. P. Pokrovskii published a polemic[18] in answer to the series of official histories of the ministries issued in 1902 on their hundredth anniversary. He viewed even the best of those official histories as "tendentious" volumes "alien to the scientific spirit" and "possessing an entirely official (*kazennyi*) character." Unlike earlier critics, however, Pokrovskii saw the ministries not at odds with eighteenth-century traditions but as a continuation of a traditional Russian political culture stretching far into the Muscovite past. He saw them, in fact, as representing the highest stage in the centuries-long history of Russian government institutions. Pokrovskii reified the historical fact of the ministerial hegemony and its ethos into a theoretical principle expressing the nature of Russia's constitution and the state ideology of autocracy. He used the phrase "ministerial power" to represent both the institutions and their ideology. To Pokrovskii, the ministries and their supporting institutional components affirmed and perpetuated the historical gulf between state and society in Russia. He aimed to clarify the "essence of the bureaucratic organization of ministerial power" as a spokesman for a society dissatisfied "with the all-consuming guardianship" of that power.[19]

Pokrovskii was a supporter of the Union of Liberation who welcomed the revolutionary events of 1905, and obviously his political position influenced his analysis of "ministerial power." He looked back to the patrimonial principles of the crown prince and the well-elaborated bureaucratic regime centered in the *prikazy* of Muscovy as the historical sources of ministerial power.[20] In his view, Russian governing power had for centuries pursued its own interests and viewpoints and by its very nature had never served the people. Although Peter I had created the colleges and Senate, and Alexander I the ministries to "restrain the despotism of our government," ministerial power had proved too strong. It continued to follow its own path, "creating for itself an exceptional position in Russian state life." Ministerial power "did not permit the development within state life of the foundations of society's initiatives. In its strivings to secure its uncontrolled and irresponsible position, Ministerial power sacrificed everything. It even sacrificed the best of the reforms that woke the nation from its lethargic sleep—the reforms of Alexander II."[21] Pokrovskii attacked that power for undermining the Great Reforms, for fighting society's growing consciousness at every step, and for inactivity or bankrupt policies that left the crucial issues of state life unresolved until the landmark events of 1905 spurred on by the liberation movement.

Pokrovskii portrays a government that tried to perpetuate, under rapidly changing conditions, an interventionist and regulatory police power based on bureaucratically written and enforced positive law. From its self-proclaimed position above estate interests, Russian autocracy, through its ministerial apparatus, sought to perpetuate its independence and the separation of state and society.

Pokrovskii's analysis fades into a rather standard and superficial survey of Russian political history from pre-Petrine times through the counter-reforms of the late nineteenth century, and is written from the liberal point of view. He offers no information about the government or, more specifically, about the ministries as institutions. His categories, though potentially valuable, are vague and his research limited.

Pokrovskii's notion of "ministerial power" can, however, be developed as a concept embracing both the institutional and ideological aspects of Russian government. A study of the history of ministerial government in Russia during the nineteenth century can provide a deeper understanding of Russian institutions as reservoirs of tradition, as defenders of ideology and interests, and as shapers of men. It is important to state at the outset a working definition of ministerial power, or of the synonyms for it used by nineteenth-century bureaucrats, administrative or police power. The doctrine of ministerial power that permeated the Russian government during the nineteenth century was an amalgam of Muscovite tradition and practice, European police state ideologies of the seventeenth and early eighteenth centuries, and borrowings from the Napoleonic regime in France.[22]

The apparatus of Muscovite absolutism, inherited by Peter the Great and reshaped with the aid of the police state and mercantilist doctrines, differed from its European counterparts in both the bureaucracy's greater independence from the social estates and in the fact that the social estates themselves were far weaker politically and economically.[23] While it is possible to argue that in European absolutism, the bureaucracy, though nominally independent, represented government of and for aristocratic interests, even recent Marxist scholarship has admitted the possibility of distinct types of absolutism in Europe, eastern Europe, and Asia.[24] These models prudently reject any dogmatic or facile connection between state power and particular social groups in areas of the world that did not share in the historical experiences of classical antiquity and feudalism.

Discussion of the features of Russian ministerial or police power must begin with the often underestimated fact that Russian lands had been ruled since at least the fifteenth century by a bureaucratic apparatus that possessed a high degree of organization and considerable professional skill.[25] The traditional viewpoints embodied in this apparatus and handed down to subsequent generations included a belief in the primacy of state power and the legitimacy of state intervention in virtually all aspects of social and economic life (and, indeed, in intellectual and religious life as well).

Although intervention did not always occur, it was ever present as a moral category, a legitimate function of those who monopolized political power. The Russian tradition of police state interventionism was expressed in the terms "guardianship" or "tutelage" (*popechitel'stvo* or *opeka*) as applied to society as a whole or to particular groups within it.[26] It had remarkable staying power and adaptability and, indeed, legitimized Peter's reforms and also survived them. Russian state interventionism was well established before the European police state ideologies that many historians still believe came to Russia with the Petrine reforms. Traditional interventionism in Russia was reinforced, strengthened, and relegitimized during the European enlightenment and French Revolution at the very time that the police state came under attack in Europe and underwent a process of radical, though subtle, transformation.[27]

The doctrine of ministerial or administrative power rejected an autonomous legal order.[28] Autonomous legal order (sometimes called "rule of law") refers specifically to the type of legal doctrine that arose only in Europe as the product of compromise between the crown, the powerful social estates of the aristocracy and the bourgeoisie, and the bureaucracies that claimed growing independence from crown and society. The primary characteristics of autonomous legal order are the theoretical separation of administration from adjudication and legislation, the growth of a method of legal reasoning independent of the mode of reasoning that prevails in the political sphere, and the existence of a corporate body of professional jurists and civil servants to operate the legal system. The development of an autonomous legal order in European states weakened the legitimate police power of the state and increased the individual's power to defend himself against the state through new legal means. In contrast to autonomous legal order, ministerial power in Russia was based on a type of bureaucratic positive law that remained the ideal of tsars and most officials throughout the eighteenth and nineteenth centuries.[29] This public law of the classic bureaucratic empires' conceived of and implemented by the crown and its minions, had served to justify the exigencies of the moment but had not proven its political adaptability under the greater pressures of the nineteenth century.

An outstanding characteristic of high ministerial officials in Russia throughout the nineteenth century was the deeply rooted belief that political matters were their concern solely and that political acts outside the chancery walls were illegitimate if not treasonous. Further, society, in its uncivilized and selfish condition, could not be trusted to participate in politics. A corollary of this thinking was co-optation, the tendency of the state to make official, or bureaucratize, any budding political association. This widespread characteristic of the ministerial power ethos mitigated against expedient political solutions to problems inherent in renovation of the traditional regime.

Since it was believed that all politics were subsumed under administration, it followed that legislation and reform in all areas were believed to be matters of administrative adjustment.[30] This attitude was held even by some of the nineteenth century's most noted reformers, such as P. D. Kiselev and L. A. Perovskii, whose reform projects stopped far short of necessary political transformation while promoting demonstrable improvements in administrative technique.

The tsar was widely seen as a symbol of legitimacy and as the center of a web of personalized power relationships in Russian political culture. Several recent studies have shown with precision how allegiance to the tsar's personal authority and to kinship bonds persisted over the centuries in the minds of career officials and other elites competing for political power.[31] These traditional attitudes persisted and coexisted with other characteristics that would most often be associated with a more rationalist or modern bureaucratic ethos that upheld the primacy of institutions or of rule of law.

A comment by Valuev (minister of internal affairs, 1861-1868) that the tsar's ministers were no more than his oriental slaves or personal servants, an anomalous situation considering their positions as heads of powerful government institutions, cannot be dismissed.[32] But in nineteenth-century Russia, even at the height of the power of ministerial government, this was incontrovertible fact. Obviously, the tsar could not personally control all affairs of state and he depended on the ministerial apparatus for policy making and implementation. Still, he could appoint and dismiss ministers at will, elevate men who were not ministers (and therefore outside the regular government institutions) to positions of influence, and accept or reject the collective wisdom of all advisory or law-making bodies. This arbitrariness in Russian political life was noted often by contemporaries of the last four tsars. A personalized form of political power began with the tsar and was reproduced in the hearts and minds of officials and those who were co-opted into a state of semi-officialdom at all levels of the state hierarchy. It resulted in the clearest expression of the tension between government by personalities and government by institutions. Further, widespread adherence to the personalized power principle in Russia suggests a strong reason for the obstinate willingness of her last autocrats to resist necessary and self-evident political changes.

As T. Taranovski so aptly put it, the tsar was caught in a bind. No longer fully master of his house because of the growth in complexity of government and the degree of institutionalization that it entailed, the tsar could still stubbornly obstruct the development of those institutions while making certain that the personal-power principle embedded in them was never extinguished. Whether one speaks of Alexander II or his supposedly more conservative son, Alexander III, the dynamics of royal defense were similar. Indoctrinated with traditions of personal duty to the exalted position of tsar, with its images of patriarchal paternalism, Alexander II worked hard to keep at bay the forces of institutional and political change. Although in some measure limited by the high bureaucracy, Alexander II successfully played factions against one another and never permitted individual ministers or groups of officials to institutionalize, and therefore possibly perpetuate, their fleeting victories. Reformers and visionaries, as hateful as they might be, could be used to shore up the system, particularly in times of great stress, but only so long as their activities and projects did not threaten the operational political culture and its ministerial power ideology. Taranovski's conclusions about the nature of autocratic power as personal power and its implications for Russian politics seem to be valid for the entire nineteenth century as well as the early twentieth. What existed, then, on the eve of the Great Reforms was a bureaucratic ethos that, with minor adjustments and reformulations, had become internalized over a long time period by a great many ministerial officials close to the center of power.

An underlying assumption of the present study is that in any polity, and especially in Russia where the bureaucratic tradition was so entrenched, governmental institutions themselves act as reservoirs of tradition and of deeply held tenets of political culture.[33] Though the ethos of ministerial power was expressed well before the creation in 1802 of executive organs called ministries, the ministries from the beginning performed the dual role of promoting not only the traditional political culture but also change. The ministries (and particularly the MVD) never relinquished this dual role. The resulting tension was most harmful to the political stability of the empire.

The Structure of the Ministry of Internal Affairs, 1802-1881

2

Despite the contributions of prerevolutionary and contemporary scholars, little is known about the organization, operation, or personnel of the ministries.[1] Further, no systematic effort has been made to trace their evolution after 1802 or to examine how their development influenced events. How and when the ministries attained political hegemony remain obscure, as do the strengths and weaknesses of ministerial government.

The ministries created on September 8, 1802, were more innovative in name than in structure.[2] Though ostensibly the 1802 law represented the re-creation of monocratic authority in central government executive institutions, in fact it simply placed ministers at the head of eight deteriorated collegial organs that had not disappeared during the late eighteenth century.

The ministries were reservoirs of bureaucratic tradition, an embodiment of forms and procedures inherited directly from the Muscovite prikazy through the Petrine colleges. Though much could be written on the similarities between the prikazy and the ministries, a look at the intermediate phase of the Petrine colleges suffices to establish the institutional continuities.[3]

The Petrine colleges have been portrayed as a distinct phase of the history of Russian executive institutions—as Peter's attempt to create more efficient and less arbitrary central government organs on the basis of Western models.[4] Scholars generally accept Peter's explanation of the advantages of the collegial principle over the monocratic, as is found, for example, in the spiritual regulation of 1721.[5] This view recognizes the immediate reason for the creation of the colleges as the autocracy's fiscal and military needs. Peter knew that these requirements were not being met by his earlier decentralization of the government or by the new Senate, which was inadequate as an administrative organ.[6]

Thus, the colleges are portrayed as a break with the past, as a new beginning or a qualitative leap into an era of intensive bureaucratization that lasted throughout the eighteenth and nineteenth centuries. The colleges are seen as an expression of the "regulated" Petrine police state, and in form and function they appear comparable to the institutions of the European absolutist monarchies.

Yet the collegial principle, as embodied in Peter's colleges, contradicts the Weberian concept of bureaucratization. In theory, collegiality, or decision-making by majority vote, is the opposite of monocracy, the sine qua non of Weberian bureaucracy. As Weber put it, "collegiality is a means of limiting monocratic authority rather than of promoting efficiency."[7] He noted that monarchs often used collegiality in highest government councils to play off interests and points of view to get the widest possible spread of information, and to keep all the members in check. He also, however, emphasized that in executive organs collegiality almost inevitably involved obstacles to precise, clear, and above all rapid decisions.[8]

One might still argue that in Russia, as in the West, collegiality was only transitional and used for a period of time by absolutist monarchs set on maintaining the independence and supremacy of the crown.[9] In Prussia, for example, monocracy rapidly replaced collegiality during the late seventeenth and early eighteenth centuries as the bureaucracy attained its quasi-independent status in relation to both crown and aristocracy. Such an interpretation might be applied to Peter's establishing the colleges at least in part to end the arbitrariness and willfulness (*proizvol*) of the *starye sud'i*, the powerful men in command of the *prikazy*.[10] As a representative absolutist monarch, Peter certainly did much to eliminate possible rival centers of power within the new empire.

A brief examination of the organization and history of the Petrine colleges, however, makes apparent the problems inherent in using them to define a distinct stage in Russian institutional history. First, Peter had eliminated some of the prikazy earlier in the eighteenth century at the time of his provincial reforms (1708);[11] and similarly, certain prikazy, such as the Siberian prikaz, continued to exist under Peter's successors. Second, the structure of the colleges as expressed in the *General'nyi reglament* (1720) and other Petrine legislation reveals a fundamental connection to the organization of the prikazy. Both the legislation and Petrine administrative practice reveal that the name "college" for Peter's executive institutions is misleading. The actual *collegium*, or the group of men—councilors and assessors—who were to make decisions by majority vote, was only the highest level of formal decision-making authority. In addition to the collegium, the colleges consisted of a president (appointed by the tsar), a vice-president, and a staff of professional career officials organized into a chancery directly subordinate to the president.[12] Because the higher-ranking members of the collegium had little administrative experience, the chancery officials were responsible for setting agenda, preparing materials for decision, and keeping written records of day-to-day operations. This permanent "chancery element," headed by the secretary, was inherited from the prikaz system with its *d'iaki* and *pod'-iachie*, and must be viewed as an essential element of continuity in Russian institutional history.[13]

The chanceries immediately began to dominate the conduct of affairs within the colleges.[14] The slowness inherent in the collegial decision-making procedure was compounded by the general unsuitability of collegium appointees for serious roles in deciding the affairs of state. Peter's institutions foundered, as would often be the case in the future. He could not find enough competent or literate Russians (of sufficiently high social standing) to occupy the eighty to ninety positions at the collegium level.[15] While setting up the colleges, Peter was to seek out foreigners suitable for these positions. Solov'ev describes the complaints of the president of the Justice College, Matveev, about the shortage of competent collegium personnel. According to Matveev, the best people had been attracted to other colleges, and the notables (*znatnyi osob*) left to his organization were undermining the efficiency of the college because of their inability to cope with the decisions they were called upon to make. Matveev claimed that although the Justice College combined the functions of at least seven of the old prikazy, the former *Moskovskii prikaz* was able to decide "ten times the number of cases" completed in the new college.[16]

A. D. Gradovskii has shown that the collegium rapidly became a haven for men often illiterate, unfit for military or other service, and unsuitable for high-level administrative work.[17] He recognized that the colleges were dominated by the chanceries and their secretaries, but there was another element in the colleges inherited from Muscovy that undermined the collegial principle it was supposed to serve. This was the office of the president. Although the president was theoretically first among equals, with the right to cast a decisive vote in case of ties, he dominated his peers from the very beginning. Peter wanted the most reliable men possible as the first presidents and he chose either trusted members of the established social elite or personal friends whom he had raised to prominent positions.[18] Despite the detailed *General'nyi reglament* and other laws, the presidents, and in

some cases the vice-presidents, had enormous authority when compared to collegium members. Their higher level of competence, proximity to the tsar, direct control over the chanceries, and powers of
appointment, nomination, and reward combined to make the presidents more representative of the monocratic (*edinolichnyi*) tradition
in Russia than of a distinctly new principle (collegiality) borrowed
from the West.

To manage the affairs of state, Peter and his successors were forced
to rely upon men and the established practices and forms of the past as
expressed in the chancery element and monocratic principle. The stub-
bornness of tradition and operational weaknesses caused Peter to
create the General-Procuracy and provide background to the igno-
minious fate of the colleges during the eighteenth century.[19]

The *general-prokuror* was an office created by Peter the Great to
unify and control the major central provincial and government institutions created by his reforms. Although the office declined in power
under Peter's immediate successors, by the 1770s under Catherine the
Great (1762-1796), and under her successor Paul I (1796-1801), the
general-prokuror had become something very close to a prime minister for domestic affairs.[20] Because of the weakness of the colleges, the
empire's central executive organs, the general-prokuror had assumed
during Catherine's reign responsibility for virtually all major branches
of domestic administration. By the end of the eighteenth century, the
general-prokuror acted as a combination of the future ministers of internal affairs, finance, and justice.[21] His authority, however, did not
have strong institutional underpinnings. It derived from the tsar's personal commission (*poruchenie*) to a trusted and capable individual.
The general-prokuror was technically attached to the ruling Senate
and had to rely upon the chancery officials of the Senate departments
to translate his will into actions.[22] By the 1780s neither the general-
prokuror nor the central government as a whole had viable executive
institutions for the conduct of domestic administration. The situation
had deteriorated so much that Catherine simply closed down many
colleges and transferred their functions to departments of the Senate
under the general supervision of the general-prokuror. Thus the College of Manufactures was closed in 1779, and the Main Salt Bureau in
1782.[23]

During the reign of Paul I there were important developments with
regard to the neglected and decayed central executive institutions.[24]
Paul believed in a centralized state administered by soldiers and officials who placed the autocracy ahead of class interests. In addition to
relying heavily on the general-prokuror, Paul reopened the colleges
closed by his mother, and began to transform them into organs quite

close in structure and function to the ministries created by his son
Alexander I in 1802. He unified the colleges concerned with financial
and economic matters into a larger Expedition of State Economy, and
at the head of several executive institutions he placed a new official,
the main director (*glavnyi direktor*). Subordinate officials of the colleges reported to the main director, who, in turn, reported directly to
the tsar.[25] Further, Paul created new organs, such as the Department
of Crown Properties (*udelov*) and the Main Post Directorate, that
were ministerial in everything but name.[26]

Paul I intended to create an entire system of executive ministries. In
his undated "Memorandum on the Creation of the Various Parts of
the State Structure," he outlined a set of central ministries very similar
to that which would be created in 1802. His plan called for "seven
main departments" each with its own minister. These were Justice,
Finance, War, Navy, Foreign Affairs, Commerce, and Treasury.[27]
Paul's plan did not include a ministry of internal affairs. Although the
plan foreshadowed the adoption of ministerial forms for central executive organs, it looked back in its division of functions to the original
Petrine colleges. Internal affairs meant mainly fiscal affairs, or administration geared to supply the state with the manpower and economic
resources to support the military and foreign policy establishments as
well as the court and the remaining governing apparatus. Three of the
seven proposed ministries had responsibility for fiscal or economic
matters, and their functions seemed designed to carry out the goals of
the eighteenth-century mercantilist police states. Neither political
police nor common law enforcement functions were included in the
jurisdictions of Paul's proposed ministries. Here, too, Paul's system
looked backward, rather than toward the new developments in European administration that influenced the authors of the 1802 law.

The origin of the 1802 plan to introduce either a unified cabinetlike
"ministry" or the separate executive ministries remains clouded.[28] According to A. N. Filippov, a prerevolutionary expert on Russian institutions, the idea was first proposed by Alexander's Swiss tutor, La-
Harpe, in response to the tsar's sense of helplessness at the news of
widespread famine in Siberia. Filippov argued that it was impossible
to determine precisely the origin of the ministerial plan because such
ideas were in the air at the time and may well have been mentioned by
any individual member of the "unofficial committee." Filippov viewed
Novosil'tsev's memorandum on administrative reform (April 1802) as
the immediate basis for the creation of the ministries in September of
that year.[29]

The Stroganov papers, published in 1903, make clearer the steps
leading to the creation of the ministries and simultaneous reform of

the Senate.[30] Apparently, the idea of ministries was first mentioned in a Stroganov memorandum as early as May 1801.[31] At that time there was no disagreement on the need to create either a unified ministry (or cabinet), or the individual executive ministries. These ideas were mentioned again in memoranda by Stroganov, Kochubei, and Novosil'tsev between July 1801 and March 1802. The final manifesto was worked out in two sessions, April 11 and 21, 1802, at which Novosil'tsev read a draft paper on the creation of a unified ministry divided into eight branches of administration.[32]

The lack of debate on the proposed reform can best be explained by the deep historical roots of the monocratic principle in Russian executive institutions, the concrete steps taken to solidify this tradition by Paul I, and the proclivities of the "young friends," in whose name the ideas for ministries were submitted, for western European ideas and institutions. The memoranda and discussions of the young friends indicate that European models, most notably France and, to a lesser extent, England, figured heavily in their recommendations.

Similar suggestions came from outside the tsar's immediate circle of young friends. S. Vorontsov suggested a unified ministry be modeled after the British cabinet.[33] Vorontsov, a supporter of the old aristocracy, thought such a cabinet would limit, or at least influence, the power of the autocrat in much the same way as the Supreme Privy Council from 1726 to 1731. In addition, the cabinet would create a unified and energetic policy.

That the unified ministry promised by the 1802 Manifesto was not created during Alexander's reign was due, in part, to the fears of the tsar and his young advisers that the ministry might become a stronghold of oligarchic interests.[34] At the very least it might inhibit any further reform plans of the young friends who viewed themselves as spokesmen of a state power above class interests. The 1802 ministries, therefore, grew logically from the Russian administrative tradition and statist ideology hostile to oligarchy. They were heavily imbued with tradition and they became the apparatus of an autocracy that rejected attempts of traditional social elites to place limits upon it.

According to the law of September 8, 1802, the mandate of the minister of internal affairs (the law was not an institutional charter) was "to look after the well-being of the people everywhere, the tranquility, peace, and public services of the entire Empire. He has under his direction all sectors of state industry, with the exception of mining, and also the construction and maintenance of all public buildings. Above that he is given the responsibility to endeavor by all means to avert shortages of food and all other life necessities."[35] Although a single executive organ had never been charged with such a broad mandate and variety of functions, the monocratic authority of the minister of internal affairs clearly was rooted in the structural tradition of the prikazy. In personal power and prestige, the office was similar to the General-Procuracy of the eighteenth century.

In functional terms, the College of Manufactures and the Main Salt Bureau and the *Preobrazhenskii prikaz* in the police sphere were the MVD's closest antecedents. The MVD was to function in three major areas of administration. First, the provincial governors were to act as ministry agents to enforce the will of the central government in the provinces.[36] Second, the MVD was to operate as a ministry of trade and industry and as the government's executive organ for relations with various social estates (*sosloviia*). The legal status and economic activities of the estates, agriculture, the cities, and internal trade and manufacturing were regulated by the MVD. It also was to administer the autocracy's rudimentary public health and philanthropic services. All these functions derived from the MVD's mandate as guardian of society and its economic well-being.

A third and closely related area of MVD responsibility was the maintenance of public order. Enforcing the laws and apprehending criminals were the sphere of a "lower" executive police that also had considerable administrative duties, while the upkeep of public morals and the active prevention of subversion and other crimes was the responsibility of the "higher," or political, police.[37] With the MVD, general administration, economic and social matters, and various kinds of police work were merged within a single central executive institution. Giving these broad police functions to the MVD was fully consonant with both the Russian tradition of ministerial or administrative power and the old European notion of the police state.

The uneasy coexistence of various economic and police functions in the MVD would remain a constant theme in Russian prerevolutionary institutional history. Here Russia differed markedly from western and central Europe, where there was a gradual professionalization of both police and bureaucracy. Petty administrative duties were taken away from ordinary policemen, while responsibility for major state social and economic policies was shifted to more specialized bureaucratic organs as well as to parliamentary institutions. In Russia, however, the less perfect separation between the police and the bureaucracy came much later in the nineteenth century, and there were severe consequences (see Chapter 5). The ministry's role as agent of social and economic change and its role as guardian of order conflicted, greatly influencing MVD ideology and policy. The MVD was in a state of constant tension during the first half of the nineteenth century, but, as will be shown, the tension became particularly acute during the reign of Alexander II.

The earliest MVD organizational changes included the gradual elim-

ination of collegial structure and culminated in the 1811 institution of
the ministries. At the same time, certain police functions were removed from the MVD and assumed by an independent Ministry of
Police.

Basically, the 1802 statute expressed the traditional personalized
power of commissions (*porucheniia*) by which a specific problem or
an entire branch of administration was assigned to an individual who
was in the tsar's confidence. The wording of the manifesto corrobo-
rates this. It reads as an order to the minister, and outlines his responsibilities instead of those of an institution. Because the minister
reported personally to the tsar and also because such important ministries as the MVD were initially headed by the tsar's young friends, the
Senate's theoretical control over the new ministries was quickly undermined. Thus, there existed another source of tension—between older
personalized authority and that firmly rooted in institutions.

The manifesto created no monocratic departments to fulfill the various administrative functions assigned to the MVD. Instead, the minister simply inherited a potpourri of old colleges and bureaus. The
manifesto did not specify the interrelations of the minister, the colleges, the provincial administrative organs, or marshals of the nobility. The major structural innovation of the manifesto was the creation
of a chancery to aid the minister in controlling the ministry's subordinate parts.[38] This chancery, the Department of Internal Affairs, was
the seed from which the MVD and its departments would grow. When
the department was created in 1803, it exhibited a hierarchical organization with responsibilities delegated according to administrative subject. The director was subordinate to the minister. Four subsections,
called expeditions, were headed by chiefs (*nachal'niki ekspeditsii*) who
reported to the director.[39] Unlike the minister or assistant minister, the
director was a permanent career official. (Speranskii was the first to
hold this post in the MVD). The director, experienced in administrative matters and able to prepare memoranda for the minister's use,
was the functional heir of the d'iaki in the prikazy and the secretaries
in the eighteenth-century colleges.

In addition to the old colleges and the new department, the 1802-
1803 laws provided for one assistant minister (*tovarishch ministra*)
and an advisory group of the nobility who had close ties to the provinces.[40] This group was to gather historical and statistical materials on
the provinces and act as a reservoir of trusted co-workers available for
special missions.[41]

The absence of structural innovation in the 1802 legislation was recognized by contemporaries who viewed the new ministries as little
more than the old executive organs under a new name.[42] The minis-

tries lacked departmental structure and had few levels of authority. Structural transformation of the new ministries required only the elimination of the old colleges and bureaus by absorption into the new expeditions (*ekspeditsii*), as was done in the Department of Internal Affairs.

To this end a memorandum that reaffirmed monocracy in government executive institutions[43] was issued and accepted by the tsar on July 18, 1803. Though submitted in the name of the first minister of internal affairs, Prince V. P. Kochubei, its author was M. M. Speranskii, one of imperial Russia's most outstanding statesmen. The Kochubei report provided a model for a series of structural reforms in all ministries that culminated in the redefinition of the ministerial system in 1810-1811. It tackled the deficiencies of the old colleges and the newly created ministries, focusing on the relationship of the MVD to the College of Manufactures and the Main Salt Bureau. Kochubei stated that he could act only as a main director of the type that existed during Paul's reign; that is, he passively received weekly reports from the colleges and was called upon to decide the most trivial matters. After a review of the historical origins of the colleges in the eighteenth century and their subsequent decline, Kochubei listed the weaknesses revealed in the first months of MVD operations.[44] The shortcomings cited were (1) slowness, (2) inadequate or absent division of functions and hierarchical gradations of decision-making authority, (3) excessive formalism and enormous amounts of meaningless correspondence, (4) inadequate responsibility of officials. Kochubei claimed that these problems prevented his carrying out his mandate as minister of internal affairs. His solution was to unify functions according to rational criteria and to install the monocratic principle at all ministry levels: "The proper movement of affairs through the levels of government (*postepennost'*) and the division of labor is the true rule for the completion (*sovershenstvo*) of all varieties of affairs."[45] The report proposed to abolish the colleges and to transfer their executive responsibilities to the expanded monocratic expeditions of the Department of Internal Affairs.

But the report did not stop with this bare outline of a new structure. It defined *postepennost'*, rendered in English as departmentalism, as the justification for adopting monocratic and hierarchical forms. Within its own competence, each level of authority to be established must remain autonomous, yet fully answerable for its performance. The levels would form a ladder leading up to the minister, and, if each performed according to the theory, vast improvements in administrative procedure could be anticipated.

The report defined in detail the limits of each level of authority within the new expeditions of the Department of Internal Affairs.[46] It also gave concrete examples of the forms for all legitimate written communications. The definitions of authority and forms were direct and simple, and as a practical guide for officials they went beyond the discussions of procedure in such documents as the Petrine general regulation (general'nyi reglament).

The disorder which had plagued Russian executive institutions throughout the eighteenth century and particularly the decline in effectiveness of the colleges had to be overcome. However, it should be remembered that Speranskii's solution called for revival of pre-Petrine chancery principles that had persisted in muted form during the eighteenth century.[47]

A word should be said about the men who were the first ministers of internal affairs and the major MVD activities under their guidance. Alexander's choices of Prince V. P. Kochubei as the first minister and Count P. A. Stroganov as assistant minister left no doubt that the MVD had been created to play the leading role in domestic administration.[48] Both belonged to the select group of young friends, the tsar's closest advisers during the early years of the reign. The most notable presence was M. M. Speranskii, the first director of the Department of Internal Affairs. The son of a village clergyman, Speranskii was an experienced career civil servant who had already served in the General-Procuracy and the chanceries of the Senate and governor-general of St. Petersburg. Kochubei used Speranskii's fertile mind as a source of ideas and projects (such as the 1803 memorandum) which were presented to the tsar in the minister's name. Speranskii performed the role of the professional seventeenth-century d'iak in relation to his aristocratic superior. After 1807 Speranskii became the tsar's personal adviser, and the man most responsible for the transformation of Russian institutions in 1810-1811.[49]

Speranskii well understood the intimate connection between men and institutions. His writings consistently emphasized both the rational organization of executive institutions and the need to raise the level of culture in Russian society to bring about innovations within institutions.[50] Speranskii idealized the possibilities of effective bureaucratic government. He knew the goals of departmentalism and defined levels of authority were impossible without first producing trained and educated officials to serve at all levels of the bureaucratic hierarchy.[51] Without a large increase in the number of such officials, Russia would repeat the experience of Peter and the collegial system in the eighteenth century. Without a transformation in the nature of Russian officialdom, the finely wrought hierarchies and procedures would never be actualized. Speranskii proposed to meet the need for hierarchy and division of labor by creating the ministerial departments.

To transform officialdom, he proposed new universities and other institutions of higher, elite education (most notably the Imperial Lycée at Tsarskoe Selo), and laws such as the 1809 decree that made examinations compulsory for middle- and high-ranking civil servants.[52] He also established as a legal principle the idea that education brought service benefits (such as automatic rank). Speranskii first articulated the ideas behind these plans during his early service as Kochubei's department director in the MVD.

Ministers displayed a variety of social and career characteristics, but remained the personal appointees and servants, though not always the personal friends, of the tsar. They were dependent usually on the tsar's continued support to remain in office or to carry out programs. Directors tended to be experienced career officials who almost never became ministers. Ministers who had exceptionally able directors and who knew best how to use their talents found that their own power and influence were enhanced.

Under Kochubei and Kurakin (1801-1810), MVD activities involved mainly basic administrative tasks and internal reorganization.[53] On a day-to-day basis, ministry officials were concerned with supervision of grain stores, agriculture, tax collection, army recruitment, philanthropy, manufacturing regulation, the collection of civil obligations (*zemskie povinnosti*), public health, and the maintenance of law and order.[54] In the legislative sphere, Kochubei participated in the sessions of Alexander's Permanent Council (*Nepremennyi Sovet*) which wrote the law of February 20, 1803, creating the possibility for landowners to free their serfs as "free cultivators."[55] The MVD was responsible for supervising this voluntary manumission, but it was also responsible for averting the twin evils of peasant uprising and gentry *fronde*. Kochubei immediately addressed a circular to provincial governors instructing them to assure landowners that the law was in no way intended to "weaken the existing order between landowners and peasants."[56] Not surprisingly, the 1803 law had no impact on the institution of serfdom. Although the MVD would remain a necessary participant in any attempt to alter fundamental social relationships in Russia, it was not yet ready to advocate and assist in the abolition of serfdom as it would fifty years later.

From the beginning, the MVD had potential as a power base for those who wished to unify and direct government domestic policy. The minister was one of the autocracy's highest domestic policy-makers. In these early years, however, the ministry remained a weak institution. The power of Kochubei and his successor, Prince A. B. Kurakin, derived more from their personal standing with the tsar than from the institution they commanded.

From 1810 to 1819, the tension eased between the MVD's economic and social functions, and its police role. In 1810-1811, all ministries were reorganized according to Speranskii's ideas.[57] Functions were redistributed among and within the ministries, and their structures and procedures were codified in detail. These laws marked the triumph of departmentalism as the organizing principle, and the departments as the basic structural components of all the ministries. The most significant change for the MVD, however, was the removal of most executive and political police functions from its jurisdiction. The law of July 25, 1810, created a separate Ministry of Police under the direction of the former military governor of St. Petersburg, A. D. Balashev.[58]

This law, wordily titled "On the Distribution of State Affairs to Special Branches of Administration with the Signification of the Subjects within the Jurisdiction of Each Branch," declared the MVD's primary responsibility to be "care for the spreading and stimulation of agriculture and industry." In addition to general administrative functions relating to the provinces, the MVD was to be mainly a ministry of agriculture and industry.

The 1811 appointment of O. P. Kozodavlev as minister of internal affairs symbolized this change in the MVD's mandate. Kozodavlev had been assistant minister under Kurakin. During his nine years as minister (1811-1819), Kozodavlev became the leading government formulator of economic policy. A rigorous protectionist, he, like Speranskii, believed that state power should be used to foster private entrepreneurship and native industry.[59]

At the same time, under the umbrella of the Napoleonic threat, Balashev's Ministry of Police and that of his successor, Count S. K. Viazmitinov, earned society's enmity by reviving harsh and arbitrary traditional secret police techniques.[60] Nonetheless, the existence of a separate, though short-lived, Ministry of Police permitted Kozodavlev to concentrate on economic and social matters.

Speranskii certainly hoped that the nascent division of responsibility between police matters and economic and social concerns would be workable. He developed the idea in various memoranda written prior to the 1810-1811 laws. In his "Introduction to the Code of State Laws (1809)," he argued that the proper organization of ministries and departments was of the utmost urgency. According to Speranskii, it was impossible for anyone, "even with the best intentions," to manage such large ministries as Internal Affairs, Finance, and Justice without improving their structure. He reviewed the need for departmentalism, claiming that it was impossible to manage a "large circle of affairs where no levels of authority exist other than ministers, readers of reports, and scribes." After remarking that the MVD had expeditions concerned with finances, salt, national economy, and police, he claimed that this caused "apparent confusion and incoherency of affairs; salt, factories, and police have little in common."[61]

Unfortunately, the 1810 redistribution of functions failed to result either in a clear-cut separation of administration from police, or in the creation of executive ministries concerned with distinctive types of economic or social questions. The new Ministry of Internal Affairs, for example, was set up to include the Department of Manufactures and Internal Trade, but administrative responsibility for the state salt monopoly was given to the Ministry of Finance.[62] Similarly, in addition to its police functions, the new Ministry of Police took over many of the old MVD's general administrative functions as well as a variety of its agricultural, economic, and social matters.[63] These included supervision of the provincial administration, foodstuffs, city and rural economy, public health, philanthropy, and all relations with the military—including recruitment, quartering, and the use of troops to maintain public order.

After 1810, ministry jurisdictions still overlapped, particularly in the areas of industry, trade, and agriculture, and the reforms failed to create independent ministries for each of these vital economic policy areas.[64] The autocracy had neither the will nor the institutions to formulate or implement systematic policies in these areas, and remained fearful of the possible social repercussions of changes in policies.

The 1810 division of functions served as an introduction to the 1811 Institution of the Ministries, the General Instruction to the Ministries, and the detailed specific instructions to each ministry. These represented the "constitution" of the autocracy's executive institutions until the October revolution. They standardized for all ministries the departmental organization and procedure first defined in Kochubei's 1803 memorandum.

In the 1811 General Institution of the Ministries, the degree of authority and responsibility of each office in the ministerial hierarchy was carefully defined.[65] A large section was devoted to administrative procedure (deloproizvodstvo) in which a typical case was dissected into its component parts. The administrative process was traced step by step, from the arrival of an original communication at the ministry to the final resolution of a case by either the minister or a lower officeholder with requisite authority.[66] Formal record- and bookkeeping procedures were also outlined.[67]

The ministers' dual role as trusted servants of the tsar and as heads of executive institutions was emphasized. The laws attempted to create both a unified government in which ministers would cooperate and consult with their colleagues on matters of mutual interest, and a rudimentary separation of power and system of checks and balances. The ministers' power was executive only. They could not create new or abolish old laws and institutions. The ministries were the "institutions by which the Supreme Executive Authority acts upon all sectors of administration." The ministers, however, could propose creation or abolition of laws and institutions to the State Council, and in this capacity were indispensable to the legislative process. Further, ministers in extraordinary circumstances could act with all the means at their disposal without prior consultation with other ministers or permission from the tsar. The specific instructions to each ministry (nakazy) listed the functions of all offices down to the desk level.[68]

The ministries and their departments had been created on paper. Several decades would elapse before actuality resembled the prescription. Even then, "ministerial power" would remain within the fabric of institutions, ready to combat or influence new departures.

The second phase of MVD history—1819 to 1837—was characterized by subtle changes in structure and procedure and by political weakness. In 1819, the Ministry of Police was abolished and its departments and special chancery were absorbed into the MVD.[69] The unification of the two ministries resulted in a unique concentration of institutional power in domestic administration. It also, however, represented a rejection of Speranskii's views on the proper distribution of functions. At the same time, the enlarged MVD gave up its pretensions in the economic sphere by yielding the Department of Manufactures and Internal Trade to the Ministry of Finance. Henceforth, the Ministry of Finance would have primary responsibility for the empire's industry and commerce.[70]

The MVD was not to be completely cut off from internal trade matters, however. On March 19, 1820, the section of the Department of Manufactures and Internal Trade, which administered Russia's trade fairs (iarmarki), was regained from the Ministry of Finance.[71] Fairs such as the annual event at Nizhnii Novgorod were vital to Russia's economy. MVD jurisdiction over them guaranteed its participation in future legislative work on credit institutions, railroads, taxation, joint stock companies, and factories.

Additional structural changes during Kochubei's second ministry included the transfer in 1819 of the Postal Department from MVD jurisdiction to the Ministry of Religious Affairs and Education.[72] Also, public health affairs were further centralized within the MVD when on May 30, 1822, the Medical Council of the Ministry of Religious Affairs and Education was absorbed into the MVD's own Medical Council.[73]

The ministries' roles were reduced during the last years of Alexander I's reign. Alexander shifted away from reliance on the ministries and other high government bodies that he had created earlier in his reign because they had not proven themselves indispensable to government policy-making. Ministers who were close to the tsar had some influence, but the failure of key ministries, such as the Ministry of Police, to fulfill their responsibilities—and the inability of many ministerial departments to complete their tasks without delays and growing backlogs—put pressure on the tsar to seek extra-institutional solutions. The prime example, of course, was the rise of Count A. A. Arakcheev from secretary in the tsar's chancery to a dictatorial position in domestic affairs. (Speranskii had already fallen from a position of power and was in exile.)[74] Arkcheev's emergence was a symptom of institutional weakness in the central government.[75] It was another sign that personalities, not institutions, were in charge of the government. It would not be the last time that such figures would emerge to "save" Russia from either real or imagined institutional weaknesses.[76]

The reign of Nicholas I brought no improvement in the status of either ministries or legislative institutions. The shock of the Decembrist uprising solidified Nicholas' proclivities for both personal rule and the transferral of military forms of discipline and patterns of authority to all areas of public life. Although historians usually view Nicholas' reign as the pinnacle of "bureaucratization," they agree that he profoundly distrusted what he regarded as a thoroughly corrupt and incompetent set of institutions and their personnel.[77] Nicholas promptly expanded the private chancery of the tsar, and within it created the notorious Third Section, a political police organ with an expanded mission to supervise and regulate the entire bureaucracy and society.[78] To avoid the "legislative order" epitomized by the State Council, Nicholas relied upon ad hoc committees and commissions, consisting of people drawn from all sectors of the civil administration, the court, and the military. Personal inspection tours by the tsar and his trusted special agents overshadowed institutional gathering of information and control (nadzor).[79] Nicholas limited the power of individual ministers within their ministries, which together with the existing weakness of the ministries effectively diminished the institutional role further.

It was still too soon after Speranskii's reforms and the creation of new universities and other elite institutions of higher education for the necessary mixture of structural development and an influx of significant numbers of young, well-educated career officials to have taken place. The enlarged MVD was unable to implement the principles of departmentalism. Further, the existing departments were unable to act effectively either as conduits of information from the provinces or as creators of legislative projects—two roles which they fulfilled with skill by the late 1830s. The MVD and other ministries continued to play a minor role in domestic policy-making from 1825 until the ministry of state domains was set up and provincial administration was reformed in 1837.

Further structural changes and redistributed functions served to define more carefully the authority inherent in the highest ministerial offices. In 1831-1833 the first major attempt to simplify the administrative process was undertaken to decrease the paperwork that was hindering operations.[80] These changes occurred during the ministries of V. S. Lanskoi (1823-1828), A. A. Zakrevskii (1828-1831), and D. A. Bludov (1832-1838).[81] None, with the possible exception of Bludov, could be included among Russia's most talented nineteenth-century officials. Lanskoi was born in 1753, and had first served during the era of Catherine the Great. He was minister of internal affairs during the transition from Alexander I to Nicholas I and had little influence on domestic policy. Zakrevskii is best remembered for his inept direction of government efforts against the severe cholera epidemic of 1830-1831 during his ministry.[82]

Throughout the 1830s Bludov was forced continually to adjust the MVD's table of organization (shtat) because of the growing bottlenecks in ministry operations. He also reorganized the ministry press and reaffirmed the special role of officials of special missions (chinovniki osobykh poruchenii).[83]

One of the primary functions of the ministry press was publication of the monthly Journal of the Ministry of Internal Affairs, which contained official announcements, decrees, and various articles. In 1828 this journal succeeded earlier ministry publications which had disappeared during the reign of Alexander I.[84] Designed to bring official news and "enlightenment" to MVD officials throughout the empire and to communicate government intentions to society, this dry journal never became popular in educated circles. Although it always lost money, it endured with minor modifications in format and content until replaced in 1861 by a daily newspaper, the Northern Post.

The new table of organization for officials of special missions issued on April 28, 1836, was indicative of important trends within the bureaucracy.[85] The positions, meant for high- and middle-level rank holders of the fifth, sixth, and eighth classes, carried full salaries, pension rights, and other service benefits. These officials of special missions were personally selected by the minister to troubleshoot, to gather and analyze information, and to enforce the minister's will in departments and provinces. Naturally, the Minister selected people he trusted and in whose skill he had faith. Directors of departments and provincial governors were allowed their own officials of special missions as provided by the tables of organization. The 1836 law stipulated fifteen officials for the minister and five for each department. They provided necessary help to provincial administrators who usually were not as able as those in St. Petersburg. Because the developing central departments in the capital were overburdened with work, the officials could sometimes circumvent problem areas and hierarchical "red tape" to carry out assignments.

During the first four decades of the MVD's existence, the detailed procedures for processing papers and cases degenerated into the kind of institutional formalism that had plagued the colleges during the eighteenth century. The formal rules of administration came to be viewed less as standards of efficiency than as means for imposing limits on arbitrary, incompetent, or negligent officials. (There seemed to be a notable lack of officials capable of taking initiative and making independent judgments.)

Formalism was fostered in the government by the detailed impersonal rules of procedure, which had become necessary for organizational stability. Thus, impersonal rules in Russia differed in meaning from their place in the Weberian bureaucratic model where they represented rationalization. Red tape, routine, and slowness were especially hampering at the lower levels of the office and rank hierarchy, where the least educated or skillful men worked with little hope of advancement. Speranskii had originally declared successful completion of cases and decreases in number of cases as criteria of efficiency. His successors, however, took this too literally and often counted quantities of paper rather than searching for deeper causes of inefficiency. Though Bludov gamely tried to decrease the MVD's correspondence and casework, the results were meager and momentary. The volume of business continued to grow, as did the number of MVD officials and expenditures.[86] High officials continued to believe that the way to improve efficiency and cope with expanding workloads was to increase manpower and expenditures at the levels where bottlenecks appeared. Already in the 1830s the factors present in the MVD institutional crisis of the 1860s were evident.

The importance of the minister's power to appoint, promote, or otherwise reward MVD officials must not be underestimated. Under Nicholas, a series of laws strengthened the independence of all ministries from the supervision of the Department of Heraldry of the Senate which formally administered the Russian civil service. The ministers were slowly becoming the complete masters of their own houses. Only the Committee of Ministers, which was composed of the ministers themselves, and the tsar, who could certainly not have personal knowledge of all men nominated for departmental directorships or provincial governorships, could formally block the decision of a minister to appoint, promote, or reward within the framework of the service statutes. The minister of internal affairs became more and more powerful in these respects. Those of his nominations which did require approval became a matter for the rubber stamp of either the Committee of Ministers or the tsar. At the lower levels within the ministry, the minister and his directors were completely independent in personnel matters. The directors and the minister could single out promising young men and promote them quickly to positions of responsibility— sometimes in violation of the service statutes. This was a continuous feature of ministry personnel policy from the 1840s and into the Reform Era (see Chapter 4).

The ministry's rise to political prominence was due, in large part, to the ability of those in power to recognize and utilize the talents of young career officials. On the other hand, the system also left room for appointments made as results of naked nepotism, imagined trust, shared political philosophy, as well as administrative skills. In the mid-nineteenth-century Russian civil service, the traditional phenomenon of "protection" cut both ways. The Committee of Ministers retained the right to approve many appointments and awards, and the dispersal of certain funds. Yet the initiative on most important policy or appointment matters belonged to the individual ministers. The Committee of Ministers was nothing more than these ministers acting in consort.[87] The empire's laws and government practice were combining in the name of expediency to accomplish the business of government, to build a central ministerial government that would eventually overshadow most institutional counterweights within the autocracy.

The next period of MVD history was inaugurated by events of far-reaching implication. During the late 1830s and 1840s the tsar's relationship to the ministries changed, as did the ministries' political position within the central government.[88] Signs of these changes included (1) a major reform in 1837 of the provincial administration and a reordering of the lines of authority between the MVD and the provinces; (2) the creation in 1837 of the Ministry of State Domains under Count P. D. Kiselev, with its mandate to carry out extensive social and administrative reforms on state lands; (3) the passage in 1839 of permanent tables of organization for all ministries; (4) the 1841 appointment of L. A. Perovskii, one of the most energetic and far-sighted nineteenth-century officials, who, in his eleven-year tenure as minister, set the MVD on the reformist course it would pursue during the early reign of Alexander II; (5) the 1842 reform of the State Council that further weakened that organ in relation to the ministries; and (6) the emergence of a new generation of highly educated career officials at the lower and middle levels of ministry departments.

The 1837 provincial reform was part of a process initiated early in Nicholas' reign. The committee of December 6, 1826, had discussed the need to reform provincial administration and strengthen its connection to the central government.[89] In April 1828, governors were obliged to submit yearly reports directly to the minister of internal affairs. In 1831 the minister of internal affairs, A. A. Zakrevskii, traveled through various provinces and submitted to Nicholas I a report that emphasized the poor condition of local administrative and police institutions in terms of both organization and the low competence and dishonesty of their personnel.[90]

The 1837 laws served to extend departmentalism down to the provincial level. The goal was to make the civil governor a powerful, monocratic figure with authority over all subordinate administrative and police organs in the province. The governor, in turn, was to be directly subordinate to the minister of internal affairs and fully responsible for executing his decisions. To this end measures were taken to convert the collegial provincial governing boards (*gubernskoe pravlenie*) into executive institutions subordinate to the governor.[91]

Another significant feature of the 1837 law was the elimination of the governors-general in all but the border provinces and the two capitals. The governors-general had been established by Catherine the Great in 1775 to act as mechanisms to control her new provincial administration.[92] With the introduction of ministries in 1802, however, the governors-general represented an independent authority outside the ministerial bureaucracy. Usually military men, they were the equals in rank and status of the ministers, and they jealously guarded their prerogatives and independence.[93] They viewed the tsar as their only superior, and sometimes because of formal seniority in rank or length of service, they felt they had greater authority than even the minister of internal affairs. The elimination of most of these offices in 1837 was a bow toward institutions. It therefore meant an important upgrading of MVD authority and status and was intended to foster a unified administrative hierarchy extending into the provinces. The control function of the governors-general was passed over to the civil governors, who were authorized to make inspection tours of their provinces and to report their findings to the MVD.[94]

The creation of the Ministry of State Domains in 1837 and its subsequent reform activities had a profound effect on both the evolution of ministerial government and the MVD.[95] Nicholas' decision to create a *ministry* to "emancipate" the state peasants (approximately 40 percent of the peasant population) and to introduce a new administrative system to state lands reversed his earlier approach toward ministries. In 1835 he commissioned the elderly Speranskii and P. D. Kiselev, the author of successful agrarian reforms in Wallachia and Moldavia, to work out a project for reforms on the state lands.[96] At first Nicholas concentrated this work in the Fifth Section of his own chancery, but two years later transferred the work to the new Ministry of State Domains. Kiselev, and his able young staff took over the new ministry, and in the following ten years carried out an aggressive program of social and administrative reform.[97]

The Ministry of State Domains, with its determined leadership, departmental hierarchies, and brilliant young staff, proved at least superficially effective as a government tool for instituting social change from above. The authority of Kiselev and his ministry rose as it became more apparent that, because of their departmental structure, organizations, and staff, ministries had become indispensable state agents of social and economic change. Many bright young men in the Ministry of State Domains in the 1840s would later serve in the MVD after the Crimean War when it helped launch the emancipation of the proprietary serfs and other "Great Reforms."[98]

The tables of organization issued on February 15, 1839, for the MVD and all other ministries gave final form to the piecemeal structural changes of the 1820s and 1830s.[99] The new MVD table represented the triumph of departmentalism and it remained in effect until the mid-1860s. As a result of departmental elaboration, the late 1830s and 1840s witnessed assistant desk chief positions going to young officials who were graduates of the institutions of higher education. These men were hereditary noblemen who, because of the rank (chin) which came with their diplomas, were eligible to hold significant departmental offices soon after entering the service.

Count Lev Alekseevich Perovskii was able to use this 1839 structure for political advantage, and he led the ministry to its powerful position on the eve of the Great Reforms. Perovskii, born in 1793, was the illegitimate son of Count A. K. Razumovskii.[100] He graduated from Moscow University in 1811 and after early service in the military and the Ministry of Foreign Affairs, Nicholas I transferred him to the Department of Crown Properties (departament udelov). This department (later the Ministry of the Imperial Court), not to be confused with the Ministry of State Domains, administered court affairs and the royal family's personal properties. In 1826 Perovskii launched a series of successful land and social reforms on crown properties, and his reputation as a brilliant administrator was born. After twelve years as assistant minister of crown properties, Perovskii was appointed by Nicholas in September 1841 to succeed Stroganov as minister of internal affairs.

As the minister, Perovskii tried to improve departmental effectiveness and the central MVD's relationship to the provinces by combatting formalism and other remaining dysfunctions. To further these goals, he pursued a vigorous and novel personnel policy which brought into the ministry many young career administrators, writers, and intellectuals. In the Kiselev pattern he also began to use the MVD and its departments as a power base from which to generate administrative reforms. Perovskii's contributions enabled him to maintain the tsar's confidence—and his post. For almost eleven years, his influence in the highest councils of government and his activities set a pattern for subsequent ministers. Using as a basis the table of organization of 1839, Perovskii strengthened the ministry departments and prepared them for the implementation of the kinds of reform that would be the MVD hallmark later during the Reform Era.[101]

The best example of how an MVD department prepared for and helped to secure State Council passage of administrative reforms is the St. Petersburg city reform of 1846.[102] This reform shows the connections between structural changes, the influx of new personnel, and the minister's effective use of his ministry to attain political goals. A special commission to reorganize the administration and economy of the empire's cities had existed since the mid-1820s.[103] On March 27, 1842, responsibility for this work was shifted to the new Temporary Section for the reorganization of municipal government within the MVD Economic Department.[104] This section was staffed by 31 men and given a mandate to prepare materials for the projected reforms. The director of the section was N. A. Miliutin, who had already acquired a reputation as a talented young administrator and statistician. He believed it necessary to gather reliable information on city conditions before writing concrete reform provisions.[105]

To this end, Miliutin and other officials of the section made numerous trips around the empire, requesting detailed reports from city officials on their precise duties and activities. During 1843-1844 ten officials of special missions were added to the section to help. Miliutin also believed in controlled transmission of the views of interested parties to the government. The disarray in city administration and the difficulties of gathering the requisite data, however, caused Miliutin to narrow his focus to the municipal administration of St. Petersburg. Perovskii authorized Miliutin to prepare a project for the State Council. Largely through the efforts of Miliutin and other talented young career officials in the Temporary Section, a compromise reform law was passed by the State Council after considerable debate and infighting, and published on February 13, 1846.[106]

As in the Ministry of State Domains, young MVD officials learned valuable lessons about the preparation of reform projects, acquired drafting skills, and gained experience in the autocracy's legislative process. Miliutin, who was Kiselev's nephew, and others such as A. K. Giers, K. K. Grot, D. P. Khrushchov, and A. D. Shumakher became important figures in the legislative process leading to the emancipation of serfs in 1861. At various times Miliutin employed intellectuals, thus providing an important meeting ground for bureaucracy and intelligentsia that was a further impetus for reform after the Crimean War. The Temporary Section was reorganized on February 18, 1849, into two permanent sections on city affairs within the MVD Economic Department, and the 1846 St. Petersburg reform served as a basis for the successful 1870 empire-wide reform of municipal administration accomplished under the stewardship of Shumakher and the Economic Department.[107]

Perovskii, greatly concerned with improving provincial administration and rationalizing its relationship to the central MVD, made the problems in these areas known in reports to the tsar during 1842 and 1843.[108] His first efforts went toward improving the control and flow of information by direct intervention by officials of special missions and high departmental officials. He also believed that only the most capable men should be appointed as provincial governors.

Perovskii continued the policy of integrating provincial administration into the MVD hierarchy by further extending MVD organizational principles down through the provincial offices. This was accomplished by the law of January 2, 1845, largely written by the philologist V. I. Dal', at that time director of the MVD's Department of General Affairs.[109] This law permitted the vice-governor to act as chairman of the Provincial Directorate (*gubernskoe pravlenie*) as well as head of the directorate's chancellery. It therefore increased the bureaucratic element in the provincial administration and freed the governor from the burdens of many less important matters.

Provincial affairs were divided into three categories for consideration by the provincial directorates: (1) juridical—to be decided collegially; (2) mandatory (*rasporiaditel'nyi*)—to be decided by the directorate according to fixed procedures, but with the governor's approval; and (3) executive (*ispolnitel'nyi*)—to be decided by the vice-governor and his advisers according to field of competence.[110] This law represented a major attempt to define the role of the provincial directorates, as well as to tighten MVD control over provincial administration.

Perovskii also continually tried to overcome the glaring dysfunctions in the ministry's operations, particularly corruption, incompetence, and excessive adherence to formal rules. To alleviate them, he proposed procedural changes and increased salaries.[111] He recognized the need to reform the provincial police and understood that competent officials were needed at all levels.

Once the MVD's authority was established in domestic affairs, Perovskii felt secure enough to expand into the Third Section's jurisdiction of political crimes. Perovskii bested the Third Section by uncovering the Petrashevskii affair;[112] this represented one more victory of the regular ministerial organs over competing personalized institutions of the autocrat. At the end of his ministry, Perovskii realized that despite the new political strengths and the proven abilities of middle- and high-level departmental officials of the MVD, the ministry was losing ground in the battle against formalism, excessive paperwork, and inefficiency. In a report to the emperor in March 1851, he wrote, "It is impossible not to recognize that bureaucratic formalities have reached the point of absurdity; endless official correspondence absorbs all the attention and energies of those who execute policy, and instead of true supervision and administration we have, for the most part, only recordkeeping and accounting for documents."[113] In April 1851 the acting minister of internal affairs, S. S. Lanskoi, introduced measures to decrease correspondence within the departments. Later in the same year a special committee of representatives from all ministries met to formulate procedural improvements. The committee's project, passed by the State Council and approved by the tsar in 1852, required all ministers to seek ways to reduce paperwork and simplify procedures at all levels of authority including provincial offices.[114]

When Perovskii departed in 1852, the MVD was dominant in the Russian domestic administration, and its officials had acquired valuable experience. The ministry's activities during the 1840s revealed both the capabilities and limits of ministerial institutions as instruments of social and political change. Many policy problems were placed on the agenda, but most remained unsolved. In spite of the advances under Perovskii, questions of structural and procedural reform within the ministry, administrative and police reform, and vital social and economic policy matters were passed on to his immediate successor, General D. G. Bibikov. Bibikov, former governor-general of Kiev, was described by the official historian of the MVD as a "typical representative of the Nicolaevan era."[115] Bibikov had blind faith in state power and believed all forms of social organization to be inherently evil. As governor-general of Kiev, he introduced the inventory system to define the obligations of the orthodox peasantry to the landowners, who were mostly of Polish nationality. The tsar authorized Bibikov as minister of internal affairs to introduce the inventory system in the western provinces. The nobility was hostile to the inventories; thus as Nicolas' reign ended it was clear that the MVD was involved in the "peasant question."

The Bibikov years also brought changes in structure and procedure. The ministry's power to issue circulars and instructions to provincial officials was expanded, and the operative instructions and circulars dating back to 1802 were codified according to the statutes of the digest of laws they amplified. The published collection of circulars was to serve as a guide to the daily administrative activities of ministry officials.[116]

The growth of the discretionary powers of the minister of internal affairs to issue circulars, instructions, and edicts having the force of law (or in amplification of already existing laws) on subordinate officials and society was one of the most important factors in the growth of ministerial power during the nineteenth century. Until 1825 the weakness of the ministries may be seen in the low number of circulars issued. Varadinov offers the following figures for the MVD:[117]

1810	2		1819	5
1811	8		1820	10
1812	3		1821	5
1814	0		1822	4
1815	2		1823	8
1816	6		1824	14
1817	6		1825	16
1818	6			

Ministry of Police (1811-1819)   98

Varadinov points out that these figures are not complete, owing to missing and destroyed papers and ambiguities in classification. The fact remains, however, that the data make it difficult to conclude that "any real centralization" had taken place. The minister's power was still inadequately clarified, and the ministry had not developed as an institution. The tsar's signature was still required for edicts that would later be issued by the minister acting alone.

During the years 1826-1853, the situation changed drastically, when approximately 4,870 circulars and instructions were issued—approximately 180 per year. This growth in the law-making power of the MVD continued unabated during the reign of Alexander II. After the peasant emancipation, the ministry published a large volume of circulars for each year (these did not include several categories classified as secret). It was difficult to distinguish between circulars and laws (za-kony) since most were viewed as amplifications of articles contained in the Digest of Laws. These circulars attest the inordinate strength of administrative power (and administrative law) in prerevolutionary Russia. The circulars should be viewed as one of the underpinnings of the Russian ministerial form of government and one of the primary factors inhibiting the development of separation of powers or the rule of law.[118]

The MVD departments and their young officials had shown that at their levels the ministry was fully capable of producing sophisticated administrative reform projects. The last half of Nicholas' reign saw Perovskii, Kiselev, and others raising ministerial government to an unassailable and indispensable position within the autocracy. The Crimean War and the change of monarchs in 1855 were only momentary interruptions in basic patterns of institutional development and behavior. The Great Reforms themselves, therefore, may be seen as the end point of processes that began well before the Crimean defeat that supposedly engendered them. It is important to remember, however, that despite the gains, ministerial officials still operated within the ministerial power framework. Administration still equaled politics, and even among "enlightened" officials there was no notion of political transformation.

In the reign of Alexander II (1855-1881), the major changes in MVD structure reflected the ministry's powerful position within the autocracy. The problems it was called upon to resolve, were complex and diverse. Although the MVD departments appeared organized by 1855, the emancipation of the proprietary serfs and other high policy matters resulted in a proliferation of new internal organs. Burgeoning areas of administration that required immediate government attention gave birth to new structures. Growth and change marked the yearly reports of the minister, S. S. Lanskoi. Nonetheless, even at the time of its greatest triumphs early in Alexander's reign, the MVD (and indeed ministerial government as a whole) was headed for a profound structural crisis. As early as the mid-1860s the bureaucratic apparatus found it increasingly difficult to fulfill its administrative and legislative responsibilities. The greater workload exacerbated inherited structural and procedural problems. Between 1861 and 1881, many highly specialized administrative subjects came under MVD jurisdiction. These were handled by newly created committees or directorates, such as the Main Directorate for Press Affairs or the Main Prison Directorate. Those in charge of the new committees were directly subordinate to the minister but were outside the regular departmental hierarchy. The number of reliable officials and the financial resources proved inadequate for the tasks at hand. Structural problems com-

bined with the ideological cleavages within the ministry to influence
strongly MVD and government policy. It was obvious late in Alexander's reign that the search for political solutions and, indeed, domestic
policy-making in many other crucial areas had come to a standstill. In
large part this was caused by structural crises within the MVD and the
larger central government.

The minister's ability to supervise personally the affairs of the expanding ministry continued to diminish. The competing claims on his
attention, both from within the MVD and from his participation in
legislative and other policy-making councils of the government, increased markedly.[119] The departments created by Speranskii remained
the backbone of MVD structure. But the existence of a galaxy of these
new, technical, and specialized organs clamoring for the minister's
attention undermined the clean lines of authority and streamlined
division of labor envisioned by Speranskii. To contemporaries and
especially to rival ministers, it appeared that the MVD was empire-
building, particularly if MVD plans to attain complete domination of
provincial government were taken into account. But the archival record indicates that both Valuev and his successor, A. E. Timashev,
complained about the excessive burdens placed upon the minister of
internal affairs. Timashev, in fact, tried unsuccessfully to divest the
MVD of its newly won censorship responsibilities. These burdens
motivated Timashev to add a second assistant minister with expanded
powers in 1869.[120]

The growth of the MVD is shown by contrasting regular and specialized departments in 1855 and in 1881 under the aegis of the minister.

MVD Structure, 1855

Regular departments	Specialized organs or officials responsible directly to the minister
Department of General Affairs	Chancellery
Economic Department	Assistant minister
Department of Executive Police	Council of the Minister (four or
Department of Religious Affairs of Foreign Faiths	five members)
Medicine Department	Medicine Council
Department of State Medical Preparations	Officials of special missions and others attached to the ministry
	Typography

MVD Structure, 1881

Regular departments	Specialized organs or officials responsible directly to the minister
Department of General Affairs	Assistant ministers (two after (1869)
Zemskii otdel (1858)	Chancellery
Department of State Police (includes Third Section and Corps of Gendarmes) (1880)	Council of the Minister (about 15 men)
Economic Department	Main Directorate of Press Affairs (1865)
Department of Religious Affairs of Foreign Faiths	Medicine Council
Medicine Department	Veterinary Committee (1868)
Department of Post and Telegraph (1868)	Technical-Construction Committee (1865)
	Central Statistics Committee (1858)
	Statistics Council (1863)
	Main Prison Directorate (1879)
	Council on Prison Affairs (1879)
	Jurisconsult Section (1866)
	Typography
	Pravitel'stvennyi vestnik (all-government daily newspaper) (1869)
	Officials of special missions and other attached to the ministry

On March 4, 1858, in conjunction with the emancipation process, a new Central Statistics Committee was formed from an already existing Statistics Committee. The new organ was subdivided into two collegial sections, a Statistics Section and the Zemskii otdel.[121] The Zemskii otdel, under the direction of Ia. A. Solov'ev, who had served his apprenticeship under Kiselev in the Ministry of State Domains, became the focal point for the MVD's work on the emancipation. Agricultural and peasant affairs were centered in the Zemskii otdel, and on July 27, 1861, it became an independent body organized as a ministerial department.[122] The Statistics Section, which had been headed by A. G. Troinitskii (after 1861, assistant minister), became the responsibility of the famous geographer and future memoirist, P. P. Semenov (later Semenov-Tian-Shanskii), who held the directorship for two decades.[123] On April 30, 1863, the section was merged with and renamed the Central Statistics Committee and reorganized along bureaucratic lines.[124] Simultaneously, a new Statistics Council was created, its membership consisting of academicians and the heads of statistics departments of other ministries and government organs.

The much-needed centralization and unification of government efforts in gathering and interpreting statistics was placed on the council agenda in 1873. In so doing, Timashev tried to elevate the council to the status of an all-government body with full authority for statistical matters. The objections of other ministers defeated the proposal, and although the law of May 24, 1875, reformed the Statistics Council, it was left with no control over the statistical work of other ministries.[125]

The most important additions to the MVD following the creation of the Zemskii otdel and the Central Statistics Committee were (1) the Main Directorate of Press Affairs (September 1, 1865); (2) incorporation of the Ministry of Post and Telegraph (late 1868); (3) a small Jurisconsult Section (1866); and (4) integration of the Corps of Gendarmes from the eliminated Third Section (August and November 1880).

The empire's press law ended preliminary censorship of certain categories of publications. This 1865 law completed the assignation of responsibility for censorship to the MVD.[126] The Ministry of Education had previously been responsible for censorship, but in the 1860s transfer of authority to the MVD began (see Chapter 5).

The Ministry of Post and Telegraph was incorporated in late 1868 when its minister, A. E. Timashev, was appointed minister of internal affairs.[127] Within the MVD the former ministry was divided into two departments. The first postal director was Baron I. O. Velio, who had been director of the Department of Executive Police.

In 1866 a small Jurisconsult Section was created. Both Adrianov, official historian of the MVD, and the Soviet institutional historian N. P. Eroshkin have ignored this organ. Yet its importance was disproportionate to its size since it gave institutional expression to the growing conflicts between the administration and the courts and helped to defend the principles of ministerial power during the remainder of the 1860s and 1870s. After the 1880 police merger, the Jurisconsult Section was combined with a similar section of the Corps of Gendarmes to form a larger Juridical Section.[128] Its function was to provide the MVD with legal expertise and to represent its interests before the courts (see Chapter 3).

The last major structural change took place in August and November 1880.[129] The Third Section was eliminated, and its higher police functions and the Corps of Gendarmes were integrated into the MVD. All police activities were centered in a new Department of State Police; its first director was the same Baron Velio of the Department of Post and Telegraph. The unification of police in the MVD was the inspiration of Count M. T. Loris-Melikov, who, at the same time, engineered his appointment as minister of internal affairs on August 6, 1880. His goal was to unify police activity and end the arbitrary and counterproductive handling of political crimes by the independent Third Section and Corps of Gendarmes. The merger added greatly to the MVD's power and was an important element in Loris' plan to use the MVD as a base from which to unify and lead the government (see also Chapter 6).

The phenomenal growth of the MVD during Alexander's reign did not, however, provide the necessary structure to accomplish the ministry's assigned tasks. I strongly doubt whether the MVD (and the government as a whole) could have solved its structural crisis without some form of partnership with elites outside the bureaucracy. And this, of course, was precisely what the doctrine of ministerial power was set against.

The structural and operational problems of the MVD, as evidenced in reports submitted by S. S. Lanskoi and P. A. Valuev during the initial years of Alexander's reign, became even more pressing through the 1860s and 1870s. All bureaucracies want more men and money, but the manner in which the requests for them are made, the types of solutions proposed, and the fate of the proposals say much about the capacity for institutional change within given organizations in larger societies. The case of the MVD is well documented. How key figures within and outside the ministry viewed its problems and how they tried to solve them tell in microcosm the frustrating and fateful story of failed institutional change in late imperial Russia.

Lanskoi's annual report for 1858 contains complaints about shortages of money, personnel, and buildings, but the overriding concern is understandably with the emancipation process and particularly with supervision of the provincial committees called upon to assist the Editorial Commission with its work.[130] Lanskoi was optimistic about the new Miliutin commission created for provincial administrative and police reform. His 1859 report gave figures indicating that the minister of internal affairs and his subordinates were having difficulty keeping up with workloads. Further, the 1860 report by Lanskoi and 1861 report, the first by Valuev, emphasized the number and diversity of administrative and policy problems that the MVD had undertaken in addition to emancipation.[131] Valuev's report contained a detailed analysis of the MVD's major completed projects, those stalled owing to the absence of necessary approval or cooperation of other ministries and institutions, and those not yet begun but approved in principle by higher authorities.[132] According to this report, the two burning questions for the MVD remained the implementation of the emancipation, and the reform of provincial and district administration. Also, Valuev called attention to the need to reduce correspondence in the MVD—a problem which led him to solicit suggestions from the department directors. He dwelled at some length on the problem of decentralization, which he was careful to define as a process that must result in an "indivisible and general provincial administration" completely under government supervision and with the state's interests fully guaranteed.[133]

From this time until 1874, continual attempts were made to reform the table of organization of the MVD. In a confidential memorandum on October 12, 1861, Valuev solicited suggestions from department directors on how to effect reductions in correspondence. He expressed concern with the departmentalism that had been prominent in the MVD since 1802. He asked what matters could be decided by provincial officials without prior communication and approval of the central ministry—and which might be decided by the ministry without communication with other ministries or representations to the highest governing bodies.

There were many levels of formal authority, or instances, in the ministry, but actual decision-making power had not been extended throughout the hierarchy in any clear fashion. Enormous increases in correspondence resulted since the administrative process required the movement of materials and requests from instance to instance up the hierarchy both within the central departments and from province to St. Petersburg. Also, official communications with other ministries and institutions were increasing, thus slowing the resolution of many problems.

Valuev claimed that there was no clear understanding of what decentralization was to mean in practice, but he felt that experienced officials were in the best position to understand ministry operations and suggest alternative procedures.[134] Though the directors' responses are not on record, the same kinds of questions and the same solicitation of suggestions were explicit in all the attempts to reform the MVD table of organization.

During his first year as minister, Valuev also tried to strengthen various institutional supports of the ministerial office. In a memorandum of July 6, 1861, he requested authority to add ten more officials of special missions to the 24 already at the minister's disposal. These men were to be in service classes V, VI, and VII with full service rights, but no salaries. Valuev portrayed them as absolutely essential to the fulfillment of his mandate. They were to travel throughout the empire because "at the present time the ministry is having difficulties in finding the means of implementing its various directives." Valuev required experienced officials for these missions because regular MVD departmental officials were often unsuited for the tasks and their "service qualities" unknown to either their chiefs or the minister. Apparently, Valuev's request was approved. He usually appointed personal acquaintances to these positions to circumvent institutional bottlenecks within the ministry's regular hierarchical institutions. Two people he appointed were D. N. Tolstoi and V. I. Fuks (see Chapter 4).

Valuev collected comparative materials on the councils of his own ministry and the ministries of Finance and State Domains. The minister's council had certain advisory and other formal functions, but its main purpose was to act as another reservoir of trusted, experienced officials who could be used to carry out the minister's personal commissions. Valuev observed that his council, according to an 1852 law, had salaried positions for only four men (two received 2,000 rubles, and two others 1,715 rubles), whereas the councils of the other two ministers had a greater number of higher salaried positions. M. Kh. Reutern, soon to become minister of finance, was listed as a member of the Council of the Ministry of Finance with a salary of 8,545 rubles, of which 4,145 rubles were paid by his former employer, the Naval Ministry. Ten members of this council had salaries of over 4,000 rubles. The Council of the Ministry of State Domains had eight members with salaries that averaged just slightly below 4,000 rubles. This absence of uniformity was certainly distant from the Weberian ideal type.

Valuev devoted an entire section of the voluminous 1861-1863 report to MVD procedural and structural problems.[135] He mentioned the need for a thorough reform of the table of organization in accordance with the tsar's wishes and the ministry's requirements. He cited the increases in quantity and complexity of MVD functions, his necessary personal role in many matters, and the weaknesses of provincial administration requiring him constantly to send supervisory and investigatory officials out from the center. Clearly, Valuev had already initiated work on table of organization reform, and in this report he presented pertinent statistics on the ministry's activities as well as general insights on major operational problems in the empire's administration.

Valuev stated that, on January 1, 1864, the MVD had 396 permanent officials on its central table of organization, with another 328 attached to the ministry in a variety of roles. In the provinces the estimate was approximately 30,000 officials. These figures compared to the figure 27,766 for the year 1857 as recorded by the temporarily defunct Inspection Department in charge of civil service records.

Valuev gave the following figures for the movement of communications and cases in the central ministry.

	1861	1862	1863
Cases	31,580	30,400	27,900
Decided or completed	21,480	20,500	19,700
Undecided	10,100	9,900	8,200
Communications			
Incoming	104,260	105,690	120,440
Executed	103,380	104,770	119,210
Signed by minister	38,970	37,250	47,530
Signed by directors	43,980	45,920	52,420
Representations of the MVD to the Highest Governing Bodies			
State Council	167	170	185
Committees: of ministers, Caucasus, etc.	621	424	676
Senate	2,651	2,285	2,808

Although the number of cases decreased slightly during the three-year period, a considerable backlog remained. Further, the number of official communications, which had increased slowly during the late 1850s, increased at a rapid pace by 1863. The number of representations (legislative projects) to the highest governing bodies was also increasing. Valuev mentioned the shift of the administration of civil obligations from the MVD Department of Executive Police to its Economic Department, approved by the tsar on May 4, 1862. He noted that a more rational division of functions would be one of his primary goals in any structural reform of the ministry.

Valuev concluded by calling attention to some features of Russian society which added to ministry burdens. Here he cited the scores of petitions, requests, and complaints submitted to local authorities and to various offices all the way up the hierarchy to the minister himself. He saw these referrals as an incredible waste of MVD time and resources, both spent on many requests not even within the jurisdiction of ministry officials. Valuev thought the explanation lay in a deeply ingrained habit of the Russian people to seek from the state the fulfillment of all of their needs. According to Valuev, many citizens simply wanted to live off the state treasury, and when petitioners were refused at the local level, their distrust of local officials caused them only to resubmit the petitions at higher levels. During the three years 1861-1863 almost 20,000 requests reached the minister alone.[136] Of these, 10,755 were fulfilled partially or completely and another 7,234 declared incorrect and rejected.

Valuev's solution was state promotion of industry and economic development in order to lift the populace out of what he regarded as "parasitism." This intuitive policy recommendation by one of Russia's leading nineteenth-century officials reveals his sensitivity to the relationship between Russian society and its institutions. Valuev, however, did not stop to consider the state's role in fostering and perpetuating the inordinate dependency of its citizens that he lamented.

During the early years of Alexander's reign the 1839 table of organization remained the basic MVD charter. Although some minor reductions in central ministry personnel had been accomplished in the early 1850s in conjunction with the attempt to reduce correspondence and simplify procecures,[137] the number and types of officials in each department, their salaries and other service rights, and the budgetary allowances for each component of the central ministry had remained fixed according to the 1839 law despite the new conditions and larger workload of the late 1850s and early 1860s.

The table of organization for government institutions was its structural blueprint for current operations. In effect, the table represented a legal amendment to the 1811 founding legislation. The table of organization and the annual budgetary process reveal how the MVD tried to adjust to administrative realities and how limited resources were allocated within the autocratic system. Without a final table of organization approved in the legislative order by the State Council and tsar, any internal structural changes, or changes in the division of labor or allocation of resources, had to be made ad hoc, on a temporary basis. This could be done only by the quiet redistribution of available funds or manpower, or by direct appeal for temporary help to the tsar or State Council. It had taken an entire decade to achieve the 1839 product despite the relative tranquility of that period. The complex process of reform of the table of organization called into play the opinions and interests of high MVD officials as well as rival ministers and others outside the MVD. Only with the presentation of yearly budgets for State Council approval and in certain highest-level policy- and law-making forums was there a comparable examination of MVD activities by outside forces powerful enough to effect its development.[138]

Alexander II placed table of organization reform for all ministries on the agenda in January 1860. He had just reviewed proposals for the Naval Ministry submitted by his reform-oriented brother, Grand

Duke Konstantin Nikolaevich.[139] These reforms called for strengthening the decision-making powers of local Naval Ministry officials, simplifying procedure, cutting superfluous personnel, and using the
money thus saved to increase the salaries of remaining officials. The
goal was to increase administrative efficiency at no cost to an already
strained state treasury. The method involved centralization of control, record-keeping, and finances within the ministry, further decentralization with the departments, and the trimming of extraneous personnel who occupied their positions by virtue of the various legal
guarantees of the service statutes. In December 1859 the Naval Ministry was given five years to introduce the new system—after which the
State Council was to review the results. The Crimean defeat, the lack
of central government unity, and the growing demands upon the ministries showed the weaknesses in naval administration to be common
to all central ministries. Alexander, therefore, ordered all ministries
and equivalent organs to prepare reforms based on the Naval Ministry
model. The first to comply were the ministries of Finance and Education, and their projects were reviewed and approved in the State
Council in April 1863.[140]

Although the order to prepare the reform had been given in 1860,
Lanskoi's ouster and the MVD's preoccupation with emancipation and
other matters delayed starting on the project until the spring of 1863.
When reminded of the tsar's original edict, Valuev created an internal
commission to gather the necessary material and prepare the project.
He chose as chairman A. D. Shumakher, director of the Economic Department, one of the bright young career officials of the 1840s, because of "his long service in the MVD and his acquaintance with the
structures of the ministry's various organs." In addition, the commission included Valuev's own official of special missions, V. A. Fuks, a
financial expert, actual state councilor Gurko, and all departmental
vice-directors. Valuev requested that they carefully consider all resources and expenditures. Each department was to assess its manpower and financial needs in accordance with past experience and
projected workloads. Directors were to determine the manpower
necessary for required work, and to keep in mind the goal of possible
cuts, as in the Naval Ministry.[141]

The first results of the commission's labors were expressed in Shumakher's memorandum to Valuev dated March 22, 1863. Shumakher
assessed the ministry's problems and prospects in light of the Reform
Era's new demands. His analysis was most unusual for a mid-nineteenth-century Russian civil servant. Instead of the usual claims for
more men and money, Shumakher wrote that "the reduction of the
existing number of 'tenured' officials not only will not cause incon-

veniences, but on the contrary might be quite useful for the conduct of business."

According to Shumakher, the departmental structures and levels of authority established by the 1839 table of organization broke down below the desk chief (stolonachal'nik) level. While section heads (nachal'niki otdeleniia) and desk chiefs had fixed responsibilities in managing and controlling their bailiwicks and in the administrative process, the table of organization provided for a group of lower offices (assistant desk chiefs, bookkeepers, and controllers) without defined administrative responsibilities. Shumakher complained that this permitted these lower office-holders to treat their obligations too lightly, especially if they lacked motivation. The absence of observable diligence at these levels, he argued, was also caused by meager salaries. An avalanche of work upon the responsible and more highly motivated section and desk chiefs resulted, which, in turn, caused bottlenecks in operations.

After noting that the service statutes made removal of the laggards next to impossible without proof of actual crimes or severe negligence, he pointed out that removal was a poor solution in any case, as the officials would only be replaced by others with the same deficiencies. Shumakher proposed to restrict to the table of organization only those offices with defined responsibilities. Instead of maintaining the group of "tenured" and incompetent lower officials on the table of organization, he proposed that a sum of money be allotted to the section heads for dispersal to each desk to hire workers for administrative and all other desk tasks including correspondence.[142] These workers would be given the service rights of those "attached to the Ministry" (sostoiash-chii pri ministerstve) with posting to a given department. Shumakher wanted to send these men where they were most needed and even to use them temporarily to replace ill or otherwise indisposed higher "tenured" men. Their tasks were to be well defined and they were to be fully answerable for their work. He portrayed this system as a vast improvement over the existing one in which men were paid fixed salaries for indefinite tasks.

Shumakher wrote optimistically of the regime's accomplishments during the early years of Alexander's reign and of its promise. The number of regular officials in the central ministry could be nearly halved, he believed, and the salaries of those departmental officials remaining on the table of organization could be significantly increased at no extra expense to the State Treasury. He wished the salaries of his own department, and throughout the MVD, to be raised to the level already approved for equivalent positions in the Naval, Finance, and Education ministries. The salaries of the director and vice-director would become 7,000 and 5,000 rubles respectively, with similar raises effected down through the hierarchy. Shumakher believed that the imminent creation of provincial social institutions (the zemstvos), the projected reform of municipal administration, the centralization of all MVD personnel and archival matters in its Department of General Affairs, and improvements in the bookkeeping and disbursing sectors of the ministry would all alleviate the pressures on ministry departments. Higher salaries would allow departmental officials to devote full time and energies to their bureaucratic duties. A more rational division of labor, such as that resulting from the transfer of the administration of civil obligations (*zemskie povinnosti*) from the Department of Executive Police to the Economic Department, ultimately would improve MVD performance.

The Shumakher proposals and other commission materials formed the basis of Valuev's reform project for the central MVD table of organization submitted to the State Council in January 1865.[143] Valuev's project, however, did not go nearly so far in its proposed alterations of the existing system. His analysis of the existing shortcomings may be summarized as follows: (1) outmoded division of functions within the ministry; (2) low salaries, in some cases lower than those for comparable positions in other ministries, and resulting difficulties in attracting and keeping talented personnel; (3) excessive formalism in procedure. His solutions included a redistribution of functions within certain departments, and small-scale personnel cuts resulting in higher salaries for remaining permanent officials at no cost to the Treasury (in some cases salaries would remain below those for corresponding officials in the Naval Ministry). Valuev rejected a Naval Ministry innovation (seconded by Shumakher) namely, that of combining sections and their subordinate desks into new and more numerous instances called *deloproizvodstva*.[144] This would have meant an increased concentration of higher-ranking officials immediately below the vice-director level, and therefore fulfillment of Shumakher's vision of meaningful decentralization. Yet, because the MVD had so many departments, this would have meant a substantial increase in salary costs, and Valuev most likely was unprepared in 1865 to press for such advantages.

The Valuev project was reviewed in the State Council in April and May 1865. The results showed that although the State Council and Ministry of Finance could impose budgetary restraints upon ministries, the council of the empire's highest legislative organ had neither the will nor the power to demand or enforce a structural transformation of the ministerial bureaucracy.

After noting that the MVD project lacked budget cuts and failed to introduce the deloproizvodstva, and therefore did not follow the pattern of the Navel Ministry reform as ordered by the tsar, the members of the combined departments of the State Council expressed willingness to take into account the increased demands made upon the MVD as a result of the emancipation, zemstvo reform, the Polish uprising, maintenance of the exile system, and so forth. Accordingly, the council approved all the budget increases and redistribution of functions sought by Valuev. The State Council gave its approval, however, on only a "temporary" basis. Despite the budgetary restraint and the fact that ministry leadership had to argue logically and forcefully to get an adequate slice of the pie, it should be noted that some MVD officials resisted steps that might have led to structural transformation.

Nonetheless, for the ministry the 1865 decision had favorable elements. Salaries were raised and functions redistributed in a more rational way. It was reasonable to expect that improvement in MVD operations and slowdown of the growing pressures on the ministry would result. The State Council in 1865 requested that the MVD prepare another "final" project for submission no later than the first half of 1867. They insisted that Valuev make more personnel cuts and simplify procedures before that time. In the two-year interval the council hoped that the MVD could fulfill the tsar's wish for reform along Naval Ministry lines as well as prove its capacity to cope with its growing duties on the basis of the 1865 temporary table of organization.[145]

The archives record in detail the fate of MVD table of organization reform from 1865 through 1874.[146] Two "final" projects were submitted, one by Valuev on July 8, 1867, the other by A. E. Timashev in 1869. Finally, in 1871 Timashev created a commission to make one last attempt to solve the table of organization puzzle. The results in all three cases were as negligible as those in 1865.

Some notable trends emerged during the preparation of the projects, however. For example, departmental directors such as I. O. Velio (Executive Police) and Shumakher (Economic Department) argued for the creation of the deloproizvodstvo instance. Though in Velio's case this was little more than the familiar request for more men and money, for Shumakher it represented a major shift in position. Shumakher, in effect, admitted the naiveté of his good intentions of 1863-1864. Though he spoke for the Economic Department, his arguments expressed the quandary of the entire MVD. Basically, the grim administrative realities of the Reform Era had shattered his hopes for rationalization. By 1867 he argued that the Economic Department had acquired administrative responsibility from other departments for civil obligations (*zemskie povinnosti*, 1862), road-building (1864),

crown peasants (1865), state peasants (1866), zemstvo economic affairs (1886), and insurance (1867). Shumakher lamented the fact that
the zemstvos had not brought expected decreases in correspondence
and casework. Rather, the opposite occurred—more casework of increasing complexity. Furthermore, the many legislative projects which
were the department's responsibility required considerable labor at all
departmental levels, from project formulation to the clerical work of
incessant copying. In 1866 alone, the Economic Department presented
76 legislative projects to the State Council. That Shumakher, too, was
forced to ask for more personnel and money is further evidence of the
structural crisis in ministerial government. The rapidly changing Russia of the 1860s was no longer amenable to administration by Karamzin's "50 good governors."

Though the Valuev (1867) and Timashev (1869) projects were more
in line with the original Naval Ministry proposals, they generally expressed minor shifts in function and increments of money for especially hard-pressed MVD sectors. The Valuev project was caught up in
its sponsor's fall from grace and was never presented to the State
Council, while his successor's version, though examined in the State
Council during 1869 and 1870, was again approved provisionally for
three years. The council handed down a new mandate to prepare a
"final" project, and Timashev promptly created a commission to do so
under F. A. Beklemishev.[147]

The Beklemishev commission symbolized the fall, by the 1870s, of
ministerial government into entirely traditional and formalistic patterns of behavior and perceptions. Its work reveals neither the vision
of Shumakher nor the healthy skepticism of Valuev. Rather, the discussions focused on petty jurisdictional jealousies, label-changing,
and absurd formulae for determining workloads and the allocation of
scant resources. The sense that departmental work had become un-
manageable, that the ministerial office itself was overburdened, and
the absence of imagination and innovative spirit all showed that MVD
officials were prepared to allocate resources and meet their problems
in ways least likely to upset the traditional ethos and formal rules of
Russian bureaucracy. The Beklemishev commission proposals were
neither taken to the State Council nor implemented within the MVD,
and there is no further archival or legislative record of table of organization reform work during Alexander's reign.[148] From 1871 to 1881
nothing more was done. The MVD operated according to the temporary 1865 Valuev table of organization (as amended by the 1869 Timashev project), and its yearly budgets. With the exception of some
minor changes made by Loris-Melikov when he unified the police in
1880, in a period that demanded innovation MVD structure and procedures remained anchored in the past.[149]

This failure was symptomatic of the government's inability to complete much of the work on its agenda. The State Council had grown so weak in relation to the ministers that it could not enforce its order that the work be completed. Timashev, minister from 1868 to 1878, was not interested and did not understand the issues involved. Departmental officials were under great pressure and basically were opposed to change. After 1861 the MVD and the autocracy were on a collision course with political and administrative realities but, like the government of which it was a part, the MVD was unable to make structural and operational changes necessary that would provide a smooth transition into handling the problems of the new era.

The abortive table of organization reform was more significant than myopic institutional concerns of the MVD might indicate. The manner in which MVD bureaucrats addressed structural problems—and the solutions they proposed—were typical of the way in which policies and legislation were formulated within the MVD and the ministerial bureaucracy as a whole. The majority of MVD officials often treated other policy matters as they did the structural and procedural reforms described above. They tried to solve administrative and social problems that had political implications by incorporating solutions into formalistic organization. It was easier to co-opt social groups or institutions into the bureaucratic system they understood best than to identify and eliminate deeper causes of problems. The results, all too often, were superficial, formalistic, and politically counterproductive —the product of narrow and traditional bureaucratic vision.

According to P. A. Zaionchkovskii, the "crisis of autocracy" of 1878-1881 meant the autocracy's "inability to govern the masses on the basis of the existing laws and by means of the existing government."[150] The experience of the MVD during Alexander's reign lends another dimension to the idea of institutional crisis, though it began well before 1878.

The Impact of Leaders

3

Central to the political power of the Ministry of Internal Affairs and its policies were the ministers themselves. Though structure and tradition had their influence, institutional history requires that leadership also be examined. Five men served as ministers of internal affairs during the reign of Alexander II. These men were Sergei Stepanovich Lanskoi (1855-1861), Petr Aleksandrovich Valuev (1861-1868), Aleksandr Egorevich Timashev (1868-1878), Lev Savvich Makov (1878-1880), and Mikhail Tarielovich Loris-Melikov (1880-1881). They had remarkably diverse social backgrounds, career experiences, political viewpoints, and personalities. During their terms of office they exhibited varied political abilities and administrative competence. Each had successes and failures in the circumscribed political arena of domestic policy-making. They ranged from the charismatic war hero Loris-Melikov, who held the office for eight months, to the obscure and stolid Timashev, minister for over ten years.

The analysis that follows concentrates on the ministers' activities, ideas, and leadership rather than on the laws that governed their powers and responsibilities.[1] The laws set the general parameters of the ministerial role, but within the legal framework, other factors, in addition to the institutional concerns of individual ministries, determined how the ministers used the office. His personal relationship to the tsar, the configuration of forces within highest official and court circles, the minister's political vision, subjective conception of the ministerial role, social origin, education, and career experience all affected an individual's performance in office.

Sergei Stepanovich Lanskoi (1855-1861)

Of the ministers considered here, S. S. Lanskoi was the only representative of an earlier generation of Russian civil servants. He was born on December 23, 1787, into an old and noble family with a long history of state service. His father had been a marshal of the imperial court and a member of the State Council. His uncle, V. S. Lanskoi, had served during the 1820s as minister of internal affairs. Lanskoi was educated at home, as was common for young noblemen of his generation, and in 1800 (at age 13!) he entered state service as a translator in the College of Foreign Affairs. His career developed rapidly. Lanskoi did not receive a lycée or university education, but he held varied positions in many institutions, from the College of Foreign Affairs to service as civil governor in Kostroma and Vladimir provinces. Apart from brief early service in the Ministry of Finance (1815-1817), he did not work in any other central ministry offices concerned with domestic administration until his brief term in 1851 as acting minister of internal affairs. Lanskoi climbed the service ladder quickly, and when he was 32 he had become an actual state councilor (rank 4).

From Lanskoi's pre-1855 record a picture of lifelong dedication to state service in various secondary posts emerges. He had a 55-year service record prior to his appointment as minister of internal affairs. Although he had been a senator for many years and was a State Council member in 1850, his bureaucratic career was distant from the ministries. As was common in the Russian bureaucracy, Lanskoi became one of the realm's senior statesmen (sanovniki) without lengthy service in the ministries. During what should have been his career prime (the 1830s and 1840s), he worked mainly on state philanthropy (prisons, hospitals, orphanages, and so forth) and women's education. Although concerned with MVD structural and procedural problems as acting minister in 1851 and, again, as a member of the Commission to Reduce Correspondence and Simplify Administration, Lanskoi had little experience with the type of administrative and social issues he would face after 1855.

One of Alexander's first acts as tsar was to appoint Lanskoi minister of internal affairs.[2] There is no concrete evidence to explain the choice.[3] Lanskoi, already 68 years old, was a member of the State Council at the time. It is unlikely that Lanskoi was appointed expressly to lead a government emancipation effort. In August 1855 Alexander had not yet appealed to the Moscow nobility to offer its own program for emancipation. In his first public statement as minister, Lanskoi announced that the tsar had ordered him "to preserve inviolate the rights granted to the nobility by his laureled predecessors."[4]

Once Alexander decided to pursue "reform from above," however, Lanskoi and the MVD became indispensable to emancipation. The MVD was the logical ministry to provide initial government leadership and expertise because of its jurisdiction over the noble estate, provincial administration and police, and aspects of the provincial economy. Lanskoi used the MVD as a power base from which to pursue emancipation against opponents within and outside the government. Because of his unswerving support for emancipation "from above" and his tactics, Lanskoi and the MVD were reputed to be hostile to the nobility.[5] Under Lanskoi, the MVD also earned a reputation as a haven for progressive and, in some minds, radical officials whose dynamism and expertise were instrumental in enacting emancipation.

From 1855 to 1861 the MVD was in the hands of men who believed that autocracy stood above estate interests. They were ready to redress the injustices and flaws of Russian society and institutions and emancipate the empire's productive forces. Lanskoi's ministry appeared to reenact the Prussian reformers' example of the Napoleonic era, and men like Miliutin thought and acted in a manner reminiscent of the Hegelian "universal class" of civil servants.[6]

Lanskoi has been portrayed by some as an elder statesman dedicated to state service and morally committed to reform. Others have argued that he lacked the energy, will, and authority to have attained his goals without the help of talented subordinates. According to P. P. Semenov, Lanskoi at 70 was not equipped to be the minister. Although Lanskoi was "a man of high honor who frankly sympathized with the magnanimous intention of his sovereign in the affair of the emancipation of the peasants," even Alexander recognized that his minister had

neither creative thought and the clear, well-defined views of a statesman, nor a firm will in executing his own decisions—and given those facts, could not be the independent leader of the Great Reform undertaken by the tsar, or even the powerful bearer of the principles or program worked out by the more skillful state officials of his own ministry. Similarly, Lanskoi could not put across well his assimilated views in the highest state institutions, and in general in highest circles, because he was neither a gifted speaker nor a clear thinker. As a result he did not have sufficient authority among his colleagues.[7]

The French publicist A. Leroy-Beaulieu similarly praised Lanskoi's character, but more severely denigrated his talents:

Lanskoi, the minister of internal affairs at the moment when that ministry had to prepare the emancipation, acted under those circumstances in a way that did the greatest honor to his character and patriotism. A straightforward man, modest and sincerely devoted to the public welfare, he was justly frightened by the immensity of the task which officially fell to him. For his advocacy of the Great Reform, he wished to secure the assistance of a man of intelligence and energy. Far from fearing a talent which might eclipse his own, he appealed to Miliutin. He offered him the post of assistant minister which would assure Nikolai Alekseevich the upper hand in the elaboration of the liberation of the serfs.[8]

In his desire to eulogize Miliutin, Leroy-Beaulieu overlooked the fact that Lanskoi first turned to A. I. Levshin, his assistant minister and prime mover of the MVD's emancipation policy until the end of 1857. Nonetheless, Lanskoi's intelligent delegation of responsibility within the MVD to men whose talents he respected and whose views he shared stands out in all accounts of the emancipation process. The astute observer P. A. Valuev, Lanskoi's successor as minister and in the late 1850s an opponent of the MVD's position, understood the nature of the bureaucratic triumph within the Editorial Commission which made emancipation possible. He also understood the roles of Lanskoi and of the MVD. According to Valuev, Lanskoi's commitment to reform and his initial willingness to devote himself to the fulfillment of Alexander's wishes gave him and his MVD subordinates the initiative within the government: "Only Lanskoi [among the sanovniki and other ministers] fully gave himself to realizing the sovereign's idea. But Lanskoi alone was not powerful enough to bring it to fruition. He depended upon his subordinates and opened the way for these second-ranking figures to direct influence on the movement and direction of the reform. These men, of the second level according to their service position, were, on the other hand, higher in intellect and ability than their service chiefs, and they hastened to make use of their superiority."[9]

Despite the tendency to view Lanskoi as weak, vacillating, and overshadowed by younger men, the historical record indicates that he pursued emancipation and other goals with considerable tactical skill and vigor. Lanskoi adroitly defended positions taken by the MVD against competing government institutions and leaders, and he tried to retain for the MVD as much initiative and control in the emancipation proceedings as possible. His manipulation of the talents of his subordinates—such as Levshin and Solov'ev, experts on the peasant economy and veterans of long service in Kiselev's Ministry of State Domains, and Miliutin, Kiselev's nephew and the architect of the 1846 St. Petersburg municipal reform—was notable. When, for example, Levshin expressed reservations about the rapidity with which the MVD and the government were moving toward reform, and about antinobility implications of the Nazimov Rescript that he had been obliged to draft, Lanskoi removed him from effective participation in the reform work, opening the way for the growing influence of Miliutin and Solov'ev.[10]

Lanskoi's maneuvers in the Main Committee and Editorial Commission, his relationship to Alexander and the deputies of the provincial nobility, and his spirited defense of the autocracy and its ministerial government indicate that he was more than an ineffectual old man under the sway of progressive and energetic subordinates. Lanskoi had come to office at a fortuitous time, when numbers of talented men were for the first time in the nineteenth century available to serve in high ministerial positions. Whether or not Lanskoi composed his proposals to the tsar and the commissions is immaterial. His views coincided with his subordinates and, in any case, he could have altered or rejected statements expressing MVD policy. He could and did remove and replace dissenters. Indeed, "the guardian of the state interest" turned out to be more formidable than most of his opponents.[11]

How can Lanskoi's steadfast support of emancipation, administrative reform, and the views of his subordinates be explained? How did this quiet and rather obscure Nicolaevan official suddenly become a symbol of antinobility policies and state-initiated and state-directed social change? Perhaps this question can be answered by viewing Lanskoi's early life, family ties, and long record of service in philanthropic and educational matters.

During his first St. Petersburg service years, Lanskoi had been a member of various masonic lodges, and in 1819 he was inducted with A. N. Murav'ev's help into a secret society, the Union of Welfare (Soiuz blagodenstviia).[12] This organization succeeded the Union of Salvation and was a seedbed for the organizations that subsequently carried out the Decembrist uprising. At the time of Lanskoi's membership, however, such societies were avowedly apolitical. They provided meeting places where young noblemen serving in the military or bureaucracy could discuss masonic teachings and the new Western political ideas brought back to Russia from the European campaigns.[13]

Masonry first appeared in Russia during the mid-eighteenth century. Initially its teachings stressed the notion of the individual's moral perfection as opposed to any concrete political or reformist notion. Its adherents spanned the political spectrum, although as the French Revolution drew closer there were in some lodges whispers of republicanism and the need for social justice and humane treatment of the serfs.

The French Revolution and subsequent reaction in Europe brought the suppression of masonry in Russia and elsewhere. But during the first decade of the nineteenth century, under the protection of Alexander I, royal family members, and certain high officials, Russian masonry again came to life. The lodges were reopened, and it was rumored that the emperor himself was a mason. The number of lodges grew rapidly, but in the aftermath of the Napoleonic invasion and wars, the tsar and his government became more and more intolerant of the political implications of masonic ideals and began to use police surveillance as a control measure. Finally, on August 1, 1822, the lodges and all other secret societies were outlawed.

Lanskoi's society, the Union of Welfare, borrowed organizational principles and rites from the masonic lodges. It was, in theory, egalitarian and open to members of all social estates; its written constitution, the Green Book, was closely patterned on that of the German *Tugendbund*. The charter called on all members to lead a "socially virtuous" life and to assist fellow members when necessary. Taken literally, the Green Book was a moderate document with no political implications. Society members were authorized to work in four fields: philanthropy, education, justice, and national economy. Approved activities included the creation or improvement of hospitals and orphanages, prison reform, help to the indigent, aged, and invalid. Members were obligated to work for the humane treatment of serfs, the construction of schools and libraries, amelioration of the conscription and military colony system, and growth of the national economy. Although the Green Book required members to support the government, the Decembrist A. N. Murav'ev claimed that the organization did have tacit political aims but that these were known only to the highest-ranking members. It is supposed that the aims included the destruction of serfdom, establishment of equality before the law, and limitation of monarchical power.

Lanskoi withdrew from the society well before the Decembrist uprising, but his subsequent career reveals a pattern of effort to further certain masonic ideals within the framework of loyal service to the autocracy. This may help explain his years of work on philanthropy and education during Nicholas I's reign. As minister of internal affairs under Alexander II, he viewed the state apparatus as the single legitimate and most effective means to attain reform objectives. He therefore worked to improve the apparatus entrusted to him.

Some of Lanskoi's attitudes in his later life have been attributed by Semenov to the fact that Lanskoi's brother-in-law was Prince V. F. Odoevskii. Odoevskii was a prominent writer, patron of the arts, and scholar at the center of Russian intellectual life from the 1820s through the emancipation. Semenov regarded Odoevskii as one of "the most educated and humanistic people of the entire period." Naturally, Lanskoi would have been aware of critical currents from contact with Odoevskii and his friends.[14]

Although Lanskoi devoted most of his energy to the emancipation battle, his views on the related problems of provincial administrative and police reform shed further light on his conception of autocracy, institutions, and ministerial power. S. Frederick Starr has portrayed Lanskoi as an advocate of decentralization or the deconcentration of the central government's authority in provincial affairs. Starr cites the opposing position of "bureaucratic centralizers" who advocated "the far-reaching administrative control and concentration in all security functions," as well as Lanskoi's opposition to M. N. Murav'ev (minister of state domains), who had submitted a plan to reintroduce temporary governors-general throughout the empire. Starr and others also view Lanskoi, however, as a staunch defender of MVD authority in the provinces, in relation to the other central ministries and provincial society.[15] Lanskoi advocated strengthening the office of civil governor as the linchpin of MVD (and government) authority in the provinces. In 1845, as mentioned earlier, the MVD, through the governors and vice-governors, had already extended its control over the provincial governing boards.[16] By the late 1850s other ministries, particularly Finance, State Domains, and Justice, feared further extension of civil governor authority (and therefore MVD authority) over their own provincial officials.[17] If Lanskoi advocated decentralization while supporting the civil governors and MVD power in the provinces, one must still ask what decentralization meant for Lanskoi and precisely how his position differed from "bureaucratic centralization." Clarification of Lanskoi's views is found in his long memorandum to Alexander on August 1, 1858.[18]

Murav'ev's plan expressed the concern of certain high officials that a necessary precondition for emancipation was creation of an effective means of maintaining public order. As such, the plan was clearly directed against the civil governors and regular provincial administration (which were seen as unfit for the role) and any extension of MVD authority in the provinces. Within the Main Committee, only Lanskoi and Grand Duke Konstantin Nikolaevich, the tsar's brother, opposed the proposal, but MVD reformers greeted the plan with determined opposition.[19]

Lanskoi and the MVD reformers defended government by the autocracy's regular and lawful ministerial institutions, as opposed to the ad hoc creation of new pockets of personal power outside the regular institutional framework. Lanskoi argued that legality resided in the civil governors, and although he admitted that the provincial administration and police had incompetent and corrupt elements, he pointed out that the temporary and personal power of governors-general would not in any way ameliorate these conditions. In Lanskoi's opinion, the governors-general would create new jurisdictional disputes, unclear lines of authority, and increased paperwork.

Lanskoi also felt that the creation of governors-general would be a political mistake for the autocracy. He noted that the tsar's sanction of emancipation meant much to the Russian people, and that the best guarantee of a successful and orderly emancipation would be the government's willingness to proceed legally toward the goal. The creation of military governors-general was an extraordinary measure implying that the government was taking a defensive position against the people. Lanskoi believed the plan would be viewed as a threat, as a sign to many that the emancipation terms would be against their interests and that they had to be forced to comply.

Lanskoi claimed society had greeted warmly the earlier elimination of the governors-general as a sign of lawfulness (*zakonnost'*). Their reintroduction would oppose "the tendency in Russian legislation to limit or eliminate personal arbitrariness"; it would violate the established procedures and structures of government to create personal satrapies instead of strengthening regular provincial authorities.

Alexander's response to Lanskoi reveals much about the tsar's attitude toward institutions and places some of his actions in the 1860s and 1870s in better perspective: "I read this all with great attention and I should tell you that this memorandum has made a completely distressing impression upon me. It was probably written not by you, but by one of your departmental or chancery directors who is very strongly opposed to the suggested new institutions because these would weaken their power and significance which they are accustomed to and often use wrongly." The tsar emphasized that the situation in Russia on the eve of emancipation was "abnormal" and that certain extraordinary, precautionary measures were therefore absolutely necessary. Alexander disputed Lanskoi's claim that the governors-general were unlawful, arguing that because they were his personal agents endowed with his confidence, and because they would have written instructions, jurisdictional disputes and violations of the regular lines of authority would be avoided. According to Alexander, provincial civil authorities were incapable of handling potential disturbances.

In answer to Lanskoi's proposal that emancipation and related administrative and judicial reforms be enacted before taking extreme defensive measures, the tsar claimed it would then be too late to send governors-general to the provinces to pacify the peasantry. Lanskoi had claimed that the government need not fear disorders if the emancipation truly improved the lot of the peasantry, but Alexander emphasized that he always feared such disorders. Alexander viewed Lanskoi's defense of the integrity of the regular administrative structure as nothing more than "a civilian and, better said, *chancery* view . . . completely opposed to mine." What he did not understand was how deeply his own view permeated the *"chancery* view" of large sectors of ministerial officialdom.

Lanskoi's eight-point program of "legal measures" to strengthen the regular provincial authorities consisted of the following: (1) Pay more attention to the personal qualities and skills of men chosen as civil governors. Closely supervise their activities in relation to the reforms and give them more means to fulfill their responsibilities. (2) Appoint supporters of government reforms from the provincial committees to civil governorships and other high offices without regard to formalities of rank that only hinder the choice of capable and practical people. (3) Expand civil governor authority on the basis of the material already collected by the MVD on the tsar's authorization. (4) During implementation of emancipation, free the governors from the chairmanship of all subordinate provincial bodies and give this authority to the vice-governors. This would allow governors to supervise more easily the implementation of the reform as well as maintain public safety and order. (5) Authorize the civil governors to eliminate all elected and appointed police officials who prove untrustworthy, incompetent, or who act in a partisan spirit during the introduction of the new order. (6) Give the governors special funds for extraordinary expenses. (7) Give clear and definite special instructions to the governors on how to deal with the provincial committees—and clarify measures that may be used against both landowners and peasants in case of difficulties during emancipation. (8) If troops prove necessary, carefully inform the commanders of their correct relationship to civil authorities.

Although Alexander agreed with the first point, he maintained that the governors-general obviated most of the others. In any case, the tsar argued, the governors-general could outperform the civil governors in the emancipation functions Lanskoi outlined. Lanskoi was shaken by the sharpness of Alexander's rebuke. In his letter to the tsar of August 7, 1858, he reaffirmed the memorandum as his own position and claimed that he had been "loyally speaking from many years of state service experience." Lanskoi offered to resign, but for unknown reasons (possibly the perception that Lanskoi and the MVD were essential to secure emancipation), Alexander relented, asked Lanskoi to remain in office, and forced the Main Committee to drop the Murav'ev proposal.[20]

Lanskoi supported the integrity of the regular government institutions which he equated with the MVD's hierarchy of offices. In the late

1850s decentralization meant for Lanskoi (and for Artsimovich and Miliutin) the fulfillment of Speranskii's principle of departmentalism. This view, therefore, implied an alteration of traditional ministerial power away from the personal element without compromising central government authority. It was thoroughly statist but in an institutional sense, and it became the credo of several later nineteenth-century European and Russian bureaucratic reformers. It is misleading to inflate this position, as Starr does, to a full-blown ideology of decentralization that implies a lessening of the bureaucratic grip on the provinces. It is also misleading to label Alexander II and Murav'ev bureaucratic centralizers without drawing attention to their contemptuous view of those government institutions that they were supposedly strengthening.

Clarification of the problem is difficult if one reads the conflicts of the 1860s and 1870s back into the late 1850s. Because the zemstvos did not exist in 1858-1861, a defense of the civil governors against governors-general appears progressive. Later, from 1864 to 1878, Valuev and Timashev also tried to strengthen the civil governors and MVD control of the provinces. Scholars view their policies, however, as designed to secure central administrative domination of the zemstvos, the new judicial organs, and the provincial offices of other ministries.[21] In short, the later MVD policy of strengthening the civil governors is presented as a triumph of bureaucratic centralization. Although the policies of Lanskoi and Valuev may have been conceived in very different spirits, in practice the distance was not great between the former's "decentralization" and the latter's "centralization." Lanskoi and his subordinates had little faith in Russian provincial society, and particularly in the nobility, and they meant, by and large, to reshape the existing government apparatus and introduce social and economic reforms from above.

Lanskoi expressed his statism and hostility toward the nobility by doing everything in his power to deny to the provincial deputies, called to St. Petersburg, substantive participation in the emancipation legislative process. He also instructed the governors to forbid discussion of emancipation in the nobility's regular provincial assemblies. Effectively evoking the image of a conspiratorial noble opposition to emancipation based on narrow class interests, he astutely played on Alexander's fears of the nobility's political pretensions and oligarchy to keep firm the tsar's will.[22]

These tactics are visible again in Lanskoi's memorandum to the tsar of August 31, 1859.[23] Lanskoi was responding to the hints of landowner publicists that their estate be granted political rights. Lanskoi warned Alexander that strong state power was necessary to keep such pretensions in check. He wrote, "My relationships, official and private, have convinced me that the general mass of the nobility cannot and should not dream of representative forms of government, as these are completely opposed to our habits, levels of education, and basic state interests." Lanskoi spoke of aristocratic arrogance and love of power, and he warned that members of the provincial committees already were viewing themselves as representatives and trying to organize deputy meeetings. For Lanskoi, these aspirations were based on narrow estate interests; these and European examples proved that compensation (for emancipation) can "only be decided by government power." Lanskoi compared the government's position to the historical example of Peel's in Great Britain, and claimed that emancipation would benefit the nobility, whether or not they realized it, by raising land values and rationalizing provincial life. To be sure, administrative reform was necessary, he argued, but among the main culprits in the provinces were the elected judicial and police officials of the noble estate. Lanskoi concluded by claiming that the low level of Russian social development precluded constitutional government—and that any concessions in that direction at the present were "incompatible with and unworthy of the supreme power." Lanskoi's words were well chosen; Alexander noted, "I agree completely with all you have said."

Emancipation was enacted on February 19, 1861.[24] For Lanskoi and the MVD, enactment was but a momentary triumph—then the immense problems of implementing emancipation, along with handling the related social and economic questions, had to be managed. Lanskoi had retained just enough of Alexander's confidence to secure emancipation, but the tsar was not committed to the ideas of the reformers. With enactment secure, Alexander made an expedient gesture toward the nobility's wounded pride and interests.[25] In April 1861 he forced Lanskoi, then 74, and Miliutin to resign. Alexander felt that new men, untainted by the sometimes bitter proceedings of the past four years, were needed, and he had always been wary of Miliutin.[26] Lanskoi was given the title of count, and died shortly thereafter in January 1862.[27]

Lanskoi left a lasting legacy as minister, however—his comprehension of the office and the ministry's great power as an institutional base within the autocratic government. He was fortunate to have arrived in office just as the MVD had matured as an organization, and when younger, more competent (and, in some cases, visionary) personnel were available. As minister, Lanskoi understood the links between the institution and its staff, and how to attain political objectives within the autocratic context. It was a lesson not lost on future ministers of internal affairs, whatever their political persuasion or vision of Russia's future.

Petr Aleksandrovich Valuev (1861-1868)

The administrative career of P. A. Valuev, one of prerevolutionary Russia's most talented and enigmatic statesmen, spanned five decades (1834-1881); his tenure as minister of internal affairs began shortly after the emancipation in 1861 and lasted until 1868, when enemies in high government and court circles engineered his dismissal.[28] During his ministry, Valuev oversaw the implementation of the emancipation statutes and secured the legislation creating the zemstvo organs of local self-government. Valuev headed the MVD during the fateful post-1861 period with its mounting pressures of new duties and expectations. He presided over the transfer of censorship and many other functions to the MVD, and he articulately and forcefully defended the administration and the autocracy against a variety of perceived threats.

Alexander II had such great respect for this career official that Valuev participated in virtually every important domestic policy decision from 1861 to 1881. His loss of ministerial office in 1868 was only a temporary setback and did not exclude him from active government participation. Like many other fallen ministers, Valuev remained a member of the State Council, a largely honorary post. In 1872, however, Alexander gave him another chance to participate more decisively as minister of state domains, an office he held until he was appointed chairman of the Committee of Ministers in 1879. In addition, between 1872 and 1881, Valuev chaired the well-known commissions on the Condition of Russian Agriculture (1872) and Preparation of Legislation Governing Hired Workers and Servants (1875). Both commissions were politically significant and closely linked to P. A. Shuvalov's plans to institute a modest form of representation in the Russian legislative process.[29]

Valuev also chaired or participated in many special conferences (osobye soveshchaniia) during the 1870s, and particularly during the "crisis" period 1878-1881, that formulated government responses to terrorism and other threats to public order. In 1879-80, conferences under Valuev's guidance enacted such extraordinary measures as the temporary governors-general (April 1879), and the Supreme Executive Commission (February 1880).[30]

Although Valuev ardently defended autocracy and the primacy of the administration, he also penetratingly criticized the autocracy and an entire generation of Russian public figures. He wrote prolifically:

memoranda, diaries, newspaper and journal articles, even novels and mystical treatises. Yet the enormous published and archival record he left behind has still not been fully analyzed, and the nature of his political vision remains clouded. In the words of P. A. Zaionchkovskii, "The political views of P. A. Valuev are highly complex. He never fully joined any single government group—neither the liberal bureaucrats, the proponents of bourgeois reforms, nor the reactionary serfowners."[31] In fact, Valuev had few illusions about the autocracy's ability to adjust to the demands of the post-Crimean War era, and as Alexander's reign wore on, Valuev became more and more pessimistic about the regime's survival chances. He knew that a new kind of autocratic politics was necessary to harness the social and economic forces threatening to shatter the rigid system inherited from Nicholas I. But he understood the characteristics of the autocracy and of ministerial power that worked against creation of the required new political framework.

Although contemporaries viewed Valuev as a postemancipation defender of the nobility and its interests, and as a critic of the peasant-oriented MVD positions of Lanskoi, Miliutin, and other so-called progressives, his relationship to the nobility was highly complex and never one of pure support.[32] Valuev fiercely opposed gentry oligarchy, even the mildest forms of gentry constitutionalism, and most other political initiatives of the corporate bodies of the nobility or other sectors of society. State initiative and control could never be compromised in such matters.

Because he was aware of the political problems faced by the autocracy early in Alexander's reign, in 1863 Valuev made a proposal to transform autocratic politics in conjunction with the creation of the zemstvos. As a first step, Valuev wished to reform the State Council to provide representatives of interested and responsible social groups at least a minimal consultative voice in the legislative process.[33] Such State Council participants were to be chosen from among zemstvo members; their authority was to be strictly advisory. Valuev's aim in 1863—to expand the political framework of Russian autocracy—remained constant in his actions and writings through 1881. He pursued it while minister of internal affairs, later as a junior member in Shuvalov's bloc, and again in 1879-80 when his 1863 proposal was reconsidered, rejected, and finally overshadowed by Loris-Melikov's similar 1881 project. Valuev envisaged an active government, which could co-opt the opposition's support, and "stand at the head of the social movement." He thought Russia required a form of representation "as all European governments have," but he believed, or at least found it necessary to reassure the tsar, that this participation was possible "at no infringement on the supreme rights of autocratic power."[34]

This attempt to "square the circle" or increase political participation within an autocratic framework reveals the dilemmas faced by Russia's most farsighted prerevolutionary statesmen. Valuev's activities and ideas help explain the ambiguities and complexities of autocratic politics during Alexander's reign, and they also shed light on the autocracy's fate after 1881. His career background, the reasons for his appointment as minister of internal affairs, and his use of the ministerial office offer instructive contrasts to the Lanskoi example.

Valuev was born in Moscow on September 22, 1815, into an old noble family traceable to the fourteenth century.[35] He received a superb private education at home. In 1831 he entered state service in the chancery of the Moscow governor-general, and in 1832 he passed the examination for rank required by Speranskii's law of August 6, 1809. His meteoric career was launched when Nicholas I noticed Valuev and a friend at a ball and put them to work in the First Section of His Majesty's Own Chancery. Valuev's first marriage to the daughter of the poet P. A. Viazemskii brought him into contact with many well-connected aristocrats and St. Petersburg writers. Among these was Alexander Pushkin, who allegedly was so taken with Valuev as to model after him the hero of his "Captain's Daughter," Grinev. During these early St. Petersburg years, Valuev belonged to a group of young officers, career officials, and university graduates called the Society of Sixteen. These men met regularly for dinner and frank, far-reaching conversation with apparent disregard of the threat of Nicholas' political police. During the 1830s, therefore, Valuev had already caught the attention of the tsar and many influential individuals. Although he had many socially prominent contacts, Valuev had neither money nor property of his own. He was one of the young noblemen who found state service a necessity for both livelihood and status. His lack of wealth and critical nature always kept him at some distance from the aristocratic circles he would be accused of courting while minister of internal affairs.[36]

Valuev's career differed from those of Lanskoi and earlier ministers in several important respects. First, he was born later (1815) and must be included among the younger generation of Russian officials whose formative early service was entirely during Nicholas' reign. Second, he had much relevant career experience to prepare him for the kinds of problems he would face as minister. He was actively involved for 25 years with legislative and executive problems pertaining to provincial society and economy, and with administrative reform. Under Speranskii, Valuev's work in 1836 on codification established a direct connection to the individual most influential in shaping the ministerial institutions he would later direct. This work with Speranskii also exposed him to the tradition of creative and critical thinking within the bureaucracy that Speranskii represented. Significantly, Valuev also served many years in the Baltic region. There, in a variety of capacities close to the center of executive power, he gained experience in the general administration of a large geographical area. His attachment to the governor-general's office meant that much of his work was conducted without interference from St. Petersburg, and his experiences fostered independence and initiative—traits rare in the older generation of St. Petersburg officials.[37] Long service in the Baltic also provided Valuev a standard of comparison to Russia, a means of acquiring firsthand knowledge of Germanic institutions and social structure. Knowledge of non-Russian institutions deepened his understanding of Russian problems, and throughout his career he tried to discern the relevance of European history and contemporary events for Russia.

Before his appointment as minister of internal affairs, Valuev also served as the civil governor of Courland Province and as director of two departments in the Ministry of State Domains under M. N. Murav'ev. Valuev's penetrating memoranda and mastery of a variety of problems brought him to the attention of powerful individuals close to the court (such as Grand Duke Konstantin Nikolaevich, Grand Duchess Elena Pavlovna, and Prince V. A. Dolgorukov), and by 1859 he had become indispensable to Murav'ev. Valuev seemed destined for a ministerial portfolio. By 1859 he was already a privy councilor (rank 3), one of the empire's highest-ranking officials—a rare accomplishment for a department director.

Valuev's appointment as minister of internal affairs reflected the changes that had occurred in both the nature of Russian officialdom and ministerial government. Valuev was neither the tsar's personal friend nor a man of widespread social connections to either the court entourage or high officeholders. Although his appointment was in some measure engineered by Count V. N. Panin, Dolgorukov, Murav'ev (and Grand Duke Konstantin Nikolaevich),[38] their recommendations and Alexander's approval resulted from Valuev's demonstrated abilities and political views, particularly on emancipation and the nobility.[39]

Valuev was ambitious. He directly competed in 1858 with Nikolai Miliutin for the post of assistant minister of internal affairs after the removal of A. I. Levshin. Rumors of Valuev's appointment as assistant minister, in fact, circulated in St. Petersburg in March 1859, shortly before the tsar relented and appointed Miliutin on a temporary basis. From 1859 to 1861, Valuev complained often in his diary about his role as Murav'ev's subordinate in the Ministry of State Domains and his lack of independence. In January 1861 Dolgorukov helped engineer Valuev's appointment as manager of affairs of the Committee of Ministers. During the following two months more rumors circulated that he might be named minister of finance or minister of state domains.[40]

Alexander's appointment of Valuev as minister of internal affairs in April 1861 and the dismissal of Lanskoi and Miliutin were deliberate decisions to compensate the nobility after emancipation. Lanskoi had not requested retirement. With the emancipation legislation safely in hand, Alexander believed it best to remove the two men most directly associated with the ministerial bureaucracy's triumph in the Editorial Commission. For implementation of emancipation, Alexander favored Valuev, whose appointment would prove acceptable to the nobility who had been denied meaningful participation in the legislative process. In the words of P. D. Stremoukhov, at the time a deputy from Nizhnii Novgorod Province (later a high Valuev appointee in the MVD), "The appointment of Valuev signaled a shift in our internal politics to a more attentive relationship to the nobility and its interests."[41]

It would be wrong to assume that his attitudes toward the nobility and emancipation were the only factors in Valuev's appointment. The enormous task of implementing the complicated arrangements between landowners and serfs still lay ahead, as did work on many other programs. Valuev's reputation as a constructive critic of existing government and social institutions and as a brilliant and energetic administrator would certainly have made him an attractive choice. This would be especially true for a tsar still committed to a program of "change from above." And in 1861 Alexander remained committed to reform. In their first meeting after Valuev's appointment, Alexander told the new minister of his desire for "order and improvements which will not alter the foundation of the government."[42] Thus, from his first days in office, Valuev was faced with the traditional MVD dilemma— how to reconcile order and change without undermining the autocracy. Valuev's response to this dilemma shaped the history of the MVD for the entire postemancipation era.

Like Lanskoi and Perovskii, Valuev understood the importance of the ministry as a power base for his participation in autocratic politics. He saw the minister's role as broader than managing MVD business, and he used the office to make an effort to shape government domestic policy. In a conversation with V. A. Dolgorukov he once described the Russian autocracy as a "ministerial oligarchy." And Valuev played the oligarch role better than most. He was a far more active minister than Lanskoi had been. He did not permit either his assistant minister or his directors to take initiatives in general policy matters or even in important ministry business. Valuev wished to stamp his own political conceptions on the MVD, and he expected the ministry's highest officials to share these conceptions. He was a prolific drafter of penetrating memoranda and legislative projects, and he wrote many important MVD position papers himself. He sought competent, loyal, and politically reliable men to fill the central ministry's highest offices. In staffing the ministry with quiet and conservative career functionaries, Valuev profoundly changed the political orientation and image of the ministry that had been a haven for progressives of the Miliutin stripe. Valuev could not have tolerated as his assistant minister a man as dynamic and politically outspoken as Miliutin, regardless of his political convictions. This may be seen in his appointment of A. G. Troinitskii as assistant minister and in Troinitskii's relatively minor role throughout the Valuev ministry.[43] This is not to say that Valuev did not make use of memoranda writers, officials of special missions, and departmental directors. Their contributions were made, however, in strict accordance with his own political views and policy objectives. Valuev was a tremendously active man whose workdays, as reflected in his diaries, indicate the growing burdens placed on the shoulders of ministers as well as their key role in the functioning of the autocracy. Typical days for Valuev included sessions of the State Council, Committee of Ministers, committees of Poland and the Caucasus, and any number of special conferences, legislative commissions, and the like. It is a wonder that he had time to conduct any MVD business at all, and here the contributions of MVD officials were indispensable.

Valuev understood the power of the ministerial bureaucracy. The tsar's power was limited (though not always predictably) by the complexity of state affairs and the bureaucratic skills and organizational strength of the ministerial oligarchy. Valuev believed that there were profound impersonal forces at work in history which further limited the autocrat's power after the Crimean War. As he put it, the tsar could abolish laws with the stroke of a pen but was helpless to change the worth of the ruble on the St. Petersburg exchange by even one kopeck.[44] As a minister, however, Valuev knew that he could go only so far in the realm of high autocratic politics without the tsar's unequivocal support. He also must have substantial support from ministerial colleagues and others in the inner circle of domestic policy-makers. Valuev's diaries reflect obsessions both with the tsar's attitudes toward his minister and with what he perceived to be the shortsightedness, incompetence, and bad faith of the empire's highest dignitaries with whom he had to work. Whereas Lanskoi had a moral commitment to emancipation and other reforms, Valuev applied his political vision to saving autocracy from its internal weaknesses and from the external forces threatening to overwhelm it. In so doing, he influenced the MVD's future to a much greater degree than did Lanskoi.

Valuev's political views shed light on the evolution of the autocracy and the MVD after 1861. His ideas are a point of departure for comparing the views of other high Russian officials on many issues. His ideas may be distinguished from those of the "enlightened" group (Konstantin Nikolaevich, Miliutin, Golovnin, and even Loris-Melikov) as well as from such hard-line conservatives as D. A. Tolstoi and K. P. Pobedonostsev. Valuev occupied a position somewhere in the middle of a variegated political spectrum, but his brand of "enlightened conservatism" did not exist in a vacuum.[45] Despite his brilliant analyses and innovative programs, the new challenges of the 1860s and the legacy of traditional autocratic politics and institutions combined to strengthen his support of an unyielding autocracy inspired by a steadfast and only partially revised view of "ministerial" and administrative power. In this sense the tensions of Valuev's thought accurately mirror those built into the mandate and structure of the MVD as an institution.

Valuev established himself early as a scathing critic of the autocratic system inherited from Nicholas I. His 1855 memorandum "Thoughts of a Russian" brought him to the attention of Konstantin Nikolaevich and Grand Duchess Elena Pavlovna during the second half of 1855.[46] The grand duke issued a circular with excerpts of Valuev's criticisms to his subordinates in the Naval Ministry. In discussing the causes of Russia's Crimean War defeat, Valuev posed the following question: "Does the present structure of the various branches of our state administration favor the development of the spiritual and material forces of Russia?" His answer was pessimistic:

The administration's distinguishing feature is a lack of truth everywhere, in the government's lack of faith in its own apparatus and in its contempt for all other means. The numerous forms overwhelm the essence of administrative activity and guarantee the official lie. Look at the yearly reports. Everywhere all possible has been done, everywhere successes are gained, and the required order will be established—if not immediately, then at least gradually. But look at affairs, and separate paper appearances from actuality, truth from falsehoods and half-truths. Seldom will permanent and fruitful benefits be found. Above, there is a brilliance, below, rot.[47]

In "Thoughts of a Russian" and in a memorandum of October 2, 1856, which he submitted as governor of Courland to the Commission on Reducing Correspondence and Simplifying Procedures, Valuev attacked formalism, excessive centralization within the ministerial system, and the lack of unity among the institutions and highest officials of the central government.[48] Valuev argued that excessive centralization had stifled Speranskii's departmentalism, or the legitimate powers and independence of the various administrative instances. But even in the 1850s Valuev made a careful distinction between decentralization of ministerial authority and autocratic power. For Valuev, the latter was, and remained, inviolable. On the subject of unity, he decried the fact that the ministers acted as far as possible alone, without coordination or common ends. The Russian ministers in his view were "upholding the rules of the ancient system of appanages."[49]

Such criticism by Valuev of the autocracy as a system of government remained remarkably constant over the next 25 years. Writing in 1882, he called Russian ministers the domestic servants of the tsar. "My colleagues and I were *les grandes domestiques*, and not *les grandes serviteurs* of the state." He described the situation of ministers as an "Asiatic, half-slavish or primitive patriarchal relationship of the state servants to the sovereign which was incompatible with the conditions of the times." This relationship was not so much "a matter of form, as one of habits and understanding."[50]

Valuev criticized his fellow ministers for failure to transcend their institutional interests and to take broader views of political issues. Although he portrayed his own willingness to support others in the best possible light, his observations on the nature of politics in the highest governing circles are substantiated by many other sources.[51]

Valuev's political thought depended heavily on examples drawn from both Russian and European history. His opinions of Nicholas I and Peter the Great, for example, were central to his conception of autocracy and the role of government power in the postemancipation era. For Valuev, Nicholas' rule represented stagnation, ignorance of elemental historical forces of change, chauvinism, and blind anti-Westernism. Often Valuev attacked nonthinking conservatives, Slavophiles, and "political Old Believers," whom he associated with the Asiatic and dark forces of pre-Petrine Russia. He despised chauvinism and the foreign policies inspired by these elements. This led him to adopt a moderate position on the Polish question, and to oppose Russian involvement in the Balkans during the late 1870s.[52]

Valuev advocated that the government energetically take the initiative in social, economic, and political questions, in contrast to Nicholas' system of immobility. Valuev's writings show a preoccupation with change, movement, and development—ideas common to certain early and mid-nineteenth-century European conservative and liberal thinkers. But here his model was also Peter the Great. Valuev wished to re-create the Petrine police state, bring institutions to the fore within the old ministerial power framework, and institutionalize the idea of creative, but selective, borrowing from the West. He admired Peter for comprehending the benefits of Western enlightenment for Russia.

Peter's reign was dominated by two great ideas: "the enlightenment and enrichment of the state, and the strengthening and security of autocracy."[53]

Valuev clearly set out his views on the relevance for Russia of European experiences in an addendum to his diary dated November 12, 1868:

I don't find grounds for the antagonism between European and Russian understandings and strivings as is so readily suggested among us. I consider Russia a part of the Christian world and a part of Europe, although I do not consider her to be England, France, or Germany, and do not wish to transform her into any of those countries. But I don't consider that Russia, remaining Russian, should reject that share of general European education that would be useful to her. I don't think that Russia was fated to invent at the eleventh hour completely new state and social forms and I don't find in Russia's thousand-year history the basis for such invention. I suggest that Russians can, and even must, use several bases and ideas not developed by Russians.

Valuev's critical Westernism fed directly into his political programs while he was minister of internal affairs, as can be inferred from the following revealing statement: "I think that in each country and in each people there are given elements which must be acknowledged and mastered. Some of these elements must not be transformed, and others must not even be considered transformable. But the *methods* of governing these forces are, to use an expression, more or less general. They are the result of many experiences, over long time periods, in many places." Valuev sought to master European political techniques and forms in order to control the changes engulfing Russia and to secure the future for autocracy. His most important reform proposals must be seen in this light. These included plans to reform the *volost'*, district and provincial administrations, and the zemstvos, and plans to reform both the Council of Ministers and State Council to unify the government and provide political participation for provincial elites. European models were also behind his desire to free Russia's productive forces, loosen estate distinctions, promote economic development, solve the agrarian question, and abolish the peasant commune.[54]

In a memorandum dated September 22, 1861, "General View of the Situation of Affairs in the Empire from the Point of View of Safeguarding the Internal Security of the State," Valuev made his first encompassing statement of his political views.[55] The memorandum, only recently discovered among the personal papers of P. E. Shchegolev, is noteworthy for its comprehensiveness. Valuev's thoughts and government activities for 20 years followed the principles set down in the memorandum, in which he stated that Russia, like all other states, was undergoing fundamental change, and that the government had been unable to influence the people or direct the social movement because of its lack of political vision and because of its many inherent structural and institutional weaknesses. Valuev reviewed the nature and potential value to the state of each social group. He maintained that it was critical to solve the agrarian question and to transform the nobility and the state's relationship to that estate. With great foresight, Valuev linked these economic and social problems to the realm of politics and institutional reform. He understood that the working apparatus of the autocracy had to be renovated in order for the ministerial bureaucracy to keep autocracy alive. In his mind, reform of the executive branch, the Committee of Ministers, and the individual ministries was unmistakably tied to plans for representation in the legislative process, local self-government (the zemstvos), and provincial administrative reform.

For the government to win the hearts and minds of the people, Valuev proposed creation of a government press as an effective censorship weapon against dissent. The spirit and tone of his arguments are captured in the following passage:

I consider it my duty to express my deep conviction that this movement that is present now and rapidly growing must be given an outlet. It cannot be contained in a closed circle. It can be directed, but must not be suppressed by force. Ideas, even those that are lies, may be contained with ideas. I refer as evidence not only to generally known European conditions, but also to the experience of our own history— to the centuries-long experience of the schism and the 30-year experience in the western provinces. World history testifies to the fact that in the development of states there are times when the suppression of ideas that are undermining social order cannot be accomplished by the use of government power alone precisely because of the limited number of unconditionally subordinate weapons at the government's disposal. What is needed is the cooperation of that part of society that is imbued with or may be imbued with opposing ideas. Pitting one side against the other, the government may rule over both and retain for itself appropriate space for its own power.[56]

It must be noted that, even at this early stage in his ministry, there were ominous signs in his thinking of an unconditional reverence for state power. Later this thinking would exemplify his ministry as the pinnacle of police power. The defeat of his most sophisticated plans was due in large measure to the power structure and ideological justification he had promoted. Valuev qualified his demands that government power not be weakened and that police and censorship be strengthened by recommending that institutional reform neither challenge nor undermine the traditional roots and foundations of autocracy. After 1861 it became increasingly difficult for Valuev to avoid the kinds of rhetorical and policy commitments that strengthened the ministerial power ethos and worked against realization of his plans to transform autocracy.

Valuev developed general plans to reorient autocratic politics in a memorandum to the tsar of June 26, 1862, "On the Internal Condition of Russia." He reviewed the growing isolation of government and tsar from all the social estates and hinted that the army's loyalty was questionable. He felt that the central government had no support in Russian society and was losing control of its provincial organs. Among his main concerns were the problems of government finances, Poland and the western provinces, and Russian youth's attraction to materialist and radical doctrines.

Valuev proposed that the government take the offensive:

We have taken the first step with the project for local economic institutions, but it is more than doubtful that this step will be sufficient. We must make an analogous attempt in the central administration . . . In an era of social agitation it is more important than at any other time for the government to take possession of the social movement and stand at the head of the social movement which creates three-fourths of history. For this notable boldness is necessary in activities which will surprise the masses and impress them. To this end it would be fruitful to return to the well-known idea of reforming the State Council on bases analogous to the Austrian Reichsrat and the State Council of the Polish Kingdom. This measure offers the advantage that it does not deliver a single blow to the full power of the sovereign, and secures for him all legislative and administrative authority. Besides which it would create a central institution which would embody some form of representation of the country.[57]

A plan to reform the State Council was drawn up in a detailed project submitted by Valuev in April 1863.[58] It proposed to institutionalize within the State Council a form of national representation based upon the zemstvos. That the plan was based upon the zemstvos was crucial. In his project of November 18, 1863, Valuev outlined the creation of a "Congress of State Deputies" (S"ezd gosudarstvennykh glasnykh) which would act as a consultative department of the State Council.[59] The deputies were to be elected by the provincial zemstvos, although there would be some representation from the capital and other significant cities. Special regulations were to govern elections from areas where zemstvos had not yet been introduced. The president and vice-president of the Congress and 14 of its members were to take part in State Council proceedings on specific issues defined in the project.[60]

Valuev's plan went further than Grand Duke Konstantin Nikolaevich's 1866 plan for representation and even Loris-Melikov's so-called constitutional project of 1881. Valuev proposed a permanent and institutionalized form of society's participation, whereas the grand duke's plan called for ad hoc consultations. But, more important, Valuev's deputies were to be elected only by the zemstvos, not by the corporate assemblies of the nobility and the zemstvos as projected by Konstantin Nikolaevich. Valuev, basing his plan on European models (particularly Austrian), wanted the new proto-representation to express the predominance of the nobility. The nobility was to retain its position in society as the only educated and propertied estate, but its representation in government affairs would be based more on economic function and wealth than on corporate status. To be sure, the nobility dominated the zemstvos in the 1860s and 1870s given the property qualifications governing the electoral laws, but Valuev openly rejected the old corporate bodies of the nobility as the basis for his plan for representative institutions. Feeling that the nobility's extant assemblies leaned toward oligarchy or constitutionalism, Valuev encouraged transformation of the Russian nobility into an economically viable, cohesive, responsible class that might act as the autocracy's principal support in society. Despite the enormous potential benefit to autocracy of Valuev's plan, Alexander ultimately vetoed it after it had been voted down in a special conference of high officials.

Valuev's views toward the nobility definitely show ambivalence. As early as December 1859 he wrote that the nobility was only "a *caste*, not a state estate [*gosudarstvennoe soslovie*] that had to be transformed in a rational sense."[61] Later, during his ministry, he was to reiterate that the nobility ("or what is to be taken by that name") did not understand its own economic and political interests or positions.[62] Nonetheless, he persisted in his view that only the provincial nobility could have the enlightenment, moral authority, and economic strength to aid government in preventing "the apocalyptic breakup of Russian society."[63]

To Valuev, property, education, religion, and family were the bases of a healthy social organism. He believed that neither the peasant masses nor the nobility in their present state could supply a stable foundation for the state in its attempt to reunify society. Yet his support of the nobility ended whenever any group within that estate attempted to organize, associate, or even discuss political issues independently of the government. As minister, Valuev quickly and decisively smothered political initiatives from both the assemblies of the nobility and the zemstvos. Also, he was extremely hostile toward the new peace mediators drawn from the nobility to assist both peasants and landlords in fulfilling the 1861 emancipation statutes.[64]

For Valuev, the government had to retain the initiative and control in all *political* matters, and as new challenges to the government arose during the 1860s he fell back more and more on his deeply held belief in this cornerstone of traditional ministerial power and the indivisibility of autocratic authority. By 1866 Valuev's earlier fears about the radical threat and the decline of government authority were far more pronounced. The initial Great Reforms—emancipation, the judicial reform, and the creation of the zemstvos—had opened a Pandora's box, and Valuev feared that the government was losing control over both society and the historical forces at work. After the Karakozov affair in May 1866, he could write to Urusov that his State Council reform project was meant to "save the autocracy."[65] But by that time his projects and memoranda displayed a primary commitment to reestablishing government authority as a prerequisite for even more tightly controlled political change. Aspects of "ministerial power" previously muted or implicit in his writings now began to take precedence over his more optimistic plans to expand the framework of autocratic politics. In 1867 he wrote about the "indefinite and pathological strivings of society." In his words, "The Russian people have been for centuries accustomed to strong power and to its universal application everywhere. Only government power, balanced in its gravitation and with equal and forceful influence on all the far-flung parts of our state, will be able to guide society to its further development on a true and lawful path."[66]

As the primary transitional figure in the MVD's evolution from the Lanskoi-Miliutin era to the conservative Timashev and Makov years, Valuev almost unwittingly furthered the cause of the traditional ministerial power ethos. His advocacy of unbridled administrative and police authority survived Alexander's reign and was carried on by D. A. Tolstoi, V. K. Plehve, I. L. Goremykin, and P. N. Durnovo, later ministers. Although Valuev never attained an unchallenged leadership position during his ministry, his articulate and spirited defense of the administration and police and his policies that strengthened them profoundly influenced the future of the MVD.

In reasserting administrative and police authority, Valuev sought to justify anew the traditional interventionist and regulatory state power and the bureaucracy's continued domination of Russian political life.

He restated and reinforced the equation of MVD, administrative, and government interests, and he linked these to autocracy itself as the only legitimate constitutional principle in Russia. This relegitimation of autocracy reinforced its anti-institutional biases and this in turn promoted paralysis in domestic policy-making and a heightened sense of governmental crisis during the last 15 years of Alexander's reign.

After 1861, structural additions to the MVD, particularly the Jurisconsult Section, the growing discretionary powers that allowed Valuev to issue circulars with the force of law, and other laws and policies that sought to strengthen the government's administrative and police powers attest Valuev's role in the reformulation of MVD ideology. The massive ideological rift between the administration (and ministerial power) and the alternative principles represented by the zemstvos and 1864 judicial reform colored Valuev's perception of the Reform Era. In 1881, after Alexander's assassination and the Loris-Melikov ministry, Valuev reflected:

The varied reforms of the previous reign have not brought the desired results and several have had consequences completely inconvenient for the monarchic principle . . . We must add that in our legislation there still exists a dualism of new and old institutions and charters which are still not in accord. The police and the administration have been pushed far to the rear under the pressure of the judicial and social institutions, and there is an antagonism and discord between the powers of the judiciary and administration that is completely harmful to the state order.[67]

The dualism of institutions and principles became more noticeable after the initial Great Reforms of the early 1860s. The growth of an indigenous radical movement, the more articulate public opinion, and the 1863 Polish uprising placed advocates of traditional ministerial power on the defensive. Valuev and the MVD defined the administration's attitude toward the new principles and institutions and the perceived threat from society itself. Under Valuev, the MVD intensified its earlier attempts to strengthen the provincial governors' authority both in relation to the provincial organs of other ministries and to the zemstvo organs of local self-government. Valuev worked to restrict zemstvo activity to local economic matters and to deprive zemstvos of the executive authority and financial means necessary to fulfill even these meager functions.

Valuev's role in the relegitimation of "ministerial power" and of the administration's hegemony during the Reform Era was not lost on contemporaries.[68] The censor A. V. Nikitenko, a subordinate in the MVD, noted Valuev's growing reliance on police power in defining the MVD role in censorship, provincial administration, and the new judicial system.[69] Nikitenko thought that Valuev and P. A. Shuvalov, head of the Third Section and Corps of Gendarmes, were moving Russia toward full-scale police rule. According to Nikitenko, Valuev saw the press more and more as his personal enemy. The censor also accused the minister of wishing to subvert the new judicial institutions and place them under firm administrative control. Nikitenko called Valuev a "pure bureaucrat" who "understood only reports" and consistently ignored "the spirit of the people," one of Russia's worst enemies.[70]

The progressive minister of education A. V. Golovnin, one of the immediate casualties of the ministerial changes after the Karakozov assassination attempt, also assessed Valuev's performance. Golovnin met Valuev in 1845 while both were serving in Livonia. Though he thought Valuev was a highly educated and brilliant administrator whose opinions were valued highly during the 1860s by Alexander, Golovnin sharply criticized Valuev's ministerial policies. Golovnin pointed out that for five years in the 1840s he had served in the MVD under Perovskii and thus was well acquainted with MVD responsibilities and operations. Golovnin's criticisms of Valuev centered on the minister's policies in the area of political justice. Spying and denunciations were becoming functions of the MVD, undermining the noble and pure reputation of the ministry, and in Golovnin's opinion these activities rightfully should have remained activities of the Third Section.[71]

Golovnin claimed that emancipation and creation of the zemstvos had placed greater burdens on the MVD, but that Valuev had sought even more power, having added the construction section and other organs to the already overloaded ministry. Golovnin accused Valuev of wishing "to have influence and to intervene in all areas of the administration" and "to participate in all possible commissions and committees including those on finance, education, Poland, railroads, etc." This cost him precious time and worked against improvements in the matters within the jurisdiction of his own ministry. MVD involvement in political police work, according to Golovnin, also cost valuable time and money and, worse still, gave all MVD activities "a police and investigatory character instead of a highest administrative character." In addition, Golovnin castigated Valuev's MVD appointments and his ostensible attempt to build a party of support in high court and aristocratic circles. Reviewing administrative actions against the zemstvos and the judicial institutions, Golovnin criticized Valuev's popularity with and guardianship of the nobility.

In an effort to be fair, Golovnin praised Valuev's policies toward the Poles and schismatics. Rather optimistically, he stated that all of Valuev's administrative actions "could only wreck the details," but not "the whole structure of laws" created by N. A. Miliutin and other authors of the Great Reforms. Golovnin maintained that Valuev was "neither evil nor a flatterer and didn't use his position or the tsar's confidence to harm others." That was "an enormous quality and it is completely possible that given the increase in power of his successor, many will frankly regret Valuev's departure."

Police power, during Alexander's reign, served as legal and moral justification for state intervention and regulation. Russian society was believed to be insufficiently developed to look after its own affairs or to uphold state interests. The legitimacy of the police function and the attitudes it engendered among even the most articulate high officials were inseparable from the institutions of ministerial government that evolved between 1802 and 1881. As minister of internal affairs, Valuev understood his mandate to develop and utilize the police powers inherent in the office. That the broad view of police power permeated his thinking may be seen in his writings and policies dating back to his ministry's earliest years. In his official Report for the years 1861-1863, he wrote that despite ideological rifts, "The real danger is from the economic crisis already tangible to all and which may develop very rapidly."[72]

Recognizing that economic backwardness threatened society by promoting the revolutionary movement, Valuev persistently defended the administration and its police power. In several memoranda written in 1866 and 1867, he argued that the government and its police authority were on the defensive against an internal enemy, namely, the rival principles of separation of powers, rule of law, and self-government and freedom of expression inherent in the new institutions and statutes of the Great Reforms.[73]

Valuev's long struggle against the political threat to bureaucratic hegemony of the zemstvos and judicial institutions began almost from their creation. A focal point for his defense of the police function against these new institutions was the office of provincial governor. In 1866 Valuev joined with Shuvalov and the minister of state domains, A. A. Zelenyi, in submitting to Alexander a special memorandum advocating substantial increases in the provincial governors' authority. They argued principally that the governors' power had been significantly weakened by the new competing reform institutions. They argued that the long-postponed reform of provincial administration was of the utmost urgency because of the growing sense of zemstvo and judicial independence in both the public and the official consciousness. Although Russian legislation referred to the governor as the "master" (*khoziain*) of the province, the authors complained that the office had lost status. It did not have authority over non-MVD officials and institutions, was unable to influence provincial appointments below the seventh class in non-MVD organs, and had lost concentrated supervisory power (*nadzor*). The loss of supervisory power was a critical issue, involving the separation of powers and the relationship between the provincial judicial institutions (particularly the *prokurory*) and the administration as represented by the governors and the MVD. In essence, the memorandum advocated that the governor control all provincial government and justice. Lawsuits, citizens' complaints, and inspections would all become the governor's responsibility as chief of the province. Since final reform of provincial administration and police would be a protracted affair, the authors requested immediate action on their proposals outside the State Council.

Alexander granted the request, and after hasty discussion in a special commission, the memorandum recommendations were debated on July 5 and 12, 1866, in the Committee of Ministers. Police authority of the governors was expanded and reaffirmed as proposed by Valuev. The governor's control function over all administrative offices and personnel was stated clearly, not simply as a reaffirmation of principles already existing in Russian legislation. The governor was given power to close meetings of private associations, clubs, and artels whose activities were considered hostile to "the state order and the security and morality of society" by merely informing the MVD of their action. The validity of many laws permitting and governing the dispensation of political justice in so-called extraordinary circumstances was reaffirmed. The committee journal emphasized that these laws were neither abolished nor superseded by the 1864 judicial reform and its guarantees of due process. Reaffirmed also were the discretionary powers of all ministers, and particularly that of the MVD minister, to emphasize and expand police authority by means of circulars and instructions.[74]

Valuev defended the government's police powers and the legitimacy of administrative justice in a memorandum written sometime in 1867. He attacked again the new judicial organs and their underlying principles. The governors, he reiterated, had lost administrative and moral authority, thereby leaving the state with less protection than western Europe. Valuev singled out the peace mediators and prosecutors (prokurory) for their hostility to the state's interests in the provinces. The prosecutors, in his view, were inhibiting the legitimate executive power (*rasporiaditel'naia vlast'*) of the governors, who were reduced to observers rather than active protectors of "the state interest and autocratic power." Valuev cited the rise of individualism and the threat of materialist and critical ideas as particularly dangerous in Russia because of the low level of society's development. The role of government power, he argued, was changing from a traditional guardianship (*opeka*) to a regulator of individual aspirations. The state had to make sure that these aspirations did not clash with its interests. In Valuev's view, such assurances could be realized only by the use of new methods.[75]

The challenges of society's criticism and the dualism of principles and institutions within the government itself were met by Valuev's revitalization of ministerial power. The Great Reforms had placed the administration in a "completely new" position, and both state and society were undergoing fundamental redefinition. Valuev aimed to salvage the integrity of administrative and police authority amidst the renovations and to secure what he regarded to be their rightful primacy within the state structure.[76] This position was taken over eagerly by his successors and became, after 1868, an MVD institutional hallmark.

After 1864 Valuev clarified the conflict boundaries between the principles of administrative and police authority and the rule of law principles promised by the 1864 judicial reform. This conflict between rival principles and institutions, which persisted through the 1870s and even through the revolutionary upheavals of the early twentieth century, had profound implications for Russian autocracy. The ministerial bureaucracy's desire to retain a police monopoly and to dominate legislative and judicial functions contributed to the paralysis of domestic policy-making and the regime's inability to broaden its political base. To maintain the ministry's authority over the independent and new judicial institutions, Valuev created a special MVD organ—the Jurisconsult Section.

Historians have ignored or overlooked the creation of the Jurisconsult Section and its functions. It is not mentioned in the official MVD history until its merger in 1880 with a similar organ of the Corps of Gendarmes to form a larger Juridical Section. Historians have also neglected the series of special conferences and commissions between 1865 and 1878 that attempted to shore up administrative power and define a better working relationship between administrative and judicial institutions at the provincial level. Instead, they have focused on some of the laws and edicts (sometimes called counterreforms), passed during the 1870s, that expanded the administration's ability to dispense political justice for so-called state crimes without interference from the prosecutors or regular courts. The reassertion of administrative authority represented by these edicts was closely related to provincial administrative reform and the role of the governors—and the attempt after 1864 to define a working relationship between the administration and judiciary in which the former would dominate. The defense of administrative and police authority that Valuev helped initiate forms the backdrop for MVD activities throughout the 1870s. It also establishes a vital continuity between the middle years of Alexander's reign and Loris-Melikov's activities in 1880-81 as chief of the Supreme Executive Commission and minister of internal affairs.[77]

After the passage of the 1864 judicial reform, the ministerial bureaucracy moved quickly to establish a modus vivendi with the new institutions and principles. During 1865 a commission chaired by Count Adlerberg, the minister of the imperial court, met to discuss the relationship between the administration and the new judicial system. The work of this commission was inconclusive, however, and on February 14, 1866, Valuev independently moved to define the MVD's position in relation to the 1864 reforms by submitting to the State Council a proposal to create a Jurisconsult Section within the MVD. The presence in other central ministries of "specially trained" jurists with this title was not a new thing, as Valuev pointed out in the preface to his proposal: "For a long time several institutions have recognized as useful to have in their central organs an official, especially familiar, by virtue of his juridical training and practical experience with the judicial sphere. With this goal jurisconsults were established in the following ministries well before the judicial reform of 1864: Ministry of the Imperial Court, War, Navy, Holy Synod, and State Bank." The competence of these organs was limited to property and contractual matters directly involving the parent institution. In light of the "completed reforms of the government administration and new legislation, and especially because of the fundamental reforms in the judicial system," Valuev held that it was now necessary to create such a jurisconsult at the MVD. He framed his proposal in terms of the established raison d'etre of the office: "On the basis of the judicial statutes of November 20, 1864, the ministries have been placed in a completely new relationship to the judicial power . . . as regards answerability of administrative officials for losses incurred to state properties entrusted to them and for the activities of officials accused before the courts." The new judicial statutes had increased direct contacts between the administration and courts. Administrators now had to make personal appearances before the courts as plaintiffs, defendants, and witnesses in suits brought against other officials.[78]

Valuev also raised the issue of the relationship to the judiciary of MVD (and therefore government) provincial administrative and police organs. He claimed he had already conducted a "complicated" four-year correspondence with the Ministry of Justice on all subjects pertaining to the separation of judiciary from administration, including the MVD's role in constructing the new institutions. The correspondence was meant to work out instructions for MVD administrative and police offices on the new relationship between administration and judiciary and to prepare legislative proposals for solving all questions that might arise from the application of the new judicial statutes to the administration. Valuev thought it was most important to have an official to represent the MVD in the courts and before the judiciary as a whole on matters relating to the MVD's responsibilities.

It must be remembered that Valuev's proposal was made at the same time that the MVD was attempting to reform its table of organization which was itself a response to growing responsibilities and workload. Since the government's budgetary resources were severely strained, his proposal is a measure of the seriousness with which Valuev viewed administrative-judicial relations. In his arguments for the creation of the office, he considered budgetary limitations. Although the functions outlined, except for MVD representation in the courts, might be fulfilled by the regular departments, the extraordinary technicality of legislative and judicial matters called for administrative coordination of efforts. In short, he envisioned the jurisconsult as "a specialist in legislative matters" and an "intermediary [organ]" between the MVD hierarchy and judicial power.

He went on to outline in detail the functions of the proposed "intermediary." The jurisconsult was to work with the departments to ensure that all legislative proposals were in the proper form and that all judiciary-related matters were handled expeditiously. The jurisconsult would be equal in service status to the department directors and members of the Council of the Minister. Specific duties of the jurisconsult were set forth as (1) participation in the writing of all projects to be approved by the legislative authority or those requiring instructions that develop the law; (2) examination of all affairs that central ministry departments decide require legal opinion (on the basis of prior report to the minister); (3) participation, including voting rights, by order of the minister or assistant minister in ministry special councils; (4) appearance in St. Petersburg, Moscow, and, when necessary, in the provincial courts on civil and criminal matters relating to the MVD, or its subordinate organs and officials; (5) participation in the writing of contracts or agreements between the MVD and private individuals; (6) cooperation with the provincial administration in judicial cases involving MVD interests; (7) fulfillment of all duties and special missions ordered by the minister of internal affairs.

Clearly, Valuev had in mind a much more significant jurisconsult than those of other central government organs. He wanted to create a separate reservoir of juridical expertise to defend administration and MVD interests before the new judicial system and principles. Moreover, the new office would function as the minister's personal supervisory agent in departmental legislative work. In essence, the jurisconsult would be a highly skilled and specialized official of special missions, but with a higher rank and service status and the assistance of a modest staff. In addition, the jurisconsult would have the service rights of a department director in matters involving central and provincial MVD organs, and the right, with the minister's approval, to use officials of the ministry (sostoiashchii pri ministerstve) for special jobs. Valuev stated that the jurisconsult and his assistant had to be graduates of either the juridical faculty of a university or a special juridical institute. (An adequate substitute for this formal training, however, would be completion of a successful examination in the juridical sciences, or proof of the requisite knowledge through service experience.) For this post, designed to promote the MVD's interests, Valuev chose P. O. Kititsyn, a staunch defender of administrative and police authority. Kititsyn was to remain jurisconsult for 14 years and write several important projects for both Valuev and Timashev.[79]

The Valuev proposal was discussed in the State Council's Department of Laws on April 23 and May 23, 1866. It was met with hostility by council members who immediately linked its creation to the table of organization reform. Only if a final table of organization were enacted could the MVD expect approval of the jurisconsult office. Furthermore, council members decreed that there must be corresponding cuts in personnel and expenditures. The State Council borrowed from Valuev's 1865 argument, claiming that the zemstvo and judicial reforms should decrease MVD correspondence on judicial matters and that the MVD departments of General Affairs and Police, and the Economic Department already handled such matters.

The council viewed the proposed jurisconsult functions as encroaching upon established duties of other MVD departments. They warned that such wide authority would lead to disconnectedness in MVD activities, and perhaps even to harmful antagonisms among individual MVD officials. The council believed that final revisions of legislative projects should be made in the Council of the Minister, as required by articles 27 and 98 of the 1811 Institution of the Ministries. The necessary preliminary work, they argued, could be done by the department directors and officials of special missions. Thus the State Council at first rejected Valuev's jurisconsult proposal and its implied adversary relationship between administration and judiciary. Valuev, however, was not to be denied; and in May the State Council reversed its stand

and approved the proposal as a "temporary" measure, pending completion of the table of organization reform.[80]

Along with the Department of Executive Police, the MVD Jurisconsult Section became directly concerned with defending the hegemony of the ministerial bureaucracy and the primacy of administrative authority from 1866 to 1880. It too was a promoter of ministerial power. Kititsyn wrote the MVD projects on provincial reform during the late 1860s and early 1870s and participated in all the special conferences and commissions that considered the growing conflict between administration and the judiciary. He and Valuev expressed similar opinions as to the administration's need to defend itself against the court system and the prosecutors. Throughout the 1870s they argued that the police and administration were consistently placed at a disadvantage by judicial officials in their attempts to secure public order.[81] They believed that the new 1864 judicial procedures demeaned administrators and policemen, lessening their prestige and authority in the eyes of the citizenry. They also believed that the judiciary no longer served state interests.

In summary, Valuev recognized the need for autocratic Russia to solve the same problems faced by the regimes of western Europe—expansion of the political base (and eventually mass politics), and the need to generate social support and maintain conditions favorable to economic growth to satisfy the relevant elites. Following the Crimean War, Valuev was the first in a line of visionary Russian bureaucrats who understood the problems of and offered solutions for modernization by means of institutional change and state-directed reform. Valuev's proposals and other writings foreshadow the later attempts of Loris-Melikov and Stolypin to come to terms with the requirements of modern statehood within an institutional framework burdened by tradition and structural weakness. What distinguished Valuev's political vision from Loris-Melikov's, however, was the distance each was willing to go in order to meet the changing political requirements of their times, and the spirit with which each approached the legitimacy of politics. It is one of history's ironies that Valuev's preoccupation with police authority and administrative hegemony after the mid-1860s strengthened traditional ministerial power, serving as a catalyst for the defeat of Loris-Melikov's 1881 plan to "save the autocracy."

Aleksandr Egorevich Timashev (1868-1878)

The appointment of Aleksandr Egorevich Timashev as minister of internal affairs in March 1868 is an indication that administrative skill and political vision were not required for ministerial office. Unlike his immediate predecessors, Timashev was a career army man, a general, and a police official, formerly chief of staff in the Third Section and Corps of Gendarmes, and a wealthy landowner of 100,000 *desiatiny* in Orenburg Province. Valuev's replacement by Timashev expressed the growing conservative strength of the autocracy.

Timashev was born on April 3, 1818, into a family of wealthy landowners and military service men in Orenburg Province. His father, Egor Nikolaevich, had served during Nicholas' reign as the Ataman of the Orenburg Cossack troops. Earlier ancestors were Smolensk service men ennobled in the mid-sixteenth century. Members of the Timashev family had served as d'iaki and voevody for the Muscovite tsars during the seventeenth century. Timashev received his formal education at the boarding school attached to Moscow University and at the School of Guards, Junior Ensigns, and Junkers. (He thus did not have the university or lycée education that had become prevalent among civilian officials of his generation.) Upon completion of his schooling, Timashev entered active military service as an *unter-ofitser* in the Izmailovskii Regiment.[82]

During his term as minister Timashev, unfamiliar with and uninterested in many ministerial matters, displayed little political skill, even within the closed circle responsible for domestic policy. He came to the MVD as an outspoken opponent of Alexander's early reforms and as an advocate of Russian autocracy as epitomized by the reign of Nicholas I. Timashev had been so displeased with the emancipation statutes, activities, and antinobility policies of enlightened officialdom that for a time he resigned from state service to brood over the situation. In a March 17, 1861, conversation with Valuev, Timashev had spoken of his intention to leave the service and stated his motives. "To remain in service at present, it is necessary to have unlimited personal devotion. I felt this for Emperor Nicholas. I don't feel it for Emperor Alexander. For the principles [of autocracy] yes, for the person, no. The emperor is suffering from illusions about what is happening. He is a despot at the bottom of his soul. He told me himself that he would sooner die than capitulate, and now we march toward capitulation."[83]

Only two years later, however, Timashev answered Alexander's call and took an appointment as temporary governor-general of Kazan, Perm, and Viatka provinces, a post created to control social unrest and the activities of exiles in the wake of the Polish uprising. By 1867 he was back in St. Petersburg as minister of post and telegraph. Only a few months later he was appointed minister of internal affairs. In fact, Timashev was doubly rewarded, because he retained the post and telegraph portfolio, that institution being incorporated into the MVD.

How can one explain the return to service, the rise to power, and the remarkable longevity in office of this man? Compared to Miliutin, Valuev, and Loris-Melikov, Timashev remains an obscure figure. He avoided the political squabbles of highest officialdom except to act as an ally of more forceful and articulate officials. He was a quiet man for whom personal service to the sovereign remained a deep and dominant motivation. In other words, he was a perfect exponent of traditional ministerial power, fitting Valuev's description of ministers as the tsar's domestic servants, a relationship encouraged by tsars and ministers alike.

Timashev's activities are further obscured because his ministry came in the interval between the Karakozov affair and the intensified governmental crisis at the end of Alexander's reign. Examination of government policies sheds some light on Timashev's ministry, but does not substantially change his contemporaries' harsh judgments.[84]

Timashev returned to service because he was patriotic and had a deep sense of duty. D. A. Miliutin viewed his elevation to ministerial office as follows: "The appointment of Timashev clearly expressed the current direction of our internal politics. A man who revealed himself during the epoch of the emancipation of the serfs as an open opponent of that great state measure, who then went abroad loudly and furiously abusing all the liberal reforms of Alexander II, now becomes minister of internal affairs! This appointment was a new and outstanding step along the path of reaction and a new victory for the Shuvalov party."[85]

V. G. Chernukha and I. V. Orzhekhovskii have recently argued that Shuvalov needed an assistant and ally to realize his plans to build a unified governing bloc and institute a form of representation during the early 1870s. Chernukha maintains that because of his great power, the minister of internal affairs should have been Shuvalov's ally. But, in Chernukha's opinion, Timashev was not suited for such a responsible and delicate role. Timashev's official colleagues observed that he seemed little interested in MVD affairs and that he often appeared in the Committee of Ministers or the State Council unprepared to discuss the matters under consideration. A. N. Kulomzin, the assistant minister of state domains, said that Timashev "could give basic clarifications only with extreme difficulty." State Secretary D. M. Sol'skii commented on the new minister of internal affairs in an 1869 letter to Valuev: "Your chair, as happens, is occupied by another. But from him the former spirited discourse does not resound. To put it better, nothing resounds."[86]

The ultraconservative Prince Meshcherskii, the moderate bureaucrat A. A. Polovtsov, the liberal theorist Chicherin, and Valuev all criticized Timashev's performance as minister and later as State Council member. On March 10, 1874, in a moment of exasperation, Valuev wrote in his diary, "Today I saw Timashev and Shidlovskii. Minister and assistant minister. Where else but Russia could they last?" Writing in 1889, Polovtsov commented on Timashev's role as a conservative member of the State Council during the 1880s: "Such people as Palen, Timashev, and Count Bobrinskii vulgarized and made hateful what conservatism gloried in."[87]

Though Timashev's administrative and political abilities were limited, certain officials who served under him in the MVD defended him. V. K. Lutskii, for example, recounts how Timashev paid for his daughter's funeral.[88] Lutskii recognized that Timashev had little experience that suited his MVD appointment. Lutskii, however, thought that Timashev's bad reputation resulted from his service in the Third Section. The talented A. D. Shumakher, director of the MVD Economic Department, saw his superior as "an honest and completely direct" man. Shumakher even published a defense of Timashev's MVD policies toward the zemstvos from 1868 to 1878. By citing all legislation, he tried to prove that contrary to public opinion, Timashev and the MVD consistently expanded the rights and legitimate activities of the zemstvos. According to Shumakher, Timashev approved many zemstvo petitions, was responsible for introducing zemstvos into other parts of the empire, and was committed to local self-government. As proof of this, Shumakher cited Timashev's approval of reworking Valuev's earlier municipal reform project in order to give the cities even more rights, and claimed that State Council passage was secured because of Timashev's "great tact."[89]

It is possible that Shumakher was justifying the role of the ministry he had served for decades and his own acts as director of the department responsible for zemstvo and city affairs. But even Valuev praised Timashev when, in 1861, he described him as "intelligent, irascible, one-sided, ambitious, and steadfast." Fifteen years later, complaining of the small-mindedness and intrigues of his colleagues, Valuev wrote, "General Timashev! At the least he is personally above reproach as a comrade, and in general does what he is capable of doing."[90]

Timashev had little general administrative experience and virtually no exposure to many of the social, economic, and political problems he would encounter as minister of internal affairs. In the Third Section (1856-1861) he had worked on the Main Directorate of Censorship. That experience provided him with a fund of ideas to which he would revert after 1868, including subsidizing progovernment publications and authors, creating an all-government daily newspaper, and nurturing intense hostility toward the press and intelligentsia.[91] As the tsar's personal representative to Kazan, Governor-General Timashev was to encourage peace and guard against possible subversive activities by Poles exiled there after the 1863 uprising.[92] In 1864, he left Kazan with thanks from the local merchant estate for bringing order to the territory and for promoting trade and industry.

Timashev's early career reflects his ideas about personal service, administrative and police authority, and military discipline. As a young man he had served Alexander as a member of the tsar's suite and commander of his escort. Timashev showed distaste for the Great Reforms, but his temporary rejection of service could not diminish the magnetism of the tsar. After 1866 Alexander was far more ambivalent toward legislative change and he did not offer outright reformers positions of authority. Timashev realized that the balance of forces within the government had shifted toward pure autocracy, a position he could support. As Shuvalov wrote at the time of Timashev's appointment as minister of post and telegraph: "You have been away a long time. The alignment of forces in favor of this or that has changed. This is not an illusion; it is palpable . . . I assure you that the principles of stability, order, and propriety are represented with a force and majesty so grand that the two or three voices which still flounder will be absorbed entirely."[93]

As minister of internal affairs, Timashev supported that part of Valuev's program (and Shuvalov's) which stood for the sanctity of the autocratic principle and the primacy of administrative and police authority. The combination fit well into the old ministerial power framework. Significantly, Alexander felt sufficiently secure with this loyal minister. Timashev complained about lack of unity and direction in government policy, but he could not conceive of anything resembling a cabinet or representative institutions. For Timashev, institutions meant the old, safe, personal-service relationships within their rigid legal frameworks, and he would have agreed with Karamzin that Russia needed 50 good governors more than law or institutions. Timashev's view of institutions is apparent in a July 18, 1863, letter to Valuev from Kazan: "The fatherland is in danger as never before, and in spite of that what do we see. Half measures. Nothing but half measures. If patriotic sentiments are a bit recharged, it is due to Katkov . . . Extraordinary measures are necessary, the nation needs to be electrified. The emperor must go to Moscow, to the Nizhnii Fair. It is necessary to supplement this with the formation of a homogeneous government which doesn't squander precious time in sterile discussions."[94]

Timashev went on to discuss the practical problems of creating a unified government and voiced his fears that a single minister might become too powerful. Behind a unified ministry, he wrote, "one sees the phantom called a prime minister." He proposed that the tsar choose two acceptable individuals who were in agreement on principles. The two would choose a third minister, the three a fourth, and so on, until the complete cabinet was approved by the tsar. This fear of strong domestic leadership from someone other than the tsar was common among Russian officials and helped to promote the government disunity and absence of political leadership that Timashev and other conservatives decried.

When Timashev first assumed office, Valuev gave him at the request of the tsar four memoranda outlining the most significant problem areas faced by the government in 1868.[95] These were: (1) curbing the new elements introduced by the zemstvo and judicial reforms, (2) the peasant and agrarian questions, (3) Poland and the western provinces, and (4) censorship and the press. Valuev observed that Timashev was not interested in these vital questions, and that Timashev's three main concerns were to create an all-government newspaper, to introduce a second assistant minister who could substitute for the minister in the highest governing bodies, and to separate the censorship apparatus from the MVD.

Shortly thereafter Timashev became greatly concerned with censorship, and he proceeded to pursue objectives in the 1870s similar to those of Valuev. Unlike Valuev, however, he gave little thought to censorship as an institutional problem. Timashev wanted the whole MVD censorship apparatus returned to D. A. Tolstoi's Ministry of Education, but he did not believe that the government should ease its control over censorship. Valuev, who had been responsible for the 1865 laws that transferred primary censorship responsibility to the MVD, was outraged. He believed that Timashev only wanted to avoid the many "difficulties and inconveniences" connected with this task.[96] Valuev felt that press affairs "by their very essence" and political significance belonged under MVD jurisdiction regardless of the inconveniences. He believed that Timashev wanted to give Tolstoi the responsibility not because of the latter's administrative abilities "and not because he was minister of education, but because of his personal qualities." Valuev commented with his habitual acerbity: "That is also a completely unique way to decide basic questions. And who still take over press affairs tomorrow if Tolstoi, with all his personal qualities, becomes ill with colic?"[97] It is worth noting that in 1858-59, when Timashev was the Third Section representative on the Main Directorate of Censorship (at that time under the jurisdiction of the Ministry of Education), he proposed creation of a new Fifth Section of His Majesty's Own Chancery to oversee and unify censorship functions.[98] During his decade as minister of internal affairs, Timashev, unlike his predecessors, could not be accused of empire-building.

Despite his limitations, Timashev retained Alexander's confidence. In October 1872 Timashev caused a diplomatic incident while visiting Paris. At a state dinner given by President Thiers, he outspokenly remarked to a stranger that the Russian government deplored the activities of French radicals, and particularly of Gambetta, since they inspired radicals in all lands. The story was played up in French and British newspapers, and Timashev submitted a lengthy explanation of the incident to the tsar.[99] He said that on meeting Thiers, he had complimented the French president on France's internal stability and on the good order of its army. After the dinner conversation with the stranger, who was apparently a confidant of Thiers, Timashev was invited the next day for another audience with the president. Thiers emphasized that although the spirit of parties was harmful in France, his own position was stable, and that Russia need not be concerned with the radical threat. Thiers said that the remark made by Timashev would be forgotten soon and expressed interest in cultivating Russia's friendship.

In his report to Alexander, Timashev pointed out that Thiers was bent on demonstrating the stability of his position so that nobody could guess the opposite and that his words on radicalism were not consonant with his actions. He cited various severe actions taken by the French government and concluded that the situation was indeed serious. In spite of the diplomatic uproar caused by the leaks to the press, the tsar wrote on the report, "All you have said is true," and Timashev continued in office.

In January 1874 there were rumors in St. Petersburg of Timashev's impending ouster because of alleged indiscretions.[100] Timashev wrote to Alexander requesting permission to resign as minister of internal affairs and from state service completely.[101] Alexander denied Timashev permission to resign from state service, saying that only after the conclusion of diplomatic negotiations then taking place in St. Petersburg could Timashev resign from the MVD. Both Alexander and his minister changed their minds, however; Timashev continued in office for four and a half years, apparently in the tsar's good graces because at several times during those years rumors circulated that Timashev was to take over the Third Section.[102]

The document that best contrasts Timashev with his predecessors Valuev and Lanskoi is his memorandum to Alexander, written sometime in the early 1870s, on the proposed extension of military obligations to the nobility.[103] It should be remembered that universal military service was enacted by the military reform of 1874. It was an ambitious measure based largely on European experience. Among the government's complex aims was a desire to ease the onerous service burden on the peasantry and to promote a sense of common obligation and sacrifice on the part of all citizens, including noblemen. It was hoped that, among other things, the reform would improve the army's morale and combat capability.[104]

Universal military service touched on one of the most important issues faced by the autocracy after the Crimean War—the future of the estate (*soslovie*) system, particularly of the nobility. As minister of internal affairs, Lanskoi had attacked aristocratic privileges and political aspirations. And in fighting doggedly for peasant emancipation, he had helped deal the nobility its most serious blow. Valuev, less hostile to the nobility, envisaged a productive and politically reliable social group less dependent on caste privileges and sought ways to shape an ineluctable process of social change.

But Timashev adhered to a vision of the nobility and Russian society as they had existed prior to the Great Reforms. He therefore opposed extending obligatory military service to the nobility and presented his arguments to this effect to the tsar. He wrote that the proposed measure would be of little practical consequence, as there were already on active service 32,000 officers and 10,000 junkers of the noble estate.[105] He said Sevastopol had shown that the army's spirit was superb and was not the reason for its Crimean War defeat. Russia's defeat was purely a question of organization and armaments.

Timashev emphasized the current strained relationship between the nobility and the government. He pointed out that for well-known reasons there was even noble opposition to the monarchic principle. "In its current mood, the nobility sees all appearances of monarchic power as despotic tyranny." Timashev distinguished between government measures resulting from state or social necessity (for example, militia service when Russia was invaded and the setting up of quarantines), and those not resulting from "circumstances." The burdens of the former were acceptable to all, but the latter brought only "grumbling and irritation" as did all tyrannical measures. Timashev argued that this was especially true when the state trampled on rights and privileges granted by charters and written into the basic laws. Universal military service would, he wrote, inculcate in the entire estate the current and widely held view that the sentence on its survival had already been pronounced.

Timashev saw the reform as the product of the War Ministry alone, and not, as society would believe, as a conscious or deliberate policy of the entire government. If the tsar really meant to decide the nobility's fate, he argued, it must be thoroughly considered at the highest government levels:

[How] could such a suggestion be made in an ordinary committee to reexamine the recruitment code consisting of *chinovniki*, when the matter is about a principle of such importance that it means for Russia's highest estate the question—"To be, or not to be." You [Alexander II] may say that such a proposal could be overturned in the State Council. Yes, but for a single institution even to raise such a question is remarkable to the highest degree. Who would believe that such an idea could be worked out in a single ministry, if it is not in accordance with the program of the entire government and the will of the sovereign himself. I will answer—Nobody!—except perhaps those who recognize and lament the complete lack of like-mindedness and unity of action in our government.[106]

Timashev concluded that the destruction of estate rights would cause great indignation and have incalculable political consequences.

Aside from his inability to grasp the full political and social import of Miliutin's proposals, Timashev adhered to a static view of society. He looked backward to re-create a mythic nobility already overtaken by political events and social change. Although the military reform was passed, the autocracy did try in succeeding decades to prop up the nobility through generous financial support and ostensible attentiveness to that estate's political interests. This effort proved futile, however, and during the Stolypin era the nobility remained too weak to wrest power from the autocracy but was just strong and organized enough to help block such important plans as Stolypin's provincial reforms.

On nationality and foreign policy questions, Timashev's views derived from his blind patriotism and sense of duty. Here he differed from Valuev, who took moderate positions on the Polish and Baltic questions and who viewed intervention in the Balkans and war with Turkey as disastrous adventurism. Timashev despised the Poles, was much less sympathetic to the Baltic Germans, and patriotically supported the Turkish War in 1877-78 with no thought of the domestic consequences.[107]

The censor E. M. Feoktistov recorded an example of Timashev's foreign policy view. In 1871, after the Prussian victory over France, Timashev called in the editors of St. Petersburg periodicals to inform them of the government's decision no longer to abide by the Treaty of Paris provisions governing access to the Black Sea. Timashev told them to show the "required patriotism" in presenting or discussing this action in their periodicals. In a long speech, he attacked "ultrapatriots" who stirred up opinion against imagined German threats to Russia, and he claimed that Russia's 1871 reversal of the European imposed humiliation of the 1856 Paris Treaty was possible only because of Prussian support. The tsar, he advised, would tolerate no criticism of Prussia in the press, and "any hostile tone toward Prussia will be punished severely."[108]

Timashev supported the military and police traditions of Nicolae-van Russia and the ethos of ministerial power. As minister of internal affairs he was a transitional figure, serving after the period of greatest MVD growth and creativity under Perovskii, Lanskoi, and Valuev and before the extreme reaction of the Tolstoi era. Timashev's leadership served to push the MVD further in the police-oriented direction that had begun under Valuev. He shared none of Valuev's political vision and mastery in administrative matters, however. There is no evidence that he gave systematic consideration to the fundamental problems of the autocracy, or to the institutional structures of the system he revered.[109] His appointment and long term as minister of internal affairs expressed the internal weakness of autocracy, and did not bode well for its ability to adapt and survive in a changing world. To Timashev, Europe's political experiences and social traumas—the revolutions of 1848, the Paris Commune, the growth of working-class movements, and so forth—were nightmares only to be avoided. He spent his greatest energies strengthening the forces of administration and police in order to reconstruct a largely mythical past.

Lev Savvich Makov (1878-1880)

When Timashev left office in November 1878, the *Government Messenger* praised his successor, Lev Savvich Makov. The newspaper emphasized Makov's long career in the Ministry of Internal Affairs under Miliutin, Solov'ev, and Timashev in St. Petersburg, and M. N. Murav'ev in the western provinces. Makov's suitability for the sensitive and difficult office of minister of internal affairs remained in question, however.

Little is known of Makov's family background or childhood.[110] He was born in 1830 into the hereditary nobility of Kharkov Province. Unlike most high MVD officials of his generation, he was educated in the Corps of Pages and spent his initial service years (1844-1856) on active military duty. By 1856 Makov was serving with a guard regiment present at Alexander II's coronation in Moscow. In May 1858, at the age of 28, he was discharged from the army because of illness. Three months later he entered the civil administration and the Ministry of Internal Affairs with the civil rank of court councilor (rank 7, *Nadvornyi sovetnik*).

Makov's service record is typical of the generation of successful Russian central ministry officials discussed in Chapter 4. The only aspect of Makov's record that distinguishes him from other high MVD officials of the era is his military education and initial military service. This service was brief, however, and Makov entered the civil service and MVD after severing completely his military connection. This occurred in 1858 at the young age of 28; therefore Makov should not be

counted among the small percentage of military men who served in
the MVD. In effect Makov was a career MVD official—a man who
rose through the hierarchies of rank and office by a combination of his
own skill, industriousness, and reliability, and with the protection of
superiors who valued his abilities.

In the words of one well-informed contemporary chronicler, "By his
capabilities and character, Makov was precisely 'the average man'—
hard-working and obliging, intelligent, a good writer, and animated,
even when he spoke. He was the type who would succeed in life, and
especially in administrative circles."[111]

Like his predecessor Timashev, Makov has remained obscure, a
career *chinovnik* best remembered as Loris-Melikov's predecessor and
for his February 1883 suicide, apparently in response to a charge of
misuse of government funds while minister.[112] Despite his meager
written legacy and the fact that he served as minister less than two
years, Makov is important for several reasons. He was the only man
appointed from within, from the MVD's career bureaucrat ranks. He
was a member of the younger generation of career officials who advanced to high positions in the central MVD organs during the 1850s
and 1860s. A skillful, loyal functionary, he was elevated by Valuev.
During the Reform Era Makov worked diligently on those MVD matters that should have prepared him well for the ministerial portfolio.
His appointment coincided with the spread of revolutionary terrorism
and the government's growing sense of helplessness, a situation that
severely tested all Russian high officials, but particularly Makov as
minister of internal affairs. In fact, the challenge of the office over-
whelmed him; he was quickly overshadowed by Loris-Melikov after
the creation of the Supreme Executive Commission in February 1880.

Makov's performance and fate as minister reveal much about autocratic politics and about the nature of the man. As minister of internal
affairs, Valuev had appreciated Makov's abilities, character, and performance in a variety of subordinate positions including director of
the minister's chancery.[113] During the crisis years of 1878-1881, however, Valuev often lambasted Makov's efforts as minister, particularly
decrying his lack of vision and political skill. After a special conference session on April 15, 1879, Valuev wrote: "I am alone, completely
alone. Even the new minister of internal affairs, a well-intentioned
force, doesn't have the desired rapport with me. He may be minister of
his own institution, but he is not a minister in general. He lacks the
kind of vision which I call panoramic." After attending meetings of
the State Council and Committee of Ministers on March 24, 1880, Valuev wrote (in English), "The Home Secretary is quite below the mark;
however, he is not the only one."[114] The state secretary, E. A. Peretts,

expressed a similar view on December 15, 1880: "Now it is clear that Makov duped us. Here is the difference between Makov and Loris: that is between a skillful *chinovnik* and a truly wise man."[115]

Makov's ministerial policies and various official documents corroborate these views. He consistently took positions colored by the ethos of ministerial power in support of the administration and police. These policies softened only during the six months prior to his removal (February through August 1880) when the strong policies and government leadership of Loris-Melikov did not tolerate MVD recidivism.

Makov's successful MVD career began in the Zemskii otdel, the organ created in 1858 and given primary responsibility for peasant affairs. In 1861 Valuev appointed him official of special missions, VI Class, for peasant affairs, responsible to the minister. Valuev then sent him to participate as the MVD representative in Senator Kapger's revisions in Kaluga and Vladimir provinces;[116] this was undoubtedly a crucial assignment in furthering Makov's career. In 1863 Valuev sent Makov to work on various peasant affairs with the governor-general of the western provinces, M. N. Murav'ev. Murav'ev apparently regarded Makov so highly that he fought his subsequent transfer to new duties in Kiev.[117]

Valuev promoted Makov several times "for excellence." On January 1, 1865, he received the rank of actual state councilor (rank 4), and was rewarded further with appointment as director (*pravitel'*) of the minister's chancery. This appointment was a career milestone, as he was now privy to all MVD business including secret matters handled directly by Valuev. With the expansion of MVD activities and workload in the mid-1860s, Valuev depended heavily on his personal chancery director. Makov served in that capacity until 1876, when he was appointed as one of two assistant ministers. Valuev, meanwhile, maintained his ties with Makov, who was chosen to serve as MVD representative on Valuev's well-known agrarian and labor commissions of the early 1870s. Early in 1878 Makov participated in the special conferences on state security chaired by Valuev. It must have seemed logical to Alexander and others to appoint Makov as Timashev's successor. At first the appointment was temporary, but on February 19, 1879, Makov was confirmed as minister of internal affairs.[118]

Makov continued in his earnest and industrious ways. He apparently worked day and night and had a fine grasp of the MVD's administrative responsibilities. Before Makov officially took office as minister, on June 9, 1878, Alexander signed into law his project to introduce a 5,000-man force of mounted rural guards (*uriadniki*). This was the

culmination of a 20-year process of police reform begun in the late
1850s under Lanskoi, Miliutin, and Solov'ev. In February 1879 the
tsar expressed pleasure at the reform and thanked Makov for his efforts. In 1880, in his 25-year report on MVD activities, Makov proclaimed that the ministry's goal of transforming the provincial police
into a specialized body concerned with state security had been realized.[119] Makov's contemporaries and recent scholar offer a different
picture, however. M. S. Kakhanov wrote in 1882 that the mounted
guards had no organic ties to the police structure, had serious deficiencies of many kinds, and did not represent an improvement over the
old *stanovye pristavy*.[120] A contemporary critic of Russian police reform put it more simply by concluding that the provincial police in
1880 "were still the dregs of Russian society."[121]

Although Makov's administrative talents might have resulted in the
amelioration of various problems under MVD jurisdiction, the rise of
terrorism and deteriorating economic conditions forced all ministers
to spend time developing plans to combat the perceived threat to public order. In the series of special conferences organized for this purpose, and in the Committee of Ministers, Makov supported the hegemony of administrative and police authority.[122] As months passed, he
grew increasingly hostile toward society. After an attempt on the
tsar's life in March 1879, Makov and Tolstoi recommended that all
suspicious persons be removed from St. Petersburg.[123] Makov also
restated the old MVD complaint that the judiciary's provincial prosecutors were interfering with MVD police work and the administration
as a whole. In order to soften the effect of the government's various
extraordinary measures, Makov appealed to society to the *Government Messenger* of August 19, 1878.[124] He called on all estates to support the government against the revolutionary evil. What such support meant in practice, however, was left unclear, and when the Kharkov and Chernigov zemstvos petitioned to the tsar in answer to the
appeal, the MVD quashed the petitions and placed their initiators
under police surveillance.

On April 4, 1879, Makov called to his apartment 30 leading St.
Petersburg editors. According to two participants, E. M. Feoktistov
and M. I. Semevskii, Makov made a long speech about the condition
of the Russian press. The minister accused the press of destroying the
moral fabric of Russian society and of causing the evil that was threatening Russia. He accused the press of publishing only derogatory
statements about the government, and claimed that the first duty of
the press was patriotism. He concluded with a threat: "The press must
be patriotic, and I warn you that it will be such, or it will cease to
exist! From this moment there will be leniency toward nothing and

nobody."[125] Makov would continue to support administrative control of the press when serving on Valuev's special commission to rewrite the censorship laws in the fall of 1880.[126]

Makov was hostile to the plans to reform the State Council and to introduce a form of representation. At a meeting of the special conference held on January 23, 1880, to discuss Konstantin Nikolaevich's 1866 plan, Makov said that the time was not ripe for such reforms.[127] He believed that only after ending extraordinary measures (such as the temporary governors-general, appointed in April 1879) could talk of such reform begin. And talk was exactly what he had in mind, for Makov wished to proceed only according to the formal behavior patterns of the autocracy he had so faithfully served.

When it came to matters of general state policy, Makov always insisted on the full participation of all concerned government institutions and the endless passing around of projects and commentaries on projects which so often hindered decisive government action. Makov was not the type to assume leadership in the government, or to try to set its course in domestic policy. In fact, he regarded those who would play this role as immoral. This became evident in Makov's relationship to Loris-Melikov and his attempt to redefine the politics of autocracy.

In February 1880, when Loris-Melikov was appointed chief of the new Supreme Executive Commission, Makov was wary. Within the Russian government it quickly became clear that Loris had become a virtual dictator of domestic policy and that he planned to use his position to put forth a unified and coherent program. Makov recognized that the advent of the Loris-Melikov "system" could only result in a decrease of his own authority as minister. During the six months that he headed the Supreme Executive Commission (that is, the entire six months of its existence, from February to August 1880), Loris had to rely upon Makov and the MVD apparatus to enact many of his most important policies. Makov and the MVD had to carry out all of Loris-Melikov's edicts on political crimes, police matters, relations with the zemstvos and cities, press affairs, and various economic questions. The MVD archives contain many examples of Loris' informing Makov of Supreme Executive Commission decisions that required him to send circulars or instructions to the provincial governors outlining the new policies.[128] Makov performed out of a sense of duty.

Makov did not agree with Loris-Melikov's policies, however, and as the months wore on his wariness of Loris turned into growing hostility.[129] Loris-Melikov began to regard Valuev and Makov as his two most dangerous government enemies. By the summer of 1880 he felt strong enough to dispense with Makov at least, and he eliminated the need for this domestic-policy middleman by convincing Alexander to abolish the Supreme Executive Commission and to appoint him as the new minister of internal affairs.[130] Loris had momentarily succeeded in gathering the reigns of domestic policy into his own hands, but Makov was not to be dismissed so easily from the highest government councils. Alexander, and at least one powerful protector, V. A. Dolgorukov, felt that Makov deserved compensation. The tsar chose to separate the Department of Post and Telegraph from the MVD and elevate it once again to an independent ministry with Makov as minister. As if this were not enough, Alexander also removed the Department of Religious Affairs of Foreign Faiths from the MVD and gave Makov the title of director of this now independent department. (After Alexander's death, this department again became part of the MVD.) Various sources mention that Loris was unhappy with this because he feared Makov's new power to examine correspondence.[131]

Makov's ministerial power ethos, narrow political vision, and view of autocracy are well expressed in two documents, a lengthy memorandum written to Loris-Melikov shortly before Makov's ouster as minister of internal affairs, and a personal letter to K. P. Pobedonostsev written immediately after the March 8, 1881, conference which first postponed Loris-Melikov's plan to introduce a form of representation.[132] The memorandum to Loris-Melikov was written in response to Loris' plan to publish a brochure by the Slavophile General R. A. Fadeev as a way of initiating discussion of its content in the Russian press. Fadeev had attacked the bureaucratic foundation of Russian state institutions, calling it bankrupt and "directly harmful to the general good and to the lawful development of the state's moral and productive forces." Makov summarized the argument and responded that it obviously meant that Fadeev regarded Russia's lawful institutions as harmful. He went on to say that Fadeev was correct only "in that the mechanism of our state institutions is complicated and unwieldy, and that the mass of affairs could be decided locally." While he did not "completely disagree with General Fadeev," Makov chose to address himself to the possible consequences of openly discussing the matter in the press. Russian bureaucracy had been a product of internal Russian life and conditions, said Makov, and as such had been nurtured by the tsars. He stated that criticism of the bureaucracy was tantamount to criticism of the supreme power that created and supported the bureaucracy. For this reason, and because Russian journalists "have for a long time—and particularly in recent times, tried to criticize and discredit state power and institutions and also to attack the goodness and charity of autocratic power," Makov said that he could take no responsibility for any discussion in the press.

Makov further developed his idea of autocratic power. He castigated the zemstvos which did not "satisfy the expectations and views of the government, or the interests of the population." In response to the demand that zemstvo activities be widened, Makov claimed that the development of all social institutions "must come directly and solely from the government and autocratic power." According to Makov, "Only the power of the sovereign can be called upon to satisfy the vital needs of the people and only to that power belongs the initiative to show the direction and the borders for changes in this or that law. This indivisible right of autocratic power creates its charisma and is the source of the love, devotion, and faith in its goodness with which the people surround the Russian sovereign as the foundation of all that is good and useful for the state." Makov argued that publicists and journalists "cannot be allowed to discuss the fundamental laws, which can only be reworked in the legislative order by permission of the sovereign himself."[133]

Makov feared that Fadeev's pamphlet would raise hopes, causing agitation in the zemstvos ("Thank God they have been quiet for the past three to four years"). The need to prevent possible illegitimate thoughts or deeds and, indeed, any politics independent of the bureaucracy, a habitual desire of the conservative Russian bureaucratic mind, was expressed when Makov raised the following issue: "And what can the government do if the discussion [in the press and zemstvos] goes beyond the proper borders? Repressive measures would have to be used to stop a discussion which the government itself had allowed." As this memorandum indicates, Makov held firmly to the old ministerial power formulas and did not envisage expansion of the autocracy's political base.

The assassination of Alexander II and Loris-Melikov's "insensitive" attempt to secure his program immediately under the new tsar drove Makov into outright opposition. At the March 8 conference, Makov spoke against adopting Loris-Melikov's plan for representation. In his letter to Pobedonostsev, written in the evening following the daytime meeting, Makov explained his actions. He told Pebedonostsev, Loris-Melikov's most outspoken opponent at the meeting, that although he disagreed with many of Pobedonostsev's views, "I bow before the truthfulness and civic courage of your words today." Makov exclaimed, "We are surrounded by a circle of lies, lies, lies, yes actually lies that filled and charged that government bubble that, in spite of brilliant phrases and the eulogies of newspaper articles, burst with an explosion, taking with it into eternity the tsar-martyr mourned by us."[134]

Makov disclaimed personal interest and reviewed his own speech at the meeting earlier in the day. He attacked not only Loris-Melikov's project but also his motives: "No single minister has the right to portray himself as the benefactor of the people—that right belongs exclusively to the monarch." In siding with Pobedonostsev at the meeting, Makov also argued that the matter required careful review and should not be decided that day.[135] Alexander III fulfilled this wish, and in fact the Loris-Melikov plan was never adopted. Although Makov took his own life in 1883, he probably would have been pleased that "careful review" meant postponement of State Council reform or introduction of the representative principle until after the 1905 revolution.

Mikhail Tarielovich Loris-Melikov (1880-1881)

Mikhail Tarielovich Loris-Melikov was born in Tiflis in 1825.[136] His family, of Armenian origin, had joined the Georgian nobility in the seventeenth century. Loris belonged to the Armenian-Gregorian Church, a fact that later certainly did not endear him to St. Petersburg advocates of official nationality. His father was a trader of considerable acumen, who apparently conducted business with various European nations. Loris received a cosmopolitan upbringing and enrolled at the Lazervskii Institute of Eastern Languages in St. Petersburg to pursue his education. Forced to withdraw from the institute because of a disciplinary problem, he subsequently enrolled in the military School of Junior Ensigns of the Guards.[137] He graduated in 1843 and entered active service as a cornet in the Life Guards Grodno Hussar Regiment.

Loris had little in common with his four predecessors. He *chose* to become minister in August 1880, after serving six months as the head of the Supreme Executive Commission, a post that gave him dictatorial powers in domestic affairs.[138] Furthermore, his social background, service experience, and political ideas set him apart from the four earlier ministers. Loris, a career military officer, had served for decades in the Caucasus, Dagestan, and other areas far from the St. Petersburg bureaucratic and court world.[139] He was a war hero, famous for commanding the capture of the fortress at Kars during the Turkish War (1878). Throughout his many years of military service he had demonstrated considerable administrative and political skill, tact, independence, and energy.

As the chief administrator of border regions inhabited by non-Russian nationalities he had governed independently of St. Petersburg—without the various institutional formalities and blockages that encumbered the central bureaucracy. He was used to having complete command over his troops or the areas under his administration. The only other minister who had somewhat comparable executive experiences in non-Russian areas was Valuev, who had served a long apprenticeship in the Baltic region. Loris-Melikov's formative and career experiences were far different from those of the St. Petersburg dignitary Lanskoi, the gendarme general Timashev, or the ministerial bureaucrat Makov. Many of the ideas and techniques that he tried to put into practice in St. Petersburg in 1880-81 had proven successful during his earlier service.

Loris-Melikov was thrust onto the stage of high autocratic politics during the crisis years of 1878-79 immediately after his Turkish War victories. Ironically, his first two positions as temporary governor-general of Astrakhan, Saratov, and Samara provinces and governor-general of Kharkov Province resulted from the regular government's failures, particularly those of the MVD. In the first instance, Alexander appointed Loris in January 1879 to direct efforts against a plague epidemic that had broken out in Vetlianka.[140] Rumors of an empire-wide epidemic had spread to St. Petersburg and Moscow and to Europe. Loris immediately determined that the threat was purely local, thus quieting the fears of St. Petersburg society. At the same time, he selflessly recommended the abolition of his temporary governor-generalship, a gesture that also impressed contemporaries. His later service in April 1879 as temporary governor-general of Kharkov Province resulted from terrorist activities and the central government's fear of revolutionary upheaval. Loris was given unlimited powers "to combat the internal enemies of the state." His methods were so effective that it was from this post that Alexander chose him to head the Supreme Executive Commission, created just a few days after the bloody terrorist bomb attack on the winter palace (February 5, 1880) that left the tsar, its primary target, unharmed.

In appointing Loris-Melikov head of the Supreme Executive Commission, Alexander gambled on decisive, energetic, and charismatic leadership. This was the kind of leadership Loris had displayed in the past, the kind so conspicuously absent among St. Petersburg bureaucrats and courtiers. The tsar's willingness to accept this type of leader as the arbiter of domestic affairs is perhaps the best evidence of his momentary recognition that the autocracy could no longer rule according to the old patterns and through the old institutions. Loris' appointment was another sign of recognition of the long-simmering "crisis of autocracy."

Despite his unique talents and experiences, Loris-Melikov built on the foundations laid by Lanskoi and Valuev. He wished to use the organizational strength of the Ministry of Internal Affairs as a power base from which to realize a political vision. And in the process, he would try to elevate the office of minister of internal affairs to one comparable to the prime minister's office in a cabinet system. Thus, the MVD became vital to his plan to redefine the nature of autocratic politics.

It is difficult to generalize about the five ministers of internal affairs during the reign of Alexander II. Their social origins, education, career experiences, administrative skills, and political vision differed greatly, and in a sense they may serve as symbols of the spectrum of available talents from which a tsar could choose his highest-ranking government officials. The fact that the tsar could choose must never be forgotten in assessing the workings of autocracy as a set of related institutions. He could and did appoint to the most sensitive and powerful positions men who he believed conformed to his perceptions of momentary needs. The wide spectrum represented by these men and their accomplishments in office shed light on the weakness of political leadership and fragility of a centralized bureaucratic government purported to be all-powerful. The structure of government and institutional traditions acted as powerful constraints upon the activities and leadership potential of the ministers. Of course, individual initiative was possible, but the combined influence of the bureaucratic and court components of Russian political culture would remain very difficult to overcome. The experience of Alexander's ministers shows clearly the odds against sustaining long-term changes in the fundamental political wisdom of Russia's official world.

It is clear that Alexander's most important expectation from his ministers was personal loyalty to the autocrat. In three of his five appointments, he appears to have ignored the minister's political skills. Ministers were expected, at best, to be competent in their institutional affairs, and not to express broader political views or attempt to speak for tsar or government. Alexander was quick to isolate or eliminate those who infringed on his personal power. Thus, he shelved Valuev's proposed State Council reform and eventually, in 1868, the minister himself. Similarly, when it became apparent that Shuvalov had grown too powerful, and that he had consciously built a bloc of support with the intention of creating a representative mechanism, "Peter IV" was sent off as ambassador to London.

In his study of the ministerial appointments of Nicholas I, W. Bruce Lincoln has shown that of the 52 ministers during the reign, 61.5 percent held the military rank of general or higher, and 71.8 percent held aristocratic titles.[141] Lincoln concluded that the prime criterion for appointment to ministerial office was service, broadly conceived. For the 52 men considered, the average length of service prior to appointment was 37.2 years. This service, however, was in a wide variety of capacities, and Lincoln concluded that ministerial appointment was due in part to factors other than career success in domestic administration. Among these factors, he listed chance encounters with the tsar, family connections, valor on the battlefield, and successful completion of a major task assigned by the tsar.

It would appear that little had changed during the Reform Era and its aftermath.[142] Although the ministers of internal affairs were no longer personal friends of the tsar, as under Alexander I, the same factors that Lincoln noted are evident. All the ministers were career-long state servants. If any change can be noted, it would be the slightly greater emphasis given to career success in domestic administration. Certainly, Valuev, Makov, and, to a lesser extent, Lanskoi exemplify this. Yet even these men had vastly different career experiences, and their inclusion under one rubric would be misleading. Makov, in particular, represents the special case of an MVD departmental official elevated to ministerial office with unfortunate results.

Because of his ambivalence and inconsistency in making ministerial appointments, Alexander helped to undermine the institutional structure of the Russian autocracy. Ministers and ministries never clearly understood their political function or possibilities. During the first half of the reign Alexander elevated the MVD's political importance and chose ministers, Lanskoi and Valuev, capable of using the office for political ends. Alexander then for 12 years placed the MVD in the hands of Timashev and Makov, both of whom lacked the authority, political skill, and vision to promote MVD leadership within the government. Institutions remained subordinate to personalities and the personal-power principle, and the bureaucracy's potential as initiator of political renovation was severely damaged.

In 1880 Alexander sought to alleviate Russia's social and political crises by gambling on Loris-Melikov's energy, charisma, and proven pacification skills. Never before had he ceded so much authority to a single minister, and it appeared that he would permit the MVD at last to fulfill its purpose as guardian of the welfare of all inhabitants of the empire. Alexander acted to offset weaknesses in the structure of ministerial government and autocracy that his own earlier actions had only intensified. Nonetheless, had Alexander lived, it is questionable whether Loris-Melikov's "dictatorship of the heart" and MVD hegemony would have persisted much beyond Alexander's perception of immediate and uncontrollable crisis and the continued utility of the devolution of his own authority.

High Officials and Their Careers, 1855-1881

4

During the Reform Era the history of changes in the nature of MVD personnel was closely related to the kinds of policies the ministry adopted. To illustrate this I consider in this chapter the biographical characteristics and career patterns of a group of 87 civil servants who reached positions of responsibility and influence within the regular hierarchy of the MVD's central organs.[1] Generally, at the time they held these offices, these men held ranks 5, 4, or 3 on the Table of Ranks, the offices being assistant minister (*tovarishch ministra*), director and vice-director of the various departments, and positions in the highest ministry collegial organs (such as the Council of the Minister and the Main Directorate of Press Affairs). These men, successful career officials, were highly educated administrators who served below the rank of minister but far above the army of petty scribes and others who never attained even the lowest (14th) rank, or who remained mired at the lowest levels of the Table of Ranks hierarchy engaged in menial and mechanical tasks. The skilled career civil servant began to emerge in the ministry during the 1840s and 1850s as a result of earlier government educational reforms, the rapid growth of the ministerial system, and the increasingly complex administrative tasks faced by ministries.[2]

This analysis of the MVD officials themselves serves as another element in the structural approach to institutional history set out in earlier chapters. Here I explore the role of personnel in the ministry's evolution from leading instrument of the peasant emancipation and haven for "progressive" bureaucrats, to conservative supporter of immutable autocracy, a static gentry-dominated society, and the traditional principles of ministerial power.

Marc Raeff and Hans-Joachim Torke have drawn attention to the dissimilarities between the Russian civil service during the first half of the nineteenth century and the bureaucracies of western Europe.[3] They single out the nature of Russian officialdom itself as one of the clearest manifestations of the Russian "deviation" from classic Weberian norms. In education, ethos, and efficiency, the Russian official seemed a poor, distant relative to the specialized, ethically charged, rational *Fachmänner* of the West. Raeff emphasizes the use of court favorites—often military men—"to fill important bureaucratic posts or to expedite major policy decisions or reforms."[4] Below these elite decision-makers, he sees the mass of Russian officialdom, which was separated from the top level by an unbridgeable gulf, and concludes that "while Russia had a host of minor executive clerks busily writing papers they never fully understood, it had no homogeneous, efficient, alert, and politically conscious policy-making bureaucracy comparable to the Prussian, French, or even Austrian."[5] Torke, while sharing many of these views, sees an evolutionary process, a movement closer to the western standard, which resulted in noticeable improvements after the Crimean War. Torke considers the Great Reforms in part a result of the process of the bureaucracy's emancipation from the tsar. This emancipation paralleled the earlier (Torke says circa 1800) and equally important emancipation of the bureaucracy from the nobility.[6]

In recent years the work of American and Soviet scholars has shown that imperial Russian bureaucratic realities were more complex than the above views suggest.[7] We now accept the existence by midcentury of an increasing number of nonlanded career civil servants, primarily of noble origin, who occupied middle- to high-level positions. These men viewed themselves as bureaucrats, as servants of the state (*dolzhnostnye litsa*), rather than as members of their hereditary legal estate. Their political views and career concerns began to diverge noticeably from those of other members of the nobility. While there was surely a great distance between the notables at the top of the earlier nineteenth-century government apparatus and the scribes at the bottom, by mid-century there was something substantial in between. A great deal of the substantive legislative and administrative work of the government was now conducted by a new generation of men occupying the many key positions in the ministries and other central government organs. The trend is evident in the following percentages offered by P. A. Zaionchkovskii for 1853.[8]

	Land and Serf Owners	Born Nobility	Titled
Committee of Ministers	94.4	100.0	66.6
State Council	92.2	98.2	53.7
Senate	72.7	95.4	13.3
Assistant ministers and directors of departments	63.6	86.3	5.2
Ambassadors and special envoys	52.6	100.0	47.3

In the category of assistant ministers and department directors there was a substantial decrease in property ownership, titles, and even noble origin. Furthermore, 69.5 percent were younger than 60, and 71.8 percent were educated at home. This departed significantly from the profile of the older men sitting in the highest governing institutions. In the State Council, 67.2 percent were older than 60 (23.6 percent over 70), 69 percent were educated at home, and 49 percent were military generals. The corresponding figures for the Committee of Ministers were 77.7 percent older than 55, 61.9 percent educated at home, and 55.5 percent military generals.

W. Bruce Lincoln has noticed among the younger career officials a small group of "enlightened" bureaucrats, men unselfishly serving more abstract notions of the state and willing to speak for and act in the interests of society.[9] These men looked to western European ideas and experience and might have qualified for inclusion in the Hegelian "universal class"—the theoretical formulation of the Prussian bureaucratic ideal.[10] The influence of these men on the Kiselev reform of the state peasantry, the St. Petersburg municipal reform, and at least three of the Great Reforms, the 1861 emancipation of the proprietary serfs and 1864 judicial and zemstvo reforms, has already been demonstrated.[11]

In the MVD, the enlightened men constituted a small though influential minority that first gained prominence during L. A. Perovskii's tenure as minister (1842-1852).[12] These officials, perhaps best exemplified by Miliutin, reached the summit of their power during the legislative process leading to the 1861 emancipation. Shortly thereafter, Miliutin, then assistant minister, was eased out of office. A similar fate awaited Ia. A. Solov'ev, head of the Zemskii otdel, two years later. Others preferred to transfer to institutions where their particular skills and opinions might be more appreciated. Thus, A. K. Giers, a specialist in financial matters, transferred to the Ministry of Finance under M. Kh. Reutern, a former colleague of the reformist Grand Duke Konstantin Nikolaevich at the Naval Ministry.[13] Of the 87 men in this sample, very few (perhaps six to eight) can be included definitely in the subgroup of "enlightened" bureaucrats.

The majority of new career civil servants in the sample first entered the ministry as appointees of Valuev and Timashev. They did not share the theoretical and political concerns of the "enlightened" minority, preferring instead to view society as a growing adversary.[14] In their unequivocal support of the regime, they adopted a kind of bureaucratic statism very close to the traditional ministerial power ethos. It was less articulate and more conservative than might be expected from Reform Era officials.

These men, not the more transitory "enlightened" bureaucrats, are indicative of the evolution of high Russian officialdom in the ministry after the emancipation. The existence in Russia by mid-century of a new generation of highly educated career officials is an important fact of social and institutional history. But this fact, taken alone, does not permit assumptions about the impact of such men within a specific institutional context. To determine in what sense, if any, these administrators brought "rationalization" to the ministry, one must move beyond the information contained in personnel records and learn as much as possible about the ideas and labors of the men while members of the ministry staff. Only by combining demographic data with more traditional types of historical evidence can one arrive at a balanced assessment of the officials' impact on the Ministry of Internal Affairs.[15] With this is mind, one can examine the various types of biographical data and the career patterns of the officials as a prelude to some generalizations on the role of these men in the history of the ministry during Alexander's reign.

The ministry officials fall into three distinct age groups. The first (oldest) group (I) consists of men whose careers peaked during the late 1840s or 1850s and extended no further than the early 1860s. The second group (II), which comprises the majority of the sample, includes most occupants of high ministry offices during the reign of Alexander II. The youngest group (III) includes men who usually did not attain high positions until the very end of the reign, and who often went on to play leading roles in the ministry in the decades after 1881.[16]

I (born 1785-1815)	II (born 1815-1835)	III (born 1835-1850)
16 men (18.6%)	62 men (72.1%)	8 men (9.3%)

The average age of the officials upon promotion to rank 5 (*Statskii sovetnik*—equivalent in the military to a rank between colonel and general) was 36.5 years.[17]

The emergence of a new generation of bureaucrats (group II) shows the pivotal nature of the reign of Alexander II in Russia's institutional and social history from 1825 to the October Manifesto of 1905. This 25-year period (1855-1881) saw the rise and decline of "enlightened" bureaucrats, the attainment of high office by their more conservative contemporaries, as well as the formative early careers of such later ministry conservatives as V. K. Plehve and P. N. Durnovo (represented in group III). That progressive bureaucrats had their formative career experience under Nicholas I while reactionaries had theirs under Alexander II suggests that developments within the bureaucracy were more complex during both reigns than is often implied by uncritical periodizations and labels.

The high officials of the MVD were predominantly the sons of hereditary members of the nobility. Of the 87 men, 77 were born into the nobility, 4 were born into the merchant class, 3 were the sons of clergymen, 1 was the son of a noncommissioned officer, 1 was the son of a low-ranking *chinovnik* who had not attained hereditary noble status, and 1 was the son of a foreigner who later became a Russian citizen. So far as can be ascertained, only three men were born with titles, although another three earned the title of count during their careers.

That so many of the men were born into the nobility may mean that they were only second-generation noblemen. Or it may mean that their ancestors had acquired hereditary nobility status as a result of service at any time during the preceding three centuries. The information is difficult to trace because it is not provided in the personnel records. A check of several genealogies (*rodoslovnye knigi*) reveals that only a relatively small percentage (perhaps 15 percent) of the family names are traceable back before 1600. Among these, direct ancestral links can be established in only a handful of cases. Another modest group (10 percent) had identifiable ancestors who acquired hereditary status after 1600. Approximately two-thirds of the men had family names that do not appear in the various genealogies.[18] This indicates that many of the ministry officials descended from families that acquired hereditary status as recently as the eighteenth or early nineteenth century. The ennoblement of most of these families therefore resulted from the continuous expansion of the service nobility in the eighteenth century beginning with the policies of Peter the Great.[19]

Memoir literature reveals that some of these men came from provincial families of small or medium landowners or local officials.[20] These men were imbued at an early age with the need to attain *chin*, to pursue their educations, and to make a successful career in the state apparatus, preferably in St. Petersburg. With a few exceptions, even the officials whose direct lineage can be traced as far back as the thirteenth century, such as Valuev, shared the financial problems and career ambitions of the offspring of the more recently ennobled service nobility. In a society marked by its lack of corporate institutions, professional associations, and employment opportunities in private enterprise, both older and newer hereditary noblemen were dependent on state service for livelihood and status. This fact helps explain the enduring statism of many bureaucrats and their willingness on specific issues to sacrifice the interests of some members of their legal class.

If 100 souls or 500 *desiatiny*, the amount required to gain voting rights in the provincial assemblies of the nobility, are taken as a standard of what was required for the maintenance of an extremely modest life-style on income from the land, two-thirds of the officials may be considered as falling below that standard, or landless. The following table shows the breakdown of hereditary property of 71 ministry officials.[21]

No property of any kind	44 men	62.0%
Less than 100 souls or 500 desiatiny (whichever listed)	4 men	5.6%
100-500 souls or 500-2000 desiatiny	14 men	19.4%
Over 500 souls or 2000 desiatiny	9 men	12.9%

In a number of cases a small amount of property was later acquired either by purchase or by award, and a very few men married women possessing small amounts of property. As Walter Pintner has shown for the mid-century civil service as a whole, there is no correlation between landownership and the attainment of either high office or high rank or, conversely, between the holding of high office and the subsequent acquisition of land.[22] Not only were most of the men not tied to economic interests based on property ownership, but the lack of property obviously did not hinder their careers: they could and did attain any of the highest posts in the ministerial hierarchy.

The religious affiliation of these officials was solidly Russian Orthodox. Seventy-six (88.3 percent) were of this faith, and most of those remaining were Lutheran—nine men (10.3 percent). One man was listed as a member of the Uniate Church and one as a member of the Armenian-Gregorian Church. While telling us nothing of the depth of religious feeling of the men, the figures reflect the existence of an important German-Lutheran group in the Russian bureaucracy as well as the discrimination against other minority religions in the service statutes.[23]

By the end of the Crimean War, the formal educational attainments of Russia's civil servants had been radically transformed.[24] High officeholders of the first four decades of the nineteenth century would most likely have been educated in private institutions, in the military, or at home. Their formal education consisted of the most basic and general subjects, and their preparation for administrative work was developed on the job. This trend was a holdover from the late appearance in Russia of a developed system of higher educational institutions and the seventeenth- and eighteenth-century Russian tradition of on-the-job training that has been described in the recent work of S. M. Troitskii.[25] As Pintner has shown, with the various educational reforms accomplished during the reign of Nicholas I, the situation began to change rapidly. New universities, such elite institutions as the Imperial Lycée at Tsarskoe Selo and the Imperial School of Jurisprudence, and a system of state secondary schools were established. The goal was to provide educated servitors for the rapidly growing state apparatus—both at the center and in the provinces,[26] and by the 1840s the new system was already bearing fruit for the Ministry of Internal Affairs, as can be seen from the following statistics on the education of 85 MVD officials:

Imperial Lycée, Tsarskoe Selo	13 men	15.3%
University (Russian)	39 men	45.9%
Imperial School of Jurisprudence	6 men	7.1%
Other elite lycées or schools	2 men	2.3%
Military schools	15 men	17.6%
Religious institutions	2 men	2.3%
Institute of the Corps of Engineers	2 men	2.3%
Privately educated	2 men	2.3%
University (foreign)	1 man	1.2%
Other (secondary education only)	3 men	3.5%

The figures indicate that approximately 75 percent of the officials were graduates of higher, nonmilitary institutions of learning, and that a very small number, about 6 percent, had received only secondary educations.

The statutes on state service in the Digest of Laws provided the legal mechanism for rich and poor noblemen alike to launch their careers with advantages largely unavailable to the other estates. The state needed officials, and noblemen had both the legal right to enter the service and either a monopoly or high priority on admission to the state institutions of higher education. (One should remember, however, that the universities had significant numbers of non-nobles as students and that this was the best and practically the only way for them to rise in society.) Graduates of these institutions were immediately given the 12th, 10th, or 9th chin depending on their standing in the graduating class. These graduates thus began their careers at levels hardly, if ever, attainable in a lifetime for most chinovniki.[27]

From a formal point of view, Russia seemed to be emulating Prussia, where the state universities, particularly the juridical faculties, were producing a professional class of technically competent civil servants. Yet the Russian institutions of higher education were not successful in instilling either the technical competence or the ethos of their Prussian counterparts. Hans-Joachim Torke has shown that the Russian system in the first half of the nineteenth century failed to produce bureaucrats on the Prussian model for several reasons. First, beginning with Speranskii's early reforms there was an overemphasis on general education as opposed to specialization. The curricula were unfocused and aimed at providing a smattering of general knowledge; juridical and other subjects relevant to future administrators were either ignored or underemphasized. Although the establishment of juridical education came to be regarded as an important goal of the state, and separate faculties and schools were created, the quality of the training proved to be formalistic, dry, and uninspiring, largely unsuited to the creation of a class of critically thinking jurists, the backbone of the classic *Rechtsstaat*.[28]

Memoirs of student life offer a stark picture of Russian legal training, which consisted often of rote memorization of sections of the Digest of Laws. In the words of the art critic V. V. Stasov, a graduate of the Imperial School of Jurisprudence, the students were mainly concerned with their career prospects, not with substantive legal issues. Although some recipients of Russian legal education are counted among the "enlightened" bureaucrats of the Reform Era, it is a mistake to view the fact that Russia had more civil-servant graduates of juridical faculties as a sign of an overall increase of progressive views within the bureaucracy or a trend toward a "jurist monopoly." Some of the most notorious upholders of the autocratic principle, statism, and various traditional views were, as will be shown, not only graduates of these faculties but men who worked for a time in the new judicial organs created in 1864 that they later tried so diligently to undermine.[29]

Although a small number of MVD positions required specialized or technical education (medical degrees for work in the Medicine Department or Council, engineering training for construction and public works, formal academic training for geographical surveys, statistical work, and certain kinds of censorship), the majority of high ministry officials must be considered generalists.[30] There is little evidence that the formal education of these men imparted either expertise or technical competence, or that they were seen by their service superiors as having such skills. Officials became "expert" on certain kinds of administrative problems after they had acquired working experience. V. I. Insarskii, one of the young successful career officials from the provinces, whose rise began in the Ministry of State Domains under Count P. D. Kiselev and who later served as director of the Moscow Post Office and in the council of the minister of internal affairs, summarized the situation well: "What was required [in the Russian bureaucracy] was able men [*sposobnye liudi*], not experts or specialists, that is, people who could get things done whatever they might be and however necessary." Insarskii thought that the specialists who did exist within the ministry were largely incompetent when it came to "affairs" and that they should be kept from both current matters and anything outside their own narrow fields of competence. The Ministry of Internal Affairs with its diverse and growing functions and general police and administrative responsibilities would become more and more a suitable home for this kind of "talented" official.[31]

Valuev once write that the laws on promotion in the Digest of Laws were "outworn arithmetic formulas" and were largely responsible for the low quality of the civil service during the first half of the nineteenth century. According to Valuev, the system instituted by Peter the Great was called forth to meet specific historical requirements and factors, such as the persistence of *mestnichestvo*, no longer relevant for Russia as a European state. (Mestnichestvo was the Muscovite system of place-ordering for servicemen that emphasized the prior position of their families in determining their current service status. The system was abolished, in theory at least, in 1682.) For him, the only result of the "time-in-grade" requirements was that the highly talented no longer held any advantage over the incompetent—"who remain in their positions by that unlimited indulgence which pervades the spirit of all Russian administrative chiefs [*nachal'niki*]."[32]

Valuev's claims, echoed by his contemporaries, are generally accepted by today's historians as expressing one of the pervasive weaknesses of Russian administration. The problem may be formulated as follows. Did the so-called men of talent find insurmountable legal obstacles to the rapid attainment of either rank or responsible positions in the civil service hierarchy? The evidence for the MVD, at least, indicates that this was not the case. The personnel records of ministry officials reveal a pattern of rapid promotion, often in contravention of the laws, beginning in the earliest stages of their careers. This trend may be observed in the administration as a whole throughout the 1840s and 1850s, but it becomes even more pronounced in the ministry after the 1861 peasant emancipation during Valuev's tenure as minister.[33]

According to law, promotion from rank 14 through 5 (collegiate assessor to state councilor) was to be governed by time-in-grade intervals (*vysluga*) applied "equally for all servitors":[34]

From rank	To rank	Interval (years)
14	12	3
12	10	3
10	9	3
9	8	3
8	7	4
7	6	4
6	5	4

All promotions to rank 4 (actual state councilor) and above were to be awarded without reference to time-in-grade and were subject to the tsar's approval. According to these rules, if a man entered service at rank 14, it would have taken 24 years to reach rank 5 (state councilor), the rank which prior to 1856 secured hereditary noble status and which, by the tables of organization (shtaty), was the prerequisite for holding a position at the vice-director level of a ministerial department. Most of the ministry officials, by virtue of their education, entered service at ranks 12, 10, or 9. Assuming that most officials began service at age 20, we see that higher civil service positions were not attained until a man was in his late thirties or early forties after as much as two decades of bureaucratic labor.[35]

The service statutes provided possibilities for propelling "skillful people" or outright favorites up the service ladder at a much faster rate. The most important legal alternative to time-in-grade was that of meritorious promotion ("for excellence" (*za otlichie*). By this concept (*zasluga* as opposed to *vysluga*) the law allowed time-in-grade intervals in specific cases to be "shortened by one year" for chinovniki "distinguished by their special labors and talents" (*darovaniia*). The mechanism by which such promotions were made was petition of the immediate superior listing specific cause, followed by approval of the main chief of the institution. This gave ministers considerable power to promote men more rapidly than prescribed by the vysluga intervals. Personal relationships with one's superiors were often decisive in influencing the course of a career.[36]

The evidence reveals a pattern of intervention by superiors and ministers to promote men in this way. The possibility of such intervention, of course, invited abuses as well as the rapid advancement of genuinely talented men. To illustrate how the laws were both used and circumvented and how these ministry officials reached high positions beginning in the early 1840s, the rates of their promotion may be examined. Let us assume rank 9 (titular councilor, equivalent to military captain) to be the take-off point for a successful career. This was the rank given to the highest graduates of the elite schools as they entered the service. For those beginning at ranks 10, 12, or 14 (11 and 13 were never used), attainment of rank 9 meant the end of one's apprenticeship and the opening up of possibilities similar to those open to men beginning at that rank. Rank 5 (state councilor, equivalent to a military rank between colonel and brigadier general) was the legal prerequisite for the class of Ministry of Internal Affairs offices under consideration here. According to the vysluga system of promotion, the time-in-grade intervals for the four promotions between ranks 9 and 5 add up to 15 years. If we assume that each of the four promotions was "for excellence" (the zasluga principle), one year can be subtracted from each interval, resulting in a period of 11 years. By law it was thus possible for a man to reach rank 5 at quite an early age, especially if his career began at rank 9. The *average* period between these two ranks for 62 officials for whom data exist was 10.9 years. In addition, almost all of the men received the next highest rank (4—actual state councilor—outside the vysluga system by definition), within another two or three years. Of the four promotions necessary to attain rank 5, for all the men anywhere from two to four were recorded "for excellence." What is even more striking is that 10.9 years, already less than the minimum legal interval, is only an average. There were no less than 24 examples of men progressing from rank 9 to 5 in even shorter periods, ranging from 6 to 10 years (for example: Makov, 6 years; Barykov, 7 years; Zaika, 8 years; Palen, 8 years; Shumakher, 9 years).

These rapid promotions were not peculiar to the MVD, since some men served elsewhere early in their careers. However, the increasing pressures on the state apparatus and particularly on the ministry after the Crimean War (and emancipation) are reflected in a marked increase in rapid promotions during the years of the Valuev ministry (1861-1868). The chronic shortage of capable administrators could not be solved solely by the gradual influx of the generation of highly educated men. The demands made upon the ministry were increasing almost geometrically, and ministers chose to adhere selectively to the formal aspects of the service statutes.

Two other important points in the service statutes permitted ministers a degree of freedom from the excessive formalism of the law requiring equivalence of rank and the class of office (*klass dolzhnosti*). First, an individual could hold an office (*dolzhnost'*) whose class could be up to two ranks higher than his chin. This decision was left to the minister "on the basis of current needs" within the ministry. In addition, a man could be promoted one rank above the class of his office, thus setting up the possibility of his being given an even higher office should the "need" arise. Furthermore, one did not have to be the legally confirmed (*utverzhdennyi*) occupant of an office in order to carry out its functions. The personnel records offer many instances of appointments as "acting" holder of a given office. These features of the service statutes help account for the dynamism in career patterns of the successful ministry officials.[37] Men moved temporarily up the functional ladder, and kept moving upward rather than either stagnating at middle level posts or moving back down one step in the hierarchy. In short, in the MVD at least, "temporary needs" were a permanent condition.

And this was not all; the records contain examples of promotions that seem to defy even these elastic rules. There are cases of men receiving as many as five promotions in rank in the short period of five years. This circumvention of Russia's elaborate laws was hardly a paradox to the ministers involved. In order to attain any degree of efficiency or even simply to have "reliable" men to implement his policies, the minister, whose own position was precarious, had to promote "skillful and trustworthy" men who might facilitate the realization of the minister's own political goals. This was the only alternative to mediocre performance or transformation of the institutions and men of the Russian administration, a possibility never considered realistic during the reign of Alexander II.[38] There was pressure from within to promote those men capable of producing quality work, especially if they appeared to be either apolitical or supporters of the regime. Later, Loris-Melikov would focus on the problems implicit in such an approach when he called for a new bureaucratic ethos as a prelude to completion of the Great Reforms in Russia.

In addition to the rules on promotions an elaborate system of awards and gifts was written into the Digest of Laws.[39] There were orders (each with several degrees and decorations), medals, marks of excellence, monetary awards of various kinds, and other gifts ranging from land to gold snuff boxes. Often in the personnel records there are simple notations of approval or thanks for specific services either in the name of the minister or of the tsar himself. Each order carried certain legal privileges, usually of no practical meaning, and the recipients often had to pay sums of money, at times not readily available, to receive the medals and ribbons. Cash awards or salary supplements would probably have been more appreciated by the already financially pressed officials.

Why then did the nonmonetary awards exist, and why are the personnel records littered with perhaps a dozen awards for each successful ministry official? The answer must be sought in notions of esteem and approval important both to the servitor and to the society in which he lived. Awards were constant reminders to the official and his colleagues that he was valued by his superiors. If an official failed to receive expected rewards, he and his colleagues took it as a sign of trouble or stagnation in that career. Wearing the dress uniform of the administrative institution, with orders and medals displayed for all to see, the individual enhanced his self-esteem and sense of belonging.[40] These and other intangibles made up to some degree for the low salaries, the sense of precariousness, and the ever-present curse of domination from above that constantly threatened career prospects. In any case, it is clear from personnel records that a constant flow of awards always accompanied a successful career.

For the bureaucrat whose career had already been launched during the decades of Nicholas I's reign, a "reputation" for capability and personal knowledge or awareness of this reputation by people who mattered were the best guarantees of continued success after the Crimean War. In its extreme forms this was the notorious principle of protection (pokrovitel'stvo) which seems to have been always operative in Russian bureaucratic history. The government's mobilization for reform provided new fields for careerism and ever-increasing amounts of work for existing institutions. Protection would be practiced on a larger and less personal scale to provide staff for a ministry that had expanded greatly and accumulated many new functions during the 1850s and 1860s. The personnel records reveal a quickening pace in the advancement of bureaucratic careers as men were brought into the ministry to work on or implement the peasant emancipation, to gather statistical information and reliable intelligence on conditions in the provinces, to serve as provincial governors, to work on the multitude of legislative proposals for further reform, and finally, to staff such important new institutions as the Main Directorate of Press Affairs. Though the quality of their education may be questioned, there is no doubt that these men had skills which improved the work performance at high levels of the ministry.[41] There is also no doubt that they gave conservative support to the autocratic principle and acted as a brake on the reformist tendencies displayed by ministry officials prior to Valuev's ascendancy. The relationship of these men to the political concerns of the MVD and the autocracy can best be explored in conjunction with their career patterns and the appointment policies of the ministers of internal affairs during Alexander's reign.

It is hard to generalize about the extraordinarily diverse career patterns of the ministry's officials. Very few men served their entire careers in either the central or the provincial organs of the MVD. Frequent transfers from institution to institution within the government were prevalent at the lower and middle levels of the civil service hierarchy. Once a man had reached one of the middle- or higher-level positions in the ministry, however, he usually remained in the MVD for the remainder of his active career. It was normal for men to be enlisted from outside the ministry to occupy such important posts as assistant minister, member of the council of the minister, or member of the council of the Main Directorate of Press Affairs. The best examples of longevity and career stability are found within the ministerial departments, where, for example, Miliutin (1853-1859) and Shumakher (1859-1879) held the directorship of the Economic Department for a total of 27 years. Yet even in the highly specialized departments, where expertise in particular matters would have been important, there are examples of outside appointments to directorships and vice-directorships. Although in some cases these outside men had relevant prior experience, it was not unusual for them to have had little knowledge of either departmental responsibilities or procedures.

For most high-level appointments, personal connections, recommendations, prior work with the minister in another institution, or the minister's political motives were of primary importance. For example, Valuev appointed many men (Tolstoi as director of the Department of Executive Police, V. I. Fuks as member of the council of the Main Directorate of Press Affairs, and so on) to high posts on the basis of personal knowledge of their talents and political views gained during periods of joint service in both the Baltic region and in the Ministry of State Domains. Although administrative and drafting skills, as well as political reliability, were of the utmost importance to Valuev, he also reserved certain appointments for socially prominent members of the nobility. This drew criticism from the progressive minister of education A. V. Golovnin, who accepted the commonly held view of Valuev as defender of nobility interests after the abolition of serfdom in 1861. Golovnin singled out the appointments of several members of the Shuvalov family, Prince A. B. Lobanov-Rostovskii and a large number of provincial governors and vice-governors, and claimed that Valuev "was guided often not by the skills of the individual, but by his court and social connections, position in society . . . and that he tried to create for himself at the court and in the aristocratic section of society a party and support."[42] Timashev, himself a general and former second-in-command of the Third Section and Corps of Gendarmes, liked to appoint conservative military men to certain high ministerial posts. Similarly, Loris-Melikov appointed trusted subordinates from earlier assignments who shared his reformist political conceptions.

The early careers of the ministry officials were marked by frequent transfers from ministry to ministry and between the provinces and St. Petersburg. Once an individual had attained a place in one of the central St. Petersburg organs, however, it was rare for him to return to a provincial post. Any subsequent work he performed in the provinces, a frequent occurrence, would be as an agent of a central ministry department. Usually the official would be on a special mission of a supervisory or information-gathering nature. In some cases, the official's early career was spent in the military and a transfer to the civil service arranged because of "poor health" or for other personal reasons. An examination of the first civil service positions held by the ministry officials reveals that the path to the highest posts in the ministry was winding. Aside from a small number (approximately 7 percent) who began service in the central ministry organs, officials began their careers in such diverse places as the chanceries of provincial civil governors and governors-general, the various departments of the senate, the various sections of His Majesty's Own Chancellery (particularly the Second Section, responsible for codification), the central and provincial organs of other ministries (particularly State Domains, Finance, and Justice), the Diplomatic Corps, the State Controller's Office, the State Chancellery, the provincial and district corporate bodies of the nobility, the Corps of Engineers, and the postal institutions.

After these initial posts the officials usually made several changes in order to find positions offering the best potential for security and future advancement. In these early stages, the civil servant had minor, if any, responsibility; even with his university or lycée education he was usually little more than a clerk or copyist, and was not yet trusted to "expedite affairs" (that is, participate in the administrative process, or deloproizvodstvo). Any special interests or particular skills of the young official were rarely taken into account for work assignments. Memoirs reveal that the young officials often viewed their initial work assignments as a burdensome necessity.[43] It is only later in the career, after several promotions, that specialization or accumulation of substantive work experience in a given area of administration may be discerned. Although a reputation for skills in a given area was often a decisive factor in further advancement, it was always possible for an official to be shifted to a new area in the same or another ministry.

Although the high officials in the ministry had diverse career experiences, it is possible to categorize these careers by taking into account all the offices held by an official, both in the MVD and elsewhere. From information in the personnel records and published materials, six categories that represent distinct types of career patterns can be established.

1. Career MVD men. The career man usually specialized in an area

that required either a professional educational qualification (such as a medical degree for high-ranking positions in the Medicine Department) or concentration on certain types of mixed administrative and economic problems involving the social estates, the cities, or even religious sects and non-Orthodox faiths. Most positions were in the Economic Department, the Zemskii otdel, or the Department of Spiritual Affairs of Foreign Faiths. These men entered the service directly in central ministry organs, and served their entire careers in those organs. Their service records indicate, however, that they often spent time on missions in the provinces to collect data, conduct investigations, and supervise subordinate provincial officials. Interestingly, these departmental officials never rose above the level of office attained by virtue of their reputation for competence and specialized skills. They never became ministers, although their departmental work and service on legislative commissions often helped shape significant legislation.[44]

2. Administrative generalists. Generalists were highly skilled administrators and personal aides to the minister. They were often brought into the ministry at mid-career to occupy such offices as assistant minister, director of the Department of General Affairs, or secretary of the minister's chancellery. In the Department of General Affairs they coordinated the disparate parts of the ministry and acted as the central ministry authority in personnel matters, finances, and other kinds of record-keeping. The secretary of the chancellery set the minister's agenda and assisted in ordinary and secret matters requiring his personal attention. The assistant ministers acted as troubleshooters for the minister, although in several cases they also became trusted coworkers responsible for generating policy or legislative proposals.[45]

3. Military officers. An insignificant minority in the post-Crimean War MVD, these men rarely worked in the central organs and therefore were out of the mainstream of administrative work. They were used most often as especially trusted officials of special missions or as provincial governors (and, of course, as military governors-general). Sometimes their early careers involved investigative or police work in either the military or the Corps of Gendarmes.[46]

4. Censors. According to the empire's censorship law of 1865, primary censorship responsibility was shifted from the Ministry of Education to a new MVD organ, the Main Directorate of Press Affairs.[47] The work of the council and its chief were closely supervised by Valuev, who regarded censorship as one of the ministry's most important functions.[48] The censors had varied service backgrounds and were usually enlisted into the ministry specifically for this work. Transfers between regular ministry departments and the Main Directorate were

rare, but as trusted appointees of the minister, the censors often performed a variety of special missions for him.[49] Censors often sat concurrently on the Council of the Minister, or did editorial or supervisory work on the ministry newspaper (*Northern Post*, 1861-1868;
Government Messenger, 1868-1917). The censors' career backgrounds
included general administrative work, information-gathering, and
academic or literary pursuits. Although several had prior experience
as censors elsewhere in the government, it is difficult on the whole to
discern specific qualifications for these posts.[50] Significantly, Main
Directorate censors appointed during Alexander's reign enjoyed great
longevity in office and many continued to serve under his successors.[51]

Until the brief ascendancy of Loris-Melikov, the ministers of internal affairs used their censorship apparatus to combat "critical tendencies" among the educated classes. The Main Directorate put at the
minister's disposal from six to eight relatively high salaried positions
guaranteed by the table of organization. Thus talented men of known
political views could be hired to help the minister enforce his notion of
what was permissible in print.[52]

5. Generalists with extended service in state provincial organs or in
corporate bodies of the nobility. After the emancipation, such men
were brought into the ministry by Valuev and Timashev in their search
for fresh talent and for people with close ties to the provincial nobility, who might be willing to subordinate their sympathy for that class
to state interests. Their willingness to seek or accept positions in the
ministry and their espousal of the ministry's brand of statism that was
opposed to both Slavophilism and gentry oligarchism made them
especially important. Such appointments provide better understanding of MVD attitudes toward society during the Reform Era.[53]

6. Men with experience in police and jurisconsult organs. Here the
generational changes in ministry personnel and the relationship between personnel and ministry ideology and policy are best illustrated.
Throughout the 1860s and 1870s the directors of the Department of
Executive Police were chosen according to criteria similar to those of
the other career categories.[54] General administrative skills, personal
connections, political reliability, and experience in police or investigative work gained on the job were most important.[55] These directors
held any number of high ministry posts. Diverse career experiences,
ranging from service in the diplomatic corps to provincial governorships, place these men within the parameters of the ministry career
sample. Police officials were men of narrow political vision. None was
ever appointed either assistant minister or minister of internal affairs.

By the end of Alexander's reign, new men appeared in the police
organs who would leave an indelible mark on subsequent ministry his-

tory. These were younger men, born in the 1840s, and are best exemplified by P. N. Durnovo and V. K. Plehve.[56] They received their education and early career experiences entirely during the reign of Alexander II. Both attained high ministry office only in 1880. Their early careers differed from their predecessors in that both had juridical training and served as Ministry of Justice prosecutors (prokurory) in the regional courts created by the 1864 judicial reform. Both, therefore, had participated in the momentous struggle between the administration and the courts even before entering the MVD. Clearly, both sided with the primacy of administrative power.[57] Plehve and Durnovo dominated the ministry police structure during the 1880s, and their policies helped solidify the ministry's position as a bulwark of autocracy. Most significantly, their ministry careers extended into the twentieth century and may be seen as a link between the Reform Era autocracy and that which survived the 1905 revolution. Both men became ministers of internal affairs, Plehve in 1902 and Durnovo in 1905. While they held that office they earned reputations as enemies of reform, advocates of police repression, ardent believers in Russification, and supporters of landed-gentry interests.[58]

The social profiles and career patterns of the ministry officials indicate that despite the influx, beginning in the 1840s, of younger, highly educated men, there is no evidence that there were enough "skilled" men to fill the most responsible positions in the MVD hierarchy. Ministers and their departmental directors and section chiefs had to take an active and personal interest in middle- and high-level appointments in order to ensure a share of loyal and competent young career officials for the key positions. Without an aggressive appointments policy (such as those of Perovskii, Lanskoi, and Valuev), the formalistic promotions laws would have made operations exceedingly difficult.

Higher education was less important for imparting knowledge than as a means of controlling the entrance of potential high officials to the closed bureaucratic world. Neither technical nor professional training, however, was a requirement for career success. General ability to get things done within the system, expertise gained from work experience, political reliability, and personal relationships were most important.

The history of ministry officialdom clearly reflects the history of the MVD as an institution with a political viewpoint during the reign of Alexander II. In the early 1840s the MVD central departments were managed by members of an older generation who lacked the motivation and skills to cope with the increasing administrative and legislative demands. At that time a younger, highly educated generation entered the ministry and other state institutions and arose quickly through the ranks. The influx of new men continued throughout the

1850s and 1860s. The ministry's administrative and legislative capabilities increased immediately as these men moved into middle- and high-level departmental positions. The rise of these men and their successful work coincided with and was related to the general elevation of the ministry's political role within the autocracy. The most progressive and vocal of these men—the so-called enlightened bureaucrats— were a small but influential minority in the ministry that virtually disappeared after 1861; they were replaced by a silent but growing apolitical or overtly conservative majority. These were ideal *apparatchiki*, loyal supporters of the system, men of muted ambition willing to work behind the scenes to cope with the growing pressures of politics and workload. Their official papers and memoirs reveal a natural affinity for the ethos of ministerial power quite opposed to the spirit of militant state-initiated change one might expect from Reform Era bureaucrats. As entrenched and willing servants of their institution, these men helped move the ministry toward a final commitment to a police-power ideology. Ministerial power, relegitimized, had triumphed.[59] Although the social and educational profiles of the MVD officials would include them in the professional bureaucracy described by Pintner, placing the men in their institutional context suggests that their impact on Russian history was by no means uniform or predictable. It also suggests that the institutional context itself can exert a powerful influence on the political views of officials.

Policies of the Guardians

5

With the end of the Crimean War and the accession of Alexander II, Russia entered an era of rapid social and economic change as well as intellectual and political ferment.[1] The Crimean defeat made clear to Alexander and the educated elite the military and administrative weaknesses fostered by Nicolaevan autocracy. Russia's status as one of the great European powers had been severely undercut. To regain parity with these powers, Alexander infused with new energy the already well established and tested formula of reform from above. In this he was supported by a broad spectrum of social groups and the younger "enlightened" officials who believed that national regeneration required the immediate development of Russia's human and material resources.[2]

In 1855, however, reform from above remained problematic. The government, after all, consisted of the same institutions that were drawing heavy criticism in the wake of Russia's defeat. A program of national regeneration on the Prussian Stein-Hardenberg model required a motivated and efficient bureaucracy and visionary leadership, and there was good reason to doubt their existence in contemporary Russia.[3]

As has been shown, the ministerial power ethos remained entrenched, in ministerial institutions, coexisting uneasily with the newer reformist attitudes of younger officials. Also, despite the growth of departmentalism, grave operational deficiencies remained that would likely be exacerbated under the pressures generated by a large-scale reform effort. Nonetheless, the ministries with their departments and new generation of officials were the only possible executor of an activist reform movement from above. The reach of the departments into the countryside and the attitudes, administrative techniques, and reform experiences of "enlightened" officialdom had prepared the ministries to sponsor and implement an accelerated program of national regeneration. This was true despite the ministries' operational shortcomings and the possibility that the ministerial power ethos might infect the reforms themselves. Bureaucratic momentum and the tsar's will reinforced each other, and the result was the Great Reforms.

Most studies of Alexander's reign, divide it into periods of reform and reaction. Alexander gave the ministerial bureaucracy his approval to enact certain reforms beginning with the abolition of serfdom.[4] The reforms emerged from a complex legislative process that involved not only the tsar and ministerial bureaucracy but also other high officials and dignitaries, members of the royal family and court entourage, and, to a more limited extent, the intelligentsia.[5] Historians correctly argue that until the emancipation, reformist officials held the upper hand because the tsar agreed with their desire for regeneration of national power (though certainly not with all aspects of their vision), and their tradition-bound rivals were dispersed, lacked power bases within the ministries, and were generally less effective in the legislative process.[6] Supporters of the status quo had neither the bureaucratic skills nor the institutional strength to overcome the officials of the early Reform Era, centered in the ministries.

Most historians would also agree that the reformers' influence diminished quickly after 1861.[7] Alexander and many high officials feared peasant unrest and the nobility's political pretensions. With the growth of a radical opposition in the wake of emancipation and the Polish uprising in 1863, the supporters of traditional autocracy began to gain strength. The Karakozov assassination attempt in 1866 confirmed Alexander's basic conservatism, and he gave to the traditionalists the initiative in domestic policy and, more important, a power base within the ministerial bureaucracy. Alexander removed several reformist ministers of widely divergent views (such as Golovnin and Valuev) and appointed men loyal to the traditional ministerial power ethos: A. E. Timashev as minister of internal affairs, D. A. Tolstoi as minister of education, and K. I. Palen as minister of justice. He chose the politically astute Count P. A. Shuvalov to direct the Third Section and Corps of Gendarmes. Though these men differed on particulars, their fundamental beliefs were in harmony, and Alexander began openly to express solidarity with their values and policies. The result was a relegitimation of a conservative course in domestic policy. What had already begun in the MVD under Valuev was now recapitulated in a more pronounced way in the government as a whole. The traditional ethos of ministerial power came to dominate the government, though during the 1870s a muted struggle for some form of representation or society's participation in the legislative process continued.

The creator of the Great Reforms—the ministerial bureaucracy—appeared to be subverting them at worst, at best failing to develop them.[8] The autocrat rather easily blocked the few plans to give Russians more political rights and alter the ethos of ministerial power by incorporating into the legislative process representatives of society (Valuev in 1863, Konstantin Nikolaevich in 1866, and Shuvalov in the early 1870s). Even the regime's record in straightforward administrative reforms began to pale in comparison to its achievements early in the reign.

Although this view of the period is essentially accurate, problems arise when the reign is considered from an institutional perspective. In the deeper structures of the reign's political history, basic continuities are apparent. There were significant reforms after 1866—the 1870 municipal reform and the 1874 military reform, for example—just as the 1845 criminal code, administrative justice and exile, continued in effect throughout the Reform Era and its aftermath.[9] Preparations for the 1870 municipal reform went on throughout the 1860s within the MVD's Economic Department and other bureaucratic forums, and of course much was based on the 1846 St. Petersburg municipal reform. In several areas policy evidently developed in a slow, logical fashion with a certain immunity from much-publicized political events. Throughout the reign, in fact, the ministerial bureaucracy worked on many problems closely related to the more prominent Great Reforms. A recent outpouring of first-rate Soviet and Western scholarship has provided the basis for a reassessment of the political history of Alexander's reign, but gaps remain, particularly for the years 1866-1878.[10] These make it difficult to gauge accurately the relationship of institutions to policy.

Early in Alexander's reign the MVD and other ministries began work on a variety of administrative, social, and economic problems that remained on the agenda until 1881, and in most cases even into the twentieth century.[11] The reasons for the slowness and modest results of much of this work deserve the scrutiny of those who would understand the old regime's political shortcomings. Structural problems and ideological tensions made consensus elusive among those engaged in policy-making at the highest level. Indeed, policy often expressed the lowest common denominator of institutional interests. The connection of domestic-policy concerns and the heavy pressure placed upon the small, closed bureaucratic world made indecisiveness and postponement logical outcomes. The result, during the 1870s at least, was a dysfunctional legislative system. A clearly discernible paralysis of domestic policy-making was already apparent by the end of the 1860s.

In a recent monograph, Chernukha provides a subtle analysis of the autocracy's efforts during Alexander's reign to generate structural reform.[12] She uses three elaborate case studies: (1) attempts to introduce a form of representation (here she develops a model termed "government constitutionalism"); (2) the question of a unified cabinetlike organ to unite executive power; and (3) plans during the late 1860s and 1870s to introduce tax reforms, including an all-estate income tax. From Chernukha's arguments the following conclusions emerge. First, the autocracy was plagued by structural problems in its executive and legislative branches. Second, high officials perceived these problems clearly and were influenced by European developments in formulating their own solutions. Finally, with help from upholders of the ethos of ministerial power, Alexander used his authority to support the prevailing institutional and ideological conflicts and structural weaknesses within his government, thereby effectively blocking reform. This analysis is supported by the work of I. V. Orzhekhovskii, who outlines the regime's growing commitment to police power after the mid-1860s (with the MVD leading the way), a commitment designed to weaken reforms already under way.[13] Similarly, E. A. Tvardovskaia, in her monograph on M. N. Katkov, develops a model for the ideology of dynastic conservatism that serves as another analytic tool for understanding autocratic politics and domestic policy.[14]

The policies of the MVD during Alexander's reign emerged from a delicate balance of institutional interests and the abilities of its leading officials. The personal element dominated when the ministry was led by individuals able to translate their political visions into coherent programs. Institutional continuity carried the MVD along during periods of weak leadership. It should be remembered, however, that to claim that the MVD was Russia's most powerful ministry of domestic administration is not to say that it dominated the government or that its views were necessarily congruent with those finally adopted as state policy. As will be remembered, state policy represented the interaction of many institutions, individuals, and the tsar himself. The MVD position often diverged sharply from that of the other policy-making participants as well as from the policies finally adopted. The institutional strength of the ministry guaranteed it a voice, but the limitations that autocracy placed upon it and the changing nature of its own leadership resulted in a certain tenuousness in MVD impact on specific policy questions.

The first stage of MVD policy development in Alexander's reign (1855-1861) included the years of the emancipation process and initial work on administrative and social reform in the provinces and cities. These were the years of Lanskoi's ministry, when Miliutin and the other enlightened officials propelled the MVD along a probureaucratic path that emphasized institutions over personalities. They enunciated basic MVD positions and a pattern of involvement in policy areas that no future minister could ignore. The second stage, Valuev's ministry from 1861 to 1868, was easily the most important in terms of the MVD's future. Valuev inherited many policy initiatives and added many of his own. In so doing he defined the MVD position toward the zemstvo, the new judiciary, agrarian and labor questions, and other social policies, and the all-important question of politics. Valuev's policies offer the best possible illustration of the nexus of tradition, institutional influence, and the role of the personalities in Russian political history.

The legacy of a revitalized ministerial power dominated the third period of MVD policy (1868-1880) under Timashev and Makov. Leadership was routinized and bureaucratic, and political vision was nonexistent. Valuev's personnel policies and relegitimation of administrative power reinforced the narrowly conceived police-oriented policies of his successors. MVD performance deteriorated, as did that of the central government. The impact of structure and officialdom on politics is especially clear here. Without energetic leadership the increasingly rigid behavior of MVD officials just below the minister reinforced and was reinforced by weak ministerial directives. Ministry projects may have remained technically competent (though this was not always the case), but MVD and high government policy increasingly took on the gray, narrow, defensive characteristics so often associated with late imperial autocracy.

The final period of MVD policy embraced the brief (1880-81) ascendancy of Loris-Melikov. Here, once again, the leader and his vision dominated, and Loris, using the MVD as a power base, began seriously to renovate ministerial government and complete the Great Reforms. This period will be treated in detail in Chapter 6.

Central to the MVD's concern at the outset of Alexander's reign was emancipation. The MVD's role in the formulation of the edict of February 19, 1861, offers an instructive paradigm of the ministry's strengths and limitations in the context of autocratic politics. It also provides a key to the MVD's attitudes toward the political aspirations of social groups.[15]

The post-Crimean War impetus for a major assault on the institution of serfdom came directly from Alexander. In an 1856 address to the Moscow nobility, he emphasized the advantages of emancipation from above as opposed to having the issue decided by force from below. At this early point in the proceedings, Alexander, who still hoped for gentry voluntarism, gave the MVD primary responsibility for the vaguely defined goals of emancipation. It appears that he selected the MVD because of its established functions and recent reform activities.

MVD policy on serfdom was defined by Lanskoi and a small group of "enlightened" bureaucrats. A. I. Levshin, who had gained considerable experience in land reform in Kiselev's Ministry of State Domains, formulated initial MVD positions.[16] Levshin, assistant minister in 1856-57, accepted Alexander's mandate but argued that if the government were to wait for gentry initiative there would be no movement toward a just solution. Levshin suggested that the government take the lead by presenting guidelines for emancipation. These could serve as models for detailed plans corresponding to local conditions that would be developed by the provincial nobility. At this point, Levshin's position, and therefore the ministry's, was understandably fuzzy, though the outlines of certain general principles of reform, such as emancipation with land, compensation to landlords, and redemption payments, were already visible. These represented a curious mixture of far-reaching land reform tempered by more conservative financial and administrative arrangements that would severely compromise the solution of Russia's agrarian problem. Even as late as August 1857, the government, spearheaded by the MVD, was no closer to a solution to the problem than were the secret committees of Nicholas' reign. Nor should this have been surprising. That the MVD had not produced a clear "solution" to serfdom was due in part to the complexity of the issue but also to the fact that the governing institutions of autocracy worked against rapid consensus.

Though Lanskoi and, to a lesser extent, Levshin desired that the MVD retain the initiative and produce a concrete plan, older patterns of autocratic government intervened. Alexander created the secret Committee on Peasant Affairs, a traditional semilegislative body apart from the ministerial bureaucracy and State Council. Ironically, the MVD had proposed the secret committee. But it was meant to mediate between top ministry officials, who for drafting purposes needed information about local conditions, and "technical" committees created to collect data in the countryside. The ministry clearly wanted to control the data. Here Alexander stepped in and exercised his personal authority. He created the secret committee, but not the technical committees vital to the MVD proposal. Also, he subordinated the MVD to the secret committee, and thus tied the MVD to a powerful and independent ad hoc committee capable of blocking ministerial initiatives in agrarian policy—a situation that was to endure throughout the reign.[17]

From an institutional perspective the emancipation became a function and product of the MVD's attempt to define a working relationship with the Main Committee and later with the Editorial Commission that drafted the edict. The ministry constantly had to assert its influence in the legislative process and use its institutional and personal strengths to impress its views upon government and tsar. The tensions between the Main Committee and the MVD should not, however, obscure the ministry's advantages in the legislative process. From its inception, the Main Committee respected MVD authority over its own hierarchy of officials in the countryside as well as over the nobility and its spokesmen. The committee authorized the ministry to collect the data that all agreed were lacking from governors, marshals of the nobility, and "experienced *pomeshchiki*."

The preparation of the Nazimov Rescript provides an example of how MVD views merged into government policy. The secret committee adopted with modifications, Levshin's program calling for emancipation that would provide land allotments for newly freed serfs and the creation of provincial landowners' committees to assist in the reform process. Though the ministry's views were still unclarified, Lanskoi gained Alexander's approval to extend the rescript and the type of land reform it implied to the interior provinces. The secret committee offered no opposition, extending with only minor modifications the Nazimov Rescript, intended solely for the western provinces, to the Petersburg area itself. Even Levshin was appalled at Lanskoi's success in reasserting MVD leadership and maneuvering his program to acceptance as government policy. Levshin feared the government was becoming the "prosecutor of the nobility" and that rash commitment to transformation of the countryside would provoke peasant uprising. Though Levshin remained assistant minister through 1858, he was summarily removed from participation in the reform as Lanskoi turned to his younger, more radical subordinates, Miliutin and Solov'ev.[18]

During the next few months the ministry pressured the provincial nobility to petition Alexander for permission to set up committees according to the rescript guidelines. A pattern was set in which the MVD encouraged the unreliable nobility to submit proposals as a fictional act of political participation. The nobility had to appear to MVD bureaucrats as willing initiator and partner in its own transformation while the MVD managed the entire process. What has been called a constitutional innovation—the plan to institutionalize the participation of nobility and experts in the legislative process through the provincial committees—was an act of overt manipulation.[19] Substantive political power, initiatives, and decisions were to remain state monopolies exercised by the ministerial bureaucracy.

A consistent thread of MVD policy in many areas, during the early years of Alexander's reign, was the promotion of institutionalized solutions to political problems and the promotion of the regular ministerial bureaucracy against the personal power and anti-institutional bias of the ministerial power ethos. Yet even in the early months of the reign the ministry's reliance on political fictions had much in common with contemporary political trends in France, Austria, and Prussia.[20]

In practice, the MVD overtly manipulated and co-opted the provincial nobility. The Main Committee agreed that provincial committees were to be treated as collegial "bureaucratic" organs of the state. Bureaucratic edicts from St. Petersburg set in motion the process Field so aptly termed "the engineering of assent" as local authorities in their answers to the rescripts struck balances "between the demands of their superiors and the apprehensions of their neighbors."[21]

Apart from the provincial arm-twisting and preparation of local projects that provincial deputies would carry to St. Petersburg, important changes were taking place in the capital. Once again, Main Committee sanovniki placed the MVD on the defensive, as did Ia. A. Rostovtsev, the tsar's new hand-picked emancipation manager. In April 1858 the Main Committee, speaking for the government, adopted a new program which was primarily the work of M. P. Pozen. This raised the possibility of a landless emancipation with greater authority given to the provincial committees. This signaled a departure from the MVD position. The ministry's own proposal was rejected, though Solov'ev had the audacity to distribute one hundred copies of his draft project. Nonetheless, the MVD exerted its influence administratively by limiting the power of landowners over their serfs through use of ministry circulars. The committee countered by limiting the publicity of the circulars though they could not question the legality of the MVD initiative. Lanskoi also raised the issue of publicity. He wished to publish articles favorable to the government point of view, thereby creating a kind of artificial and bureaucratically managed debate of the type that Konstantin Nikolaevich and his "enlightened" co-workers had wished to make permanent procedure in Russian politics. Though this airing of government views was hardly a debate, the nobility opposed it and the Main Committee tried unsuccessfully to appease them. Commentary in the periodical press grew in an unprecedented fashion, resulting in political problems that the advocates of controlled debate failed to anticipate.[22]

The imperial orders of October 26 and December 4, 1858, and the creation of the Editorial Commission on February 17, 1859, signaled Rostovtsev's preeminence and another attempt to harness the MVD to the autocrat and his representatives. In the October order, the committee promised evenhandedness in its treatment of peasantry and nobility, and made a commitment to write a general statute for all of Russia. The means of reviewing provincial committees' proposals was also discussed. The main procedural change was that the government could call "experts" to supplement the testimony of provincial deputies. Because it was obvious that these experts would be in favor of landed emancipation, a pro-government view, the provincial projects would be reduced from the status promised in the rescripts and in the April program. They would constitute traditional petitions and not be building blocks in an expanded legislative process.

In the December order, Rostovtsev set out emancipation principles which turned out to be similar to those of Solov'ev and Miliutin. For serfs, Rostovtsev demanded economic and juridical freedom from the tutelage of the nobility. Redemption was established as the first goal, and to some this negated the notion that land had to be kept in possession of the nobility. Redemption would be gradual, but on its completion the interim obligated status of serfs would end. Juridically the peasants would acquire "civil rights" upon publication of the emancipation statutes and, most important, landlords would no longer hold administrative or police authority over the peasants. Such authority would go to the peasant commune and the officials of the peasant administration under the direct supervision of provincial authorities of the government. These points directly contradicted the rescripts and the April program, upon which all provincial draft projects in preparation were based.

With the creation of the Editorial Commission to draft the complex emancipation legislation, the MVD again had to seek new ways to mediate between the provincial deputies and government. Although the Editorial Commission was placed under Rostovtsev's jurisdiction, key MVD officials were immediately appointed to play a leading role in its work. Thus institutional victory over the rather disorganized, and less bureaucratically competent, voices of dissent would be won. The Editorial Commission was dominated by an alliance of abolitionist MVD officials and gentry intellectuals who shared Rostovtsev's belief in landed emancipation. The considerable debates within the Editorial Commission took place behind closed bureaucratic doors among essentially like-minded men. For example, Miliutin could vote with Samarin and others against the more radical positions of Solov'ev, who appeared as a lone and self-appointed advocate of peasant interests. Yet, on the whole, unity existed against real and imagined enemies of the sacred emancipation goal within and outside the government. Many MVD views prevailed, passing through the Editorial Commission, and, with the tsar's approval, emancipation laws were enacted.[23]

In the final statutes the government made a variety of concessions to the nobility in order to avoid the charge of destroying that estate by removing its economic underpinning.[24] Redemption was decreed but so also were gradualism, monetary compensation for the nobility, and preservation of the commune and historically conditioned patterns of life. Even the civil rights promised to the peasantry were hardly absolute. The newly "liberated" serfs were subject to judicial and administrative organs that promoted the isolation of the peasantry as a caste.

Finally, the relationship between the MVD and the provincial deputies and other gentry spokesmen should be mentioned again. As has been touched on earlier, the MVD, with Lanskoi as spokesman, conducted an antigentry campaign of far-reaching implications. This was primarily for the benefit of Alexander, who, ministry officials believed, had to be convinced that the nobility was a selfish estate, hostile to emancipation and therefore to the tsar's will. Lanskoi portrayed the ministry as the guardian of the state interest against the nobility's oligarchic political pretensions. Although Lanskoi and his subordinates believed in the primacy of institutions—and particularly in those of the regular ministerial bureaucracy over personal autocracy—the MVD never became fully independent of the tsar and the autocratic legislative process. In the minds of even enlightened MVD officials there was little room for spontaneity or the free interplay of competing interests, and much room for bending social aspirations to fit state requirements. MVD officials believed that a high degree of bureaucratic management and control was necessary in the state's political relationship with society. This attitude would remain characteristic of even the most reform-minded tsarist officials until the 1917 revolution. The attitudes and patterns of bureaucratic behavior expressed at this time were not new. They merely combined with reformism in a new way that could easily be adapted by ministerial leadership of different views. Within the limits of autocratic politics, the emancipation represented an MVD triumph, though by a somewhat circuitous route. Whether belief in institutions and the necessity of political vision could overcome the patterns of ministerial power to produce effective policy remained a question.

Cursory examination of yearly MVD reports or Valuev's diaries reveals that most of the issues that persisted throughout the reign were placed on the agenda prior to 1862.[25] Though emancipation dominated MVD activity prior to 1861, it called forth discussions of such related issues as provincial and district administrative reform, police reform, the labor question, sectarian matters, and judicial reform. When Valuev took office in April 1861, the MVD had primary responsibility for implementing the emancipation edict, as well as for producing new ministry positions in the context of other ongoing reform processes.

In retrospect, Valuev divided his service as minister of internal affairs into two periods, the first from 1861 to the end of 1863, the second until his removal in March 1868:

The largest part of what I did, undertook, began, or prepared, belongs to the first year of my administration. In it I wrote the first memoranda aimed at focusing the tsar's attention on the inescapable changes in our state structure, attempted to move toward a more correct fundamental organization of administration/procedures in the Committee and Council of Ministers. I directed the preparatory work on the question of zemstvo institutions, turned my attention to the inadequacies of the medical administration, took initial steps toward reform of municipal institutions, gave a new direction to schismatic affairs, put forth the basis for a new order and direction in MVD procedures, and raised the question of improving the conditions of life of the orthodox church and the external life conditions of its clergy—also the relationship of the Orthodox church to other Christian faiths and the general bases of freedom of belief, the reform of the universities, the creation of a government press and the new legislation on press affairs.[26]

Valuev did not underestimate his own contribution, but, surprisingly, he failed to mention MVD work in implementing emancipation and other ministry concerns. Nonetheless the continuities with Lanskoi's ministry are readily apparent.[27] Because emancipation would transfer police authority and administrative responsibility for over 20 million people from the nobility to various bureaucratic and semibureaucratic institutions, consideration of administrative and police reform was called for. The administrative and political implications of an emancipation that was perceived as an attack on gentry corporate interests required further political adjustments. These took the form of zemstvos. The three areas of general provincial administration, police, and self-government were inseparable in the minds of MVD officials. Their policies in these areas during Alexander's reign provide a paradigm of structural weaknesses of autocracy and the fate of ministerial power during the Reform Era.

The inadequacies of provincial administration contributed greatly to the breakdown of state authority during the successive revolutions of the early twentieth century. The problems inherent in the MVD's relationship to the provinces during the late imperial era and, indeed, under the provisional and early Soviet governments were already discernible during the reign of Alexander II. Effective administration of the distant and poorly connected parts of a vast empire had been and would remain a problem for the autocracy. The ministry's relationship to the provinces had practical and political dimensions. Politically, the ministry faced the task of unifying disparate government offices and integrating government and society. Administration of the provinces involved transformation of various local offices of the MVD and other central ministries, bringing them into touch with the central government and with the local population to promote order, growth and fundamental loyalty.

In 1918 the official journal of the People's Commissariat of Internal Affairs, *Vestnik NKVD*, in its discussion of the problems facing the new Soviet provincial administration, referred to the materials and discoveries of the Kakhanov commission, which had examined similar problems between 1881 and 1885.[28] The *NKVD* noted that key structural problems in the early Soviet period were identical to those of the late nineteenth century, and that the Kakhanov commission's proposals were not without relevance for the young Soviet government. This is the kind of structural and institutional continuity that provides a deep dimension to political history, and once again, it is the Reform Era that sets the issues and conflicts in clear perspective. The Kakhanov commission was the fruit of the reform initiatives of Loris-Melikov in 1880.[29] Though formally constituted only in the autumn of 1881 after the assassination of the tsar and Loris-Melikov's retirement, the new commission was chaired by M. S. Kakhanov, one of Loris' closest advisers. The Kakhanov commission, with a mandate to prepare legislative projects on all aspects of provincial, district, county, and peasant administration, and on the zemstvo organs of self-government, began its work with the materials collected during the four senatorial revisions ordered by Loris-Melikov during the summer of 1880. The Kakhanov commission materials provide a rare in-depth picture of local administration drawn essentially from the end of the Reform Era and reign of Alexander II. The problems identified by the Kakhanov commission and its proposals offer an invaluable summary of the entire MVD relationship to the provinces during the 25-year period under analysis here. These materials, earlier MVD material on the reform of the provincial directorates (*gubernskoe pravlenie*), and the superb contemporary analyses drawn from the liberal *European Messenger* bring into focus the contours of the ministry's relationship to the provinces.

The MVD provincial administration reproduced in a different setting all the structural, procedural, and personnel problems examined in Chapter 2. Starr lucidly analyzed the first moves to reform provincial administration after the Crimean War.[30] The deliberations of the Miliutin commission of 1859 and of the administrative section of the Editorial Commission were closely intertwined. They created important new institutions for peasant administration, and, of course, eventually the zemstvos, but nothing was accomplished in those early years to reform the MVD's provincial and district administrative offices.[31]

The first serious attempt to treat the timeless problems of inefficiency, formalism, and inadequate personnel in the provincial directorates came simultaneously with the central ministry's work on its own table of organization reform. Valuev described the problems of the provincial directorates and of administering the provinces in general in a memorandum dated September 1, 1864.[32] Valuev began with a historical overview of provincial administration and its weaknesses, and noted that these had inspired creation of the Miliutin commission in 1859. That commission, he argued, had avoided formulating plans for the MVD provincial administration by claiming that the task was impossible at a time when the forthcoming zemstvo and judicial reforms left unclear the eventual functions of the regular provincial administration.

Valuev believed improvement to be necessary and possible if the MVD would follow the experimental reform carried out in 1859 and 1861 in the provinces of the Kiev governor-generalship. The aim in Kiev, where there had been some success in reducing correspondence and completing more cases, was to abolish the provincial directorates, which had been reduced to little more than overburdened clerical offices, and replace them with new unified directorates that would bring together under the aegis of the provincial governor all branches of the province's administration (including non-MVD branches) for top-level collegial decision-making. Valuev also railed against false formalistic collegiality and wanted vice-governors and provincial councilors to have the right to sign certain edicts without the cumbersome consultations called for by law. Just as he had argued for the central ministry table of organization, Valuev complained about the low salaries of his highest provincial officials, salaries diminished even more by the enormous increase in the cost of living after the Crimean War. Valuev pointed out that even the provincial police assistant ispravniki earned more than the councilors of the provincial governing boards, and, worse, the representatives of other ministries usually received higher salaries than governors and vice-governors. Valuev proposed the same solution for the provinces as that embodied in the table of organization plan for the central ministry, namely, to eliminate and consolidate certain offices and to work toward a more rational division of functions while using saved money to increase salaries.

Finally, Valuev treated the problem of unity, perhaps the most important issue at the provincial level. As a result of the growth of the ministries during the first half of the nineteenth century and the elaboration of departmental structures, all domestic ministries, in order to fulfill their functions and, equally important, to maintain or increase their status, began to establish provincial hierarchies, whose degree of subordination to the MVD's governor and its offices was by no means clear. The results were disconnectedness, lack of communication, and institutional rivalry. Valuev stressed the need to break down the isolation of the various offices, mixed composition boards, and committees in the provinces and get them to work together on critical local issues.[33] The State Council reacted to these proposals much as it had to the central ministry table of organization reform project, and only permitted passage of the June 8, 1865, temporary table of organization of the provincial governing boards for 37 provinces and Bessarabia,[34] which simply eliminated and consolidated a few minor offices and ignored the structural problems at the heart of provincial administration. The result was the same as at the center. Paperwork increased dramatically in the wake of the zemstvos, and the performance of the supposedly streamlined directorate became more and more inadequate.[35]

Valuev tried his hand later in another memorandum, "On the Condition of Provincial Institutions," which he wrote and gave to Alexander II in February 1868 just before his departure from office.[36] Here he developed his views on provincial administration in relation to the zemstvo and judicial reforms and the festering radical movement. Again he began by praising the conservative and constructive role of administration in Russian history. But, he argued, the central government had changed greatly from its earlier forms while the provincial administration, and particularly its head, the governor, had changed little since 1775. Indeed, the latter had hardly changed from its Muscovite predecessor, the voevoda.[37] Valuev reviewed the powers of the governors according to the 1837 law and discussed the ambiguities of the phrase "master" (khoziain) of the province, which had remained in the laws despite reforms and practices that had made mastery of the province a pipedream. For Valuev, the Great Reforms were a dividing point in the history of provincial administration, because since their enactment the governors no longer had clear authority in the province. The proliferation of rival power centers in the province, in the form of offices subordinate to other ministries and committees with no direct ties to the governor (and hence to the MVD), had made absurd the very notion of having a chief in the province. The financial and fiscal offices introduced in 1861 in the province had reduced governors to passive observers, and zemstvo boards and bureaucracy and the peace mediators had introduced an alien and hostile mediating authority between government and people. Valuev also cited the new decentralized military administrative units (*okrugi*), the local organs of the state control, and, of course, the judicial institutions created by the 1864 reform. These were all independent and rival centers of power in the provinces where there was no cooperation and permanent conflict. Valuev reviewed the 1866 law increasing the governors' authority in the provinces and claimed that it had been inadequate. What was needed was virtually complete central MVD control through its own agents, the governors, with disputes submitted to the Committee of Ministers—and not to the Senate—for arbitration.[38] He demanded an end to antigovernment actions by all members of the tsar's civil service in the provinces, regardless of their institutional affiliation.

The memorandum was passed on to Valuev's successor, Timashev, who used it as inspiration for his own proposals (discussed in Chapter 3). It was clear that Valuev had already shifted his thinking from solving the problem of unity to unswerving support of a kind of gubernatorial dictatorship in the province. Timashev, or, more precisely, his memoranda writers, merely developed this idea in their proposals but, as noted earlier, they too ran into stiff opposition and had to withdraw several projects.[39]

As the MVD entered the 1870s the structural problems of provincial administration remained unsolved. In fact, the situation had deteriorated despite obvious improvements in the functioning of individual specialized offices (particulary non-MVD financial and technical offices) and the zemstvo contribution, for the province as a whole remained fragmented and torn by ideological conflict and impediments to decision-making. Thus provincial administration had many of the problems associated in this study with the central MVD and government. Even Timashev inadvertently stumbled onto one key aspect of the problem in the provinces that paralleled the central ministry's plight when, after visiting six provinces, he reported to Alexander that the "position of our present governors depends not so much on the quantity (formal or legal) of their power as on their personal character and activity, and on the support they receive within the highest government."[40] This primacy of personal authority exemplified the diffusion of ministerial power to the provincial level. D. A. Miliutin also noted this at the same time: "In essence there has been no improvement in provincial administration, except that several governors consider themselves able to be petty tyrants (*samodurstvovat'*) even more than before."[41]

Reports from the governors and other documents of the 1870s indicate that the piecemeal and temporary table of organization reform of the provincial directorates had not begun to address the critical problems of unity and efficiency at the provincial level.[42] Nor had anything been done to alleviate the gross inadequacies of either the district or cantonal administration. True, the zemstvo had been created, but it had only complicated matters by making the weakness of the regular administration more apparent. In politics and in practice the zemstvos placed new burdens upon an already overstrained administration. Finally, the offices of the other central ministries of domestic administration invaded the countryside and established themselves as pockets of unwelcome independent authority and expertise. The power of the provincial governors, and hence that of the MVD, was cast in doubt.

The liberal *European Messenger*, in its widely read "domestic survey" (*vnutrenee obozrenie*) of May 1870, analyzed the provincial administration problem and the Timashev reform program of 1870. It noted the absolute need for provincial administrative reform despite the creation of the zemstvos. The author claimed that society and the press were almost unanimously against the MVD project which proposed to unify and decentralize but really attempted to increase gubernatorial and MVD power. Calling the project "Nicolaevan" in spirit, the author of the review attacked the vagueness of the proposed authority of the governor and the project's design to subordinate all other non-MVD branches of provincial administration to the MVD hierarchy. This was to have been accomplished by reducing these officials to inferior members of the proposed pseudocollegial unifying organ, the provincial council (*gubernskii sovet*). According to the *European Messenger*, the Minister of Internal Affairs would become not simply a first, or prime, minister, but "the only minister."[43]

The journal criticized the MVD proposal for a provincial council from a practical administrative standpoint as well. Aghast at the notion that an MVD governor might be free to intervene in all areas of provincial life including education, the liberal journal argued for a genuinely collegial, unified, cabinetlike organ that included non-MVD officeholders and zemstvo representatives at the top of the provincial hierarchy. Unity in the provinces was a necessity just as it was for the disjointed central ministerial government, but a false unity inspired and dominated by the MVD and police power was not at all desirable. Alluding to the existing provincial directorates and believing that the proposed councils would represent no new departures, the *European Messenger* lambasted the existing directorates for their close links to the governors and their status as second-rate executive organs dealing strictly with petty matters that ought properly to be handled by the governors' chancery.

After defeat of the Timashev program, the only major change made in provincial administration during the 1870s resulted from the June 27, 1874, law that abolished the peace mediators and established in their place new collegial organs of peasant administration at the district level.[44] These were the district boards for peasant affairs (*uezdnyi po krest'ianskim delam prisutstvie*). They were introduced as a first step in solving the crisis in governmental authority at the cantonal and district levels, problems that would remain at the heart of efforts by the Old Regime to stabilize the government right through the Stolypin era and World War I. The 1874 law divided the old functions of the peace mediators and conferences (*s"ezdy*) of peace mediators between the new board, a new permanent member (*nepremennyi chlen*) of that board, who was an appointed bureaucratic official, and the old police ispravnik. The board was intended to bring collegial administration and self-government closer to the peasants. Its members, however, were to be drawn from local officeholders and landowners. The permanent member would have independent authority on land questions and would fulfill certain judicial functions. The board as a whole would take over the old peace-mediator relationship with the lower peasant administration at the cantonal and village levels. This half-hearted formulation proved a disaster in practice; it provided neither firm state authority at the lower levels (as would be provided to some extent by the hated land captains several decades later) nor effective self-government that would alleviate the caste isolation of the peasantry. Furthermore, as the *European Messenger* pointed out, these new organs only compounded the most severe of all problems in the province, namely the fragmentation of administrative authority. With this new commitment to an isolated peasant administration, the province now typically had three independent overlapping and competing sets of institutions: the regular administration, the zemstvos and city dumas, and the peasant organs. These were in addition to the multitude of mixed governmental boards and councils that functioned in the interstices.

It is important to note the government's failure to come to terms with these problems at the district and cantonal levels. Recent scholarship on the Russian Revolution has shown it was here, perhaps even more than in the capital cities, that the provisional government may have ultimately lost its struggle to restore authority in 1917.[45] Even during the 1870s when the ministry's reform projects expressed growing commitment to ministerial power, there was serious talk of cantonal reform, and more specifically of creating all-estate (*vsesoslov-nyi*) institutions of either administration or self-government.[46] In fact, in 1864 Valuev proposed a bureaucratic solution to the question of peasant administration, an institution he termed the *vyt'* that was nothing less than the future all-estate canton coupled with the presence of a bureaucratic official drawn from the local gentry, clearly foreshadowing and most likely inspiring the infamous land captains of 1889.[47]

The volost' or canton had been created by the Editorial Commission during emancipation as an administrative and police unit to provide a formal link to the central ministry (as opposed to the commune that dealt with peasant domestic and economic matters).[48] Valuev presented a plan to the Main Committee on Peasant Affairs that called for an all-estate organ to break down artificial economic and administrative barriers between social groups in the countryside, and to reintegrate Russian provincial society after the emancipation. The vyt' chief was to have been a bureaucratic official chosen from among local landowners. The principal goal was to reinvolve the nobility in local administration as state agents under bureaucratic control so that there might be in Peter Czap's words, "carefully controlled expression of public needs."[49] After 1864 Valuev's plan was quietly shelved, most likely at the behest of the tsar and his brother, Konstantin Nikolaevich.

Unfortunately, though the all-estate canton plan was a prominent recommendation of the Kakhanov commission, it was not adopted in any form during the 1870s or 1880s. Stolypin, too, who had made cantonal reform a cornerstone of his entire program, was thwarted by the nobility's fear of being swamped by more dynamic nongentry economic elements in the districts, and it fell to the ill-fated provisional government to enact, though largely on paper, an all-class volost' zemstvo to be elected by universal suffrage.[50]

As the 1870s drew to a close, the MVD relationship to the provinces was more troubled than ever. By 1876 it was clear that the Timashev-led ministry had all but given up on solutions other than the clumsy and single-minded expansion of police power in the provinces. When Timashev managed to get the Committee of Ministers to enact his proposal that governors and governors-general have expanded rights to issue obligatory edicts that were the equivalent of new laws, the *European Messenger* quite correctly saw it and the entire ministry attitude as an attempt to solve deep, real problems by formalistic juggling of functions and intolerable expansion of police power.[51] The journal also understood quite well that much of the problem could be traced to the ethos of traditional officialdom, an ethos or mentality that absolutely refused to assimilate change and particularly those momentous changes wrought by the Great Reforms. This critical note would be thoroughly assimilated by Loris-Melikov only a few years later as he tried to alter that ethos and promote structural changes that would redefine ministerial power.

A few words are in order here about the social and career characteristics of the MVD's highest provincial officials. Thanks to the work of I. V. Orzhekhovskii it is possible to draw some comparative conclusions about the characteristics of these officials as opposed to those of the central ministry officials considered in Chapter 4.[52]

Basically the quantitative data for the last half of Alexander's reign for provincial governors and governors-general only confirm the picture provided by P. A. Zaionchkovskii's material for the late 1850s.[53] For example, of the 64 governors-general and governors in office on January 1, 1879, 62 were members of the hereditary nobility, and more than 70 percent owned property. In fact, 68 percent owned more than 2,000 (and 58.8 percent more than 3,000) desiatiny of land, a fact that indicates again that there was a distinction in social and economic background between the ministry's highest officials in the central departments and those in the provinces. In general, the profiles of the governors-general and governors corresponded to older service patterns in which wealth, high aristocratic backgrounds (titles), military service, and absence of higher university (only 53.4 percent had such education) or lycée education was more prevalent. Furthermore, there was little stability in high provincial service appointments. Of the 171 men who held these posts between 1866 and 1878, 31 (18.1 percent) held office only one year, 20 (11.7 percent) held it for two years, and a total of 55.6 percent held their posts for less than four years. Of the 1879 sample, 12 (19.3 percent) were titled; of 46 civilian governors, 12 (26 percent) had court ranks, while three-fifths of the considerable military representation were members of the emperor's suite. The pattern in the provinces is unmistakable. The highest provincial officeholders in the MVD hierarchy came from a segment of service society closely wedded to the tsar-centered political culture that had been challenged by the Great Reforms.[54] Though no claim can be made for direct correspondence between social background or career pattern and administrative behavior or political view, one can infer a connection between the ideological cleavage that existed between bureaucratic proponents of traditional autocracy in the provinces, as noted by the *European Messenger* and later by Loris-Melikov, and the principles and institutions of the Great Reforms that were meant to redefine Russia's political culture.

The Kakhanov commission materials, debates, and proposals offer a convenient and penetrating summary of the condition of provincial administration at the end of the reign of Alexander II.[55] For example, the 1880 revision report on Saratov and Samara provinces by Senator Shamshin begins with a review of the work of the provincial directorate. Shamshin noted that while there were few cases of outright abuses (*zloupotrebleniia*), everywhere there was weak activity, slow movement of affairs, formal relationships of officials to the legitimate petitions and needs of private persons, carelessness (*neispolnitel'nost'*) of subordinate officials, an absence of insistence (*nastoianie*), and quarrels among authorities "even when the necessity for unified action is perfectly clear."

Though Shamshin approved generally of the administrative activities of the provincial offices attached to other domestic administration ministries, he singled out the provincial directorates of both provinces as being of little significance. Despite the changes in their tables of organization, he argued, their performance lagged well behind that of other non-MVD provincial organs. In both provinces, the report portrayed the directorates as overburdened for the most part with trivial cases and useless correspondence. The result, as one might expect, was that work on important affairs slowed to a crawl. Shamshin did note that the technical agencies of the directorate were comparably better off, but he singled out the district police administration as being in disastrous shape and he excoriated the district boards for peasant affairs and the cantonal and village administrations for being totally inadequate and, in most cases, corrupt. According to Shamshin, these lower levels of the administration in no way reflected the idea of personal freedom that was to have been instilled by the 1861 emancipation legislation.

Senator Mordvinov's revision of the black-earth provinces, Voronezh and Tambov, simply confirmed this widespread pattern. In general, Mordvinov praised the governors of the provinces claiming that both were fulfilling their duties zealously and with honor, though he did criticize one of the governors for exercising little control (*nadzor*). However, he castigated the Tambov provincial directorate for its general inadequacy and, specifically, for the lack of rational leadership from either the vice-governor or the councilors. As in the Volga provinces, the district police were singled out as worthless, and the new mounted police (*uriadniki*) as a failure. Mordvinov gave mixed reviews to the other non-MVD provincial offices and committees, but he did specify that these organs were acting independently with resulting bottlenecks, slow correspondence, and thorough lack of coordination. To remedy these problems, he strongly advocated the unification of all provincial institutions (collegial and executive) in one general provincial council. Again, as with Shamshin, Mordvinov heaped abuse upon the district boards for peasant affairs ("basically indifferent and formalistic") and the lower peasant administration as a whole.

Senator A. Polovtsov's revision of Kiev Province added further evidence, this time for a non-Russian area that had been the scene of effective provincial administrative reforms at the very outset of the Reform Era. According to Polovtsov, the provincial directorate was not fulfilling its missions as (1) advisory organ to the highest provincial administrative authority and (2) a separate collegial instance with judicial and administrative functions. Basically the directorate simply followed the governor's orders despite its collegial and independent legal status. Furthermore, the laws it obeyed were of the most formalistic nature and served to reduce the directorate's activity to fruitless paper-shuffling. Slowness, poorly defined functions and responsibilities, and bad control were all criticized as well. And, of course, Polovtsov portrayed the district and cantonal administrations as in far worse condition.[56]

In summary, at each level of the provincial hierarchy, canton, district, and province, the Kakhanov commission and its special conferences wished to construct harmonious, efficient executive authorities that would be buttressed at each instance by collegial unifying organs that would have substantive advisory and general policy-making mandates.[57] Of primary importance was, of course, the solution of the riddle of the power of the governor himself and the construction of an effective provincial directorate. The Kakhanov commission envisaged elected and appointed officials serving side by side in an organ that would have the right to decide well-defined policy matters, or, at the minimum, have the right to inform the central government of its opinions. Unity was to be achieved by this new collegial directorate which would replace several existing collegial organs (such as the boards for peasant and city affairs) yet permit the highly specialized provincial organs of other ministries and collegia to continue their work subordinate to the appropriate St. Petersburg ministry, but also linked organically together and to the governor through the medium of the new collegial organ in matters of local administration. This is what foreshadowed the early Soviet mention of the Kakhanov commission proposals. It was this idea of "double subordination" that the early Soviet government chose as its doctrine to solve the very same problems of disconnectedness, institutional rivalry, and conflict that marked provincial administration under the late imperial regime.[58] Again, according to this doctrine, the provincial organs of non-MVD ministries were to be dually responsible—to their functional and hierarchical superiors in St. Petersburg and to a functioning college in the province. Clearly, the aim here was to reproduce at the provincial level what Valuev and others had argued as necessary at the national level to instill energy and direction to ministerial government as a whole.

The Kakhanov commission, having reviewed thoroughly the state of provincial administration at the end of the reign of Alexander II, developed plans for an integrated administrative system at all levels within the province. It would have been a system that aimed to unite the disparate government organs, state, and society by means of mixed collegial organs and by more effective use of the zemstvos.

On the all-important question of the power of the provincial governors and the relationship of the MVD to those officials, the commission strove for clarity in defining powers and channels of authority. Most definitely, it wanted to modify the relationship between the MVD and the governors.[59] In fact, the commission recommended ending the MVD practice, essentially illegal, of incorporating the governors into its own hierarchy of officials. Recognizing that MVD control of the governors had been established by practice rather than conscious legislative choice (a polite way of describing the realities of ministerial power and politics), the commission argued it was because of MVD control over the governors that other ministries had established their own networks of provincial officials. The commission wished to place gubernatorial appointments in the hands of the Committee of Ministers which would recommend appointment to the tsar upon nomination by the MVD. It also wished to eliminate gubernatorial interference completely from the workings of provincial judicial and control organs. And the Committee of Ministers, not the MVD alone, would also have responsibility for awards and promotions. Given the fact that the proposed collegial provincial governing boards were to be directly responsible to the senate, not to the MVD, the Kakhanov commission proposals were quite radical, at least in the eyes of upholders of the ministerial power ethos and tradition. In fact, it was precisely the commission's attacks on MVD prerogatives, as exemplified in its proposals related to the governors and repeated at all administrative levels in the province, that fueled Tolstoi's mid-1880s counterattack—discontinuance of the commission and reassertion of traditional ministerial power and the role of the MVD.[60]

It must not be forgotten, however, that the commission recognized the governor as primary representative of the highest state power (that is, of the tsar) in the province. The governor was to remain head of all provincial police, and the vice-governor an official of the MVD following the old pattern.[61] Though in theory the governor's authority would be limited by institutionalized relationships with the new collegial directorates and zemstvos in the provinces and with the Committee of Ministers and Senate in St. Petersburg, there was still a notable vagueness in formulating limits to gubernatorial authority, particularly in regard to the zemstvos, mixed institutions, and, of course, private citizens. Unfortunately, the proponents of substantive administrative and political change in the provinces could only tone down (albeit significantly) the harshest features of Tolstoi's counter-reform projects, while not at all eliminating the traditional role of the MVD in the provinces and the capacity for ministerial power and administrative arbitrariness to operate under a vague cloak of legality.

The commission's diagnoses and recommendations for the canton and district levels of provincial administration were based on the same principles as those for the provincial level itself. They represented a compendium of the considerable body of opinion and data accumulated throughout the reign of Alexander II. The volost' or canton was to be maintained, and although the commission stopped short of the all-estate unit (whether a zemstvo or some other form of mixed board), it did wish to bring monocratic authority closer to the peasantry by establishing the office of *volostel'*, or canton chief, who was to be elected by the district zemstvo assembly (this was just the kind of recommendation that Tolstoi would single out for attack). At the district level, in many ways the weakest link in the entire administrative hierarchy of the province, direction and integration were to come from a new collegial directorate (*prisutstvie uezdnogo upravleniia*). This organ was to take over the functions of most existing district mixed boards dealing with police, peasant, military, and educational matters. Three permanent members, including a chairman, would be nominated by the district zemstvo assembly and confirmed by the MVD, the district police chief (*ispravnik*) and the chairman of the district zemstvo board (*uprava*).[62]

The problems of provincial administration and the MVD relationship to that administration were well understood during the last years of the reign of Alexander II. From the beginning the MVD relationship to provincial administration was clouded by the ministry's general police mandate and its lack, compared with other ministries, of specialized functions. The MVD saw itself more and more as "master" of the provinces, as a surrogate for the state itself. An extreme form of this view, a view wholly compatible with and expressive of the traditional ministerial power ethos, was put forth by Tolstoi during the mid-1880s in his attacks upon the Kakhanov commission proposals. Again, tragically for Russia, the practical and political inadequacies of provincial administration were eloquent testimony to the triumph of ministerial power.

The MVD annual report for 1855 declared the MVD executive police to be overburdened with administrative duties related to maintaining law and order.[63] The police, the report said, were underpaid and overburdened with irrelevant matters, a situation that only compounded their traditional venality and incompetence. The essence of MVD police policy during the Lanskoi ministry was a desire to instill professionalism, or the separation of police law and order functions from administrative and judicial functions, thus improving their ability to keep peace. MVD officials wanted Russia to have the type of professional uniformed police that emerged in Europe in the wake of the Napoleonic era. When combined with projected administrative and judicial reforms in the countryside, police performance would improve as would general administration. There was another symbolic dimension to this as well. The traditional police and administrative domination of the judicial function, in fact the primacy of administrative authority, might be redefined in a manner that would promote the rule of law and institutions in the Russian polity.

The goals proved easier to establish in theory than in practice. Police reform turned out to be a policy area where the proponents of traditional ministerial power and administrative hegemony focused their resistance to change. Police reform began with a flurry of well-articulated memoranda—such as that by the young MVD official, well-known writer, and radical publicist M. Saltykov[64]—urging professionalization. Twenty years later, efforts at police reform ended with establishment of a program for mounted police (uriadniki) in the countryside. This program contradicted in almost all respects the reformers' earlier aspirations.[65] Police reform expressed the conflict within the ministerial bureaucracy and the larger government over the redefinition of ministerial power. Those who supported substantive police reform—professionalization and a narrowing of police functions coupled with improvements in education and salary levels—stood on the side of rule of law and against traditional police authority buttressed by the personal-power principle of autocracy.

In early 1858 Saltykov offered the most comprehensive statement of the institutionalists on police reform. Saltykov urged that the police must abandon economic and judicial functions and become professional peace-keepers. The proposal closely followed one by S. Gromeka in a Russian Herald article, in which Gromeka stated that police reform could not be ignored by a government about to emancipate 20 million peasants. On February 18, 1858, Alexander ordered police reform to be placed on the agenda of the Main Committee for Peasant Affairs. It was at this point that M. Murav'ev, the minister of state domains, responded with his proposal for a new district chief (uezdnyi nachal'nik), a local administrative and police agent drawn from military personnel to report to the ministers collectively, not to the MVD alone. This plan, as well as Murav'ev's related plan for governors-general, was clearly directed against the Ministry of Internal Affairs (showing, in particular, opposition to institutional domination by the MVD of the countryside), and against the altered and institution- and law-oriented ministerial government promoted by its young officials. In response Lanskoi entrusted direction of the police reform to the new Zemskii otdel under Solov'ev. Within the Main Committee, the ministry was forced to retreat as the committee adopted a statement of reform principles (May 16, 1858) very close in spirit to the Murav'ev proposals. The MVD, however, continued its push for a comprehensive reform on the Saltykov model by asking all provincial governors to submit their comments on the Main Committee proposals. This meant, in effect, the compilation of considerable anti-Murav'ev material, since his district chiefs were designed to limit the governors' (and therefore the MVD's) authority in the provinces.[66]

In the Main Committee, Rostovtsev's emergence as the dominant figure and Lanskoi's victory over Murav'ev shifted the balance back in favor of the MVD. In March 1859 Solov'ev prepared a "direct descendant" of Saltykov's earlier memorandum. It repeated the call for professionalization and the separation of administrative and judicial functions from the police. More important, perhaps, Solov'ev proposed to transfer local economic matters to new local organs composed of representatives of provincial society. He conceived of the future zemstvos as an integral part of police and local administrative reforms that were themselves made urgent by impending emancipation. Two days later the MVD, Lanskoi, and Solov'ev were rewarded with a major victory. Alexander authorized a new Commission for the Reorganization of District Institutions. Miliutin was made chairman of the new commission (which would endure until replaced by the Kakhanov commission of the early 1880s). The three parallel reform processes—local administration, police, and zemstvo—were now launched.[67]

Police reform then was absorbed into the work of both the new Miliutin commission and the administrative section of the Editorial Commission, whose members included Miliutin, Solov'ev, and Giers. The Miliutin commission issued its program for police reform on April 30, 1860, and its details closely followed the tenets of the Saltykov memorandum.[68] The Miliutin commission supported the idea of professionalism, and called for personnel decreases and higher salaries. It was hoped that higher pay and prestige would attract talented provincial noblemen to MVD police service. This was MVD "decentralization" at its best, the controlled induction of local elites into state service to provide a measure of autonomy and stability to provincial life. The Miliutin commission also called for consolidation of municipal and district police forces, a shift from elected police officers of the gentry (the old *sotskie*) to state-appointed officers, and the elimination of the police prosecutorial function, which would be transferred to new investigative magistrates responsible to the Ministry of Justice and not to the Ministry of Internal Affairs.

Unfortunately, the Main Committee managed to reduce this initiative to a series of small-scale administrative adjustments. Instead of salary increases, grants were to be made to governors for distribution at their discretion.[69] The investigating magistrates were created, but the expanded police functions of the village elders and foremen at the volost' level left "grass-roots" police work in the hands of men largely indistinguishable in ethos or career profile from the old sotskie. The landlord was deprived of his traditional police power, but the administrative measures of 1860-61, including provisions of the emancipation edict, did little to create the professional streamlined police force envisioned by the MVD reformers.

With Valuev's appointment as minister, MVD policy toward the police shifted. To suit his own purposes, Valuev altered the bureaucratically controlled "decentralization" program of Miliutin and Solov'ev. Valuev would repeatedly argue that police deficiencies were quantitative as well as qualitative, and though the notion of professionalism intrigued him, he was unwilling under any circumstances to cede any police authority to provincial society. Valuev's fear of weakening the authority of police and administration came even to overshadow his often-expressed belief that institutions had to take precedence over personal authority. He therefore worked to increase numerical levels of police strength and to secure police primacy over judicial personnel in the countryside.[70] It is difficult to miss the irony in Valuev's position, since it implied a highly centralized and bureaucratic police force that reserved the least powerful positions for gentry elements, yet Valuev's position was considered to be progentry. Conversely, the Miliutin program went somewhat further in its decentralization (though also under bureaucratic tutelage), but it was perceived as antigentry. As in many other policy areas, the distance between the two views was not nearly so great as contemporaries believed— though it must be said that Valuev was far more openly hostile to the nascent separation of powers created by the Great Reforms.

Valuev appointed D. N. Tolstoi, an open proponent of police authority—indeed another fine example of traditional officialdom and its ministerial power ethos—as his police adviser and director of the Department of Executive Police. Shortly afterward, during late 1861, the State Council asked Valuev to comment upon the Miliutin program. Valuev shrewdly procrastinated and the entire matter was postponed until completion of the zemstvo and judicial reforms in 1864. Nonetheless, Valuev secured approval of a set of temporary rules for

the organization of police and a new table of organization for the be-
leaguered St. Petersburg police. These rules created new district police
directorates (69 cities were excepted) that retained broad, mixed functions, yet offered higher salaries. They also increased the size of the St.
Petersburg police force. It was only in October 1863 that Valuev presented his own comprehensive police proposals to the State Council.
Calling for division of the St. Petersburg force into executive and judicial branches, the proposals constituted affirmation of Valuev's belief
that judicial functions should remain in the hands of the police. Korf,
Zamiatnin, and Reutern vigorously opposed this final Valuev police-
reform effort in the same way they would later oppose his zemstvo
proposals and his programs for municipal reform. After 1863 Valuev
turned his attention to clarifying the relationship of police and administration to the new zemstvos and judicial organs as well as to supporting the regular provincial administration. In all these matters he
pursued the contradictory goals of securing the primacy of police authority while promoting the renovation of autocracy as a political
system.[71]

Under Valuev, no comprehensive police reforms were begun. Timashev's police program was especially linked to his larger effort to over-
haul provincial administration. Early in his ministry he reconvened
the Miliutin commission with A. Beklemishev as head of its police section.[72] Although the MVD supplied eight of the twelve members of
that section, it took no less than three years for it to issue a police-
reform project.

Timashev and his subordinates focused on the problem of order in
the countryside; their primary aim was to strengthen the civil governor and his administrative hierarchy. They believed in restricting police activity to "the preservation of general security, peace, and
order," and for reasons of administrative efficiency proposed to transfer certain responsibilities to zemstvo and municipal institutions. The
MVD, working to curtail remaining vestiges of collegiality in the peasant administration, proposed creation of a "territorial volost' " with
appointed police officials whose purpose was to bring police power
physically closer to the peasantry. The proposal neither redefined nor
redistributed police functions. When it reached the Committee of Ministers in spring 1873, it was so watered down that it was rejected. A
revised version of this proposal, primarily in the area of financial
matters, was made by Timashev in March 1874, but it too was rejected. In 1875 and 1876 the Police Section of the Commission on Provincial and District Institutions again prepared to submit a project,
but the Turkish War and the general slowdown in domestic policy-
making intervened.[73]

It was not until 1878 that the newly appointed minister of internal affairs, L. S. Makov, offered a new plan to create a 5,000-man rural mounted police force to maintain law and order in the countryside and to expand the municipal police forces as well. Makov and his subordinates ignored the larger issues of professionalization and redefinition of police power. Instead, they concentrated on numerical increases in police, a recommendation supported by both landowners and the urban bourgeoisie.[74]

On the eve of Loris-Melikov's rise to power, the executive police remained overburdened by administrative tasks. Its officers were transient and undereducated, and its size, though larger than in 1858, still lagged behind population growth. Ministry police policy suffered from the same lack of vision present in domestic policy as a whole during the late 1860s and 1870s. The broad police power and functions of the MVD were reaffirmed rather than trimmed, and since there was no comprehensive administrative reform for the provinces, the worst deficiencies of the police were left untouched.

A study of the relationship between the MVD and the provinces is not complete without an analysis of the attitudes of the MVD toward the zemstvos and municipal self-government. Historians have cited the ministry's relationship to the zemstvos as an indicator of the government's attitude toward society and basic political reform.[75] Yet the historiography of the zemstvos during Alexander's reign—why they were created and their relationship to the state—has been confused. Preferring to concentrate on conflicts between government and zemstvos, historians have downplayed the considerable harmony and cooperation that existed between them. The political and symbolic dimensions of the problem have been defined inadequately.

To clarify government-zemstvo relations, one must recognize that from their beginnings the zemstvos became a political symbol, for administrators and members of society alike, of what autocracy might become and therefore of how Russian political culture might evolve. Although MVD officials often perceived the zemstvos as a threat to the established order, those most responsible for their creation— Miliutin, Solov'ev, and Valuev—first saw them as critical elements in redefining autocratic institutions according to their political visions. In 1859 Solov'ev and Miliutin believed the proposed zemstvos would fulfill immediate administrative and political needs. Administratively, the zemstvos would help in the management of provincial society and its economy after emancipation. From the MVD perspective, that was an administrative burden that regular MVD organs (including the police) could not handle. Even B. B. Veselovskii accepted the importance to the MVD of the role of the zemstvos by supporting N. V. Shelgunov's statement that "the zemstvos appeared not as a concession to some form of dreamy liberal demands, but as the result of necessity as recognized by the government. It was a simple question of the division of labor and inescapable exit from the difficulty in which the government felt itself."[76]

In political terms, Miliutin saw the zemstvos as a medium for government control of the political aspirations of the provincial nobility.[77] Thus, he portrayed the zemstvos as a means for educating future generations in public affairs. Miliutin emphasized that zemstvo functions must be local and limited, and that the zemstvos could not participate in matters of national significance. Here was the beginning of a pattern in which the state alone was to determine the boundaries of zemstvo activities, while politics, or those matters having implications for the future of autocratic institutions, were to be neatly and artificially isolated from specific administrative or economic functions. Miliutin thought the zemstvos were another type of "artificial publicity," characteristic of the thinking of the "enlightened" officials of the 1850s. The zemstvos were a controlled but timely *political* concession, a step toward partnership with society from a government conscious of its acts and secure in its authority. It was an act of conservative statesmanship as exemplified by the politics of Robert Peel in Great Britain. As events would prove, this kind of statesmanship, because it could alter the traditional ethos of ministerial power and redefine political culture, would always be on the defensive in Russia.

When Valuev became the minister in 1861, he was much aware of the political implications of zemstvo organs. As has been shown, he envisioned an autocracy constructed around transformed political and social institutions. Valuev's zemstvo policy closely reflected his desire to redefine autocracy while simultaneously upholding and relegitimizing the police component of traditional ministerial power. Yet, as always, Valuev's formula was administrative hegemony based upon institutions rather than personal power.

Even though many MVD officials dwelled on the zemstvos' potential to help administer the countryside, Valuev concentrated on their political implications. In the 1862-63 debates, Valuev claimed the zemstvos would help in making a reformed autocracy more hospitable to institutions. Though his attempt to give more weight to propertied interests in the zemstvo debates is well documented, his desire to shift the source of provincial political power from estate to property—even if interpreted by contemporaries as favoring the nobility—should not be underestimated. Valuev understood the political efficacy of the government's taking "possession" of and standing at the head of the "social movement."[78] In his attitude toward reform of the clerical estate and in his proposal to reform the State Council (the zemstvos and not the corporate bodies of the nobility would be the basis of representation), Valuev worked to transform traditional estate structures and politics and to renovate the political system. The notion of controlled participation of local elites in administration and the national legislative process became a central element in the thinking of those future ministers of internal affairs who speculated on and tried to avert the fate of autocracy.

As early as mid-1863, Valuev described the unity of state power and his thoughts about how the zemstvos ought to relate to that power:

There is applied as the basis of the draft bill on zemstvo institutions the idea of decentralization; but this is not intended to weaken the existing ties between the parts and the common center. The state authorities are not dividing the zemstvos from itself . . . In transferring to the zemstvos issues within certain bounds, the government does not diminish the totality of its rights but rather relieves the burden resting upon itself . . . It is essential to bear in mind the form and inviolability of our state unity. The mutual tie between various parts of the organism is possible only by preserving the firm bonds between the various units and the center.[79]

Although the passage reveals fear of gentry constitutionalism and federalism, it also renders insignificant, for this analysis, the later distinction of scholars and publicists between "state" and "society" theories of local self-government.[80] From the beginning, MVD leaders had viewed the zemstvos as part of a larger, inviolable state power. Should the zemstvos ever have a political function, the state would define it and restrict it to spheres of activity *within* the state's political monopoly. Reorientation or redefinition of Russian politics did not imply a weakening of that monopoly. Thus, MVD policy toward the zemstvos was two-dimensional as it attempted to follow the ministry's artificial distinction between administration and politics. The MVD formula was measured aid to the zemstvos as administrative units, but containment and prosecution for acts the ministry considered to be overtly political. The administrative relationship between provincial and even central MVD authorities and the zemstvos produced little dispute and rancor. It would appear that even the most highly publicized examples of government hostility and restrictive anti-zemstvo legislation were, in fact, understandable administrative attempts to respond to administrative abuses and inefficiency within the zemstvos or to define or clarify poorly written statutes.[81] Even as late as the 1890s zemstvo-government relations were marked by a pattern of noninterference from the center.[82] Between 1866 and 1870, liberal zemstvo activists, however, continued to portray MVD measures as illegal, restricting zemstvo ability to tax property and industry and eliminating the free-postage right claimed by zemstvos as "public" institutions.[83] The problem arose because the mission of ministerial power—to isolate politics from administration—could not be fulfilled. The existence of zemstvos, whatever their function, was politically significant precisely because they immediately acquired symbolic meanings within the circumscribed, but growing, world of elite opinion.

Though Valuev consistently defended the existence of zemstvos, several isolated political challenges by conservative aristocratic proponents of oligarchy and enemies of bureaucracy (for example, the St. Petersburg and Zelenyi cases in the late 1860s) who happened to be using particular zemstvos as their forums led him to reaffirm the state's political monopoly.[84] Valuev never abandoned his hope that the zemstvos would fulfill their assigned administrative and political functions. But the well-publicized appearance of a few zemstvo-based gentry political demands led him and the MVD to mount increasingly heavy-handed political attacks on the zemstvos. Once Valuev equated the zemstvos with the new judicial institutions as political threats to autocracy, a pattern of institutional perception and response was set. Henceforth, whatever the day-to-day administrative relationship between zemstvos and government, the latter, particularly the MVD, treated the zemstvos as a potential threat to the political monopoly represented by ministerial power. The MVD policy was reduced to surveillance, suspicion, and, if possible, co-optation. Symbols to the bureaucrats of society's political challenge, the zemstvos, not surprisingly, represented that same challenge to citizens who were demanding political participation.

As in many other policy areas, Valuev's less talented successors accepted his most pronounced pro-bureaucratic views. Under Timashev and Makov, the MVD cooperated with the zemstvos on most administrative matters. The government's tax-reform commission even solicited zemstvo opinions, thereby setting a precedent for zemstvo participation in the legislative process.[85] Though disputes arose over zemstvo franking privileges, the zemstvo role in the postal system, and so forth, there was a surprisingly harmonious working relationship at the local level. But the zemstvo as political symbol would not disappear. At the outset of Timashev's ministry the zemstvos were again caught up in MVD plans to strengthen administrative and police authority in the provinces and particularly to strengthen the office of civil governor. In 1867 the newly appointed assistant minister, B. P. Obukhov, while still governor of Pskov Province, said that the zemstvos were incompetent and that provincial society was too immature for any substantial administrative responsibility. Obukhov felt that zemstvo participation was inconceivable on anything other than the most tightly controlled basis. The attempt to solicit zemstvo opinions for the tax-reform commission was accompanied by an MVD demand that zemstvo discussions be carefully restricted to the economic aspects of tax reform.

The MVD believed it could control the zemstvos and their political implications. However, the realities of administrative and political life during the 1870s, exemplified by the tax-reform process, Shuvalov's plans for representation, and the subsequent Valuev agricultural and worker commissions, cultivated institutionalization of social participation in the legislative process. During the 1870s zemstvo data and expertise were increasingly indispensable to the government, and the potential political benefits for autocracy of controlled local participation were evident. Yet the ministerial power ethos of Timashev, Makov, and their high MVD subordinates worked to subvert this development and to maintain what was rapidly becoming an outdated and fictional state political monopoly. In an 1880 report to Alexander on MVD activities for the preceding 25 years, Makov praised zemstvo administrative contributions and the good relationship between zemstvo and government officials, ignoring the political dimension completely.[86] However, from 1878 to 1880, the crisis years, Makov identified zemstvo activists' political demands with the programs of revolutionaries and terrorists.[87] He was hostile to proposals to extend the activities of local self-government and reasserted bureaucratic control over zemstvo programs and appointments.[88] As an experienced administrator, Makov understood the need to rework the 1864 statutes, but when it came to larger issues of social and political transformation, he rejected any alteration of traditional Russian political culture. Only later, under Loris-Melikov, did the zemstvos again become the object of political vision.

The Municipal Reform of 1870 was analogous to the better studied creation of the zemstvos.[89] The MVD positions in the debates that brought a form of self-government to many of the empire's cities exemplify how resurgent police power came to dominate ministry policy. The ministry's evolving viewpoint on municipal reform during the 1860s was inseparable from the MVD goal of strengthening provincial administration under the aegis of its own civil governors as described above. When finally passed in 1870 the Municipal Reform was a compromise between the MVD and forces within the government opposed to any extension or strengthening of the MVD hierarchy in the provinces. In this case, the compromise brought both sides some notable successes, but the result was another ambiguous reform that reflected the structural and ideological cleavages within autocracy.

The Municipal Reform was of course a post-Karakozov Great Reform whose preparation proceeded in relative isolation from the upheavals of the 1860s. Its development may be traced back to the Perovskii ministry of the 1840s, the creation of the Economic Department in the MVD, and the St. Petersburg reform of 1846. Despite the continuity in preparatory work, the MVD could not maintain a policy-making monopoly, as with many other policies. In 1860 the MVD Economic Department published the first of seven volumes of statistical data titled *Urban Settlements of the Russian Empire*.[90] Although this compilation was a necessary first step in comprehensive municipal reform, there were still vast gaps and some inaccuracies in the data. Alexander commissioned Valuev and the MVD to gather more material, including the opinions of urban elites, and to prepare a draft project.[91]

In April 1862 the Economic Department under A. D. Shumakher and his assistant N. I. Vtorov began this major data-gathering effort. The provincial governors appointed 509 committees made up of city residents to articulate recommendations according to an agenda prepared by Shumakher. By 1864 the local committee reports had been submitted to the Economic Department for incorporation into the ministry project. Here the problems began, for it was clear that the ministry and the urban elites had quite different notions of self-government and different responses to the questions that the MVD had posed for consideration by the committees.[92]

Basically, the MVD had formulated its guidelines for discussion around four major deficiencies in municipal administration: (1) the fact that urban affairs remained in the hands of tax-paying social groups (merchants and artisans), and the failure of the 1846 St. Petersburg reform to attract talented property owners from the nobility to municipal public service; (2) the absence of all-estate municipal assemblies; (3) confusion of executive and legislative power in municipal government; and (4) poorly defined rights and duties of public officials and institutions—in short, the entire question of bureaucratic tutelage and supervision. Although both MVD officials and urban residents agreed that these were problems, the urban elites argued that effective self-government and improvement in municipal administration required a lessening of traditional bureaucratic tutelage and a genuine commitment from the administration to conduct relations with the cities in a new spirit, according to well-defined guidelines for relations between the state bureaucracy and municipal self-government.

The resulting MVD project of 1865 revealed the ministry's desire to maintain that tutelage. Among its features was placing the proposed municipal self-government institutions squarely within the regular

MVD hierarchy under general supervision of the governors, municipal assemblies that were to be strictly advisory rather than legislative bodies, and an electoral system based on a three-curiae tax qualification that was modeled upon Prussian urban self-government.[93]

It was at this point that central government personalities and institutions opposed to growing MVD power and MVD attempts to dominate the province's government rallied to the cause of self-government. The MVD's and Valuev's principal opponent, as had been the case in the zemstvo reform, was Baron Modest Korf, at that time chief of the Second Section of the tsar's chancery. Though history records Korf as a liberal, it overlooks his obvious ambition and unscrupulousness.[94] In the legislative process, Korf had maneuvered the Second Section into a mediating position between the ministries and the State Council and had already forced Valuev and the MVD to retreat during the zemstvo debates.[95] The MVD had to submit its proposals to the Second Section even before consideration in the State Council. Whether Korf was hostile toward the MVD, was exercising a personal vendetta against Valuev, or had a personal ambition to become minister is not known, but in 1865 Korf and the Second Section, assisted by D. M. Sol'skii, turned back the MVD project.[96] They portrayed the proposal as too favorable to the administration, particularly the governors (and hence the MVD). They also claimed that the excessive borrowing of German western forms, particularly the three-curiae tax-based electoral system, was inimical to Russian social estates. Korf and his successor, Urusov, proposed instead a property-based electoral system, or at least a mixed property and tax system that would strengthen representation of the nobility as an estate. Korf and his supporters were thus using defense of the estates as a means of defending the principle of independent self-government against the power of the MVD.

Between 1865 and final passage in 1870, the Municipal Reform project was vigorously debated at the highest levels of the Russian government.[97] The debates again centered around rival conceptions of self-government and the role of the MVD in urban and provincial life. The ministry wanted to co-opt and incorporate new municipal institutions into its own hierarchy, with the governors having considerable power; the Second Section and its allies, on the other hand, wanted to create new provincial boards for municipal affairs, mixed committees consisting of MVD and non-MVD bureaucrats and city representatives with extensive power to make decisions and interpret law. These would act as mediators between the municipalities and the regular administration. The ministry was appalled at this proposal to create yet another independent quasi-bureaucratic center of authority in "its" provinces. It only reconfirmed the worst MVD fears of the disintegration of unified power in those provinces and, of course, served to harden the ministry's stand on provincial reform in general and on the need for a strong civil governor.

The MVD wanted the new mayors to be purely administrative officers, separate from the dumas, whereas the Second Section and city spokesmen placed the officials at the head of the new city assemblies as spokesmen for city interests. On the property qualification, Timashev argued that the MVD would acquiesce to property as the determinant, but only if the qualifications were lowered substantially to take into account the relative dearth of urban dwellers belonging to the nobility.

These and other outstanding issues were finally resolved in the government commission that met during the first three months of 1870.[98] The MVD managed to retain control of the police in the cities and to have the three-curiae tax-based system adopted as the basis for representation. MVD opponents, however, also won major points. For example, the mayors were to be drawn from the dumas. More importantly, the provincial boards for municipal affairs were created, and the cities were given powers to gradually expand the tax base and hence the participation of urban professionals, intellectuals, and potentially even workers in municipal self-government.

It should be remembered, however, that the MVD provincial governors did retain ill-defined supervisory powers over municipal self-government. The future of self-government under the aegis of a ministry that was becoming more vociferous in its defense of administrative power could only be problematic.[99]

Again, an interesting pattern could be observed in the debates surrounding the Municipal Reform. The Second Section and the other "liberal" officials who worked against the MVD program defended some retrograde estate privileges in order to protect the larger and more important principle of self-government against the encroachments of ministerial power. These groups were successful in moderating the legislative outcome. This pattern would be repeated time and again in subsequent decades, as, for example, in the 1880s when the most extreme plans of D. Tolstoi were similarly thwarted.

In social policy the MVD had to face the question of whether it should support, dismantle, or transform the traditional estates. The policy choices were complicated by the fact that profound social and economic changes were already under way. Economic development and the emancipation had resulted in the emergence of a distinct but small urban proletariat and entrepreneurial groups that cut across traditional estate boundaries.[100] In government and at court, however, it was customary for those who supported ministerial power to defend estate society as well. Though the outlines of the post-1881 MVD policy of subsidy and forced maintenance of the nobility and the estate system were already visible prior to 1881, ministry policy wavered between support of and transformation of the traditional estates.[101] Like his more outspoken opponent M. N. Katkov, Valuev wanted to maintain a gentry-dominated estate society, but only if the gentry could acquire a new class consciousness. Ministry leaders were aware of the economic and political costs of a rigid estate society, and many tried to promote social mobility and to cater to dynamic groups within the estates. But they always came up against their own sense of the inviolability of administrative and police authority and structural constraints that further limited policy possibilities. The resulting policies increasingly supported traditional guardianship and social immobility.

Following the Crimean War, the implications of the emergence and growth of an urban working class had to be debated. Leading officials and publicists wanted to avoid the proletarianization of workers they believed responsible for the revolutionary upheavals in Europe during 1848-49.[102] The need to define a labor policy appeared on the MVD agenda as one more part of the impulse to reorganize society in conjunction with emancipation. Since the late 1840s the MVD had recognized the need to promote economic productivity; it began to consider reforms well before the Crimean War. During Nicholas' reign the ministries had debated issuing to workers mandatory employment record books as a control mechanism of worker-employer relations. The ideas of "ministerial power" and official nationality—particularly the idea that Russia was not bound to repeat the pattern of Western historical development—fostered a bureaucratic vision of Russia's ability to avoid proletarianization of the urban workers not by halting the processes of urbanization and industrial growth, but by the time-honored methods of state guardianship through administrative regulations.[103]

By 1857 a commission of inquiry had been created in the MVD to examine complaints that young apprentices had been mistreated in St. Petersburg workshops.[104] In 1859 another commission, chaired by A. F. Shtakel'berg, began to reexamine the traditional *tsekh* system and to draft a new industrial code applicable to all branches of industry.

MVD policy emerged in the Shtakel'berg commission deliberations. Among the barriers to achieving greater productivity, the MVD singled out the tsekh and the legislation restricting the urban economy. Ministry officials wished to promote a more mobile society and a free marketplace on the one hand, and state intervention and regulation in employee-worker relations to avoid European urban problems on the other. The state wished to "protect" the workers by erecting an edifice of special legislation and institutions that, practically speaking, could only keep them isolated from the other estates. The worker booklets and factory inspectors—agents of control and protection that might be compared to the peace mediators—were typical ideas of MVD officials long used to the legitimate exercise of broad police functions. Though the Shtakel'berg commission and leading "liberal" economists supported a free marketplace and attempted to remove the social and legislative obstructions, the state's guardianship of the workers was also reinforced through the legitimation of state intervention in labor-management relations.

The Shtakel'berg commission, heady with optimism, issued a comprehensive program "befitting the advent of a new era in Russian economic life." It provided for worker booklets, factory inspectors, and urban industrial courts to mediate between employers and workers. The commission failed to note, however, the contradiction between passing laws assigned to treat workers as individual "citizens," and the exercise of state intervention that brought to bear traditional police functions and estate patterns of social organization. State protection of workers embodied the dilemmas of conservative renovators and modern liberalism that must rely upon state power, hence bureaucracy, to overcome or regulate the injustices of the free market ideal of classical liberal thought. Further, as Reginald Zelnik has shown, the notion of creating a citizenry was itself inimical to pure autocracy and its supporting ethos of ministerial power. Although MVD officials feared capitalist competition and the horrors of the European experience, they desired the "clear division of labor and the development of a class of highly skilled completely urbanized industrial workers" necessary for industrialization. To this end the commission favored forms of workers' associations (*arteli* and *tovarichestva*).

The Shtakel'berg commission proposals were not adopted. The intense government activity surrounding emancipation, creation of the new zemstvos and judicial institutions, financial reforms, and so forth, lowered the priority of the labor question. More important for the fate of labor legislation, however, was the effect of the radical activity in St. Petersburg during the early 1860s. As shown earlier, the activities of the radicals hastened Valuev's reconfirmation of police authority and were in part responsible for the more conservative positions of the MVD in all areas of domestic policy. Valuev's 1862 closing of the Sunday Schools for seditious activity signaled growing MVD fear of social dissent. In Zelnik's words, political grounds were used to "end initiatives favorable to the organization of labor."

Although the labor question was shelved, it was no longer possible in the early 1870s to believe that Russia could escape the social and urban problems of Europe. As the numbers of workers grew, so did their grievances.[105] Because of its traditional police functions and policy of guardianship, the MVD viewed labor unrest increasingly as a matter of short-term prevention and punishment. In the wake of the Nevsky strike of 1870, the ministry again professed the need for comprehensive labor legislation as well as more administrative controls. That it succeeded in obtaining more controls was partly the result of pressure from subordinate MVD police and administrators in the cities. Provincial officials were given more authority to exile strike leaders to distant provinces and to increase police surveillance over both workers and factory owners.[106] Though ministry representatives advocated comprehensive labor legislation in the Ignat'ev and Valuev commissions between 1872 and 1875, the proposals were not adopted. During Alexander's reign the government failed to formulate a comprehensive labor policy, and the groundwork was laid for the extreme police-inspired labor policies of the post-1881 MVD.[107]

In its postemancipation agrarian policy, MVD police functions and growing fear of massive peasant unrest conflicted with the goal of ameliorating the inadequacies of the 1861 settlement and the burgeoning agrarian (and demographic) problems of the countryside.[108] The MVD never really had a free hand, as the powerful Main Committee for Peasant Affairs (under a new name) continued to exist throughout the reign.

Unfortunately, peasant administrative institutions were unsuccessful, as were the economic arrangements of emancipation. Furthermore, the economic pressures upon the peasantry (from redemption payments, taxes, obligations, inadequate allotments, population increases, low technology, and so forth) were increasing dramatically. Under both Valuev and Timashev, the MVD tried to reform peasant administration by assuring bureaucratic and police tutelage. At the same time, the ministry promoted private peasant landholding, apart from the restraints of the commune and joint responsibility (*krugovaia poruka*). By the 1870s agrarian productivity in the countryside was seriously hampered. In the development of MVD agrarian policy during Alexander's reign, it is remarkable that, first of all, there was great cooperation among the MVD and its later rivals, the Ministry of Finance and the Ministry of State Domains. Second, the proposals of the Valuev Agricultural Commission of 1872 (which MVD representatives helped formulate) clearly foreshadowed subsequent bureaucratic thinking on the agrarian question. For example, the removal of state support for the commune would later be found in Stolypin's agrarian program of 1906-1911. Ironically, the MVD during the 1860s and 1870s had to fight not so much rival ministries but the Main Committee on Agricultural Affairs, headed by the erstwhile reformer and sponsor of enlightened officialdom Grand Duke Konstantin Nikolaevich. While Valuev and Timashev wished to expand bureaucratic authority in the provinces down to the village level, first by controlling and then by eliminating the overly independent peace mediators (who were replaced on June 27, 1874, by the district boards for peasant affairs), Konstantin Nikolaevich steadfastly defended the commune and the peasants' "way of life" from what he perceived to be one-sided or self-interested bureaucratic encroachment.[109]

During the 1870s even MVD officials understood that punitive measures such as forced sale of peasant property to cover tax arrears would undermine future economic viability (and hence taxability) of the recently "freed" serfs.[110] Here the agrarian question intersected government fiscal policy and tax revenue requirements. In cooperation with the Ministry of Finance, the MVD pursued a more flexibile policy on the question of tax arrears. There were few forced sales of peasant property and the peasantry was offered tax advantages. Late in the decade, the MVD attempted independently to determine the tax-paying ability of peasants in several provinces, but the central government was unable to produce or uphold a unified policy. The autocratic government failed to adopt MVD supported measures such as those suggested in the Agricultural Commission report—removal of state protection of the commune and facilitation of peasant departure from the commune. The Valuev commission proposals exemplified the foresight still available to the government from its own ranks during the 1870s. Unfortunately, inadequate leadership and institutional and ideological conflict within the government once again foiled such legislative initiatives. Though the shift to a more sterile agrarian policy occurred somewhat later than the corresponding shift in labor policy, both strands reflected the ministry's growing reliance on traditional police authority. Tax reform, too, was postponed because the structurally and ideologically fragmented central government could not unite long enough to legislate fundamental reforms. At the close of Alexander's reign, Loris-Melikov and Finance Minister Greig moved to abolish the soul tax and to reinvestigate agriculture and peasant administration. Following Alexander's assassination, agrarian policy exhibited the same lack of movement and stale bureaucratism as in other major policy areas during the 1870s. Bureaucratic control of the countryside and administrative adjustments became dominant MVD goals and the more flexible and creative policies of the 1850s and 1860s were infused by the spirit of traditional guardianship and police authority that would ultimately triumph during the 1880s. During the 1880s the MVD and other branches of the administration adopted a traditional, piecemeal, short-term administrative approach to the rapidly growing and diversifying problems of the countryside. The gradual change in the spirit and goals of MVD policy and reaffirmation of ministerial power does much to remove the apparent gulf between the Reform Era and its aftermath.

The MVD censorship policy also shows the reassertion of police authority and the traditional ministerial power ethos.[111] During the early 1860s, Valuev, aided by A. V. Golovnin, then minister of education, presided over transfer of a considerable share of the administration of government censorship from the Ministry of Education to the Ministry of Internal Affairs. Valuev considered the censorship function vital to both ministry and government in their fight against independent public opinion and for continuing the bureaucracy's monopoly in legitimate politics. Valuev also wanted the state to take the offensive in publicly promoting its own views and accomplishments, that is, to build a body of public opinion at once hostile to revolutionaries and supportive of autocracy. In 1862 the MVD assumed responsibility for supervising printing presses and certain types of published materials. On April 6, 1865, temporary press regulations transferred many censorship functions to the MVD.[112] Most forms of preliminary censorship were eliminated for journals, newspapers, and books of over 160 pages, and primary responsibility for content shifted to editors, publishers, writers, and printers. Henceforth they would be responsible for violations discovered by the censors after the material was in print.

Though the new regulations promised to transfer censorship prosecutions to the courts, the MVD, through its new censorship apparatus, the Main Directorate of Press Affairs, had control, in practice, over bringing the cases to the courts, as well as rights of inspection and surveillance in most facets of the publishing industry. Furthermore, the regulations, patterned after similar rules of Second Empire France, permitted the MVD to issue warnings to publications judged to be in violation of bureaucratic standards of taste and political propriety. After three warnings, the offending publisher might be shut down for up to six months, or even completely. As is well known, Valuev used this police authority. In mid-1866, after the Karakozov attempt to assasinate Alexander, the radical journals *The Contemporary* and *The Russian Word* were discontinued permanently. Valuev did not discriminate in his hostility toward antistate publications: he used his power to harass such right-wing publicists as M. N. Katkov.[113]

Though the government portrayed the new censorship regulations as progressive, their effect was chilling, since the publishing world was now subject to penalties determined by the MVD. The notion of responsibility after the fact undoubtedly had a negative effect on creativity and willingness to publish, as is the case in any organized system of punitive censorship. Controlled public debate or artificial publicity, the goal of the reformers of the 1850s, would be transformed within the new institutional structure of the censorship. The debate might still take place, but the MVD by acting as guardian of the state interest would have the weapons to coerce the press and literary establishment into submission. Such weapons provided ready means for reasserting traditional bureaucratic values and conceptions of the state interest. Even under Valuev and most decidedly under Timashev and Makov, the MVD linked its censorship policies to its hostility toward the new judicial system and to reassertion of the administration's monopoly of political justice.

During Valuev's tenure, the MVD subscribed, to some extent, to the notion that the courts must decide certain censorship cases. In the new system of censorship, some cases did reach the courts, with results that were distressing to the MVD. In eight of the twenty-one cases that were tried in court during Valuev's ministry, the Ministry of Justice dismissed the complaints for lack of evidence. Several acquittals served only to foster administration distrust of the courts and the rule-of-law principles they represented. In censorship the bureaucracy's massive distrust of the new courts would be very similar to its reaction to the jury acquittal of the unabashedly guilty Vera Zasulich at the end of the decade.

When Timashev took over the MVD he wished to divest it of its censorship responsibilities, but it did not take him long to accept them. On November 20, 1869, he submitted a memorandum to the Council of Ministers citing the evil thought spread by irresponsible writers and publishers because of the leniency of the 1865 temporary regulations. Timashev argued that these laws needed clarification, particularly with respect to the prosecution of offenders in the courts. At the same time Timashev launched a successful drive to establish an all-government newspaper under the aegis of the MVD. His goal, in creating the paper called the *Government Messenger* (*Pravitel'stvennyi vestnik*), was not only to promote the government's point of view but also to eliminate the official or semi-official status (and resulting immunity to censorship laws) of other ministry newspapers, particularly the *Russkii Invalid* of the War Ministry, that sometimes criticized government policy.[114]

On November 2, 1869, a new commission to review the press laws was created, under the chairmanship of S. N. Urusov. This commis-

sion worked for two years and then in 1872 it issued a project that was
reviewed in a special conference sponsored by Timashev. Another legislative stalemate, characteristic of the 1870s, manifested itself. The
government passed no comprehensive legislation during the entire
decade. (Indeed, censorship reform appeared on Loris-Melikov's legislative program of 1880-81 as another pressing Reform Era legacy.)
Nonetheless, a succession of administrative edicts during the 1870s
gave the MVD and its censorship apparatus increased administrative
powers to regulate, supervise, and even close down publications.[115]
Police authority and the traditional ministerial power ethos found
ready expression in the censorship function, as they did in the administration of political justice and in the ministry's long struggle to remain independent of, yet superintend, the 1864 judicial system. Early
in Timashev's ministry, censorship was especially harsh as administrative edicts increased the powers of the Main Directorate of Press
Affairs, at that time headed by M. R. Shidlovskii, a former general.
He was replaced in 1871 by M. N. Longinov, former associate of the
poet Nekrasov, member of *The Contemporary* circle, and writer of
pornographic verses. This succession of almost ludicrous appointments was broken in 1875 when the top Main Directorate post passed
to the more bookish orientalist V. V. Grigor'ev.

Throughout the 1870s the MVD received increased authority to dispense administrative justice and to issue circulars having the force of
law.[116] Generally speaking, during Alexander's reign the MVD wavered between blatant use of this growing police authority and enactment of social and economic policies that, despite their component of
police guardianship, at least held out the hope of transforming individual estates and loosening the estate system. Ministry policy was
always marked by this ambivalence. One can point to many positive
initiatives, such as Valuev's attempt to break down the cultural isolation and economic penury of the white, or parish, clergy; his desire to
remove state support of the peasant commune; his early position on
the labor question; his promotion of joint stock companies; and his
attempts to transform the nobility.[117] This desire to unleash productive forces in society, at the same time retaining bureaucratic and
police control, was inherent in the traditions and functions of the ministry. In this sense, structure may be said to have profoundly influenced politics. The autocracy's drift from the policies of the 1870s into
the more reactionary policies of the 1880s and 1890s was in large measure institutionally determined.

This pattern of policy development was broken only during 1880-81
in Loris-Melikov's ministry. Though his programs and methods will
be treated in Chapter 6, here the background to Loris' attempt to

renovate Russian autocracy can be established as having taken shape during the Reform Era. The role of the MVD in the relegitimation of police authority, and therefore in the strengthening of the ministerial power ethos, should now be clear. The ministry was involved, during Alexander's reign, in several attempts to institutionalize participation of social elites in the legislative process. Those plans, themselves products of the tensions within the autocratic government, help to explain the origins and the ultimate failure of Loris' renovation attempt and, indeed, the fate of autocracy itself.

The first such attempt, which served as a model for Loris' 1881 plan, was the 1858-59 provincial committees and their representatives brought to St. Petersburg ostensibly to aid in the drafting of the emancipation legislation.[118] It should be remembered that the failure of this early method to become institutionalized was in large part due to the ministry's manipulation of the provincial deputies and the climate of opinion surrounding the tsar. Next came Valuev's 1863 plan to introduce 16 members of a proposed congress of state deputies (*s"ezd gosudarstvennykh glasnykh*) into the general sessions of the State Council.[119] Clearly, this was in response to manifestations of gentry political aspirations and to the appearance of radical movements and propaganda in the wake of emancipation. The Valuev plan fits neatly into a series of contemporary conservative renovation attempts elsewhere because he consciously modeled it after similar tentative movements toward quasi-representative institutions in Austria, another multinational empire.[120] Valuev believed that Russia was ready for the institutionalization of a controlled form of social participation in the legislative process to be patterned after the recently created Austrian *Reichsrat*. In Russia, as in Austria, an essentially traditional and conservative bureaucratic government was faced with the task of recasting its political institutions in order to counter internal and external challenges to their existence. This movement toward conservative renovation, a conscious desire to preserve certain elements of traditional political culture while adapting forms and political techniques of countries perceived as politically more advanced, comprised a common wave of historical experience for contemporary states in both Europe and Asia during the latter part of the nineteenth century.

The fate of Valuev's plan is well known. Alexander himself, perhaps with counsel from individuals hostile to any alteration of traditional autocracy and its ministerial power ethos, rejected the plan.[121] He claimed that, with the threat posed by the Polish uprising and revolutionary movement, such a concession to society was ill timed, and also that Russia was too "immature" for representation anyway. Another plan, by Alexander's brother, Grand Duke Konstantin Nikolaevich, was rejected in 1866.[122] Though Valuev's plan was more radical because it advocated representation based upon the zemstvos and hence upon property, as opposed to the grand duke's use of both traditional estate institutions and the zemstvos, the latter plan still fell victim to the post-Karakozov retrenchment. Alexander announced, at a meeting of the Council of Ministers on January 12, 1867, that he emphatically rejected his brother's proposal and any other similar "constitutional aspirations." Interestingly, it has been noted recently that Valuev, in negotiations with S. N. Urusov, had been offered the role of ghost-writer in the formulation of the grand duke's project. Konstantin Nikolaevich, it appears, had not supported Valuev's project two years earlier, but he now wished to claim responsibility for the first major step in renovating autocratic politics. Valuev, either because he thought the tsar would reject the idea or because he wanted to reformulate and receive credit for another project of his own, refused to prepare the grand duke's project, but he did serve as a consultant in correspondence with Urusov.[123]

The struggle of parliamentarianism against conservative revolution so noticeable, for example, in Bismarckian Germany, was taking place in Russia. Here, however, the struggle was over the first tentative steps toward establishment of quasi-parliamentary institutions. The tsar, with his stubborn belief in the indivisibility of his patrimonial inheritance of autocratic power, was the most obvious obstacle to political transformation. Other obstacles were the large numbers of powerful officials and courtiers who believed in personal authority and traditional ministerial power. Yet the ministerial institutions themselves, with their traditions and ideologies and the inadequate legislative process, also worked against political transformation.

Until recently, scholars believed that Konstantin Nikolaevich's plan of "government constitutionalism" was the last to introduce representative forms prior to the debates of early 1880 and Loris' 1881 plan. The Soviet historian V. G. Chernukha, however, has uncovered a major attempt by P. A. Shuvalov between 1870 and 1874 to create a new form of political representation.[124] Shuvalov's plan, which culminated in the Valuev agriculture and labor commissions with their social representation and similarity to British parliamentary commissions, may be linked closely to the earlier plans to reform the State Council and Loris-Melikov's later effort. All of them, including the proposal for controlled participation of zemstvos in tax-reform deliberations and the late 1870s proposals of War Minister Miliutin, were manifestations of a growing belief in the necessity of political transformation. The Shuvalov plan is particularly instructive because it represented, even more than the Valuev and Konstantin Nikolaevich proposals, an attempt from within the ranks of the traditionalists to initiate far-reaching political change. Though the events centered on the enigmatic Shuvalov, whom contemporaries sometimes called "Arakcheev II" and "Peter IV," his fate and the MVD role also say much about the importance of an institutional power base for would-be reformers and the prospects for political change within the autocracy.

Shuvalov, scion of a well-known aristocratic St. Petersburg family, burst upon the political scene when he was appointed chief of the Third Section and the Corps of Gendarmes in the wake of the Karakozov assassination attempt. Apparently a man of strong Western, particularly Anglophile, leanings, he wanted to reform the autocracy to preserve it and, perhaps more important, to assure the survival of the nobility as an estate. Shuvalov thought that the economic regeneration of the countryside should be dominated by a productive and responsible estate of landed gentry, and a new agriculture sector based upon the revived peasant commune and Western technology and methods. Shuvalov was particularly moved by the example of the Paris Commune of 1870-71 and by what he perceived to be a rising revolutionary movement in Russia. He had scrutinized the English example of conservative reform, and he believed that only timely concessions from those in power might avert upheaval.

Shuvalov launched an offensive to organize a bloc of supporters within high ministerial circles that included the minister of internal affairs, Timashev, and Valuev, whom Alexander had appointed as minister of state domains. The 1872 Agricultural Commission resulted, a commission patterned after English parliamentary commissions. It involved a relatively open and public process of gathering testimony from bureaucrats and outside experts. As in England, the government issued commission materials to the public in a form similar to parliamentary blue books. Shuvalov spoke of the need for constitutional changes and for fresh forces to overcome the static, highly routinized, bureaucratic, and structurally divided government of the late 1860s and early 1870s. Shuvalov was responding to the policy stalemate that had resulted from the government's structural flaws. According to B. M. Markevich, Shuvalov's aim was to prove that, as in England, the conservative party was really liberal in spirit and capable of leading the country forward through a well-conceived, timely reform program that would expand the political foundations and social base of autocracy. He also believed it was possible to inculcate in the zemstvos and corporate institutions of the hereditary nobility an enlightened conservatism.

The plan to involve zemstvos and noble representatives in the legislative process was discussed in late 1873 and again in early 1874 in the Committee of Ministers, where it was greeted with considerable hostility, not only by the conservatives but also, most significantly, by those usually considered reform-minded. For example, Konstantin Nikolaevich, Miliutin, and Reutern opposed Shuvalov's plans, seeing in them a conservative estate-centered attempt to establish aristocratic oligarchy. Shuvalov was portrayed as a power-hungry individual whose plans threatened the tsar's authority, and therefore autocracy. Though during the debates Timashev meekly agreed that Russia needed some form of representation, he failed to articulate a plan or effectively promote that goal. Reutern wished to call ad hoc "experts" as had been done in the past without establishing representative institutions. When a stalemate was reached, Timashev asked Valuev to draft recommendations that all could agree upon. The results were incorporated into the Valuev Commission on Labor, another ad hoc commission of experts, with zemstvo and noble representatives chosen by the bureaucracy. Shuvalov was rapidly falling from grace, not so much for personal reasons (as was believed by earlier historians), but because of his relentless pressure for political reform that threatened the autocrat's personal power.

Shuvalov viewed the outcome in the Committee of Ministers as a defeat, and he wished to make another attempt at a more grandiose and institutionalized plan. But even Timashev objected, and Alexander removed Shuvalov from the office of chief of the Corps of Gendarmes and, in effect, exiled him as ambassador to England. Subsequently, the Commission on Labor sent several experts and representatives of social institutions to testify before the State Council, but the practice was never developed. Though results were meager during the late 1870s, the government had taken important first steps that recognized the need for representation, and an efficient and regular legislative process for domestic affairs. Throughout the period of 1876-1879 several other almost forgotten plans for political and institutional transformation were presented and discussions continued in high government circles. A growing circle of government officials of diverse political views were reading widely in "constitutional" literature, and most of them, regardless of political philosophy, recognized the necessity for political change.

It was unfortunate that only extreme crisis and the emergence of the charismatic Loris-Melikov could move the vision of a redefined autocracy closer to realization. During the reign of Alexander II, MVD policy touched on virtually all the core problems faced by the autocracy. The continuities and disjunctions that resulted from a delicate balance between institutional and personal factors are clearer. Despite the

Shuvalov episode and the movement of government constitutionalism, police authority and ministerial power continued to dominate MVD policy during the 1870s. The unmistakable drift in ministry policy toward a rigid and traditional interpretation of its police mandate overshadowed the countervailing tendency toward a more moderate and flexible statism. The structure of ministerial government and the place of ministries within the larger tsar-centered government would have made another outcome most difficult, but certainly not impossible. By 1880 only an exceptionally strong, energetic individual able to promote and secure political and institutional change could have reversed the apparent victory of police authority and ministerial power. Loris-Melikov appeared and he embarked on that task. His experience proved fateful for the future of imperial Russia.

The "Dictatorship of the Heart"

6

Even before he became chief of the Supreme Executive Commission in 1880, M. T. Loris-Melikov described his method of administration and his policies as a governing "system."[1] Two characteristics of his approach—concern with public opinion and policies cutting across the functional divisions of ministerial institutions—were already evident during his many years of service as chief administrator in various non-Russian borderlands. During his twelve-year tenure in Terek *oblast'*, for example, Loris governed independently of the regular domestic administration in St. Petersburg.[2] He was able to pacify the hostile, non-Russian tribesmen, establish the Russian administrative presence, and successfully integrate the area into the empire. Loris won political support by pursuing vigorous coordinated policies designed to raise economic and educational standards. In addition, he made an outward show of soliciting public opinion and expressions of needs that he then attempted to meet.

Loris, a war hero (he was commander of the force that captured the Turkish fortress at Kars), was a charismatic leader. His name was well-known in educated and court circles, and his deft handling, early in 1879, of the Vetlianka plague crisis greatly enhanced his reputation for energetic leadership.[3]

Loris-Melikov's first attempt to govern an area closer to European Russia came with his appointment on April 5, 1879, as temporary governor-general of Kharkov Province in the Ukraine. The creation of three temporary governors-general (in St. Petersburg, Odessa, and Kharkov), with complete authority over civil administration and the military came at a time of growing terrorist attacks on Russian officials, leftist agitation among the peasants, and social unrest brought on by deteriorating economic conditions after the Turkish War. Appointment of the governors-general signaled that the crises of the 1870s had intensified. The governors-general represented "decentralization of autocratic authority"—the creation of territorial dictatorships that further weakened the power of the tsar.[4]

The appointment as governor-general gave Loris-Melikov an opportunity to apply his methods to an area that had been a seedbed of revolutionary activity. His successful pacification of Kharkov made a lasting impression on all sectors of official and public opinion and undoubtedly contributed to Alexander's decision to make him head of the Supreme Executive Commission upon its creation on February 12, 1880.[5]

In a report to the tsar dated February 2, Loris-Melikov summarized his activities as governor-general of Kharkov and outlined the basic principles of a proposed governing system. He wrote that when he arrived in Kharkov on April 20, 1879, the population was in an "excited state" and the "Supreme Administrative Power, in the person of the Civil Governor, had revealed itself powerless in the struggle with the evil. This was partially a result of the uncoordination and lack of unity in the activities of the various organs of provincial administration, and partially because of the inadequate personnel and means at its disposal." Loris reviewed the failures of the district and city police, the inept performance of an aged and ineffective commander of gendarmes, and the inadequate government supervision and broken "moral ties" between students and teachers. In describing his own policies, Loris claimed that energetic measures had been necessary to permit a turnabout in the government's stance—from a purely defensive position to an active response in the struggle against the revolutionary evil. The primary aim was to "revive" the moral authority of government power by means of a two-sided policy. First, the administration was to prosecute severely, but legally, political and common criminals. Second, Loris wanted to "calm" the reliable elements of society and revive their confidence in government power by securing their legitimate interests. These policies, in their aim to prevent social unrest, fit well with the traditional police function of the administration, yet placed far greater emphasis on the legitimacy of private interests.[6]

As in his previous posts, Loris took responsibility in Kharkov for defining all areas of government policy. He reviewed the disposition of political cases, and with great success diminished arbitrary arrests and administrative exiles.[7] He also issued plans to restore discipline in the schools and advocated creation of a technical institute "because the population of this underdeveloped area had few technical skills and as a result agriculture and manufacturing were suffering."[8] Loris claimed that the population of Kharkov was responding to his initiatives, but that ultimate success would require "a continuation of the government system which has already begun to reveal its useful results."[9]

The institutional basis of Loris' "system" was the special powers invested in the office of temporary governor-general. The nature of that office had been debated for years, but Loris argued that its special powers were necessary to restore social order under the extraordinary conditions of 1879. The office of governor-general was indispensable precisely because it permitted its occupant to control all aspects of policy and thereby transcend the institutional conflicts that had paralyzed government activities. The office of governor-general, which so often had been used to circumvent the regular ministerial institutions and basic laws of the empire, was now seen as the only viable means of unifying competing administrative organs within the province. More important, Loris-Melikov saw it as the instrument of ending the age-old arbitrariness of Russian government, restoring legality and answering to society's justifiable demands. The personal-power principle was now viewed as the only means of promoting institutions in the long run.

But governors-general—indeed, all tsarist administrators—had to become more active politically. To root out the causes of revolutionary activity, which were "complex and grounded in the various conditions of social and economic life," state power had to be "watchful and able to exert its influence wherever necessary." This was possible only, Loris stated, if the governors-general were in close enough touch with local interests to determine and fulfill their needs. This type of government would be more productive than "armed guard duty and punishment alone." The governors-general were thus indispensable in establishing a new pattern of interaction between administration and society. To do this, they needed authority over all provincial matters, and over all the provincial organs of the central ministries that in the past had proven inefficient, arbitrary, and hostile to society.[10]

The governors-general, according to Loris, had to "*appear* as the highest representative of legality and restorer of violated legality wherever, and in whatever sphere, such violated legality appears." For these new political tasks, Loris-Melikov advised that the tsar reject men who "would use only their repressive tools of military courts, administrative exile, arrest, and imprisonment." This recommendation was evidently directed against the traditional bureaucratic behavioral patterns in central and provincial ministerial institutions. Loris explicitly criticized the civil governors and provincial administrative and police personnel and argued that the expansion of the civil governors' power would not aid the government. "The authority of power," he believed, "did not depend on its prescriptive rights alone, but in the *manner* in which the representatives of power choose to utilize these rights." This did not mean that the governors-general were to meddle in the day-to-day affairs of the regular administration, but it did mean that they had to control excesses and incompetence.[11]

To a large extent, Loris-Melikov was rejecting the institutional and political frameworks of the Reform Era that had proven ineffectual in meeting the political challenges confronting autocracy. The governors-general were a first step toward transformation of administrative principles. The goal was to restore legality and establish more effective interaction with society so that "individuals, social estates, and private institutions would find in the governor-general the protection of their interests within the borders of the law and their respective spheres of activity."[12]

Three days after Alexander approved the February 2 report, a bomb exploded in the Winter Palace. In response to this incident, and to restore public order and combat terrorism, Alexander selected Loris-Melikov as chief of the Supreme Executive Commission.[13] According to the *ukaz* creating the commission, its functions appeared to be limited to "the securing of state order and social tranquility" and the suppression of the revolutionary movement. Neither the Third Section nor the regular MVD police had been able to protect the tsar, even within the walls of his palace. The main chief of the commission was therefore given direct control over state-crime investigations in St. Petersburg and its military district. The office of temporary St. Petersburg governor-general was abolished; all administrative and military institutions were ordered to fulfill the commission's demands in "affairs pertaining to state order and social tranquility." The main chief was given the power "to issue all executive orders and in general to take all measures that he recognizes as necessary for the protection of state order in St. Petersburg as well as other localities of the empire."[14]

From the first days of his appointment, however, it was clear that Loris would interpret the mandate broadly. After a conversation with Loris on February 10, two days before the appointment was announced, D. Miliutin wrote: "Count Loris-Melikov understands his new role not in the sense only of chairman of an investigatory commission, but in the sense of a dictator to whom would be subordinated all powers, all ministers." Similarly, after a Committee of Ministers meeting on February 18, Valuev commented, "Count Loris-Melikov was present at the committee. He has barely begun to enter his role, but sees before him another—as organizer of all branches of the state administration."[15]

As head of the Supreme Executive Commission, Loris followed exactly the policy described in his February 2 report.[16] On February 15 the *Government Messenger* carried his appeal for cooperation and support in an article called "To the Residents of the Capital."[17] Before he could promulgate his proposed social, economic, and administrative reforms and secure full support of the people, he had to restore public order. To accomplish this, Loris had to resolve several problems that had existed for years. Competing centers of police authority (Third Section, MVD, governors-general, and so on) often worked at cross purposes, and the handling of "political" cases from investigation through punishment was arbitrary and slow. The Supreme Executive Commission was to alleviate these problems—albeit on a superficial and short-term basis.

Loris tolerated no institutional intermediaries or opposition in his relationship to the tsar. He had regular and frequent personal audiences with Alexander, and in February and March 1880 he secured Alexander's approval of a plan to subordinate the Third Section, Corps of Gendarmes, city police (MVD), and governors-general to his own authority.[18] While he headed the commission, Loris formed the nucleus of a staff, which he would later take along to the Ministry of Internal Affairs. Among them was M. S. Kakhanov, future assistant minister and author of such documents as the January 28, 1881, "constitutional" project.

The journals of the Supreme Executive Commission reveal that Loris-Melikov's primary goal during March and April was to consolidate all police activities in the area of political crimes and to improve the autocracy's handling of investigations, sentences, and punishments for political crimes. At its first meeting, on March 4, the commission set forth these basic aims and entrusted the collection of the necessary data (such as lists of those arrested, imprisoned, or placed under police surveillance, their alleged crimes, the legal basis for administrative action, and cases in abeyance) to commission members P. A. Markov, Senator I. I. Shamshin, and General M. I. Bat'ianov.[19]

In the commission sessions of March 11 and 24, detailed reports were read on the investigated aspects of political justice. The commission had uncovered many cases of administrative abuse of the laws, particularly the laws of May 1, 1871, and September 1, 1878, authorizing the dispensation of administrative justice for political crimes. It also found disorganization and slowness in all phases of the administrative justice process. It moved with haste to review incomplete or questionable cases to assuage the prevalent opinion that justice was harsh and arbitrary. Loris wished to free the innocent, or those guilty of minor misdemeanors so that people would know that the autocracy respected and observed its own laws. It is important to emphasize that he did *not* contemplate weakening the legitimacy of administrative justice or police authority. Rather, his goals were efficiency, minimizing political costs and elimination of the institutional conflicts and duplication of functions that had hindered the effective application of administrative justice. In the police-judiciary conflict, it was clear that he sided with the police and believed in the inviolability of a morally purified administrative and police authority in the area of political crimes.

The Supreme Executive Commission's preoccupation with political crimes did not mean that Loris-Melikov had forgotten his other goals. In a report to Alexander of April 11, 1880, Loris proposed actions to alleviate the social, economic, and institutional causes of the governing crisis.[20] He reviewed the Supreme Executive Commission's activities and his initial appeals for public support. Society's response had been gratifying. Many people had expressed faith in the tsar and goodwill toward the government's program, and had made concrete suggestions for dealing with the revolutionaries and solving other problems. Loris was confident that with this public feeling "neither the false teachings of the West, nor homebred madmen endanger government power."

He went on to emphasize the need to address the causes of the revolutionaries' initial successes. Here he placed the blame squarely on autocratic institutions—on the bureaucracy he now formally commanded. According to Loris, European socialist thought entered Russia during the era of the Great Reforms. At first socialism gained few adherents, primarily because Russia lacked an agricultural and factory proletariat equivalent to that of the West. Socialism remained weak, however, because the reforms satisfied the aspirations of much of Russian society. "Government power had never appeared so brilliant and celebrated, and society had never been so well disposed toward a Russian tsar." But this solidarity depended on carrying through the reforms to their necessary conclusion, and Loris felt this had not occurred: "The new order created in many branches of administration a new situation for the representatives of power that demanded new knowledge, modes of activity, and skills. This truth was inadequately assimilated and far from all organs of power performed as required." According to Loris, the Great Reforms brought "inescapable mistakes," the result of overzealousness in government. Too often, officials had proven unable to adapt to the new order, shape circumstances, and lead the people. Extreme views for or against the reforms resulted, with nobody willing to concentrate on correcting or completing the work begun.

Loris discussed the institutional arrangements that had obstructed completion of the reforms and effective domestic policy-making:

Even the most moderate attempts to adjust the realities of the reforms and reinforce the inadequacies of the legislation by the still-untouched branches of the government met with hidden or overt opposition, and remained stagnant. This was the fate of many questions of primary importance whose solutions had been sanctioned by the tsar. A countless series of commissions and endless, fruitless correspondence irritated public opinion, and satisfied nobody. Everything was submerged in the chanceries, and the resulting stagnation affected the newly constructed institutions.

Loris listed the main areas of policy paralysis where effective government initiative was desperately needed: (1) The peasant question—there was no movement toward improving the inadequacies of the 1861 arrangements; (2) The new judicial system—the judiciary had become isolated from the general state structure. He renewed his attack on the prosecutors "who have far from assimilated their proper meaning" and also criticized the new legal profession (*advokatura*), "the meaning of which was not understood by the ordinary mind." According to Loris, the lawyers' impact on public opinion was working against the state because they had brought up much in the courts "that had gone unspoken before." (3) The clergy—with few exceptions it was stagnating in ignorance and losing what little influence it once had; (4) The nobility—weakened as an estate and existing in confusion; (5) The zemstvos—inadequate government support had caused deterioration; (6) The cities—self-government had suffered as a result of problems also common to the zemstvos; (7) Education—policies of the 1870s had no social support.

Loris accused the administration of confusing socialism and anarchism with ordinary, and beneficial, criticism of the existing order. He advocated a "softening of the methods and manner" of administrative behavior.

Loris also noted that society had long demanded a form of representation. He reviewed proposals ranging from western European forms to the calling of an old Muscovite *Zemskii sobor*. Although he mentioned the solutions proposed earlier by Valuev and Konstantin Nikolaevich—calling zemstvo or gentry representatives to participate in State Council deliberations—Loris was not yet ready to advocate such a proposal himself. He had not yet assigned to the existing government institutions their new policy tasks, and his system had not taken root within the government. He wrote, "According to my deepest conviction, no reform in the sense of these last suggestions [for representation] could be useful now, and because of their utter untimeliness, they could be harmful. The people do not think of them and would not understand them, and the government is not yet ready to answer the criticisms that representation would express."

Loris-Melikov offered the following five-point program to immediately extend his system. (1) Continue the struggle against revolutionaries but take care not to confuse them with individuals guilty only of misdemeanors. (2) Establish complete unity among all government organs engaged in the struggle. (3) Gradually return to legality in government. (4) Encourage government institutions and personnel to be more attentive to the urgent needs expressed by society's spokesmen. (The administration must be attentive to the zemstvos, the cities, and the clergy, Loris said, and it must act on old matters that remained unresolved in chanceries and commissions. As examples of matters needing resolution, he cited raising the status of the clergy, tax reform, the agrarian question, worker legislation, the passport question, provincial administrative reforms, and the schismatic legislation and censorship.) (5) Restore faith in the educational system. (As a first step, Loris recommended removal of leading personnel in the educational establishment.)

Loris recognized that as head of the Supreme Executive Commission he remained dependent on the ministerial bureaucracy for the preparation and implementation of such wide-ranging domestic policies. Most of the problems had been extant for decades; their solutions depended on leadership and goodwill from within the ministerial bureaucracy. In Loris' words,

The direction of institutions depends primarily on the individuals who head them. Their mission is to be the precise executors of the good designs of Your Excellency for the happiness of Russia and her people. Their responsibility before posterity is great, and they should deeply understand that they are the servants of their affairs, and that one of their most essential aims is that of attracting hearts to the source of power in Russia. In these difficult moments of state life such as we are now living through, they should stand at the very top of their profession in terms of skills and their love for the governed.

(Alexander's marginal note here was, "True, but it is not easy to find them.") Loris knew that without his leadership there would be no program, so he asked Alexander to reserve initiatives and ultimate control of the policy areas described in the report for the main chief of the Supreme Executive Commission. Alexander's written approval said,

"Thank you for the frank presentation of your thoughts which are completely in accord with my own. I see, with pleasure, that you fully comprehend the heavy burden that I have placed upon you. May God help you vindicate my faith."

Loris-Melikov's emphasis on transcending institutional bottlenecks and on demanding a new spirit or "manner" (*obraz*) of acting from high officials showed his awareness of a basic problem faced by Russian government reformers for centuries. That is, would it be possible for the bureaucracy to initiate and carry through reform programs before the nature of the institutions and personnel of the bureaucracy were transformed? Could the ministerial power ethos be altered enough to permit the ministerial system to work toward Loris' goals; could this be a lasting arrangement? These questions concerned Loris in the months preceding the transfer of his power base from the Supreme Executive Commission to the Ministry of Internal Affairs.

Loris moved quickly to establish greater dominance over the ministerial bureaucracy. In mid-April he provoked a quarrel between Makov, the minister of internal affairs, and Tolstoi, the conservative minister of education and procurator of the Holy Synod. The quarrel resulted in Tolstoi's forced resignation from both posts. Tolstoi had established the educational system derided by Loris and was a symbol of resistance to change. Loris victoriously noted that Tolstoi's resignation had "produced universal joy."[21]

Concurrently, however, Loris-Melikov was finding it increasingly necessary to work through Makov and the MVD in order to implement his program throughout the empire.[22] Although Makov dutifully carried out Loris' edicts, his basic hostility toward the new methods and goals of Loris-Melikov was no secret. Makov epitomized the tsarist administrator unable to adjust to the new era. Another key ministry, Finance, was not yet in the hands of Loris-Melikov's closest associate, A. A. Abaza. In order to develop and implement his vision of a unified domestic policy, Loris considered control of the Ministry of Finance and of the MVD essential. Makov's presence as minister of internal affairs was an obstacle, and his removal from office would probably not have surprised contemporaries. What did take them by surprise was Loris-Melikov's decision to become minister of internal affairs himself.[23]

Loris-Melikov became minister of internal affairs on August 6, 1880. At the same time the Supreme Executive Commission was abolished; its functions were transferred to the MVD. The Third Section was also abolished, and its functions were absorbed into a new Department of State Police within the MVD. The MVD also absorbed the Corps of Gendarmes with the minister henceforth assuming the title of Chief of Gendarmes.[24]

The August 6 Manifesto was calculated to make a favorable impression on the public, high official and court circles alike. The abolition of the Supreme Executive Commission was seen as a tactful and self-effacing move by which Loris was giving up his dictatorial, extra-institutional powers to become one (albeit the most powerful one) among a group of ministers. The abolition of the Third Section profoundly impressed liberal opinion. Long a symbol of autocratic arbitrariness and repression, it had always functioned outside the regular ministerial bureaucracy as part of the Tsar's Own Chancery.[25]

The arguments Loris-Melikov used to persuade Alexander to sanction these changes were contained in a report dated July 26, 1880.[26] Loris reiterated his belief that the socialist threat could be paralyzed "not in the short term, but only in the long term and only by the influence of government and social forces completely in accordance with the conditions of a given state." Fast, systematic, firm, and decisive government action, was needed, as well as a permanent government organ fighting sedition and unifying society according to the principles of the state order. Loris declared the Supreme Executive Commission inadequate as a unifying institution. With the Supreme Executive Commission at the ministerial bureaucracy's mercy, Loris feared that it might soon be reduced to impotence typical of other autocratic commissions and committees.

In Loris' view, the commission's immediate mission to restore state order had been accomplished. It was time now to "concentrate in one of the highest organs of state administration those governmental authorities which in the general legal order have the mandate of securing the state and social order in the wide sense. This organ of the Supreme Power is the Ministry of Internal Affairs which is entrusted even now with the highest supervision of the main functions of the state's internal life." Loris added that if the MVD became too cumbersome as a result of its new responsibilities, it could give up jurisdiction over Post and Telegraph, and Foreign Faiths.

Loris was proposing nothing less than the organization of the autocracy around the Ministry of Internal Affairs. He realized that the tsar's personal approval was not enough. His own position and the new policies that would result had to be institutionalized. The minister of internal affairs would function as a prime minister, and the ministry itself would finally fulfill its original broadly defined police mandate. Tsar-appointed individuals or commissions could not implement a full-scale domestic policy. The ministerial bureaucracy, and particularly the MVD with its structures, jurisdictions, and personnel remained the only suitable power base for the redefinition and renovation of autocracy. As Loris put it: "The changes suggested by me— concentrating in the person of the minister of internal affairs the direction of all the police in the state, ordinary as well as political, zemstvo and city affairs, and the press—would give him, in my opinion, the real means and the possibility, with the friendly and well-wishing support of other institutions, of creating firm power." (It is interesting to note that he felt a "dual-power" situation would result if a Ministry of Police were to be formed.)

Of all domestic-administration ministries, the MVD had the jurisdiction and apparatus to establish most easily Loris' conception of new politics. The ministries themselves had to serve as a base for the transformation of ministerial power. First, however, they had to be activated and infused with a new spirit. Furthermore, the institutional bottlenecks and dysfunctions that had contributed to the paralysis of government domestic policy- and law-making had to be overcome. Loris-Melikov's ministry occupied a position unique in nineteenth-century Russian political history. Never had one *minister* gathered so much power and so much monarchal support for a massive state-directed reform program.

In a revealing report submitted to Alexander on August 1, Loris demanded the unification of all police organs in the provinces under the civil governors and the MVD.[27] In response to suggestions that provincial police be placed under zemstvo jurisdiction, Loris said it was theoretically impossible for the state to cede police power to society. Such an act "would mean not only limitation of the state's power, but its destruction." Loris also pointed out—and here he cited Stein and other German theorists—that the very notion of self-government was limited to the extent that it was consonant with the general "benefit and improvement" of the state as a whole. Police authority in control of self-governing bodies would, in his view, be detrimental to the general welfare.

In an August 11 report to Alexander, Loris proposed to reinstitute senatorial revisions and to conduct them immediately in six or seven provinces. He was trying to break out of the autocracy's institutional bind by using a mechanism that had languished during the decades of ministerial ascendancy in the central government. Throughout the first half of the nineteenth century the Senate remained weaker than the ministries it was supposed to control. Nevertheless, during Nicholas' reign, senatorial revisions, or special investigations of provincial administration and general conditions, had often uncovered abuses that were subsequently corrected. Both central and provincial administrators tended to view the revisions as a menacing form of outside intervention. At the height of the ministries' power under Alexander II, however, revisions were rare. Between 1861 and 1880 only two revisions took place, those of Senator Kapger in Kaluga and Vladimir provinces (1861-62) and Senator Kliushin in Perm Province (1870-71). These were the result of the personal vendettas of particular ministers. During Alexander's reign, the ministries and their subordinate organs were protected from senatorial revision or any other outside control mechanism.[28]

By proposing a series of revisions, Loris-Melikov was pointing to the ministerial bureaucracy's failure in its policy-making and legislative functions. The senatorial revisions of 1880-81 were designed to overcome institutional conflicts and shortcomings and to accumulate quickly the materials and data necessary for the entire domestic legislative program. Loris intended to use the revisions to force information from and discover deficiencies in central ministry chanceries and their provincial subordinates, and to wrest from other ministries all legislative and policy initiative. He hoped by these means to assure his own and MVD domination of the central government.

The senatorial revisions were the first step toward implementation of an MVD-based governing system. The revisions, as will be seen, were directly connected to the January 28, 1881, "constitutional" project. The revision materials were to form the basis of an entire legislative program, and they were the first order of business for the advisory commissions of representatives, projected for mid-1881.

The full range of Loris-Melikov's intentions may be seen in his August 11 report and in the remarkable instructions prepared for the senators chosen to undertake the revisions.[29] In presenting the proposal to the tsar, Loris emphasized that senatorial revisions were of proven benefit, used even by Nicholas I "to check on the activities of local authorities and to learn the requirements of the various parts of the vast Russian empire." These revisions "always had completely beneficial results, and [in] providing animation to local life, had provided the central government with invaluable materials for the exact determination of the actual situation in the provinces under revision and for the clarification of the measures necessary to correct the detected disorders."[30]

Loris argued that if revisions were entrusted to the right individuals, information on public opinion outside the two capitals would be available to MVD and police officials. As minister of internal affairs, Loris claimed that he must rapidly resolve questions that had long been on the MVD agenda. Revisions in six or seven representative provinces would immeasurably aid him and other high officials faced with similar problems.

Aware of the revisions' potential impact on public opinion, Loris claimed that "the very announcement of the revisions cannot, by my conviction, fail to produce an entirely quieting impression on society as a new evidence of Your Excellency's guardianship of the people's welfare." Although Loris was careful to subordinate his role in the revisions to that of Alexander, it was clear that in educated circles Loris would receive much credit for them.

Alexander approved the plan. Four senators were chosen to undertake revisions of the following provinces: I. I. Shamshin (Samara and Saratov); A. A. Polovtsov (Kiev and Chernigov); S. A. Mordvinov (Voronezh and Tambov); M. E. Kovalevskii (Kostroma, Kazan', and, later, Orenburg and Ufa). The senators' detailed instructions were contained in a 49-point memorandum organized under six institutional headings: (1) Internal Affairs; (2) Judicial; (3) Financial; (4) State Domains; (5) Education; (6) Means of Communication.[31] These instructions summarized the backlog of legislative and policy matters. The problems directly under MVD jurisdiction were listed first, others placed into the appropriate category by domestic ministry, but all problems were presented as government problems. The instructions gave the highest official sanction to Loris' view that the problems of the individual ministries were interrelated.

The first 15 points pertained to problems formally under MVD jurisdiction. The senators were to examine or investigate the following areas of concern.

1. The degree to which socialist-revolutionary ideas and influence had been disseminated in the provinces; the causes of these ideas and influence, and possible measures for combating them.

2. The influence of the administrative exile system on local opinion, especially regarding political crimes; whether changes would be necessary, and the kind of changes needed; the surveillance system.

3. The current mood and expectations of the peasantry; peasant unrest; rumors of a new land repartition. (Special instructions were included for Kiev and Chernigov provinces.)

4. The economic condition of the populace, the causes and counteraction of decline in the local economy, the differences in the economic situation of the former proprietary and state peasants, taxation and arrears and the means by which land could more easily be turned over to peasants as private property; peasant resettlement.

5. Potential regularization of local administrative organs for peasant affairs according to the structure created by the law of June 27, 1874.

6. The structure and administration of the peasant commune so that officials of the peasant institutions could better fulfill their obligations and those of the peasant commune.

7. Removal of undesirable persons from the commune.

8. The entire zemstvo situation, their successes and failures, par-

ticularly as they related to the local economy and the well-being of the population; thorough examination of the relationship of central and provincial administration to the zemstvos. Had the government tried systematically to paralyze the zemstvos? Could an unobjectionable form be found in which representatives of different provincial zemstvos could meet to discuss specific problems of mutual interest? Could the records and debates of zemstvo meetings be published? Examination of zemstvo financial resources, taxing powers, collection of civil obligations; examination of zemstvo personnel and the election process; measures to improve relations between cities and zemstvos.

9. Application of the 1870 Municipal Reform throughout the empire.

10. The provincial administration—in order to complete the reform work that had become more and more necessary over the past 25 years; the goals were to decrease the number of individual offices, unification of functions, decentralization for certain kinds of decisions, simplification of procedures, elimination of stifling formalism, complete security of state and social order, the correct handling of all affairs, and social and individual interests.

11. The influence of the government's policy of police unification in the provinces, and suggestions for practical measures to accomplish this expeditiously.

12. The relationship between the gendarmes and general police: the new uriadniki, city and district police; the necessity of special railroad gendarmes.

13. Sanitary conditions in the cities and factories, and possible public health measures.

14. The position of the Old Believers; possible measures to further improve their legal position.

15. The "character of the influence of the Jewish element"; possible measures to implement existing laws on Jews.

Taken alone, these instructions concerning MVD responsibilities were designed to produce statistics and concrete suggestions on major problems that had proven intractable since the initial reforms of Alexander's reign. But when examined in conjunction with the instructions under other institutional headings, Loris' additional motives are apparent. Taken as a whole, the instructions reveal his attempt to break down the institutional compartmentalization that had stymied the autocratic legislative process. It was no longer possible to approach vital policy problems with narrow institutional perspectives. Rather, an overview was necessary, one that could legitimately and regularly call on society for opinions and information.

For example, the first instruction under the judicial heading addressed the intense conflict between the new judiciary and the administration. The relationship of the prosecutors to both the courts and the provincial administration and police was to be subjected by the senators to the following specific questions: "Are all state and social interests sufficiently supported before the judicial power by the activities of the prosecutors [*prokurorskii nadzor*]? Do the prosecutors have sufficient authority for the execution of their duties and the necessary cooperation from relevant provincial institutions?"

The instructions covered virtually the entire system of justice, including the prisons. Similarly, under the heading of Financial Institutions, matters to be investigated included provincial tax policy, the regulation of factories, workers, craftsmen, credit institutions, banking, the collection of arrears, the passport system, and the role of Jews in economic life.

Under State Domains, various agricultural questions were to be looked into, including the dispensation of technical knowledge through the ministry's special schools, resettlement, the regulation of agricultural labor/landlord relations, and how zemstvos and private individuals might assist the Ministry of State Domains and government with these matters.

The senators were to investigate all levels of education, from the universities through the secondary schools, teacher-training colleges, and the various local primary and other schools set up by Tolstoi during the 1870s. They were to determine whether, in particular, secondary education was responsive to local needs.

In the communications area, the main aim was to improve the relationship of the central Directorate of the Means of Communication to the city governments and zemstvos. The instructions mentioned the need for access roads to the new railroads and for other routes to domestic and foreign markets.

The senatorial revision program was ambitious—perhaps overly so. It placed in the hands of four men (and their staff) the investigation of matters that had occupied the entire ministerial bureaucracy for years. Nonetheless, it represented a fresh start, and was an indication that the new government leaders believed the MVD could solve Russia's problems. With some help from the regular ministerial bureaucracy, the revisions could provide the basis for a vast legislative program.

The four senators were able to complete the data-gathering aspect of their mission. Although these materials were never discussed in the representative commissions projected by Loris, they were discussed in the autumn of 1881 after his fall from power. At that time the Committee of Ministers created the Kakhanov commission to prepare a new reform project for provincial administration.[32] The senatorial revision material was passed on to the new commission, but the new leaders turned the materials to ends far different from those Loris had planned.

Loris-Melikov could not wait for the completion of the revisions or for reform of the legislative process before trying to extend his governing system. His own legitimacy required action and visible achievement. The office of minister was more powerful than ever. With the support of his chosen MVD staff (Kakhanov, Perfil'ev, and others) and the close cooperation of Abaza at the Ministry of Finance, Loris made a series of policy decisions between August 1880 and January 1881 designed to further his overall objective of adjusting the autocracy to changed conditions.[33]

The policies set forth by Loris-Melikov are difficult to assess. For the most part, they represented only beginnings toward the resolution of many problems. The policies were never fully put to the test. They were overshadowed by the January 28, 1881, "constitutional" project, and did not come to fruition because of the assassination of Alexander II on March 1, 1881.

Loris' major decisions pertained to MVD structure, the economy, the zemstvos, censorship, and education. In securing Alexander's approval for policies, Loris circumvented or ignored the collegial decision-making procedures and the formalities of the legislative process. To succeed, he too had to depend upon the personalized autocratic power he wished to transform. Each decision that was made was calculated to have an impact upon public opinion. This was part of what Loris meant by the government's need to act in a new "manner," and this deliberate interaction of government with public opinion was certainly extended to a degree unimaginable earlier in Alexander's reign.

Loris-Melikov revealed his motives when he called together the editors of St. Petersburg's leading journals and newspapers in September 1880.[34] Participants' accounts indicate that, while Loris still sought society's support, he in no way pandered to "liberal" opinion as his detractors maintained. The purpose of the meeting was to berate the journalists for publishing too many articles advocating constitutions, and assemblies of the land (zemskie sobory), and so forth. Loris said such articles only agitated public opinion and stirred vain hopes. He explained that he had not been given the authority, as minister of internal affairs, to propose a central representative body, and that in any case he personally did not favor one.

Loris favored giving more authority to existing institutions and modifying them as necessary to bring them into "conformity and harmony" with the old order.[35] He had in mind the zemstvos, other organs of municipal self-government, and the new judiciary. The final integration of these institutions into the autocratic structure required much more than establishing a form of representation under pressure from society. The institutions of the Reform Era would be revitalized and integrated during the next five to seven years.[36] Loris knew that any proposal that hinted at constitutionalism or at the slightest weakening of autocratic rule would be futile. The attitudes of the tsar, his court, and high officials prevented such a suggestion. The goal was to redesign autocratic politics and alter the traditional ministerial power ethos without threatening Alexander. Thus the myth of autocracy had to be maintained long enough to institutionalize the elements necessary for renovation.

Loris-Melikov thought that a primary way to effect firmness and viability in the autocracy was to solve its inherent structural and institutional problems. He moved to redefine the MVD division of functions in accordance with his August 6 mandate to unify the empire's police apparatus. On November 15 all police were finally merged into a new Department of State Police.[37] The merger fulfilled one of the aims Speranskii had when he redefined ministry functions in 1810-11: the unification of police functions and the separation of police from general and economic administration. As a result of the November 15 law, the political and executive police were united into one department, and 32 administrative functions were removed from that department. These functions were transferred to the Department of General Affairs, the Economic Department, and the Zemskii otdel, all better equipped to deal with them. No longer would the police be responsible for supervising the provincial administration's personnel matters, military recruitment, and other functions pertaining to schismatics, tax arrears, public buildings, and so forth.

The new Department of State Police was not to be a narrowly defined executive organ equivalent to other MVD departments. On the contrary, the November 15 law transformed the police into an elite organ with wide-ranging powers. Loris openly promoted the idea of elitism, of attracting only the most experienced, skillful, loyal officials with proven "zeal and knowledge of affairs." To attract such fully mature chinovniki to police work, Loris recommended a table of organization different from those of the old Third Section and other MVD departments. According to the new table of organization, the salaries of the highest officials in the Department of State Police were raised to levels well above those of comparable offices in the other MVD departments.[38] In addition, the new department's central offices were streamlined. Whereas the Third Section had 71 officials in St. Petersburg, and the Department of Executive Police had 57, the new unified department would have only 52. Loris defended the cuts of "tenured"

officials—an act unheard of on that scale in the imperial bureaucracy
—by claiming that the smaller number of more talented officials attracted by "good service conditions" could do a better job.

Under the terms of Loris-Melikov's police reorganization, the government did not yield any of its police authority. In fact, because of
the structural changes, police power was strengthened. The first article of the department's legal mandate restated the old police principle
of "prevention and cutting-off" of crimes and securing public safety
and order. The mandate included state crimes, passports and border
security, supervision of all police organs, and many other matters. Its
weapons continued to include administrative exile and the surveillance system. Under Loris-Melikov, the first steps were taken to
strengthen the department's foreign agents—men sent abroad to infil-
trate the groups of Russian political emigrés.

To efficiently uphold the law, Loris-Melikov had made the reorganized police the dominant organ of the Ministry of Internal Affairs. The
laws of August 6 and November 15, 1880, profoundly influenced Russian history from 1881 to 1917 and beyond. Loris unified the police
within the MVD, but not as a separate and uncontrollable ministry.
Much would depend on how the highest police officials, particularly
the director of the department, chose to interpret the mandate. Loris,
aware of this, asked for a 10,000-ruble salary for the director. He
wanted a director who could "regulate the activities of the police in
conformity with the contemporary condition of society and highest
government views."

Loris also counted on his position as minister of internal affairs to
control the police, since the department would remain technically
under his command and since under his "system" he was largely responsible for defining the "highest government view." Unfortunately,
Loris did not foresee that the Department of State Police might come
to express the traditional ministerial power ethos and dominate the
MVD as in fact occurred after 1881, under the conservative Tolstoi
and his successors. The Plehves and Durnovos, who would play such
fateful roles in the later history of autocracy, were among the first
high officials of Loris-Melikov's Department of State Police. That conservative police directors actually would become ministers of internal
affairs, as did Plehve and Durnovo, would undoubtedly have repelled
Loris.

The November 15 law also created a Judicial Section in the Ministry
of Internal Affairs by amalgamating the MVD Jurisconsult Section
and its Corps of Gendarmes counterpart.[39] The Judicial Section was
established as a result of continuing conflict between the administration and the judiciary since the mid-1860s and of the need to continue

the functions of the Supreme Executive Commission's special Judicial-Police Section. The Judicial Section would supervise and insure the legal conduct of all political cases and act as intermediary between the MVD and judicial institutions. Among other things, it would supervise prosecutions for state crimes, according to the laws of May 19, 1871, and September 1, 1878, and represent the government before the Senate in criminal matters.

The functions of the Judicial Section were similar to those established in 1866 by Valuev for the original MVD Jurisconsult Section. By 1880, however, the volume of state crimes prosecutions had increased markedly, and Loris underlined the need for procedural knowledge and juridical expertise within the MVD. For Loris this was not simply a matter of defending MVD fiscal or contractual interests in the courts (as was the case with the jurisconsults of other ministries) but of "higher interests pertaining to the vital principles of our state." The man who would head the new section must possess "not only a thorough juridical education and service experience, but complete reliability and impartiality."[40] The first occupant of the post was the over-procurator of the First Department of the Senate, N. D. Rychkov. He was replaced shortly after this appointment by P. N. Durnovo, who was ambitiously seeking the top role in the police apparatus.

In addition to setting up new structures that he hoped would guarantee the efficient and legal operation of administrative and police authority, Loris increased the salaries of provincial governors and city police chiefs (*gradonachal'niki*),[41] and directed that gendarme indictments go directly to the governors rather than to the central Department of State Police. Finally, in January 1881 Loris-Melikov placed N. K. Grot, the progressive veteran of the Reform Era, in a new supervisory position over the Main Prison Directorate.

In shaping economic policies, Loris moved to bring immediate relief to the peasantry and other sectors of the population suffering from inflation, rising prices, heavy taxation, and famine. In this effort, he was helped by Minister A. A. Abaza, appointed in October 1880, and Assistant Minister N. Kh. Bunge, of the Ministry of Finance. Cooperation between this ministry and the MVD momentarily overcame the awkward functional divisions between the two that had existed since 1819. In the autumn of 1880 Bunge submitted a program to the tsar for curing Russia's economic ailments. The program included land reform and peasant resettlement, abolition of the hated salt and soul taxes, and their replacement by an income tax.[43]

Bunge's program was a detailed expression of the general policy lines promoted by Loris. On October 14 Loris had written to Alexander advising abolition of the salt tax. He argued that, aside from financial issues involved, the act would "satisfy many expectations and be so in accord with the wishes of the nation that the moral impression produced by it would more than compensate for the temporary material loss to the state budget." Loris understood the tsar's mentality well, and again he portrayed him as the beneficiary of society's goodwill. He wrote that abolition of the salt tax was a logical step to follow emancipation—a new "favor" granted to the people from the heights of the throne that would be recognized by all estates and would "strengthen the union of tsar and people." On November 23 Alexander signed the law abolishing the tax.[44] Loris circumvented the State Council and even the Committee of Ministers—a fact which outraged such "liberal" guardians of autocratic procedures as E. A. Peretts.[45] Strict observance of the autocracy's legislative order remained an obvious impossibility for a leader who would avoid governmental paralysis.

Loris was particularly concerned with the continuing problems of famine, food supplies, and the price of bread in the capital. He initiated a review of food reserves and distribution, and proposed solutions including famine relief, loans, and the organization of public works projects on railroads, roads, and canals.[46] He called in the St. Petersburg grain merchants and demanded that they lower prices immediately.[47] When they answered that famine conditions, costs, and the market determined prices, Loris, in his capacity as chief of gendarmes, threatened them with administrative exile if the prices were not brought down within 24 hours.

Similarly, to correct major deficiencies in the organization of state finances,[48] Abaza proposed that all expenditures above estimates (smety) be examined in the State Council under direction of the Ministry of Finance, that regular estimate procedures be enforced for the army and navy, that military expenditures be reduced to levels consonant with state resources, that a working relationship be created between the Ministry of Foreign Affairs and the Ministry of Finance because of the close relationship of finances and foreign policy, and that the vital economic functions of State Domains and Means of Communication be unified under the direction of Finance.

These proposals formed an integral part of Loris-Melikov's governing system. They represented a foretaste of policy possibilities for a unified and forward-looking central government unencumbered by the institutional obstacles of the traditional policy-making process.

In regard to the zemstvos, Loris-Melikov proceeded cautiously, building upon the initiatives taken in May while Makov was still minister of internal affairs.[49] Loris gradually expanded zemstvo competence to discuss local economic questions and administrative matters pertaining to the peasantry.[50] At the same time, however, he maintained firm government control over zemstvo activities and aspirations. He rejected a zemstvo petition to call a congress of zemstvo officials from various provinces to discuss an invastion of crop-destroying insects in Kherson Province. Although Loris was already thinking of some form of statewide consultative body based on the zemstvos, he would not, in this case, permit development of the principle of association.[51] Legitimate association had political implications, and therefore change in this area could come only at the government's initiative—and at a time and in a form that Loris judged practicable.

Education and censorship were other main areas in which Loris-Melikov was active. Education matters were more directly in the province of the Ministry of Education and special legislative commissions, but Loris and his supporters (Miliutin, Saburov, Abaza, and others) worked to revise the statutes governing student life and the universities. Their goal was to win students and academics to the side of the regime through restoration of their corporate rights and stricter limits on outside bureaucratic interference.[52]

Although the MVD by no means controlled the empire's entire censorship apparatus, its Main Directorate of Press Affairs had considerable responsibility for periodicals and books under the 1865 press law and subsequent legislation.[53] Censorship was a very sensitive area in government-society relations. It was a police function that brought the administration into direct contact with the political views and aspirations of educated society. The regime feared the printed word and its effect on what it regarded as immature public opinion.

By 1880 the censorship establishment and its statutes were in disarray. Government attempts during the late 1860s and 1870s to rewrite the 1865 law had resulted in a series of piecemeal measures designed to strengthen the administration's hand. These measures had proven ineffective, however, and Loris had to confront the problem upon taking command of the Supreme Executive Commission. Since improvement in the government's relationship to society was central to his system, a more liberal censorship between February and August 1880 fit easily into his overall policy. In October he appointed Valuev to chair a special conference to reexamine the censorship laws.[54]

Loris explained his aims to Valuev, who reported the conversation as follows: "The minister of internal affairs recognizes that newspapers in the capital teem with articles that do not correspond to the interests and views of the government, but under the existing legislation on press affairs the government is not armed with the means, if not to eliminate, at least decrease this inconvenience. With this aim he suggested moving from the mixed system of administrative and judicial punishments to a more severe system, but one exclusively of judicial punitive measures."[55]

Loris did not wish to give up MVD's domination of censorship, and he did not advocate anything resembling the freedom of the press that would exist after 1905. Rather, he wanted the courts to take responsibility (and perhaps blame) for punitive measures. At the end of 1880 the special conference subcommissions worked out detailed proposals to this effect. This was to become a source of special animosity between Loris-Melikov adherents and the conservative members of the conference.

As in all other areas, Loris wanted to deal with censorship by placing the police function into a legal framework that would be both less arbitrary and more appealing to society's educated elements. The function of censorship was to remain intact, and Loris was optimistic that the courts would defend the state to whatever extent was necessary. The notion that the courts could play a positive role from the government's perspective was predicated on the realization of Loris' larger goal: final integration of Reform Era and traditional institutions and principles to produce a revitalized politically viable autocracy.

On January 28, 1881, Loris-Melikov introduced a project calling for a form of representation in the legislative process.[56] The project, best understood in light of Loris' projected governing "system," was calculated to revitalize the ministerial bureaucracy and transform autocratic law-making. Loris (and Kakhanov, who actually wrote the project) wanted to provide an outlet for the growing desire of social groups to participate in political life. In this sense, the project signified a moderate step toward expanding the political framework of the state. Scrutiny of the project reveals additional utilitarian motivations. The consultative commissions and supporting measures outlined were directed specifically at the ministerial bureaucracy and the inadequate legislative process. As was true in the matter of senatorial revisions, the project was designed to promote political change, alter the ministerial power ethos, and overcome specific institutional weaknesses of the autocratic government.

The January 28 project began with a review and defense of his policies since February 1880.[57] Loris claimed success for his system, which "showed and continues to show a beneficial influence on society in the sense of quieting its anxious condition and stimulating its faithful readiness to serve you, the Sovereign, with all its energies for completion of that great enterprise of the State Reforms undertaken by you from the first day of your accession to the throne." He emphasized the need to complete the Great Reforms, by which he meant the need to end the paralysis of domestic policy. In order to accomplish this, he argued, the government required: (1) immediate access to the voluminous data already collected in the ministries, chanceries, and commissions (this material pertaining to questions raised in the past with the tsar's permission, had become stymied in the inefficient legislative process); (2) the materials on provincial conditions currently being collected and analyzed by the senatorial revisions; and (3) the "practical knowledge of men closely familiar with local conditions and needs."

Loris was careful, as usual, to reject western European forms of representation as incompatible with Russian conditions, perhaps even harmful. He rejected the "harmful" precedent of reverting to the old Muscovite institutions such as the *zemskii sobor*. Instead, he directly linked his proposal to the precedent of the editorial commissions of 1858-59 that prepared the emancipation legislation. It was a shrewd formulation, for the tsar was less likely to reject a form that he had once approved. As Loris put it, "These commissions were already a method tested by the wise directives of Your Majesty."

Basically, Loris proposed a three-step process for the preparation and passage of legislative projects. The first stage would consist of two "temporary preparatory commissions" modeled on the earlier editorial commissions. The tsar would appoint commission members who would be drawn primarily from the central ministries and other institutions but would also include nonservice "experts" on specific issues. The function of these commissions was to process materials and write legislative projects on tsar-mandated problems. In the short term, Loris suggested that one of the two commissions be concerned with "administrative-economic" matters and the other with financial questions. The administrative-economic commission was to prepare projects immediately on the following matters within the jurisdiction of the MVD: (1) reform provincial administration and its relationship to judicial and social institutions; (2) modify the 1861 peasant legislation in light of subsequent experience and the needs of peasantry; (3) find the means to end the obligatory relationship of peasants to their former landlords and to lessen the burden of redemption payments in areas where needed; (4) review the zemstvo and municipal administration statutes with the aim of supplementing and correcting them in light of experience; (5) organize food reserves and the entire system of feeding the population; (6) formulate measures to improve cattle-raising.

The subjects for the financial commission—taxes, passports, and so forth—were to be specified by the tsar according to a report to be submitted by the minister of finance. According to the project, this report would be "based on prior agreement with the minister of internal affairs, especially as many of the functions of these two ministries are intimately related."

The second stage of the legislative process was to take place in a "General Commission" chaired by someone in whom the tsar could place confidence. The legislative projects written by the preparatory commissions were to be examined, amended (if necessary), and approved in the General Commission. This body would consist of the members of the preparatory commissions and the elected representatives of society. These representatives were to be chosen from the zemstvos and the major cities. In order to attract the most "useful and knowledgeable people," the representatives would not have to be zemstvo or city duma members (*glasnye*). In those areas where zemstvos or city dumas had yet to be opened, the representatives would be chosen by local government authorities. The total number of representatives was left unclear although the project suggested two for each of the provinces with zemstvos and an additional two for the major cities.

The third stage would take place under the usual State Council procedures. Projects approved by the General Commission were to be sent to the State Council with the conclusions of the minister in whose jurisdiction the matter lay. To assist the State Council in its legislative work, Loris proposed that, with the tsar's approval, perhaps 10 to 15 representatives of the organs of self-government might participate with voting-rights in the State Council sessions.

Loris claimed that the first two stages were purely advisory and that no change was contemplated in the method of either raising legislative matters or enacting them in the State Council. The invitation of members chosen by institutions outside the administration would only come after the projects had been prepared by government officials, with the help of small numbers of "outsiders" who would be well known in government circles. Furthermore, the entire membership of the preparatory commissions would participate in the General Commission to defend and clarify government projects. These procedures were "consonant with the interests of national life," according to Loris. "They reserved entirely and exclusively to the Supreme Power the right of legislative initiative at the time and within the borders it decides necessary for the general interest."

In the final paragraphs of his report, Loris pressured the ministries to take immediate steps to insure the success of the new legislative process. He demanded that "the most skillful and efficient" chinovniki in each central ministry begin to collect and systematize relevant materials under the correct policy headings. Loris even authorized the use of outsiders for this work if it would help guarantee success and set a deadline that would correspond with completion of the senatorial revisions. He hoped that this would allow individual ministries to send to the preparatory commissions material already shaped into legislative projects, rather than "raw materials" alone. Loris wanted the preparatory work accomplished during the fall of 1881 and he envisaged calling the General Commission shortly after the regular zemstvo sessions early in 1882.

For the most part, these sections of the project, directed at the bureaucracy, indicate that in addition to satisfying the aspirations of educated people and economic elites, Loris aimed to mobilize the bureaucracy for a unique assault on Russia's domestic problems. He aimed to create a bureaucratic quasi-parliament within an autocratic framework that was in many ways similar to contemporary political systems in Europe and Asia. He concluded his report with a reminder that society expected the further development of the Great Reforms and a claim that his project would satisfy the visible desire of Russians to serve tsar and country. The government would profit from the experience and knowledge of local men, but, most important, the project would animate public life and dampen, if not eliminate, "the indifference to society's affairs that has been the most fertile soil for the success of anarchist propaganda."

Loris-Melikov could not secure the tsar's approval for the project without submitting it to collegial examination by a group of the empire's highest officials and the heir to the throne. The project was discussed in a special conference on February 5, 1881.[58] The journal of the conference was submitted on February 16 and approved by Alexander on the following day.[59] The conference and the tsar approved the project with minor adjustments in the number of representatives, the length of commission sessions, and so forth. More significant, they eliminated the proposal to include 10-15 representatives in State Council sessions with voting rights.[60] At the end of February a final Project for Government Communication was drawn up. The tsar called Valuev to the Winter Palace early on March 1 to ask if he had any objections to the written text. Valuev said he did not, and Alexander asked him to call a meeting of the Council of Ministers for final enactment of the project into law. Valuev set the meeting for March 4. Later in the day, on March 1, Alexander was assassinated, setting off a chain of events that resulted in the destruction of the Loris-Melikov system. The project was never enacted. The advocates of traditional ministerial power, with its static and narrow view of politics, reasserted their influence and came to dominate the autocracy of Alexander III.[61]

It is difficult to imagine the shape of Russian autocracy and its ministerial form of government if Loris-Melikov's system had continued throughout the 1880s or later. The sense that Loris-Melikov's politics represented something different in the political tradition permeated the thinking of Russians of all political persuasions. The plight of reformers of the late imperial era may be seen particularly in the virulent reaction against Loris from both the extreme left and a large part of spectrum to the right of center.[62] The left believed that, given time, the Loris-Melikov system would ease Russia's social and economic crises and help build the consensus necessary for the renewal of autocratic power.[63] Supporters of traditional autocracy, such as Pobedonostsev and Katkov, and even reform-minded individuals such as Valuev and B. N. Chicherin, feared Loris' political demeanor and the implications of his policies.

Pobedonostsev and Valuev, enemies on most political matters, could together accuse Loris of seeking popularity, of hungering for power, and of egotism. In their opinions, Loris had violated cardinal tenets of the ministerial power ethos. He had crossed the border separating the legitimate political activity of tsarist officials from that associated with a European-style political culture involving parties, representative bodies, and constant interaction with public opinion and special interests.

It was this style of politics, this apparent attentiveness to public opinion and the so-called legitimate interests of social groups, that distinguished Loris-Melikov's attempt to redefine the autocracy. Had he remained in office, there might have been a more efficient, equitable, and politically conscious autocracy, supported by emerging social and economic interest groups that could make their influence felt through quasi-representative institutions. Loris-Melikov might have created a more flexible government with a degree of social participation. It must be emphasized, however, that for the short term, administrative and police authority would have remained dominant and in the central government's hands.

Loris-Melikov chose the Ministry of Internal Affairs as the institutional power base from which to create a new governing system. Like Speranskii, however, he understood the need to transform, or at least infuse with new spirit, the institutions and personnel of the bureaucracy. His governing system was also a considered response to specific institutional policy problems. That his system was viewed as a liberal dictatorship, or authoritarianism of the center, suggests connections between the 1880-1881 experience and the later political conceptions of Witte and Stolypin.[64] Soviet historians have labeled both Loris-Melikov and Stolypin "Bonapartists" who pursued policies of "maneuvering" (*lavirovanie*) to win the support of both "feudal" and bourgeois elements.[65] This is an aspect of late imperial—and indeed global—history that deserves further study.

By late spring of 1881, the new tsar, Alexander III, had forced Loris-Melikov and his supporters from office and had turned the Ministry of Internal Affairs over to N. P. Ignat'ev. Although the MVD would remain very influential in domestic policy-making, the minister of internal affairs no longer could aspire to prime minister status. The ministry reverted to its position as one among many competing centers of power and influence that grew in authority during the last decades of the Old Regime. The initiatives taken toward reshaping the foundations of autocracy during Loris-Melikov's brief ministry were not institutionalized, and within the government after May 1881 habitual ministerial conflict and weak leadership again prevailed. This rapid turnabout indicates the tenuousness of reforms emanating from partnership of the tsar and a single minister.

The one major institutional change in the MVD that survived Loris —the unification of the police within the MVD—was fateful. The MVD's police role and its direct responsibility for the regulation of political life came increasingly to influence its perception of social and political problems. Alexander III, by temperament more conservative than his father, came under the influence of supporters of traditional autocracy and the ministerial power ethos. Although Loris' brand of Russian "Bonapartism" held out the promise of winning society's support, the new tsar and his supporters rejected it. They emphasized and expressed the traditional ministerial power ethos; in particular, they reasserted support for the tsar's personal authority and narrowed the sphere of legitimate politics as much as possible. Under Alexander III, the bureaucracy took refuge behind thick chancery walls.[66]

Conclusion

7

The ministries of imperial Russia were neither monolithic nor omnipotent. Their capabilities and dysfunctions derived from their structure, personnel, and the legacy of several centuries of administrative practice. The MVD was unlike other ministries in its greater number of departments, directorates, councils, and officials directly responsible to the minister. These components had diverse functions that were not always compatible. Whereas the ministries of Finance, Education, and Justice, for example, had narrowly defined jurisdictions in single major areas, the MVD's functions embraced general administration, police, censorship, and a host of social and economic matters. Management of the MVD was therefore especially difficult. In policy matters, the diverse functions provided broad scope for the diffusion of the ministerial power ethos—hence the high visibility of the ministry as the primary support of autocracy.

Despite its large number of organs, the MVD was dominated by relatively few high officials in departments, directorates, and councils. Substantive responsibility for departmental operations lay with the section chiefs and their immediate superiors, the vice-directors and directors. During the 1860s fewer than one hundred central ministry officials dominated MVD affairs, and approximately 40,000 officials were dispersed in the provinces. The fact that operational responsibility remained with such a small group of officials in St. Petersburg showed that, in practice, Speranskii's notion of departmentalism never extended far down the administrative hierarchy during the Reform Era.

The highest-ranking MVD officials belonged to a caste of career civil servants whose self-image and political outlook set them apart from society as a whole. Their administrative abilities and ideological viewpoint, as orchestrated by the minister, helped determine MVD policies and administrative performance. By the mid-1860s the MVD at its highest levels had become a haven for a type of conservative generalist who supported fully the tenets of ministerial power and was more suited to work in police, censorship, and general administration than in such professionally oriented ministries as Finance, Justice, and Means of Communication.

By 1855 the MVD and other ministries had attained a position of momentary semi-independence from the traditional social estates and from the emperor himself. The ministries had proven themselves indispensable to the execution of reforms and domestic policy. A fortuitous combination of legal mandate, strong leadership from Perovskii and Lanskoi, the development of departmental structures, and the presence of a small but influential number of young, energetic, reform-minded people brought the MVD to a preeminent position in the government.

But this position was tenuous. Institutions had to contend not only with the tsar's personal power and the hostility to institutions that it fed in high government and court circles, but also with inherited patterns of government organization and behavior. The institutional foundations of autocracy were weak and remained so, even at the height of the Great Reforms. It was always possible for personalities and offices outside the regular ministerial system to accumulate power in given situations. Legislation and policy-making by ad hoc committee, sporadic intervention in policy debates by the emperor, his peculiar relationship to the ministers, and his frequent reliance upon officials with extraordinary powers, such as the governors-general, served to undermine the evolution of the ministerial bureaucracy as the lawful foundation of government, political innovator, and potential mediator between tsar and society. Despite the MVD's rapid growth during Alexander's reign, its ability to act as leader or unifier of the government was always subject to the above limitations, as well as to budgetary constraints wrought by the central government's almost continual financial crisis and poorly reasoned spending priorities.

The satisfactory fulfillment of its duties, apart from attempts to dominate the government, required that the MVD's heavily centralized and small St. Petersburg establishment not be excessively challenged by either the volume or the complexity of the tasks at hand. It was particularly important that there should be no political challenge, for politics was the arena in which both the ministry and the autocracy were least comfortable and ultimately most vulnerable.

The pressures of social change and great power competition unleashed after the Crimean War provided such a challenge. On the eve of emancipation the MVD began to acquire functions rapidly. The administrative and political decisions that its officials were called upon to make increased greatly in complexity, in line with the kinds of social, economic, and ideological changes taking place. The volume of business began to strain the manpower and budget of the central MVD —a situation that hindered ministry operations at the levels in which decision-making and legislative work occurred. The new generation of civil servants who occupied the key MVD posts at this time were, by and large, men of narrow administrative competence, capable of serving existing administrative mechanisms but ill suited by temperament or skills to break away from established patterns.

These men lacked political vision (in short supply in most bureaucracies), while educated and public-spirited men outside the official world had little access to the levers of power. Although some notable attempts were made (by Valuev, Konstantin Nikolaevich, Shuvalov, and Loris-Melikov) to create institutions that would bring state and society into a closer working relationship, no effective political mechanism was established during the 1860s and 1870s. The tsar was too jealous of his powers, there was too much discord, and the ministerial power ethos was too entrenched among the ministers, members of the court entourage, and other high officials for the autocracy to venture to broaden its base of support.

Had the MVD had fewer departments and a narrower range of functions, and had it been part of a united government that drew systematically upon outside sources for legislative work and general domestic policy-making, it might have been able to concentrate its efforts on the most basic problems of general administration and law enforcement. As it was, however, during the Reform Era the MVD remained a cumbersome institution not always able to perform its statutory duties.

The outmoded division of labor in the MVD reflected and helped perpetuate the ministerial power ethos. Instead of separating police from general administrative functions, all MVD activities remained infused with the broad notion of police power set forth in its original mandate. Traditional police guardianship found its way into MVD management of economic, social, political, and law enforcement matters. Furthermore, ministry components had overlapping jurisdictions and vaguely defined responsibilities. As a result, during the Reform Era, Russia did not have specialized ministries like those in other centralized European states (such as the French and Prussian ministries of Agriculture and of Trade and Industry). These would not be created until the 1890s, or, in the case of Trade and Industry, October 1905.

Such problems of government organization expressed a structural disunity that hindered completion of the policies and reforms necessary to stabilize the regime and create political consensus after the Crimean War.

The dualism of institutions and principles described by Valuev in his 1882 analysis may be seen as a contest between conservative renovation and ministerial power. In the MVD the latter was victorious; institutions and legality were often sacrificed to personal power and fealty, piecemeal administrative solutions, and the ethical superiority of police power. When decisive action was called for, most high officials found acceptable the cumbersome formalism of the legislative process. Yet when it came time to defend institutional prerogatives and ministerial power against other institutions, principles, or, especially, society, MVD officials acted resolutely and independently, using personal authority and rule by administrative decree.

After the 1861 emancipation, MVD leaders perceived a growing threat to the autocracy and the bureaucracy's hegemony from leftist groups, gentry oligarchists, and national separatists. Valuev and the high officials he brought into the MVD chose to define the ministry's role in terms of traditional police authority and ministerial power. Ministerial power provided an accepted idiom for members of the circumscribed bureaucratic world. It provided a comprehensible set of symbols and prescriptions for legitimate political action. For the post-Crimean War generation of high MVD officials, ministerial power and police guardianship were the foundations of Russian statehood.

The ministers of internal affairs had considerable influence upon these developments. Although Valuev had sophisticated ideas about society, the economy, and institutional reform, his activities resulted in the renewal and strengthening of ministerial power. He established the machinery and fostered the attitudes that were readily used by his more conservative successors. Although many of Valuev's ideas about government's role were similar to those espoused by his "liberal" predecessors, Lanskoi and Miliutin, the effect of his leadership was to make the MVD a key opponent of evolution toward rule-of-law systems such as those of contemporary European states undergoing conservative renovation.

Valuev's successors, Timashev and Makov, reflected the fragility of the ministerial bureaucracy as the foundation of Russia's government. The very fact that the emperor could choose these two men as ministers of internal affairs—men who did not grasp the importance of institutions and political change to autocracy's future—lessened Russia's chances of evolving toward even the limited forms of politically conscious bureaucratic Rechtsstaat envisaged by Valuev and later by Loris-Melikov.

Finally, the MVD's history during Alexander's reign illustrates the plight of the reformers, those who were caught between the conservatism of hostile colleagues—blind defenders of autocracy—and the vociferous, and at times violent, expressions of a society growing more organized and articulate. To realize their programs, reformers—Miliutin, Valuev, Loris-Melikov, Stolypin—eventually had to work with and through the existing government institutions and their personnel. This inevitably hindered realization of their plans. In addition, as it became more apparent that government officials had to interact with interest groups, economic and social elites, and the intelligentsia, the resurgence of ministerial power made such activity more difficult. Though Loris-Melikov was most successful at this new politics, even he had to act arbitrarily and outside the law (as in his repeal of the salt tax) to achieve certain goals.

Mid- or late-nineteenth-century Russia appears remote from England, France, Prussia (and, after 1871, from Germany), and even from Austria in social and political institutions and level of economic development. Russia is often placed at the far end of the scale of European absolutism (or as a different type of absolutism altogether)—as an unlimited autocracy with a centuries-long history of bureaucratic rule and a unique social structure (an enormous peasantry, a politically weak, service-oriented nobility, a semi-Asiatic merchantry, and so forth).[1] When compared to the Ottoman Empire, China, and Japan, to name only three non-European societies confronting enormous challenges, Russia of the 1860s and 1870s appears more advanced in terms of national power and unity, economic and military might. This suggests a framework for comparison of the historical roles of mid-nineteenth-century administrative and political elites that takes into account their political acts and ideas as well as the kinds of institutional and political changes discernible along a geographical spectrum ranging from western Europe through Asia.[2]

That Russia had an earlier, far more sustained contact with European powers than did China and Japan has obscured the fact that during the 1850s and 1860s the structure of world politics and economics had already drawn Europe and Asia closer than ever before in various relationships of borrowing, domination, and reaction to the culture, institutions, and technology of more advanced European nations. The developments in Russia described above took place at a time when comparable political and institutional change was taking place in Europe and other areas of the world that witnessed European economic and military penetration of traditional cultures and polities. The years from 1848 to 1875 witnessed the creation of a global economy, linking the disparate parts of the world in ways previously unimaginable. According to E. J. Hobsbawm, "the tightening net of the international economy drew even the geographically remote areas into direct and not merely literary relations with the rest of the world. What counted was not simply speed but the range of repercussion."[3] In that range of repercussion can be found common patterns of political and institutional change. In Europe, administrative and political elites faced similar economic, social, and political problems. Their responses, and often their theoretical justifications, influenced the programs of Russian, Ottoman, and far eastern reformers and renovators. To cite just three examples, the Great Reforms in Russia and the Tanzimat era reforms in the Ottoman Empire were formulated after rather extensive examination of European models, and the Meiji constitution in Japan was clearly based upon a mixture of Prussian theory and Japanese tradition.[4]

In each case, the task for administrative elites and political leadership (often coterminous) was to renovate traditional political institutions and, indeed, entire political cultures challenged by internal social and economic changes or by those changes in conjunction with aggressive encroachment by foreigners. The conscious adaptation of new or borrowed political forms or techniques into existing political cultures and institutions represents what I call conservative renovation. The leaders of these regimes operated within indigenous political cultures and institutional frameworks even while attempting to transform them. The common goal of conservative renovators was to permit necessary innovations in political, economic, and social life without inviting destruction of the regime by internal revolution (led by middle classes, workers, peasants, or nationalities) or by foreign conquest. This common wave of politics and administration during the second half of the nineteenth century represented a search for conservative synthesis that would permit maintenance of or dramatic increases in national power. The Tory democracy of Disraeli, the "liberal empire" of Napoleon III, Bismarck's Prussia, and later Germany, Austria during the years leading to the Compromise (*Ausgleich*) of 1867, the Ottoman Empire of the Tanzimat era, China during the T'ung Chih restoration, and Meiji Japan offer a unity of experience that transcends wide cultural diversity and differences in levels of economic development.[5]

At the center of this spectrum of conservative renovating regimes was Russia. The institutional and political history of Russia presented in this volume can provide future researchers with a focal point, in geographic terms and in terms of the relationship of bureaucratic and/ or political leadership to forms of political change and conservative renovation during the late nineteenth century. Russia, particularly during the ascendancies of men such as Miliutin, Valuev, and Loris-

Melikov (and, later, Witte and Stolypin) provides an example of a traditional bureaucratic regime struggling to renew or redefine the political culture and social institutions that support it.

The nature of the government and political leadership of the Reform Era provides an especially clear example of an internally logical and consistent pattern of political change that finds ready analogues in contemporary states of both Europe and Asia that were at vastly different stages of economic and political development. Concentration on style and implements of rule and the relationship between regimes and their political constituencies reveals a common pattern of response to essentially similar internal and external challenge. The political techniques often ascribed, for example, to "Bonapartism"—manipulation, plebiscites (or mass or other forms of electoral politics which may be seen as a functional equivalent), new and more intense dialogue with public opinion, social reform, state intervention in the marketplace, establishment of semiconstitutional and constitutional regimes—all fall neatly into place as conscious efforts undertaken in different institutional and cultural settings to move from the politics of traditional absolutism and bureaucratic routine to new institutional and political arrangements involving the controlled participation of economic and social elites.[6] What German scholars have called a struggle between parliamentarism and conservative revolution in the more advanced countries of western and central Europe (where parliaments already existed) is thus repeated with meaningful parallels of form and function in the struggle to create the first vestiges of social participation in national legislative processes elsewhere.[7] According to this view, a central unity is revealed between the gradual expansion of parliament's powers under France's Second Empire, for example, and the newly westernized and youthful bureaucracy's attempts to expand the sphere of legitimate politics in the Ottoman Empire and Japan.

A striking constant is the presence of bureaucracy as mobilized by the political leadership as a leading political force for change, and this underlines the importance of Russia as a focal point. For in Russia, as in the Ottoman Empire, China, and Japan, political leadership itself was centered in the bureaucracy as the only source of legitimate politics, apart from the crown. Within the Russian bureaucracy, the tension between those who wished to redefine traditional political culture by altering institutions and their supporting ethos and those who desired to maintain traditional autocracy was particularly notable. Similarly, the tension between the bureaucratic advocates of renovation and the tsar, the other crucial element in the political equation, offers fruitful patterns repeated in other national contexts.

Several of the Russian officials, discussed in this study attempted to redefine traditional autocracy by experimenting with new political techniques of the "mass" or "interest" politics of contemporary Europe. Significantly, these bureaucratic attempts at renovation emanated from the ministerial bureaucracy, the institutional power base described above, comprising the central ministries and their provincial apparatus. During the Reform Era and immediately thereafter, the major examples of nonroutinized, charismatic political leadership issued from either ministerial officials or outsiders using the ministries as their power base. These leaders had to contend with rival ministers, competing institutional power centers (such as the State Council), and the tsar, but they all espoused the common themes promoted by renovating ministerial officials—legality, institutionalization of an enlarged realm of politics that involved society's participation in controlled public debate, and new patterns of political behavior, particularly among officials themselves. Much of Russia's history after the Crimean War involved an intense struggle between the advocates of these renovating political changes and powerful supporters of a static traditionalism. The traditionalists' concept of politics remained firmly anchored in personal authority and police power, an interlocking web of anti-institutional, clannish political relationships, at the apex of which stood the tsar.

Russia's central position in the spectrum of renovating regimes is fixed by the clarity of the conflict between bureaucracy and tsar and by the ideological conflict within the bureaucracy itself. Russia's fate in 1917 offers ample evidence of its failure to renovate institutions. And, as I have tried to show, the experiences of one institution, the Ministry of Internal Affairs, is a viable paradigm for understanding that institutional and political failure, as well as for approaching the issues implicit in comparative history.

The institutional fabric of the ministerial bureaucracy, as exemplified by the MVD and the ethos of its officials, profoundly influenced the course of Russian history after the Crimean War. Governmental structure and ideology limited the autocracy's ability to act decisively, despite the considerable bureaucratic effort expended throughout the reign on legislative matters. Operationally, the MVD reproduced in microcosm the problems of the entire central government. Immediately following emancipation, the MVD made an ideological shift toward defense of administrative authority and away from the principles that would be embodied in the zemstvos and in the judicial system. The momentous struggle between ministerial power and the rival principles of rule of law, separation of powers, and local self-government was not visible in a single "crisis of autocracy" late in Alexander II's reign and even less so in a unique "revolutionary situation." MVD history since 1802 shows that the sources of this conflict and of the MVD policies and ideology that prevailed after 1881 are not simply to be located in the reaction to the assassination of Alexander II. Rather, these sources, rooted deep in history, came to the forefront particularly in the reign of Alexander II. Even while the Great Reforms were being issued, the ministerial power ethos and the hegemony of police authority were reaffirmed and given renewed legitimacy. Loris-Melikov's effort to use the MVD as a base to unify the government and to redefine administrative power and political culture was but a momentary reversal of organizational and ideological trends present during the previous two decades. His failure was Russia's tragedy, for it would take 25 years for the MVD, and government as a whole, to receive again, this time from Stolypin, the kind of leadership that had appeared so promising in 1880.

The MVD story during Alexander II's reign is laden with irony. In a period most often seen as one of momentous reforms that brought Russia closer than ever before to the patterns of European institutional and political development, the MVD developed a structure and modes of administrative behavior that would militate against the consolidation and extension of the Great Reforms. This structure and ethos would persist, with tragic consequences for the remainder of the imperial era.

Appendix A
Expenditures on Central Government Institutions, 1864-1866 (in rubles)

	1864	*1865*	*1866*
State Council	508,364	500,359	549,129
Committee of Ministers (Chancery)	39,731	39,505	46,298
His Majesty's Own Chancery			
I Section	21,519	23,479	25,491
II Section	96,790	96,733	100,803
III Section	56,687	56,686	52,781
Commission on Petitions	117,777	127,007	118,576
Holy Synod	237,986	248,160	250,128
Ministry of Foreign Affairs	495,208	509,444	550,741
Ministry of War	4,175,670	3,936,573	4,414,262
Naval Ministry	2,113,418	2,212,598	2,325,487
Ministry of Finance	2,170,931	1,893,060	1,862,289
Ministry of State Domains	973,304	958,655	954,899
Ministry of Internal Affairs	737,326	740,745	828,042
Ministry of Education	210,123	204,228	196,005
Main Directorate of Means of Communication	502,589	475,155	622,256
Ministry of Post	276,931	270,767	276,566
Ministry of Justice	189,165	190,431	187,527
State Controller	297,803	416,646	410,944

Valuev evidently had these tables compiled to prove his point that the MVD central organs were receiving less money than less important ministries. The figures include some categories of expenditures not covered by the table of organization projects discussed above, but it is clear that the domestic administration fared poorly in comparison to the military establishment. Furthermore, the Ministry of Internal Affairs received substantially less than the Ministry of Finance and even less than the Ministry of State Domains. Although at the time the MVD had wider responsibilities and more political power than the Ministry of Finance, its central organs had fewer fiscal resources.

The autocracy's willingness to spend vast amounts on the military, while watching every ruble when it came to the salaries of its own officials and the legitimate needs of its own institutions, is a phenomenon which continued throughout Alexander's reign (TsGIA SSSR F. 908 op. 1 d. 239 11. 1-9), but it became especially acute at the end of the reign after the expenditures for the Turkish War. See Tatishchev, *Imperator Aleksandr II*, 2:150-175; and I. F. Gindin, *Gosudarstvennyi Bank i ekonomicheskaia politika Tsarskogo pravitel'stva (1861-1892 gody)* (Moscow, 1960), 52-53.

Appendix B
MVD Budgets, 1855-1881

The budgets for the years 1855-1881 place the monetary figures revealed in the table of organization reform materials in better perspective. After the 1862 financial reforms, the MVD submitted its yearly budget estimates to the State Control for scrutiny prior to final consideration in the State Council. The estimates were also examined by the Ministry of Finance, but in general they were approved by the State Council with only minor modifications. The MVD submitted estimates of income as well as expenditures, since prior to 1862 each central government institution had its own statutory sources of income apart from its share from the state treasury. In the MVD's case, this income was, in a sense, drawn from the "land" in the form of special assessments, civil obligations (*zemskie povinnosti*), and income from the large amounts of capital set aside for state philanthropy, foodstuffs, and so forth. Prior to the 1862 centralization of the state's finances, MVD income from its own sources almost equaled its empire-wide expenditures. After 1862 the MVD was obligated to move quickly toward total dependence on the State Treasury for all its operating expenditures.

According to the yearly estimates (TsGIA SSSR F. 1152), MVD empire-wide expenditures (in rubles) for the period 1855-1881 were as follows:

1855	8,659,526
1858	8,668,986
1860	8,640,181
1864	11,793,978
1866	15,309,466

1867	15,944,529
1868	15,285,318
1869	19,386,314
1871	24,076,828
1872	25,724,398
1874	26,167,291
1875	26,193,197
1876	34,700,085
1877	34,414,612
1878	35,376,767
1879	36,892,485
1880	37,521,795
1881	39,605,013

In absolute terms, the figures reveal more than a four-fold increase in MVD expenditures from the late 1850s to the late 1870s. This may be compared to an increase in the entire regular government budget for the same period of approximately 2.3 times. The steady increase in MVD expenditures during Alexander II's reign is easily explained by the increased responsibilities acquired by the MVD during that time. The empire's growing population and the increased tempo of economic and social stratification required increased government expenditures on an empire-wide basis. For example, the integration of the State Peasants into the regular provincial administrative system in 1866 and the Kingdom of Poland into MVD jurisdiction later in the decade resulted in new categories of yearly expenditures.

The question remains, however, of how the large sums represented in the annual estimates were actually spent. There is an enormous discrepancy between the MVD total budget figures above and the table of organization totals for the organs of the *central* MVD. At all times during the discussions concerning the table of organization for the central MVD, the figures proposed remained between 500,000 and 800,000 rubles. Yet between 1864 and 1872—the years of the table of organization discussions—total MVD expenditures ranged from 11,793,978 rubles to 25,724,398 rubles. Obviously, expenditures on the central organs of the MVD constituted only 3 to 5 percent of the total MVD budget.

This minute percentage provides a clue to an important phenomenon of Russian administration and the autocratic government in general. In spite of its reputation as a highly centralized state, and the fact that its best bureaucratic talent was concentrated in St. Petersburg, the autocracy spent only a minuscule fraction of its total resources in support of those institutions most directly responsible for solving the major social, economic, and political problems it faced. This may be

seen in the following breakdown of the MVD budget for the year 1877
—a year after the major growth in MVD structure and functions
(TsGIA SSSR F. 1152 d. 657 ll. 130ob.-131).

Salaries of minister of internal affairs, assistant ministers, members of the Council of the Minister, officials of special missions and others attached to the minister	143,987
Salaries of personnel of central MVD organs	545,153
Censorship apparatus	260,398
Institutional expenditures, central MVD	123,810
Construction Institute	72,547
Salaries of governors-general, governors, city police chiefs, and other expenses for their institutions	2,434,227
Provincial and regional governing boards	2,962,662
City, district, and regional administration	7,724,860
Medical section	1,487,195
Support of quarantines and agents	85,694
Quarantine guards	43,646
Support of clergy of non-Orthodox faiths	1,877,462
Expenditures on Penal Section	8,921,081
Repair and maintenance of government buildings and prisons, heat, lighting	2,122,038
Relief benefits, assistance, philanthropy	1,961,794
Construction of churches	1,850,435
Administration of the Nizhnyi Novgorod Fair	63,252
Local military needs in the provinces of the Polish Kingdom	1,495,236
Expenditures for sending troops on leave in Russia to the Kingdom of Poland	176,752
Support of the Uniate clergy and other related expenses	28,895
Miscellaneous expenses	983,416
Security of the Orthodox clergy of the nine western provinces	12,227
Total	35,376,767

As can be seen, the government spent large amounts on administering the far-flung parts of the empire as compared to what was allotted
to the central organs of the MVD. Large sums were also spent on such
things as church construction, support of the non-Orthodox clergy,
and miscellaneous items. What is perhaps most striking is that nearly
nine million rubles went to the penal system (including the exile system and prisons). The government was spending more than nine times
on the penal system than it spent on the entire MVD central apparatus
including the censorship establishment.

Aside from the expenditures on public health and philanthropy and
relief there is no evidence of a relationship between the budget and
specific social or economic programs outside the regular allotments

for the provincial, municipal, and regional officials listed in the thick volume of tables of organization that accompanied the estimates. Whether government or society received an adequate return from the amounts spent on these officials or the other items in the budget is a question difficult to answer. Given the government's limited resources and the obvious importance of an institution like the MVD, one can only conclude that the manner in which the autocracy distributed its resources worked against the MVD's ability to fulfill the dual role of agent of social and economic change and keeper of public order.

Notes

1. Ministerial Power in Prerevolutionary Russia

1. See, for example, Geoffrey A. Hosking, *The Russian Constitutional Experiment: Government and Duma, 1907-1914* (Cambridge, 1973), and George Katkov, *Russia, 1917: The February Revolution* (New York, 1967). On the structural causes of revolution, see S. N. Eisenstadt, *Revolution and the Transformation of Societies: A Comparative Study of Civilizations* (New York, 1978); Theda Skocpol, "France, Russia, China: A Structural Analysis of Social Revolutions," *Comparative Studies in Society and History*, 18 (April 1976): 175-210; and Theda Skocpol, *States and Social Revolutions* (Cambridge, 1979).

2. *Polnoe sobranie zakonov Rossiiskoi Imperii s 1649 g. Sobranie pervoe 1649-1825*, 45 vols. (St. Petersburg, 1830), esp. nos. 20,406; 20,582; 24,686 (hereafter cited as *PSZ* I).

3. I have in mind here officials who might be included under the heading of "enlightened" bureaucrats, as proposed by W. Bruce Lincoln. These were represented in the MVD by such men as N. A. Miliutin, A. D. Shumakher, A. V. Golovnin, and A. K. Giers. See W. Bruce Lincoln, "The Tsar's Most Loyal Servitors: Russia's Enlightened Bureaucracy (1825-1881)" (unpublished manuscript); Lincoln, "The Genesis of an 'Enlightened' Bureaucracy in Russia, 1825-1856," *Jahrbücher für Geschichte Osteuropas*, Band 20, Heft 3 (September 1972), 321-330; and Lincoln, "Russia's 'Enlightened' Bureaucrats and the Problem of State Reform 1848-1856," *Cahiers du monde russe et soviétique*, 12, no. 4 (October-December 1971): 410-421. Also P. A. Zaionchkovskii, *Pravitel'stvennyi apparat samoderzhavnoi Rossii v XIX v.* (Moscow, 1978), 187-191.

4. See the highly intelligent discussion of this viewpoint in Theodore Taranovski, "The Politics of Counter-Reform: Autocracy and Bureaucracy in the Reign of Alexander III, 1881-1894" (Ph.D. diss., Harvard University, 1976), 167-227.

5. On political culture in general and its Muscovite clan- and bureau-
cratic-oriented manifestation, see Edward L. Keenan, "Russian Political Culture" (unpublished manuscript). Keenan adapts Lucian Pye's definition as follows: political culture is that set of attitudes, practices, and sentiments that
gives order and meaning to the political process in the minds of members of
the great Russian community, and that provides, or permits its bearers to generate, the underlying assumptions and ideas that govern behavior in the political system. See also Lucian W. Pye and Sidney Verba, eds., *Political Culture
and Political Development* (Princeton, 1965); Clifford Geertz, "Ideology as a
Cultural System," in *The Interpretation of Cultures: Selected Essays* (New
York, 1973); J. G. A. Pocock, "Languages and Their Implications: The Transformation of the Study of Political Thought," in *Politics, Language and Time:
Essays on Political Thought and History* (New York, 1973), 3-41.

6. The two official historians of the MVD and such eminent officials as
M. M. Speranskii and N. A. Miliutin adopt this point of view. See S. Adrianov, *Ministerstvo vnutrennikh del: Istoricheskii ocherk*, 3 vols. (St. Petersburg, 1901), 1:1-2, 47-51, 103-112N; V. Varadinov, *Istoriia ministerstva vnutrennikh del*, 3 vols. (St. Petersburg, 1858-1863).

7. Lincoln, "Russia's 'Enlightened' Bureaucrats," 413-414.

8. *PSZ* I, no. 20,406; Adrianov, *Ministerstvo*, 1-2.

9. *PSZ* I, no. 20,406.

10. Ibid.

11. Ibid.; Adrianov, *Ministerstvo*, 2-9. P. A. Valuev, minister of internal
affairs (1861-1868), repeatedly made the connection to the Petrine tradition.
See Chapter 3.

12. D. P. Troshchinskii, "Zapiska Dmitriia Prokof'evicha Troshchinskago o ministerstvakh," *Sbornik Imperatorskago Russkago Istoricheskago
Obshchestva*, 3 (St. Petersburg, 1868): 1-162 (hereafter cited as *SIRIO*).

13. Ibid., 40-50. George L. Yaney accepts the idea of senatorial government as a myth, but at the same time he portrays eighteenth-century Russian
government as somehow different from what went before and what came
after. George L. Yaney, *The Systematization of Russian Government: Social
Evolution in the Domestic Administration of Russia* (Urbana, 1973), 51-128.
A recent study of the early nineteenth-century debates over collegial government, with a perceptive analysis of Russian political culture, is by David
Christian, "The 'Senatorial Party' and the Theory of Collegial Government,
1801-1803," *The Russian Review*, 38, no. 3 (July 1979): 298-322.

14. Nineteenth-century writings that attack the ministerial bureaucracy
are too numerous to detail here. The attacks came from Slavophiles, Western-
ers, "liberals," and radicals. See, for example, the essays in A. I. Gertsen and
N. P. Ogarev, eds., *Golosa iz Rossii* (London, 1856-1857).

15. The entire story of the Council of Ministers during the reign of Alexander II is brilliantly told by V. G. Chernukha in her monograph, *Vnutrenniaia politika tsarizma s serediny 50x do nachala 80x gg. XIX v.* (Leningrad,
1978), 136-198.

16. Ibid., 150-155.

17. Ibid., 155-170.

18. S. P. Pokrovskii, *Ministerskaia vlast' v Rossii: Istoriko-iuridicheskoe izsledovanie* (Iaroslavl', 1906).

19. Ibid., I.

20. Ibid., III-LXXXVII. Here Pokrovskii reviews Russia's institutional history up to the 1802 Manifesto.

21. Ibid., I.

22. For a classic discussion of European absolutism as exemplified by the Prussian experience, see Hans Rosenberg, *Bureaucracy, Aristocracy and Autocracy: The Prussian Experience, 1660-1815* (Cambridge, Mass., 1958).

23. The question of absolutism in Russia has been hotly debated among Soviet historians, particularly in the journal *Istoriia SSSR* from 1968 to 1972. For complete citations and an excellent summary and analysis of the "absolutism" problem, see Hans-Joachim Torke, "Die Entwicklung des Absolutismus —Probleme in der sowetischen Historiographie seit 1917," *Jahrbücher für Geschichte Osteuropas*, Band 21, Heft 4 (1973), 493-508, and "Die neuere Sowjethistoriographie zum Problem der russischen Absolutismus," *Forschungen zur Osteuropäischen Geschichte*, 20 (1973): 113-133. See also Alexander Gerschenkron, "Soviet Marxism and Absolutism," *Slavic Review*, 30 (December 1971): 853-869; Leonard Krieger, *An Essay on the Theory of Enlightened Despotism* (Chicago, 1975); and the judicious Soviet treatment of Iu. B. Solov'ev, *Samoderzhavie i dvorianstvo v kontse XIX veka* (Leningrad, 1973), esp. 9-164.

24. Perry Anderson, *Lineages of the Absolutist State* (London, 1974), 15-59, 195-235. On the same theme, Gerschenkron ("Soviet Marxism," p. 868) correctly states: "There is still no clear recognition that the interests of the state are something *sui generis* and in some periods not just as important, but infinitely more important than class interests. The naive acceptance for such periods of 'axioms' of class interests as main determinants can only lead research into cul-de-sacs of sham problems and irrelevant conclusions. What is needed is an undogmatic general theory of state power in which the autonomy —the *Eigengesetzlichkeit*—of that power is no longer either disdainfully denied as 'false consciousness,' but is frankly recognized as a crucial sociological phenomenon that is indispensable for the understanding of momentous historical events and processes."

25. On the *prikaz* system, which for too long has been ignored as the very backbone of Muscovite power, and which in many ways was ahead of its time in organization and efficiency, see Borivoj Plavsic, "The Russian Bureaucracy in the Seventeenth Century," in Walter M. Pintner and Don Karl Rowney, eds., *Russian Officialdom from the Seventeenth to the Twentieth Centuries: The Bureaucratization of Russian Society* (Chapel Hill, 1980); N. V. Ustiugov, "Evoliutsiia prikaznogo stroia russkogo gosudarstva v XVII v.," in Akademiia Nauk SSSR, *Absoliutizm v Rossii XVII-XVIII vv: Sbornik statei* (Moscow, 1964), 134-167; N. F. Demidova, "Prikaznye liudi XVII v. (Sotsial'nyi sostav i istochniki formirovaniia)," *Istoricheskie zapiski*, 90 (1972): 332-354; and "Biurokratizatsiia gosudarstvennogo apparata absoliutizma v XVII-XVIII vv.," *Absoliutizm v Rossii*, 206-242. See also Peter B. Brown, "Early Modern Russian Bureaucracy: The Evolution of The Chancellery System from Ivan III

to Peter the Great, 1478-1717" (Ph.D. diss., University of Chicago, 1978).

26. On guardianship and the notion of the police state see V. Sergeevich, *Lektsii i izsledovaniia po drevnei istorii russkago prava*, 4th ed. (St. Petersburg, 1910), 247-248; David A. J. Macey, "The Russian Bureaucracy and the 'Peasant Problem': The Pre-History of the Stolypin Reforms, 1861-1907" (Ph.D. diss., Columbia University, 1976), 19-26; Marc Raeff, "The Well-Ordered Police State and the Development of Modernity in Seventeenth and Eighteenth Century Europe: An Attempt at a Comparative Approach," *American Historical Review*, 80, no. 5 (December 1975): 1221-1243; Taranovski, "Politics of Counter-Reform," 167-277.

27. Brian Chapman, *Police State* (New York, 1970), 7-49.

28. Roberto Mangabeira Unger, *Law in Modern Society: Toward a Criticism of Social Theory* (New York, 1976), 52-58.

29. Ibid., 58-133; S. N. Eisenstadt, *The Political Systems of Empires: The Rise and Fall of the Historical Bureaucratic Societies* (New York, 1969).

30. Lincoln, "The Tsar's Most Loyal Servitors," 175-185.

31. Keenan, "Russian Political Culture," 35-46; Taranovski, "Politics of Counter-Reform," 221. Taranovski's discussion of the power position of the autocrat is unsurpassed. See also Lincoln, "Tsar's Most Loyal Servitors," 25-29; V. Val'denberg, *Drevnerusskiia ucheniia o predelakh tsarskoi vlasti* (Petrograd, 1916), 432-455; Zaionchkovskii, *Pravitel'stvennyi apparat*, 182-186; L. V. Cherepnin, *Zemskie sobory russkogo gosudarstva v XVI-XVII vv.* (Moscow, 1978).

32. P. A. Valuev, "Graf P. A. Valuev o polozhenii Rossii v 1882 godu," *Minuvshie gody*, 1, no. 9 (September 1908): 29-30.

33. For an overview of the historiography of Russian bureaucracy with full bibliographic citations, see Daniel T. Orlovsky, "Recent Studies on the Russian Bureaucracy," *Russian Review*, 35, no. 4 (October 1976): 448-469. See also Hans-Joachim Torke, "Das russische Beamtentum in der ersten Hälfte des 19. Jahrhunderts," *Forschungen zur osteuropäischen Geschichte*, 13 (1967): 7-345.

2. The Structure of the Ministry of Internal Affairs, 1802-1881

1. The two published official histories of the MVD are Varadinov, *Istoriia ministerstva*, and Adrianov, *Ministerstvo*. Varadinov, an MVD official, produced a largely undigested compendium of materials from MVD archives and the *PSZ*. Adrianov wrote the jubilee history which contains important material on structure and policy but which is far too self-serving. I was able to locate a third history of the ministry by A. S. Norov, then a young MVD functionary and later minister of education. Varadinov claimed it was lost, but it is located in GPB OR F. 531 (Collection of A. S. Norov) d. 26-37, *Istoricheskie svedeniia o ministerstve vnutrennikh del ot obrazovaniia do 1830g.*

2. *PSZ* I, no. 20,406.

3. There has been no systematic study of the Petrine colleges. Yaney, *Systematization*, 63-66.

4. B. H. Sumner, *Peter the Great and the Emergence of Russia* (New

York, 1962), 111-115; Yaney, *Systematization*, 63-66, 85-90. Kliuchevskii, Gradovskii, and Wittram are more mindful of the Muscovite institutions and traditions upon which the colleges were constructed, but they emphasize that Peter was attempting to transform Russian government. V. O. Kliuchevskii, *Sochineniia* (Moscow, 1958), 4:168-192; A. D. Gradovskii, *Vysshaia administratsiia Rossii XVIII st i general-prokurory*, in *Sobranie sochinenii A. D. Gradovskago*, 1 (St. Petersburg, 1899): 108-165; Reinhard Wittram, *Peter I Czar und Kaiser*, 2 vols. (Göttingen, 1964), 2:112-118. Demidova judiciously argues that the process of bureaucratization took place over several centuries (sixteenth through eighteenth), but she still labels Peter's institutions as "new." N. F. Demidova, "Biurokratizatsiia gosudarstvennogo apparata absoliutizma v XVII-XVIII vv.," *Absoliutizm v Rossii*, 222-224.

5. *PSZ* I, no. 3,718. The spiritual regulation was largely written by Feofan Prokopovich; it contains a clear statement of the Cameralist principles behind the adoption of collegiality in Europe. The law argued that many voices could attain the truth more easily than one, and their collective decision would be less arbitrary and carry more authority than one made by an individual. Also, there was a promise of greater efficiency and the elimination of corruption. As Leibniz put it, "There cannot be good administration except with colleges; their mechanism is like that of watches whose wheels mutually keep each other in movement." According to the Cameralists, collegial administration allowed the ruler to involve the representatives of traditional estates in government in a way that made them mutually dependent and therefore more dependent on the ruler himself. See Yaney, *Systematization*, 86-90.

6. Kliuchevskii, *Sochineniia*, 4:168-171; Wittram, *Peter I*, 2:100-115. Wittram argues that the administrative reforms resulted from a mixture of traditional, practical, and theoretical considerations.

7. Max Weber, *The Theory of Social and Economic Organization* (New York, 1947), 329-341 and 402.

8. Ibid., 398. Weber writes, "Any interest in reviving the principle of collegiality in actual executive functions is usually derived from the interest in weakening the power of persons in authority. This, in turn, is derived from mistrust and jealousy of monocratic leadership . . . on the part of the members of the administrative staff."

9. Ibid., 403-404; Yaney, *Systematization*, 85-90.

10. Quoted in Wittram, *Peter I*, 2:114.

11. Many territorial prikazy were eliminated in 1708-1709 when Peter created the large provinces. Others, such as the *razriad*, were absorbed into the new Senate, while others were combined into larger units before the creation of the colleges. Similarly the collegial principle was introduced at various times before the colleges were created—and it is even argued that collegiality existed within the prikazy. Kliuchevskii, *Sochineniia*, 4:168-171. Wittram, *Peter I*, 2:101-115.

12. *PSZ* I, No. 3,532. See also the variants of the text in N. A. Voskresenskii, *Zakonodatel'nye akty Petra I*, vol. 1, *Akty o vysshikh gosudarstvennykh ustanovleniiakh* (Moscow-Leningrad, 1945), pp. 411-516. The *General'nyi reglament* details the structure and procedures of the colleges. As such it is the

forerunner of the detailed instructions prepared by Speranskii and others for the 1811 reform of the central government. A thorough analysis of the effects of the General'nyi reglament and other Petrine legislation on the colleges would assist in breaking down the various misconceptions surrounding them. See articles XVII, XXVIII, XXIX-XLVII.

13. The existence of the "chancery element" in Russian institutions has long been noted by scholars as expressive of the bureaucratic principle. Gradovskii sees the creation of the ministries in 1802 as the triumph of this element, and therefore of bureaucratization. Gradovskii, *Vysshaia administratsiia*, 280.

14. Gradovskii, *Vysshaia administratsiia*, 126-134.

15. Ibid., 126ff. Wittram, *Peter I*, 2:114-118. It is inferred that Peter enlisted German and Swedish war prisoners for work in the colleges.

16. S. M. Solov'ev, *Istoriia Rossii s drevneishikh vremen*, 15 vols. (Moscow, 1960-1966), 8 (16): 458.

17. Gradovskii, *Vysshaia administratsiia*, 126ff.

18. Wittram, *Peter I*, 2:116.

19. On the General-Procuracy see Gradovskii, *Vysshaia administratsiia*, 141-166; Yaney, *Systematization*, 56-57, 207-212. On the operations and decline of the colleges, see S. M. Troitskii, *Finansovaia politika russkogo absoliutizma v XVIII veke* (Moscow, 1966).

20. See especially Yaney, *Systematization*, 207-212; M. V. Klochkov, *Ocherki pravitel'stvennoi deiatel'nosti vremeni Pavla I* (Petrograd, 1916), 224-270; Gradovskii, *Vysshaia administratsiia*, 192-277.

21. Klochkov describes this especially well in *Ocherki*, 224-270. See also A. N. Filippov, "Istoricheskii ocherk obrazovaniia ministerstv v Rossii," *Zhurnal ministerstva iustitsii*, no. 9 (November 1902), 41-43.

22. Yaney, *Systematization*, 208-212.

23. Troitskii, *Finansovaia politika*, 33; Gradovskii, *Vysshaia administratsiia*, 251-254; Klochkov, *Ocherki*, 154-157, 312-313, 330, 341, 377.

24. Klochkov's *Ocherki* remains the best work on domestic policy and government institutions during the reign of Paul I. For his review of the earlier literature on the subject, see pages 143-160; on the central executive organs, pages 271-406.

25. *PSZ* I, nos. 19,554; 19,679; 19,775; Klochkov, *Ocherki*, 398-399.

26. *PSZ* I, no. 17,906; Klochkov, *Ocherki*, 392-396.

27. "Zapiska Imperatora Pavla I ob ustroistve raznykh chastei gosudarstvennago upravleniia," in *SIRIO*, 90 (St. Petersburg, 1894): 1-4.

28. The September 8, 1802, Manifesto created a single "ministry" that was to be divided into eight separate branches of administration, each to be headed by a single minister. As will be shown, the idea of a unified Russian ministry (or cabinet), in the west European sense, only became a reality after the 1905 Revolution. For a brilliant discussion of the historical development of European unified state ministries, see Otto Hintze, "Die Entstehung der modernen Staatsministerien," *Staat und Verfassung* (Leipzig, 1941), 265-310.

29. Filippov, "Istoricheskii ocherk," 46-48.

30. Nikolai Mikhailovich, Velikii Kniaz', *Graf P. A. Stroganov* (1774-

1817): Istoricheskoe issledovanie epokhi imperatora Aleksandra I, 3 vols. (St. Petersburg, 1903), 2:61-243.

31. Ibid., 2:11; A. V. Predtechenskii, *Ocherki obshchestvenno-politicheskoi istorii Rossii v pervoi chetverti XIX veka* (Moscow-Leningrad, 1957), 136.

32. Predtechenskii, *Ocherki*, 137-138.

33. Ibid.

34. Various political points of view expressed by members of the nobility as well as by members of the unofficial committee are reviewed in Predtechenskii, *Ocherki*, 63-130. The conflict between the "senatorial" or oligarchic party and the tsar and his young friends has been cogently summarized by Marc Raeff. He described the "constitutionalism" of Alexander and his closest advisers as "the rule of law, and the clear, logical, hierarchical organization of the administration. Law, order, clear structure of the political machine were the contents they put into such words as constitution, fundamental laws, etc. At no time did they mean representative institutions, checks and balances, abolition of the autocracy . . ." Marc Raeff, *Michael Speransky: Statesman of Imperial Russia 1772-1839*, 2nd ed. (The Hague, 1969), 29-46.

35. *PSZ* I, no. 20,406.

36. I. Blinov, *Gubernatory: istoriko-iuridicheskii ocherk* (St. Petersburg, 1904); S. A. Korf (Baron), *Administrativnaia iustitsiia v Rossii*, 2 vols. (St. Petersburg, 1910), 1:291-352.

37. For a contemporary statement of the distinctions between the different kinds of police, see M. M. Speranskii, "Zapiska ob ustroistve sudebnykh i pravitel'stvennykh uchrezhdenii v Rossii (1803 g.)," in M. M. Speranskii, *Proekty i zapiski* (Moscow-Leningrad, 1961), 89-101. See also Robert J. Abbott, "Police Reform in Russia, 1858-1878" (Ph.D. diss., Princeton University, 1971), 5-9; and P. S. Squire, *The Third Department: The Establishment and Practice of the Political Police in the Russia of Nicholas I* (Cambridge, 1968), 13-29.

38. *PSZ* I, no. 20,406, article IV, no. 4; also articles XIII, XIV.

39. *PSZ* I, no. 20,582.

40. Ibid.

41. The structural matters treated throughout this chapter are described more fully in my "Ministerial Power and Russian Autocracy: The Ministry of Internal Affairs, 1802-1881" (Ph.D. diss., Harvard University, 1976).

42. Senator Troshchinskii, for example, did not write his famous attack on the ministries until after 1811, when the system of ministerial departments and the monocratic principles were institutionalized in final form for the entire central government. Troshchinskii continued to view the 1802 Manifesto as Alexander I's attempt to improve the collegial executive organs inherited from the eighteenth century. He maintained that the 1802 ministries were designed to further the collegial principle. Troshchinskii, *Zapiska*, 34-35. Others, using hindsight, expressed their dissatisfaction with the 1802 legislation because of its vagueness, their dislike of its authors, or their feeling that the new system would eventually lead to abuses worse than those it was meant to alleviate. F. F. Vigel', *Zapiski*, 2 vols. (Moscow, 1928), 1:148-150,

157; G. R. Derzhavin, *Zapiski Gavriila Romanovicha Derzhavina, 1743-1812* (Moscow, 1860), 455-458, 472-474.

43. *PSZ* I, no. 20,852.

44. Ibid., 756-769.

45. Ibid., 769-770.

46. Ibid., 770-775.

47. Gradovskii, *Vysshaia administratsiia*, 280ff.

48. The idea that the MVD was the most important ministry in the Russian government was fostered by its official historians. According to A. S. Norov, "The Ministry of Internal Affairs is the most important in the state; all else derives its basis from the MVD. It is the foundation of the great structure of government." GPB F. 531 (Collection of A. S. Norov), d. 26 1.7. The Soviet historian I. V. Orzhekhovskii shares this view for the 1860s and 1870s. *Iz istorii vnutrennei politiki samoderzhaviia v 60-70-x godakh XIX veka* (Gor'kii, 1974), 53-82.

49. Raeff, *Michael Speransky*, 1-227; M. A. Korf (Baron), *Zhizn' grafa Speranskago*, vol. 1 (St. Petersburg, 1861).

50. Scheibert called attention to Speranskii's understanding that the success of institutional reforms depended on the prior creation of a new officialdom—efficient, well trained, and dedicated to the tasks at hand. Scheibert argued that the weakness of Speranskii's later reform projects resulted from his failure to ensure the creation of this new officialdom. Peter Scheibert, "Marginelien zu einer neuen Speranskij-Biographie," *Jahrbücher für Geschichte Osteuropas*, Band 6, Heft 4 (1958), 449-467; Raeff, *Michael Speransky*, 61-66, 381-382.

51. Raeff, *Michael Speransky*, 61-66.

52. *PSZ* I, no. 23,771. For the best analysis of this law, see Torke, "Das russische Beamtentum," 58-70.

53. Varadinov, *Istoriia ministerstva*, 1:100-250. Adrianov, *Ministerstvo*, 1:15-20, 23-32.

54. Adrianov, *Ministerstvo*, 1:23-32; "Doklad ministra vnutrennikh del za 1803," *Zhurnaly Komiteta Ministrov*, 1 (1801-1810) (St. Petersburg, 1888), appendix I, 54-79.

55. *PSZ* I, no. 20,620; Predtechenskii, *Ocherki*, 171-175.

56. Adrianov, *Ministerstvo*, 1:29.

57. Speranskii, *Proekty i zapiski*, 201-216, 228-231. The two primary laws that reorganized the ministries were the decree of July 25, 1810 (*PSZ* I, no. 24,307), and the detailed general institution of the ministries of June 25, 1811 (*PSZ* I, no. 24,686).

58. *PSZ* I, nos. 24,307; 24,326; Adrianov, *Ministerstvo*, 1:19-22, 39-45; Squire, *The Third Department*, 23-45; Varadinov, *Istoriia ministerstva*, book 1, part 2, 4-12. Squire mistakenly argues that Speranskii's and Alexander's main aim was to create a powerful Ministry of Police.

59. Predtechenskii, *Ocherki*, 295-322; Adrianov, *Ministerstvo*, 19, 23-32; William T. Blackwell, *The Beginnings of Russian Industrialization, 1800-1860* (Princeton, 1968), 130-132, 153, 163, 168.

60. Adrianov, *Ministerstvo*, 1:19-22; Squire, *The Third Department*, 23-45.

61. Speranskii, *Proekty i zapiski*, 201-202, 206-207.

62. *PSZ* I, nos. 24,307; 24,326; 24,687; 24,688.

63. *PSZ* I, no. 24,687. Predtechenskii claims that Kozodavlev wrote the specific instructions to the minister of internal affairs and a project for the organization of the ministry in 1810. Kozodavlev viewed the MVD's most important departments as the Economic Department and the Department of Manufactures and Internal Trade. Predtechenskii, *Ocherki*, 301. Raeff (*Michael Speransky*, 110) claims that Speranskii wrote the instructions and organizational plans (1811) for the ministries of Finance and Police. The 1811 organization of the MVD was fixed by the following laws: *PSZ* I, nos. 24,686, 24,969, 25,137, 25,392, 26,320. The structure is outlined in Adrianov, *Ministerstvo*, 1:21.

64. The division of labor (*raspredelenie del*) remained an intractable problem for the Russian government for over a hundred years. After 1811 the major domestic ministries, especially MVD, Finance, and State Domains (founded in 1837), acquired more and more diverse domestic administrative functions. Vital economic and social affairs responsibility was spread among all three ministries with much overlap. Both France and Prussia, for example, created separate ministries for agriculture and industry and commerce early in the nineteenth century. Russia did not establish a Ministry of Agriculture until the 1890s, and its Ministry of Trade and Industry was created only in October 1905. Russian merchants and industrialists had argued for the creation of such a ministry since the 1820s. The division of labor among Russian ministries reflected the low level of economic development as well as forms of social organization and statehood. Thus, instead of a Ministry of Agriculture to deal with the most pressing nineteenth-century problem on a nationwide basis, Russia had ministries of the Imperial Court (for the personal property of the royal family), of State domains (for state property), and of Internal Affairs (for lands owned by the *dvorianstvo* and, after 1861, by the peasantry).

On the Prussian ministries, see Hue de Grais (Graf), *Handbuch der Verfassung und Verwaltung in Preussen und dem Deutschen Reiche* (Berlin, 1906), 56-64; Herman G. James, *Principles of Prussian Administration* (New York, 1913), 67-80. On the French ministries, see Théophile Ducroq, *Cours de droit administratif et de législation française des finances, avec introduction de droit constitutionnel et les principes du droit public*, 7th ed., 7 vols. (Paris, 1897-1905), 1:93-100; Léon Duguit, *Manuel de Droit Constitutionnel*, 3rd ed. (Paris, 1918), 530-536. On the various Russian government attempts to create organs for trade and industry, see N. S. Kiniapina, *Politika russkogo samoderzhaviia v oblasti promyshlennosti* (Moscow, 1968), 197-246; V. Ia. Laverychev, *Krupnaia burzhuaziia v poreformennoi Rossii 1861-1900* (Moscow, 1974), 88-108, 225-228. On the creation in 1905 of a Ministry of Trade and Industry, see L. E. Shepelev, *Aktsionernye kompanii v Rossii* (Leningrad, 1973), 251-261.

65. *PSZ* I, no. 24,686, articles 205-206.

66. Ibid., articles 61-204.

67. Ibid., articles 178-204.

68. Ibid.; various articles from 206 to 243 relate to the laws mentioned in this paragraph.

69. *PSZ* I, nos. 27,964; 28,239; Adrianov, *Ministerstvo*, 1:22. The reasons for these changes are not fully known. The historian of the Third Section, P. Squire, cites dissatisfaction with the Ministry of Police on the part of the tsar, his advisers, and some of the citizenry. Speranskii had long since lost his influential position in St. Petersburg, and was unable to defend the central government institutions he created in 1811. It is likely that the unification was linked to the return in 1819 of V. P. Kochubei as minister of internal affairs. Kochubei, who remained minister until 1823, vociferously opposed Kozodavlev's economic policies. A free-trader, Kochubei believed that Russia must follow its own path of economic development, and that it should remain an agricultural country serving as the granary of Europe. Accordingly, the state was to keep its hands off industry, saving active sponsorship for native peasant handicrafts. It seems more than a coincidence that when Kochubei returned to office, the MVD gave up its jurisdiction over manufacturing while reclaiming its original 1802 agricultural functions from the Ministry of Police.

70. Blackwell, *The Beginnings of Russian Industrialization*, 127, 140.

71. *PSZ* I, no. 28,205.

72. Ibid., no. 27,970.

73. Ibid., no. 28,910.

74. Raeff, *Michael Speransky*, 170-203.

75. Michael Jenkins, *Arakcheev-Grand Vizier of the Russian Empire* (New York, 1969), 171-174; V. N. Stroev, *Stoletie Sobstvennoi Ego Imperatorskago Velichestva Kantseliarii* (St. Petersburg, 1912), 5-124.

76. On the theme of personalized, clannish politics versus institutions during the mid and late eighteenth century, see David L. Ransel, *The Politics of Catherinian Russia: The Panin Party* (New Haven, 1975), 73-144, 262-289; Yaney, *Systematization*, 221-229, 207-212.

77. M. Polievktov, *Nikolai I. Biografiia i obzor tsarstvovaniia* (Moscow, 1918), 209-225; A. E. Presniakov, *Apogei samoderzhaviia: Nikolai I* (Leningrad, 1925), 43; V. O. Kliuchevskii, *Sochineniia* (Moscow, 1958), 5:264, 267, 270-272; Nicholas V. Riasanovsky, *Nicholas I and Official Nationality in Russia 1825-1855* (Berkeley and Los Angeles, 1969), 184-234.

78. *PSZ* II, no. 449. This law eliminated the Special Chancery of the MVD and transferred its affairs to the Third Section of His Majesty's Own Chancery. Squire, *The Third Department*, 60-63; Sidney Monas, *The Third Section: Police and Society in Russia under Nicholas I* (Cambridge, Mass., 1961), 60-74; Adrianov, *Ministerstvo*, 1:97-101.

79. W. Bruce Lincoln, *Nicholas I, Emperor and Autocrat of All the Russias* (London, 1978), 151-195.

80. Varadinov, *Istoriia ministerstva*, 3, book 1, 48-52.

81. Adrianov, *Ministerstvo*, 1:52a, 62a, 64a.

82. Roderick E. McGrew, *Russia and the Cholera, 1823-1832* (Madison and Milwaukee, 1965), 55-158.

83. *PSZ* II, nos. 2,982; 3,351; 4,969; 7,685; 9,113; Orlovsky, "Ministerial Power," 63-65.

84. Successive ministry publications from 1803 through the *Zhurnal ministerstva vnutrennikh del* (1828-1861) are reviewed by Varadinov in *Istoriia ministerstva*, 3, book 1, 673-777.

85. *PSZ* II, no. 9,113.

86. *PSZ* II, no. 6,439; Varadinov, *Istoriia Ministerstva*, 3, book 1, 48-52.

87. On the failure of the Committee of Ministers to function as a unified cabinet, see Yaney, *Systematization*, 194-220, 249-258; S. N. Seredonin, *Istoricheskii obzor deiatel'nosti komiteta ministrov*, 3 vols. (St. Petersburg, 1902).

88. This change has gone largely unnoticed by historians. An exception is Richard Wortman, *The Development of a Russian Legal Consciousness* (Chicago, 1976), 143-234.

89. "Bumagi Komiteta 6 Dekabria 1826 goda, otnosiashchiiasia do preobrazovaniia gubernskago upravleniia," *SIRIO*, 90 (St. Petersburg, 1894): 212-358; S. Frederick Starr, *Decentralization and Self-Government in Russia, 1830-1870* (Princeton, 1972), 31-32.

90. Adrianov, *Ministerstvo*, 1:58-59.

91. *PSZ* II, no. 10,304; S. A. Korf (Baron), *Administrativnaia iustitsiia v Rossii* (St. Petersburg, 1910), 1:292-296; Adrianov, *Ministerstvo*, 60-62; Starr, *Decentralization*, 33-34; Yaney, *Systematization*, 217-218.

92. A. D. Gradovskii, "Istoricheskii ocherk uchrezhdeniia general-gubernatorstv v Rossii," *Sobranie sochinenii*, 1:299-338.

93. See, for example, "Biurokraticheskaia voina 1839 goda," *Russkaia starina*, 32 (1881): 890-895. The powers of governors-general and their relation to the MVD and the regular institutions and laws of the empire would arise as a problem during Alexander II's reign more than once.

94. *PSZ* II, no. 10,303.

95. A. P. Zablotskii-Desiatovskii, *Graf P. D. Kiselev i ego vremia* (St. Petersburg, 1882); N. M. Druzhinin, *Gosudarstvennye krest'iane i reforma P. D. Kiseleva*, 2 vols. (Moscow-Leningrad, 1946-1958), 1:504-505, 510, 521-526; Yaney, *Systematization*, 164-166, 219-220; Sidney Monas, "Bureaucracy in Russia under Nicholas I," in Michael Cherniavsky, ed., *The Structure of Russian History: Interpretive Essays* (New York, 1970), 277-280.

96. Monas, "Bureaucracy in Russia," 274-277; Druzhinin, *Gosudarstvennye krest'iane*, 1:244-299, 476-521.

97. Lincoln, "The Tsar's Most Loyal Servitors," 83-110.

98. The connection has been noted by Druzhinin as well as the leading scholars of the Emancipation. Ibid., 379-623.

99. *PSZ* II, no. 12,029. Also Varadinov, *Istoriia ministerstva*, 3, book 2, 60-64.

100. *Entsiklopedicheskii slovar' "Granat,"* 7th ed. (Moscow, 1913), 23:658; F. A. Brokgauz and I. A. Efron, eds., *Entsiklopedicheskii slovar'* (St. Petersburg, 1898), 23:348-349. Adrianov, *Ministerstvo*, 80a; Monas, *The Third Section*, 247.

101. *PSZ* II, nos. 15,373; 15,634; 16,001; 16,606. Varadinov, *Istoriia ministerstva*, 3, book 2, 81-82; Adrianov, *Ministerstvo*, 54-55; Orlovsky, "Ministerial Power," 77-79.

102. W. Bruce Lincoln, "N. A. Miliutin and the St. Petersburg Municipal Act of 1846: A Study in Reform under Nicholas I," *Slavic Review*, 33, no. 1 (March 1974): 55-68.

103. Adrianov, *Ministerstvo*, 1:72-73.

104. *PSZ* II, no. 15,432. An MVD Commission on City Economy had been created under Bludov in 1836. Adrianov, *Ministerstvo*, 1:73-74.

105. Lincoln, "N. A. Miliutin," 57-60; A. Leroy-Bealieu, *Un homme d'état Russe (Nicolas Milutine)* (Paris, 1884), 1-25. Miliutin's service record is found in TsGIA SSSR F. 1162 (State Council) op. 6 d. 335.

106. Lincoln, "N. A. Miliutin," 60-67.

107. Adrianov, *Ministerstvo*, 1:55; Varadinov, *Istoriia ministerstva*, 3, book 3, 16-19; *PSZ* II, no. 23,024. On the municipal reform of 1870, see Lester Thomas Hutton, "The Reform of City Government in Russia, 1860-1870," (Ph.D. diss., University of Illinois, 1972).

108. These reports are described in Adrianov, *Ministerstvo*, 1:63-64; Starr, *Decentralization*, 33. See also Korf, *Administrativnaia iustitsiia*, 1:324-332. The reports are published in *Materialy sobrannye dlia vysochaishei uchrezhdennoi kommissii o preobrazovanii gubernskikh i uezdnykh uchrezhdenii*, part I, *Materialy istoricheskie i zakonodatel'nye* (St. Petersburg, 1870), sec. II, para. 2-75.

109. *PSZ* II, no. 18,580; P. I. Mel'nikov, "Vospominaniia o V. I. Dale," *Russkii vestnik*, 104 (1873): 275-340.

110. *PSZ* II, no. 18,580; Korf, *Administrativnaia iustitsiia*, 1:328-335.

111. Perovskii quoted by W. Bruce Lincoln, "Daily Life of St. Petersburg Officials in the Mid Nineteenth Century," *Oxford Slavonic Papers*, n.s., 8 (Oxford, 1975): 82-100. See also Varadinov, *Istoriia ministerstva*, 3, book 3, 20-24.

112. Monas, *The Third Section*, 248-260.

113. Perovskii quoted by Lincoln, "Daily Life," 15.

114. Varadinov, *Istoriia ministerstva*, 3, book 3, 21-26 and book 4, 20-25; *PSZ* II, no. 25,944; Starr, *Decentralization*, 111-122. Simultaneous minor reductions in the central MVD table of organization are described in Adrianov, *Ministerstvo*, 1:55-56. Several vice-directorships and the Third Section of the Department of General Affairs were eliminated, as well as a variety of low-ranking departmental officials. On the eve of the Great Reforms, however, the overall size of the ministry was very close to that outlined in the 1839 table of organization.

115. Adrianov, *Ministerstvo*, 1:104.

116. Ibid.; Yaney, *Systematization*, 169-175; Daniel Field, *The End of Serfdom: Nobility and Bureaucracy in Russia, 1856-1861* (Cambridge, Mass., 1976), 41-42. In an 1851 speech to local dignitaries at the end of his four-year term as governor-general of Kiev, Bibikov expressly disavowed any intention of having sought to build bridges between state and society. He proudly proclaimed that his mission was not to seek popularity. Quoted in Torke, "Das russische Beamtentum," 256.

117. Varadinov, *Istoriia ministerstva*, 3, book 4, 22-30.

118. Ibid., 30-43.

119. P. A. Valuev, *Dnevnik P. A. Valueva ministra vnutrennikh del*, 2 vols., ed. P. A. Zaionchkovskii (Moscow, 1961), 1:172-176. TsGIA SSSR F. 1284 (MVD—Department of General Affairs) op. 66 d. 49 ll. 63-64; F. 1275 op. 1 d. 102 ll. 6-10.

120. Ibid., 2:252-254, 289. On the Timashev proposal for a second assistant minister, see TsGIA SSSR F. 1152 (State Council, Combined Departments) op. 7 d. 69 ll. 19-20. Valuev himself had made an earlier plea for a second assistant minister. See TsGIA F. 908 (Collection of P. A. Valuev), op. 1 d. 312 ll. 1-11ob.

121. All structural changes, except for the creation of the Jurisconsult Section, are treated in Adrianov, *Ministerstvo*, 1:103-112. *PSZ* II, no. 32,826.

122. *PSZ* II, nos. 37,290; 37,291; 37,292; 37,293.

123. *Entsiklopedicheskii Slovar'*, 57:435-436.

124. *PSZ* II, no. 39,566.

125. *PSZ* II, no. 54,742.

126. *PSZ* II, no. 41,990. See also Charles A. Ruud, "The Russian Empire's New Censorship Law of 1865," *Canadian Slavic Studies*, 3, no. 2 (Summer 1969): 235-245.

127. *PSZ* II, no. 45,574.

128. *PSZ* II, no. 61,551. For Loris-Melikov's report to Alexander outlining these changes, see TsGIA SSSR F. 1284 op. 241 d. 81.

129. *PSZ* II, nos. 61,279; 61,284; 61,550.

130. TsGIA SSSR F. 1284 op. 66 d. 49 ll. 74-75.

131. TsGIA SSSR F. 1284 op. 66 d. 371. The journals of these commissions are found in TsGIA SSSR F. 1275 op. 1 d. 102 and F. 1275 op. 93 d. 22.

132. TsGIA SSSR F. 1275 op. 93 d. 22 ll. 5-36.

133. Ibid., ll. 36, 40ob.-41.

134. TsGIA SSSR F. 1282 (MVD Chancery) op. 3 d. 14 ll. 3-4.

135. "Otchet po Ministerstvu Vnutrennikh Del za 1861, 1862, 1863 gg.," TsGIA SSSR F. 1284 op. 66 d. 11 ll. 169-175, 490-508. This was the last "yearly" compilation submitted by the MVD during the remainder of the nineteenth century even though such reports were required by law. On the significance of these reports, see R. Iu. Matskina, "Ministerskie otchety i ikh osobennosti kak istoricheskii istochnik," Glavnoe Arkhivnoe Upravlenie SSSR, *Problemy arkhivovedeniia i istochnikovedeniia* (Leningrad, 1964), 209-226. Yaney correctly sees the absence of these reports after the early 1860s as a manifestation of the enormous power of both the MVD and the Ministry of Finance—and their unwillingness to submit their activities to outside examination or control. His explanation of why they were able to avoid submitting the reports is confused, however. Since the tsar could have demanded such reports (and Nicholas II did, beginning in 1899) but chose not to, I can only conclude that he placed his personal relationship with the ministers above the institutionalization of any controls over the ministerial system. It also appears that the growing pressures upon the ministries and especially upon the ministers left little time for the compilation of detailed summaries of yearly operations. The MVD departments could barely cope with their administrative and legislative duties. See Yaney, *Systematization*, 301-305.

136. These petitions fell into the following categories: (1) peasant affairs—5,846; (2) municipal and zemskii obligations (*povinnosti*) and foodstuffs, and social welfare—3,570; (3) public health—652; (4) general administration and police—9,011; and (5) miscellaneous—394.

137. See note 114.

138. The tables of organization are located in special supplementary volumes of the *PSZ*.

139. On the reforms in the Naval Ministry, see Seredonin, *Istoricheskii obzor*, 3, part 2, 2-4; Jacob Walter Kipp, "The Grand Duke Konstantin Nikolaevich and the Epoch of the Great Reforms, 1855-1866," (Ph.D. diss., Pennsylvania State University, 1970).

140. TsGIA SSSR F. 1261 op. 2 d. 170a ll. 1-7, and TsGIA SSSR F. 1287 op. 46 d. 1981 ll. 1-3.

141. A copy of the official communication from Valuev to A. D. Shumakher is found in TsGIA SSSR F. 1287 op. 46 d. 1981 ll. 1-3.

142. Ibid., ll. 11-14. Shumakher proposed giving each desk 1,000 rubles— 600-700 for one *sotrudnik* with the remainder to be used for hiring clerks.

143. Copies of the project are located in TsGIA SSSR F. 1261 op. 2 d. 170a ll. 3-42; and F. 1152 op. 6 d. 208 ll. 2-87. Some of the internal MVD correspondence and materials used in preparing the project are found in TsGIA SSSR F. 1284 op. 133 d. 1 ll. 5-67. For further details on this and the other projects discussed here see Orlovsky, "Ministerial Power," 109-135.

144. In the Naval Ministry, section chiefs and their subordinate desk chiefs had been replaced by a single official with the title *deloproizvoditel'*. These men, in turn, had senior and junior assistants. The point of this change was to increase the number of responsible instances below the vice-director level. Thus, instead of a department's having four sections (*otdelenii*) it might now have six or eight deloproizvodstva. Each of the new *deloproizvoditeli* would receive salary and service benefits higher than the old section chiefs, and each would be empowered to make the same kinds of decisions as the old section chiefs.

145. TsGIA SSSR F. 1152 op. 6 d. 208 ll. 108-109. The State Council insisted, however, that Valuev try to make further personnel cuts and procedural simplifications during the next two years.

146. Mansurov to A. D. Shumakher, 9 February 1867. TsGIA SSSR F. 1287 op. 46 d. 2074 l. 67; see also TsGIA SSSR F. 1284 op. 133 d. 15. ll. 31-50; F. 1282 op. 3 d. 18 ll. 50-92, for the new projects. All projects are discussed in detail with full references in Orlovsky, "Ministerial Power," 114-135.

147. Mansurov to Shumakher, 3 June 1871, TsGIA SSSR F. 1287 op. 46 d. 2074 l. 110.

148. The archives yielded some hints that the MVD was again collecting material for table of organization reform in 1880, in conjunction with a government commission established in 1879 to seek ways to reduce government expenditures. See TsGIA SSSR F. 565 op. 5 d. 19863 l. 4. In F. 1287 op. 46 d. 2074 there was one reference to an 1881 report by actual state councillor Polivanov on improving the division of labor and procedures within MVD departments. The report, however, could not be located in the archives.

149. See M. S. Kakhanov's *zapiska* written sometime in the spring of 1880 in TsGIA SSSR F. 908 op. 1 d. 416 ll. 1-7.

150. P. A. Zaionchkovskii, *Krizis samoderzhaviia na rubezhe 1870-1880-x godov* (Moscow, 1964), 5, 475.

3. The Impact of Leaders

1. For the operative version of the 1811 statutes during the reign of Alexander II, see *Svod zakonov Rossiiskoi Imperii*, 16 vols. (St. Petersburg, 1857), vol. 1, articles 189-268 (hereafter cited as *Svod zakonov*, 1857).

2. Biographical information on Lanskoi is sparse. His service record is located in TsGIA SSSR F. 982 (Collection of S. S. Lanskoi), op. 1. This record is summarized in detail in *Russkii biograficheskii slovar'*, 25 vols. (St. Petersburg, 1896-1918), 10:70-74 (hereafter cited as *RBS*).

3. P. P. Semenov-Tian-Shanskii, *Epokha osvobozhdeniia krest'ian v Rossii (1857-1861) v vospominaniakh P. P. Semenov-Tian-Shanskago*, 2 vols. (St. Petersburg, 1911-1916), 1:5.

4. Alexander's appeal was made in the speech of March 30, 1856, in which he also claimed it "better to abolish serfdom from above than to await the day when it will begin to abolish itself from below." *Materialy dlia istorii uprazdneniia krepostnago sostoianiia pomeshchich'ikh krest'ian v Rossii v Tsarstvovanii Imperatora Aleksandra II*, D. P. Khrushchov, comp., 3 vols. (Berlin, 1860-1862), 1:103-104, 114. See also Field, *End of Serfdom*, 62, and Emmons, *Russian Landed Gentry*, 51.

5. The attitude that the MVD and its highest officials who worked on the Editorial Commission preparing the emancipation statutes were hostile to the nobility pervades the large amount of literature on the emancipation process. From the Nazimov rescript of November 1857 to final enactment in 1861, Lanskoi and his subordinates were cast in the role of bureaucratic social levelers and encroachers upon gentry corporate interests and private property. See, for example, Field, *End of Serfdom*, 102-172, 324-358; Emmons, *Russian Landed Gentry*, 209-318.

6. The term is used here generically to describe the ideal type of Prussian enlightened bureaucrat—that is, an official of the kind of bureaucracy described by Hegel in *The Philosophy of Right*.

7. Semenov, *Epokha osvobozhdeniia*, 1:4, 6.

8. A. Leroy-Beaulieu, *Un homme d'état Russe (Nicolas Milutine): D'apres sa correspondance inedite* (Paris, 1884), 20.

9. Valuev, *Dnevnik*, 1:312 (note dated April 29, 1868).

10. Levshin, "Dostopamiatnye minuty v moei zhizne: Zapiska Alekseia Irakleevicha Levshina," *Russkii arkhiv*, 23, no. 8 (1885): 521-555.

11. Field, *End of Serfdom*, 102-172, 233-264.

12. Semenov, *Epokha osvobozhdeniia*, 1:4; *RBS*, 10:70.

13. Anatole G. Mazour, *The First Russian Revolution, 1825: The Decembrist Movement, Its Origins, Development, and Significance* (Stanford, 1961); A. Pypin, *Obshchestvennoe dvizhenie v Rossii pri Aleksandre I*, 5th ed. (Petrograd, 1918), 313-464; A. Pypin, *Russkoe masonstvo XVIII i pervaia chetvert' XIXv* (Petrograd, 1916), 380-398.

14. Semenov, *Epokha osvobozhdeniia*, 1:5.

15. Starr, *Decentralization*, 120-122, 137, 144-145.

16. Korf, *Administrativnaia iustitsiia*, 1:292-296.

17. Starr, *Decentralization*, 122, 135, 137, 144.

18. The original and one copy of this memorandum with Alexander's

comments in the margins are preserved in TsGIA SSSR F. 982 op. 1 d. 97 ll. 25-45. The document was attributed to Lanskoi and published as part of the Solov'ev memoirs: Ia. A. Solov'ev, "Zapiski senatora Iakova Aleksandrovicha Solov'eva: Krest'ianskoe delo v tsarstvovanii Aleksandra II," *Russkaia starina*, 35 (September 1882): 641-642. For Alexander's comments, see Solov'ev, "Zapiski," *Russkaia starina*, 33 (March 1882): 587-592. Lanskoi's memorandum was also published without Alexander's comments in M. A. Miliutina, "Iz zapisok Marii Agleevny Miliutinoi," *Russkaia starina*, 97 (February 1899): 272-281. The authorship of the memorandum is in dispute. Miliutina believes her husband wrote it. Kornilov, the compiler of the Artsimovich materials, claims Artsimovich wrote it. Artsimovich, *Viktor Antonovich Artsimovich*, 159n. The important point is, however, that it was discussed by all three men and presented by Lanskoi under his own name as the MVD position. In later communication with the tsar, Lanskoi defended as his own the positions set forth in the memorandum.

19. Starr, *Decentralization*, 144-148; see also Solov'ev, "Zapiski," *Russkaia starina*, 33 (March 1882): 561-579.

20. Starr, *Decentralization*, 145-148; Dzhanshiev, *Iz epokhi velikikh reform*, 41-43. At the same time another Murav'ev plan—to create extra-institutional officials called district chiefs at the district level—was also defeated.

21. Starr, *Decentralization*, 330-342; Yaney, *Systematization*, 328-347; B. B. Veselovskii, *Istoriia zemstva za sorok let*, 4 vols. (St. Petersburg, 1909-1911), 3:119-140.

22. Field, *End of Serfdom*, 173-232, 265-323, 614; Emmons, *Russian Landed Gentry*, 209-318.

23. TsGIA SSSR F. 982, op. 1 d. 97 ll. 47-59. Also published in Miliutina, "Iz zapisok," *Russkaia starina*, 99:106-108.

24. Field, *End of Serfdom*, 356-357.

25. Diary of D. A. Miliutin, quoted in Zaionchkovskii, "P. A. Valuev (Biograficheskii ocherk)," in Valuev, *Dnevnik*, 1:28.

26. Alexander had been reluctant to appoint Miliutin as Lanskoi's assistant minister in 1858. Miliutin was already regarded as a radical in court and high bureaucratic circles, and Lanskoi apparently had to go to great lengths to convince the tsar of Miliutin's indispensability to the emancipation legislative process. The tsar approved Miliutin's appointment, but only as "acting assistant minister." See Leroy-Beaulieu, *Un homme d'état Russe*, 52-54; Miliutina, "Iz zapisok," 97 (January 1899): 56-64.

27. *RBS*, 10:72-73.

28. On Valuev's career, see P. A. Zaionchkovskii, "P. A. Valuev (Biograficheskii ocherk)," in P. A. Valuev, *Dnevnik*, 1:17-54, and Gordon Dale Knutson, "Peter Valuev: A Conservative's Approach and Reactions to the Reforms of Alexander II" (Ph.D. diss., University of Kansas, 1970). Both these works treat Valuev's thought and activities in a superficial fashion. Valuev's service records are preserved in TsGIA SSSR F. 1162 op. 28a d. 66 and F. 1284 op. 76 d. 70. The most important source on Valuev is his voluminous diary covering the years 1845-1884; P. A. Valuev, "Dnevnik Grafa Petra Aleksandrovicha Valueva, 1847-1860 gg.," *Russkaia starina*, 70 (May-November

1891): 167-182, 339-349, 603-616; 71:71-82, 265-278, 547-602; 72:139-154, 393-459; *Dnevnik P. A. Valueva ministra vnutrennikh del,* 2 vols. (Moscow, 1961); and *Dnevnik 1877-1884.* (Petrograd, 1919). Large archival collections in the USSR contain much additional unpublished material.

29. For the significance of these commissions, see V. G. Chernukha, "Problema politicheskoi reformy v pravitel'stvennykh krugakh Rossii v nachale 70-x godov XIX v.," 139-190; *Krest'ianskii vopros v pravitel'stvennoi politike Rossii 60-70 gody XIX v.* (Leningrad, 1972), 152-164. For the Committee of Ministers' discussion of the Valuev commission's report, see its journal reprinted in Seredonin, *Istoricheskii obzor,* vol. 3, part 2, 239-315. On the 1874-1875 commission, see V. Ia. Laverychev, *Tsarizm i rabochii vopros v Rossii (1861-1917 gg.)* (Moscow, 1972), 39-54.

30. Tatishchev, *Imperator Aleksandr II,* 2:544-573; Zaionchkovskii, *Krizis samoderzhaviia,* 58-147; journals of several of the 1878-1880 conferences are found in TsGIA SSSR F. 908, op. 1 d. 395.

31. Zaionchkovskii, "P. A. Valuev," 28.

32. In 1866, for example, Valuev closed the St. Petersburg provincial zemstvo for its political pretensions. Tatishchev, *Imperator Aleksandr II,* 2:17-18.

33. Apparently Valuev already had considered such a plan in the late 1850s. Zaionchkovskii, "P. A. Valuev," 34-37; Knutson, "Peter Valuev," 272-290; L. G. Zakharova, *Zemskaia kontrreforma 1890 g.* (Moscow, 1968), 44-55. For the text of the project, see Bermanskii, "Konstitutsionnye proekty," 225-233.

34. Valuev linked the creation of the zemstvos to reform of the State Council. He argued that the former, although an important step, would not alone suffice to solve the political problem faced by the regime—and that in order for autocracy to survive the government had to foresee problems and take appropriate measures ahead of time. P. A. Valuev, "O vnutrennem sostoianii Rossii (26 June 1862)" in V. V. Garmiza, "Predpolozheniia i proekty P. A. Valueva po voprosam vnutrennei politike (1862-1866gg.)," *Istoricheskii arkhiv,* 3 (January-February 1958): 143-144.

35. Biographical material is from Zaionchkovskii, "P. A. Valuev," 17-54, and the service record in TsGIA SSSR F. 1284 op. 76 d. 70.

36. Recently one scholar included Valuev among the aristocratic party of Reform Era ministers, as opposed to a group of poorer and less prominent *arrivistes.* This claim is based on a faulty notion of Valuev's actual social and economic position and an uncritical acceptance of contemporary accusations that Valuev had social pretensions. See Helju Aulik Bennet, "The *Chin* System and the *Raznochintsy* in the Government of Alexander III, 1881-1894" (Ph.D. diss., University of California, Berkeley, 1971), 126-127.

37. Lincoln, "The Ministers of Nicholas I," 308-323; Zaionchkovskii, *Pravitel'stvennyi apparat,* 106-142.

38. Valuev, *Dnevnik,* 1:104.

39. Starr, *Decentralization,* 178-179.

40. Miliutina, "Iz zapisok," *Russkaia starina,* 97 (January 1899): 59-64; Valuev, "Dnevnik grafa," *Russkaia starina,* 71 (August 1891): 48, 140-152,

273; Valuev, *Dnevnik*, 1:103.

41. P. D. Stremoukhov, "Iz vospominanii o grafe P. A. Valueva," *Russkaia starina*, 116 (November 1903): 274-275.

42. Valuev, *Dnevnik*, 1:104.

43. See the revealing correspondence between Troinitskii and Valuev: G. A. Troinitskii, ed., "P. A. Valuev i A. G. Troinitskii," *Russkaia starina*, 99 (July 1899): 225-240; (August 1899), 467-480; (September 1899), 697-706; 100 (October 1899): 231-239. For Troinitskii's service record, see TsGIA SSSR F. 1162 op. 6 d. 555; A. V. Nikitenko, *Dnevnik A. V. Nikitenko*, 3 vols. (Moscow-Leningrad, 1955), 3:76.

44. Valuev claims to have made this point directly to Alexander as early as August 1861. P. A. Valuev, "Graf P. A. Valuev o polozhenii Rossi v 1882 godu," *Minuvshie gody*, 1, no. 9 (September 1908): 25-31.

45. The term "enlightened conservative" was apparently D. A. Miliutin's. Quoted in Zaionchkovskii, "P. A. Valuev," 42.

46. P. A. Valuev, "Duma russkago (vo vtoroi polovine 1855 g.)," *Russkaia starina*, 70 (May 1891): 349-360.

47. Ibid., p. 354.

48. *Materialy o preobrazovanii gubernskikh, otdel administrativnyi*, 1, part 4, 197-206; Valuev, "Duma russkago," 355-356; Starr, *Decentralization*, 179.

49. Actually, Valuev was ambivalent about decentralization within the ministries because Russian officials at the middle and low levels of the hierarchy lacked competence. He was dissatisfied with the prevailing system of centralization mainly because it was not effective—that is, so many important matters were referred to the minister that he could not possibly make all the necessary decisions and many were made by section or desk chiefs (whose ability to make such decisions he evidently did not trust). The implication was that the minister should have made all the important political decisions; and that is exactly the way Valuev tried to run the MVD during his seven-year tenure as minister. Valuev, "Duma russkago," 355; Valuev, *Dnevnik*, 1:100, 120-121.

50. Valuev, "Graf P. A. Valuev o polozhenii Rossii," 29-30. See also *Dnevnik*, 1:74, 98-102, 144; 2:48.

51. See, for example, Nikitenko, *Dnevnik*, 3:1-17, 48, 90-92; Miliutin, *Dnevnik*, vol. 3.

52. Valuev, "Graf P. A. Valuev o polozhenii Rossii," 28; *Dnevnik*, 1:71, 206-211; 2:102, 363-364; *Dnevnik 1877-1884*, 5-22.

53. Valuev, "O vnutrennem polozhenii Rossii 1864 g.," 145-146; *Dnevnik*, 2:416-417. Valuev had read and admired thinkers as diverse as Lorenz von Stein and Alexis de Tocqueville. See Herbert Marcuse, *Reason and Revolution: Hegel and the Rise of Modern Social Theory* (Boston, 1960), 374-388. For a discussion by one of Valuev's contemporaries, see A. D. Gradovskii, "Chto takoe konservatizm," in *Sobranie sochinenii*, 3:313-346. Gradovskii defines a creative conservatism and points to Robert Peel as an example.

54. Valuev, *Dnevnik*, 2:416-417. See, in particular, Peter Czap, Jr., "P. A. Valuyev's Proposal for a *Vyt'* Administration, 1864," *The Slavonic and East*

European Review, 45, no. 105 (July 1967): 391-410. Valuev consistently pressed for policies that would promote the creation of an infrastructure for economic development. He wanted to ease various legal restraints on Russian social groups and estates to unleash the productive forces of the country. Throughout the period 1861-1881 Valuev maintained that financial and economic questions, or crises as he termed them, including agrarian matters, were the most important problems faced by the government.

55. The memorandum, which is located in TsGIA F. 1093 (Collection of P. E. Shchegolev) op. 1 d. 338, was discovered and extracts published and analyzed by the Soviet historian V. G. Chernukha in "Programmnaia zapiska ministra vnutrennikh del P. A. Valueva ot 22 sentiabria 1861 g.," in Akademiia Nauk SSSR, Otdelenie Istorii, Leningradskoe Otdelenie, *Vspomogatel'nye istoricheskie distsipliny*, 7 (Leningrad, 1976): 210-220.

56. Chernukha, "Programmnaia zapiska," 217.

57. Valuev, "O vnutrennem sostoianii Rossii 26 iiunia 1862 g."; Garmiza, "Predpolozheniia i proekty," 141-144.

58. Garmiza, *Podgotovka*, 155-163; Bermanskii, "Konstitutsionnye proekty," 229-230; Zakharova, *Zemskaia kontrreforma*, 52-54.

59. Bermanskii, "Konstitutsionnye proekty," 225-233; Zakharova, *Zemskaia kontrreforma*, 49-52. See also Valuev, *Dnevnik*, 1:218-219, 256-257, 261.

60. Zakharova, *Zemskaia kontrreforma*, 48-49.

61. Valuev, "Dnevnik grafa," *Russkaia starina*, 72 (1891): 146.

62. Valuev, "O vnutrennem sostoianii Rossii 26 iiunia 1862 g.," 141.

63. Valuev, "O vnutrennem polozhenii Rossii (1864 g.)," 148, 151.

64. Chernukha, *Krest'ianskii vopros*, 25-69. During 1861-1863 Valuev assumed that the peace mediators acted too independently in negotiating with landlords and peasants to prepare land charters. In 1862 he ordered a senatorial revision in Kaluga Province that was aimed at Governor V. Artsimovich, a known comrade of the Miliutin group and ostensible supporter of peasant interests against the nobility. Valuev simultaneously was sparring with peace mediators in Tver Province who had connections to Unkovskii's liberal gentry group in Tver. The peace mediators, directly linked to the Senate as well as to the MVD, clearly represented a breach in the clean lines of hierarchy that Valuev wished to establish. Though he could not eliminate the peace mediators during his ministry, he did succeed in driving many from office and in reducing their efficiency in the countryside.

65. Valuev to Urusov, May 1, 1866, TsGIA SSSR F. 908 op. 1 d. 198 ll. 52-53.

66. Valuev, "O polozhenii gubernskago upravleniia," TsGIA SSSR F. 908 op. 1 d. 277 1. 95.

67. TsGIA SSSR F. 908 op. 1 d. 277 ll. 116-117.

68. For an enlightening discussion of ideology and the symbolic dimension of political ideas during periods of rapid social and economic change, see Clifford Geertz, "Ideology as a Cultural System," in *The Interpretation of Cultures: Selected Essays* (New York, 1973), 216-220. Geertz writes: "When traditional and hallowed opinions and rules of life come into question, the

search for systematic ideological formulations, either to reinforce them or to replace them, flourishes. The function of ideology is to make an autonomous politics possible by providing the authoritative concepts that render it meaningful, the suasive images by means of which it can be sensibly grasped" (216). "Ideologies provide symbolic frames against which to match the unfamiliar . . . produced by a transformation in political life" (220). See also J. G. A. Pocock, *Politics, Language and Time: Essays on Political Thought and History* (New York, 1973), 3-41; and Karl Mannheim, "Conservative Thought," in Kurt Wolff, ed., *From Karl Mannheim* (New York, 1971), 132-222.

69. Nikitenko, *Dnevnik*, 3:49, 52, 54, 69, 71, 76, 92.

70. Ibid., 3:61, 80, 82, 90.

71. TsGIA SSSR F. 851 (Collection of A. V. Golovnin) op. 1 d. 8 ll. 9ob.-18.

72. TsGIA SSSR F. 1284 op. 66 d. 11 l. 86.

73. See especially "O merakh k usileniiu administrativnoi vlasti," TsGIA SSSR F. 908 op. 1 d. 277 ll. 40-59; and "O polozhenii gubernskago upravleniia," TsGIA SSSR F. 908 op. 1 d. 277 ll. 60-95.

74. Seredonin, *Istoricheskii obzor*, 3, part 1, 130-143. The minister of justice, Zamiatnin, and the minister of finance, Reutern, were invited to submit commentaries prior to debate in the special commission and the Committee of Ministers. Both men vehemently opposed any extension of MVD authority in the provinces. They saw the proposed authority of the governors as greater than that of the old *voevody*.

75. Valuev, "O polozhenii gubernskago upravleniia," TsGIA SSSR F. 908 op. 1 d. 277 ll. 60-95.

76. Valuev, "O merakh k usileniiu administrativnoi vlasti," TsGIA SSSR F. 908 op. 1 d. 277 ll. 40-41.

77. On the creation of the Jurisconsult Section in 1866, see TsGIA SSSR F. 1149 (State Council, Department of Laws) op. 6 d. 48 ll. 12-17. On the 1880 merger, see *PSZ* II, no. 61,551 (November 15, 1880), and TsGIA SSSR F. 1284 op. 233 d. 6, "Ob uchrezhdenii iuriskonsul'tskoi chasti pri MVD."

Materials on the Adlerberg and Butkov commissions of 1865-1867 may be found in TsGIA SSSR F. 1190 op. 16 d. 15; the memoranda and journal of the 1867 commission chaired by Tizengauzen in TsGIA SSSR F. 908 op. 1 d. 274; the journals of an 1870 commission on the relationship between the police and the courts, also in F. 908 op. 1 d. 274; and the materials of an 1876 commission chaired by Kititsyn, the MVD jurisconsult, in TsGIA SSSR F. 1284 op. 233 d. 3. See also the voluminous materials on the series of ongoing commissions on the relationship between the administration and the judiciary contained in TsGIA SSSR F. 1405 (Ministry of Justice) op. 64 d. 7614a, 7614b; and F. 1405 op. 76 d. 7185, 7186. See, for example, the laws of May 19, 1871 (*PSZ* II, no. 49,615); June 7, 1872 (*PSZ* II, no. 50,956); the rules of September 1, 1878 (not in *PSZ*) and the law of August 9, 1878 (*PSZ* II, no. 58,778). These measures served to strengthen the power of the administration and police in relation to the courts and court officials—particularly in the area of so-called political crimes. These and other laws and measures are discussed in Vilenskii, *Sudebnaia reforma*, 308-310, 322-323; Zaionchkovskii, *Krizis samoderzhaviia*, 76-79.

78. TsGIA SSSR F. 1190 op. 16 d. 15, F. 1149 op. 6 d. 48 ll. 12-17.

79. Kititsyn's service record is found in TsGIA SSSR F. 1291 op. 123 d. 102 ll. 42-59.

80. TsGIA SSSR F. 1149 op. 6 d. 48 ll. 27-30.

81. See the memoranda and other documents in TsGIA SSSR F. 908 op. 1 d. 277, collectively titled "Bumagi P. A. Valueva kasaiushchiesia administratsii, politsii, i sudebnykh reform v Rossii."

82. Material on Timashev's life is scarce, a remarkable fact considering that he served as minister for ten years. He did not capture the fancy of historians, so existing histories have little material to offer about him. Basic biographical information is found in TsGIA SSSR F. 1687 op. 1 d. 5 (his career record) and in *Entsiklopedicheskii slovar'*, 33:180.

83. GBL OR F. D. A. Miliutina No. 169 k. 11 p. 9 l. 8, quoted by P. A. Zaionchkovskii, "P. A. Valuev," 44; Valuev, *Dnevnik*, 1:89-90.

84. See, for example, Abbott, "Police Reform," 182-236; Chernukha, "Problema politicheskoi reformy," 138-191; *Krest'ianskii vopros*; Korf, *Administrativnaia iustitsiia*, 1:306-320; John G. Gantvoort, "Relations between Government and Zemstvos under Valuev and Timashev, 1864-1876" (Ph.D. diss., University of Illinois, 1971); I. V. Orzhekhovskii, *Administratsiia i pechat' mezhdu dvumia revoliutsionnymi situatsiiami (1866-1878 gg.) (Gor'kii, 1973)*, 65-92; Orzhekhovskii, *Iz istorii*, 57-134.

85. GBL OR F. D. A. Miliutina no. 169 k. 11 p. 9 l. 8, quoted by Zaionchkovskii, "P. A. Valuev," 44.

86. Chernukha, "Problema politicheskoi reformy," 146-147; Orzhekhovskii, *Iz istorii*, 57-134. Another example of his indifference to affairs is provided in the memoirs of N. G. Zalesov, who, as an official of special missions, appeared before Timashev in 1870. On all questions the minister answered, "I don't remember, check with the department as to the state of that matter etc." Quoted in Chernukha, *Vnutrenniaia politika*, 79. TsGIA SSSR F. 908 op. 1 d. 629 l. 1ob. and F. 1642 op. 1 d. 193 l. 44, quoted in Chernukha, "Problema politicheskoi reformy," 147.

87. B. N. Chicherin, *Vospominaniia Borisa Nikolaevicha Chicherina: Zemstvo i Moskovskaia Duma (Moscow, 1934)*, 94; V. P. Meshcherskii (kniaz'), *Moi vospominaniia chast' vtoraia (1865-1881gg.) (St. Petersburg, 1898)*, 126-128, 153; A. A. Polovtsov, *Dnevnik gosudarstvennogo sekretaria A. A. Polovtsova v dvukh tomakh (1887-1892 gg.)*, 2 (Moscow, 1966): 174; Valuev, *Dnevnik*, 2:250-260, 289, 303.

88. V. K. Lutskii, "Iz zapisok V. K. Lutskago," *Russkaia starina*, 118 (May 1904): 334-335.

89. A. D. Shumakher, "Neskol'ko slov o g.-a. Timasheva i otnoshenii ego k obshchestvennym uchrezhdeniiam," *Vestnik evropy*, 6, no. 12 (1893): 846-857.

90. Valuev, *Dnevnik*, 2:367.

91. Various papers and memoranda relating to the press, censorship, and plans to create a government newpaper are located in TsGIA SSSR F. 1687 op. 1 d. 23, 24, 25, and 26. Timashev was serving as the Third Section's representative on the Main Directorate of Censorship at that time. His censorship policy while minister of internal affairs is analyzed by Orzhekhovskii, *Adminis-*

tratsiia i pechat', 65-92.

92. Materials, including newspaper accounts of Timashev's service as governor-general, are in TsGIA SSSR F. 1687, op. 1 d. 30. See also Timashev's letters of May 31 and June 28, 1863, to V. A. Dolgorukov, the head of the Third Section, in TsGIA SSSR F. 1687 op. 1 d. 45 ll. 32-35ob.

93. Letter of P. A. Shuvalov to Timashev dated October 2/14, 1867, TsGIA SSSR F. 1687 op. 1 d. 45 ll. 32-35ob.

94. Timashev to Valuev, July 16, 1863, TsGIA SSSR F. 1687 op. 1 d. 44 l. 1.

95. Valuev, *Dnevnik*, 2:246-247, 496-499, 255-256.

96. Ibid., 252.

97. Ibid., 254, 289. Again, in 1874, Timashev proposed transfer of the Main Directorate of Press Affairs to the Ministry of Education. His aim ostensibly was to lesson the burdens upon the MVD.

98. "Zapiska o prichinakh neobkhodimosti sozdaniia V otdelenie Ego I. V. Kantseliarii dlia nabludeniia za napravlenie literaturoi," TsGIA SSSR F. 1687 op. 1 d. 25.

99. TsGIA SSSR F. 1687 op. 1 d. 37 ll. 35-40.

100. Valuev, *Dnevnik* 2:290-291.

101. Timashev to Alexander II, January 4, 1874, TsGIA SSSR F. 1687 op. 1 d. 40 ll. 7-7ob.

102. Valuev, *Dnevnik*, 2:312, 387.

103. "Dokladnaia zapiska Ministra Vnutrennikh Del Aleksandru II o podchinenii dvorian rekrutskoi povinnosti," TsGIA SSSR F. 1687 op. 1 d. 39 ll. 7-12.

104. Forrestt A. Miller, *Dmitrii Miliutin and the Reform Era in Russia* (Nashville, 1968), 182-230; P. A. Zaionchkovskii, *Voennye reformy 1860-1870 gg. v Rossii* (Moscow, 1952), 254-337.

105. TsGIA SSSR F. 1687 op. 1 d. 39 ll. 7-12.

106. Ibid.

107. On MVD policy in the Baltic region, see Michael H. Haltzel, "The Reaction of the Baltic Germans to Russification during the Nineteenth Century" (Ph.D. diss., Harvard University, 1971), 132-219.

108. Feoktistov, *Za kulisami*, 108-109.

109. In his retirement speech, Timashev listed the problems that he considered most troublesome for the minister of internal affairs, including (1) the Baltic and Polish administration; (2) municipal reform; (3) the 1874 law on military obligations; (4) mobilization of the army; (5) the military situation; (6) the threat of epidemic; (7) the political situation of recent years. Compare these concerns with those of Valuev in his four memoranda of 1868. TsGIA SSSR F. 1687 op. 1 d. 9 ll. 1-37.

One unusual example of Timashev's taking a position in defense of the MVD's institutional integrity occurred in 1868, several months after he took office. In a letter to Alexander of December 22, 1868, he complained about disagreements between the governor-general of Kiev and the MVD. Timashev petitioned the tsar to appoint another governor-general, one with experience in civil administration and one with whom he, as minister, could work. Timashev thus, almost unwittingly, upheld the integrity of the regular ministry institutions, a position he might well not have taken had he not been minister of internal affairs. TsGIA SSSR F. 1687 op. 1 d. 38 ll. 1-3.

110. Information on Makov's life is found in his service record, TsGIA SSSR F. 1162 op. 6 d. 309 ll. 40-67; see also *Entsiklopedicheskii slovar'*, 35: 430; K. A. Skal'kovskii, ed., *Nashi gosudarstvennye i obshchestvennye deiateli* (St. Petersburg, 1890), 220-231; "Iz obshchestvennoi khroniki—1-e aprelia 1883," *Vestnik evropy*, 4, no. 2 (1883): 892-901.

111. *Nashi gosudarstvennye*, 221.

112. See note 110. Also, Feoktistov, *Za kulisami*, 185-186; Polovtsov, *Dnevnik*, 1:55-57, 64. The reasons for the suicide are not clear. Makov was linked to S. Perfil'ev, who embezzled a large sum of money while holding high office in the MVD. The author of the sketch in *Nashi gosudarstvennye* states that Makov was too religious and upright to have stolen money. There were also accusations of bribe-taking from Old Believers.

113. Valuev, *Dnevnik*, 2:262.

114. Valuev, *Dnevnik 1877-1884*, 33-34, 51, 78.

115. E. A. Peretts, *Dnevnik E. A. Perettsa, gosudarstvennogo sekretaria (1880-1883)* (Moscow-Leningrad, 1927), 15.

116. The Kapger revision was instigated by Valuev to remove the liberal governor of Kaluga Province, V. A. Artsimovich, who was viewed as hostile to local landowners in the application of the emancipation statutes.

117. *Nashi gosudarstvennye*, 222.

118. Makov was named acting minister on November 27, 1878. It is possible that Alexander was still preoccupied with the Turkish War and its diplomatic aftermath, and that he gave little thought to the vital appointment of minister of internal affairs. It should be noted that Prince Meshcherskii was shocked at the appointment and claimed that it was greeted with "bewilderment" in St. Petersburg. Meshcherskii saw the appointment as a sad sign of the times. While Makov was an "amiable man" and a good composer of official papers, hence a good director of the MVD chancery and assistant minister, he was not cut out to be the head of the MVD. According to Meshcherskii, the office was the most difficult in the empire and its occupant had the most important political role. Meshcherskii, somewhat surprisingly, had been a harsh critic of Timashev's performance as minister as well, but with the appointment of Makov, he stated, "the prestige of the post faded and the political role of the Ministry of Internal Affairs was reduced to the palest and most passive of all government institutions." Meshcherskii, *Moi vospominaniia*, 2:412-416.

119. Makov, *Kratkii ocherk*, 73. Makov boasted that in years past there had been only chinovniki, but now there were "police in the strictest sense of the word." See also Zaionchkovskii, *Krizis samoderzhaviia*, 68n.

120. Quoted in Zaionchkovskii, *Krizis samoderzhaviia*, 68n.

121. Abbott, "Police Reform," 250.

122. Zaionchkovskii, *Krizis samoderzhaviia*, 68-143; Valuev, *Dnevnik 1877-1884*, 33-62; Tatishchev, *Imperator Aleksandr II*, 2:558-573.

123. Miliutin, *Dnevnik D. A. Miliutina 1878-1880* (Moscow, 1950), 129.

124. *Pravitel'stvennyi vestnik*, August 19, 1878; Zaionchkovskii, *Krizis samoderzhaviia*, 80-81.

125. This was quoted in "Iz obshchestvennoi khroniki 1-e aprelia 1883,"

Vestnik evropy, 4, no. 2 (1883): 900. It seems that Makov momentarily lost control. He picked up a copy of the liberal newspaper *The Voice* (*Golos*) and began reading from one of the articles. As he read, he grew angrier and angrier and ordered his assistant to issue a warning to *The Voice* on the spot. Then someone pointed out, much to Makov's embarrassment, that the article was, in fact, a telegram passed by special government censorship which had appeared in all the daily newspapers, including *Pravitel'stvennyi vestnik*.

126. Zaionchkovskii, *Krizis samoderzhaviia*, 261-269; Valuev, *Dnevnik 1877-1884*, 122-127.

127. Zaionchkovskii, *Krizis samoderzhaviia*, 140-141.

128. See, for example, the correspondence in TsGIA SSSR F. 1282 op. 1 d. 640. The pattern usually began with a secret communication from Loris-Melikov to Makov asking either for information or for appropriate edicts to be sent to provincial governors, police officials, and so on. Makov would then refer the matter to the appropriate department director. Another way in which Loris-Melikov used Makov was the ouster of Tolstoi as minister of education and procurator of the Holy Synod. Loris instigated a spat between the two men during which Tolstoi impugned Makov's honor (accused him of taking money from Old Believers for services rendered). As a result, Tolstoi was forced to resign. Feoktistov, *Za kulisami*, 185-186; Valuev, *Dnevnik 1877-1884*, 82-87. Loris-Melikov gloated over his victory, which was applauded by liberal public opinion. Miliutin, *Dnevnik 1880-1881*, 243.

129. Valuev, *Dnevnik 1877-1884*, 104-108; Zaionchkovskii, *Krizis samoderzhaviia*, 234-235.

130. Zaionchkovskii, *Krizis samoderzhaviia*, 222-227.

131. Peretts, *Dnevnik*, 1. Every day at 11:00 A.M. Makov and his predecessor, Timashev, used to present the tsar with a report on the opened mails.

132. Makov to Loris-Melikov, July 21, 1880, TsGAOR F. 569 op. 1 d. 59 ll. 5-9. Makov to K. P. Pobedonostsev, March 8, 1881, *K. P. Pobedonostsev i ego korrespondenty, pis'ma i zapiski s predisloviem M. N. Pokrovskogo*, 2 vols. (Moscow-Petrograd, 1923), 1:160-162.

133. Makov had, in fact, taken the initiative and received permission from Alexander to reopen the question of rewriting the censorship legislation. This was part of the background to the Valuev conference in the autumn of 1880. Loris was suspicious of these initiatives, which strengthened his resolve to take the post of minister of internal affairs himself.

134. Makov to K. P. Pobedonostsev, March 8, 1881.

135. On Makov's performance at the fateful March 8 meeting, see Peretts, *Dnevnik*, 32-47; Valuev, *Dnevnik 1877-1884*, 151-154; Miliutin, *Dnevnik 1881-1882*, 35-37; V. A. Bil'basov, *Byloe*, books 4-5 (1918), 185-193. See also Hans Heilbronner, "Alexander III and the Reform Plan of Loris-Melikov," *Journal of Modern History*, 33 (December 1961): 384-397.

136. TsGIA SSSR F. 866 (Collection of M. T. Loris-Melikov), op. 1 d. 1; *RBS*, 10:694-700; Skal'kovskii, *Nashi gosudarstvennye*, 201-214; M. T. Loris-Melikov, "Ispoved' grafa Loris-Melikova" (Loris-Melikov to A. A. Skal'kovskii, October 14, 1881), *Katorga i ssylka*, 2, no. 15 (1925): 118-125.

137. The incident is recounted in N. A. Belogolovyi, "Graf Mikhail Tariel-

ovich Loris-Melikov, 1878-1888," in *Vospominaniia i drugie stat'i*, 3rd ed. (Mocow, 1898), 176-177. Loris was a close friend of the poet Nekrasov during his early years in St. Petersburg. Ibid., 177-178. Loris-Melikov is one of the main characters in L. N. Tolstoi's well-known story "Khadzhi Murat."

138. The best general presentation of these events is Zaionchkovskii, *Krizis samoderzhaviia*, 148-230.

139. *RBS*, 19:694-695; TsGIA SSSR F. 866 op. 1 d. l. 64.

140. TsGIA SSSR F. 866 op. 1 d. 1; Han Heilbronner, "The Russian Plague of 1878-79," *Slavic Review*, 21, no. 1 (March 1962): 89-112.

141. W. Bruce Lincoln, "The Ministers of Nicholas I: A Brief Inquiry into Their Backgrounds and Service Careers," *The Russian Review*, 34, no. 3 (July 1975).

142. Indeed, this is borne out by another Lincoln study, "The Ministers of Alexander II," *Cahiers du monde russe et soviétique*, 17, no. 4 (1976).

4. High Officials and Their Careers, 1855-1881

1. See, for example, the essays in Pintner and Rowney, *Russian Officialdom*. In studying this small group of officials serving in one central government organ, I used demographic materials not only to shed light on Russia's governing elite as a social group, but also to explore connections between the background and experience of Russia's governing elite, on the one hand, and their ideas and performance as officials, on the other.

2. My analysis is based largely on personnel records (*formuliarnye spiski*) located in Soviet archives. A variety of published sources provided more information about promotions and the officials' own view of career prospects than did the personnel records. Although the records have many shortcomings, their use permits much more complete coverage of the holders of the offices considered (biographical material was available for only about 30 percent of the 87 men). This sampling of officials represents approximately 80 percent of those who held departmental directorships and the office of assistant minister during Alexander's reign. (Archivists were unable to locate the records of the remaining 20 percent.) In some cases, such as assistant minister or director of the Department of State Police, the representation is complete. For the lower offices (vice-directors and members of collegial bodies) the representation is lower, 50 to 70 percent depending on the office.

All the personnel records are located in the Central State Historical Archive of the Soviet Union in Leningrad (TsGIA SSSR). Most of the material is in the *fond* of the MVD's Department of General Affairs, the ministry organ concerned with personnel, or in the *fondy* of the ministry departments in which the officials worked. The following *fondy* were used: F. 1284, Department of General Affairs, MVD; F. 776, Main Directorate Press Affairs; F. 821, Department of Religious Affairs of Foreign Faiths; F. 1162, State Council; F. 1349, personnel records gathered for the Heraldry Office of the governing Senate. After 1857 the Senate no longer kept personnel records for the entire civil service. The MVD had responsibility for keeping its own records, and was particularly disorganized in carrying out this task. The inventories (*opisi*) for the Department of General Affairs do not include personnel records. An excellent discussion of the history and meaning of *formuliarnye spiski* is found in Z. I. Malkova and M. A. Pliukhina, "Dokumenty vyshikh i tsentral'nykh uchrezhdenii XIX nachala XX v. kak istochnik biograficheskikh svedenii," in Glavnoe Arkhivnoe Upravlenie SSSR, *Nekotorye voprosy izucheniia istoricheskikh dokumentov XIX-nachala XX: Sbornik statei* (Leningrad, 1967), pp. 204-208. Apart from memoirs and diaries, the best source for career information is the incomplete *Russkii biograficheskii slovar'*. Often the biographies in *RBS* are taken from the official spiski.

3. Marc Raeff, "The Russian Autocracy and Its Officials," *Harvard Slavic Studies IV: Russian Thought and Politics* (Cambridge, Mass., 1957), 77-91; Hans-Joachim Torke, "Das russische Beamtentum."

4. Raeff, "Russian Autocracy," 87-88.

5. Ibid., 68.

6. Torke, "Das russische Beamtentum," 7-48, 285-309.

7. See especially Walter M. Pintner's contribution to Pintner & Rowney, *Russian Officialdom*; Pintner, "The Social Characteristics of the Early Nineteenth Century Russian Bureaucracy," *Slavic Review*, 29, no. 3 (September 1970): 429-443. P. A. Zaionchkovskii has published another analysis of mid-nineteenth-century officialdom, "Vysshaia biurokratiia nakanune krymskoi voiny," *Istoriia SSSR*, no. 4 (July-August 1974): 154-165. The most complete study is a recently published article by W. Bruce Lincoln, "A Profile of the Russian Bureaucracy on the Eve of the Great Reforms," *Jahrbücher für Geschichte Osteuropas*, Band 27, Heft 2 (1979), 181-196. Similar material for the eighteenth century is found in S. M. Troitskii, *Russkii absoliutizm*, 155-295. For the second half of the nineteenth century, see V. R. Leikina-Svirskaia, *Intelligentsiia v Rossii vo vtoroi polovine XIX veka* (Moscow, 1971), 71-91; Orzhekhovskii, *Iz istorii*, 26-56; Zaionchkovskii, *Pravitel'stvennyi apparat*, 179-220. For the early twentieth century, Don Karl Rowney, "Higher Civil Servants in the Russian Ministry of Internal Affairs: Some Demographic and Career Characteristics, 1905-1916," *Slavic Review*, 31, no. 1 (March 1972): 101-110. Several more recent articles follow a basic prosopographical methodology: W. B. Lincoln, "The Ministers of Alexander II," *Cahiers du monde russe et soviétique*, 17, no. 4 (1976): 467-484; "The Editing Commissions of 1859-1860, II," *Slavonic and East European Review*, 56, no. 3 (1979); "The Composition of the Imperial Russian State Council under Nicholas I," *Canadian-American Slavic Studies*, 10, no. 3 (1976): 369-381; W. E. Mosse, "Aspects of Tsarist Bureaucracy: Recruitment to the Imperial State Council, 1855-1914," *Slavonic and East European Review*, 57, no. 2 (1979). The most complete study in any language to date of the trappings of service in tsarist Russia is L. E. Shepelev, *Otmenennye istoriei chiny, zvaniia i tituly v Rossiiskoi imperii* (Leningrad, 1977). More complete references to recent works on Russian officialdom may be found in Orlovsky, "Recent Studies on the Russian Bureaucracy," *The Russian Review*, 35, no. 4 (October 1976): 448-467.

8. Zaionchkovskii, "Vysshaia biurokratiia," 164. Zaionchkovskii has also located in the archives of the First Section reliable figures for the growth of bureaucracy during the Crimean War. The following figures represent the number of officials possessing *chin* (p. 55): 1847—61,548; 1850—71,819; 1856 —82,352.

9. W. Bruce Lincoln, "The Circle of the Grand Duchess Yelena Pavlovna, 1847-1861," *Slavonic and East European Review*, 48, no. 112 (July 1970): 373-387; "Genesis of an 'Enlightened' Bureaucracy in Russia"; "Miliutin"; "Russia's 'Enlightened' Bureaucrats." See also Richard Wortman, "Judicial Personnel and the Court Reform of 1864," *Canadian Slavic Studies*, 3, no. 2 (Summer 1969): 224-234; and Wortman, *Development of a Russian Legal Consciousness*.

10. G. F. W. Hegel, *The Philosophy of Right*, tr. T. M. Knox (Oxford, 1942), esp. 155-161; Z. A. Pelczynski, ed., *Hegel's Political Philosophy, Problems and Perspectives* (Cambridge, 1971); Hans Rosenberg, *Bureaucracy, Aristocracy, and Autocracy: The Prussian Experience, 1660-1815* (Cambridge, Mass., 1958).

11. See, for example, Emmons, *Russian Landed Gentry*; Field, *End of Serfdom*; Zaionchkovskii, *Otmena krepostnogo prava v Rossii* (Moscow, 1954); V. V. Garmiza, *Podgotovka zemskoi reformy 1864 goda* (Moscow, 1957); Starr, *Decentralization*; Friedhelm Barthold Kaiser, *Die russische Justizreform von 1864: zur Geschichte der russischen Justiz von Katharina II bis 1917* (Leiden, 1972); Wortman, *Development of a Russian Legal Consciousness*.

12. A. D. Shumakher, "Pozdnyia vospominaniia o davno minuvshikh vremenakh," *Vestnik evropy*, 196, no. 3 (1899): 89-128; W. Bruce Lincoln, "The Daily Life of St. Petersburg Officials in the Mid-Nineteenth Century," *Oxford Slavonic Papers*, n.s., 8 (Oxford, 1975): 82-100; Lincoln, "Miliutin"; see also Sidney Monas, "Bureaucracy in Russia under Nicholas I" in M. Cherniavsky, ed., *The Structure of Russian History: Interpretive Essays* (New York, 1970), 269-281.

13. Kipp, "Grand Duke Konstantin Nikolaevich"; S. M. Seredonin, *Istoricheskii obzor deiatel'nosti komiteta ministrov*, 3 vols. (St. Petersburg, 1902), vol. 1.

14. Many example could be cited here from the memoirs, memoranda, and other writings of the men included in this sample. For a classic statement of this point of view by one of the ministry officials, see B. Obukhov, *Russkii administrator noveishei shkoly: Zapiska pskovskogo gubernatora i otvet na nee* (Berlin, 1868); D. N. Tolstoi, "Zapiski grafa Dmitriia Nikolaevicha Tolstogo," *Russkii arkhiv*, 23, no. 2 (1885): 5-33.

15. Michel Crozier emphasizes the importance of analyzing the "bureaucratic experience" within the institutional and historical context in which officials lived and worked. I follow him in viewing bureaucracy as, first of all, a national experience, the historical product of a specific culture and society, but also as an institutional experience. See Michel Crozier, *The Bureaucratic Phenomenon* (Chicago, 1967), 1-9, 145-269.

16. All tables are derived from the formuliarnye spiski discussed in note 2, *RBS*, and memoirs.

17. This remarkable figure compares most favorably with the age span of 43-52 offered by John Armstrong as a general guideline for the attainment of high office by the European administrative elite. John A. Armstrong, *The European Administrative Elite* (Princeton, 1973), 239.

18. See, for example, P. Dolgorukov, *Rossiiskaia rodoslovnaia kniga*, 4

parts (St. Petersburg, 1854-1857); A. Bobrinskoi, *Dvorianskie rody vnesen-nye v obshchii gerbovnik vserossiiskoi imperii*, 2 parts (St. Petersburg, 1890); *Russkaia rodoslovnaia kniga izdanie "Russkoi stariny,"* 2 vols. (St. Petersburg, 1873, 1875).

19. On the history and expansion of the service nobility in the eighteenth century, see especially Troitskii, *Russkii absoliutizm*; Brenda Meehan-Waters, "The Russian Aristocracy and the Reforms of Peter the Great," *Canadian-American Slavic Studies*, 8, no. 2 (Summer 1974): 288-302; Robert E. Jones, *The Emancipation of the Russian Nobility, 1762-1785* (Princeton, 1973).

20. V. A. Insarskii, "Zapiski Vasiliia Antonovicha Insarskago," *Russkaia starina*, 81 (January 1894): 4-20; Tolstoi, "Zapiski," 5-10; "Mezhdu strokami odnogo formuliarnogo spiska 1823-1881," (signed A. K.), *Russkaia starina*, 32 (1881): 817-855; B. N. Chicherin, *Vospominaniia Borisa Nikolaevicha Chicherina: Moskva sorokovykh godov* (Moscow, 1929).

21. Assessing the significance of the property holdings listed in the *spiski* is difficult because of the absence of uniform categories in the listings. The number of serfs is listed in some and amounts of land in others. It is unclear whether those officials with land listings only did not own serfs as well. If, in fact, those with landholdings did not own serfs, it would imply that the civil servants were even less well off than the table indicates.

22. Pintner, "Social Characteristics," 440.

23. Zaionchkovskii gives the following percentages of Germans in the highest government organs for 1853: State Council, 16.3 percent; Senate, 10.8 percent; Committee of Ministers, 1.1 percent; assistant ministers and directors of departments, 15.2 percent. Thus, the number of Lutherans seems to have decreased slightly at the assistant minister and department director levels during the Reform Era. Rowney finds only 5 percent Lutherans among high MVD managers in 1905. Zaionchkovskii, "Vysshaia biurokratiia," 157, 159, 161-162; Rowney, "Higher Civil Servants," 103.

24. James E. Flynn, "The Universities, the Gentry and the Russian Imperial Services, 1815-1825," *Canadian Slavic Studies*, 2 (Winter 1968): 486-503. See also Patrick L. Alston, *Education and the State in Tsarist Russia* (Stanford, 1969); Torke, "Das russische Beamtentum," 137-173; Allen Sinel, *The Classroom and the Chancellery: State Educational Reform in Russia under Count Dmitry Tolstoi* (Cambridge, Mass., 1973), 1-33; Wortman, *Development of a Russian Legal Consciousness*, 35-50.

25. Troitskii, *Russkii absoliutizm*, 267-295. For the seventeenth century, see B. Plavsic's discussion in Pintner and Rowney, *Russian Officialdom*.

26. Functionally, the educational reforms of the early nineteenth century played a similar role to those of the eighteenth century. In both cases the state viewed the educational experience as the first step on the service ladder. Thus, the junker schools of the eighteenth century may be seen as more primitive versions of the later universities in terms of their function as preparatory schools for officials.

27. *Svod zakonov Rossiiskoi Imperii*, 16 vols. (St. Petersburg, 1857), 3, part I, "Ustav o Sluzhbe Grazhdanskoi po opredeleniiu ot pravitel'stva" (hereafter cited as *Svod zakonov* [1857], articles 1-87 (*o priniatii v grazhdanskuiu*

sluzhbu i opredelenii k dolzhnostiam). Articles 88-351 discuss the service rights pertaining to all the empire's educational institutions, including the rights to enter service and to receive rank upon graduation. See also Torke, "Das russische Beamtentum," 97-102.

28. Torke, "Das russische Beamtentum," 1-48, 102-173; Rosenberg, *Bureaucracy, Aristocracy and Autocracy,* 46-74, 137-228. My view differs from that of Wortman in *Development of a Russian Legal Consciousness* in that he finds, at least within the judicial organs, such a class of jurists to have emerged by the Reform Era from Russia's institutions of higher learning (particularly from the Imperial School of Jurisprudence and the universities). These different interpretations underline the difficulties inherent in applying generalizations based on the experience of one institution to the bureaucracy as a whole or to other institutions.

29. Chicherin, *Vospominaniia: Moskva sorokovykh godov,* esp. 1-70; K. K. Arsen'ev, "Vospominaniia K. K. Arsen'eva ob Uchilische Provovedeniia 1849-1855," *Russkaia starina,* 50 (April 1886): 199-220; V. V. Stasov, "Uchilische Pravovedeniia sorok let tomu nazad 1836-1842," *Russkaia starina,* 29 (1880): 1015-1042; 30: 393-422, 573-602; 31 (1881): 247-262; Charles and Barbara Jelavich, *The Education of a Russian Statesman: The Memoirs of Nicholas Karlovich Giers* (Berkeley and Los Angeles, 1962). Of course, one could argue that careerism among law students is hardly an unusual phenomenon. Wortman, *Development of a Russian Legal Consciousness,* convincingly shows for the judicial organs a significant increase in officials with higher legal education by the late 1850s. These men seem to have differed in ethos from many of their contemporaries with similar educations who worked in other sectors of the bureaucracy. Leikina-Svirskaia, *Intelligentsiia v Rossii,* 77, shows that by 1869, 50.7 percent of the students in Russia's eight universities were enrolled in juridical faculties.

30. In some respects, the Russian experience in the mid-nineteenth century may be compared to Britain's historical reliance upon generally educated civil servants. For an enlightening discussion of the educational background of the English, French, and German administrative elites, see Armstrong, *European Administrative Elite,* 127-251.

31. Insarskii, "Zapiski" (February 1894), 10-11; Shumakher, "Pozdnyia vospominaniia," 109-122; Lincoln, "Daily Life."

32. P. A. Valuev, "Otryvki iz zamechanii o priadkoi grazhdanskoi sluzhby v Rossii," TsGIA SSSR F. 908 op. 1 d. 24 ll. 26-31.

33. For excellent discussions of rank see Torke, "Das russische Beamtentum," 48-96; Richard Pipes, *Russia under the Old Regime* (New York, 1974), 135-137. Pipes's analysis is, on the whole, correct, but he overemphasizes the idea of automatic promotion for time-in-grade and underestimates the possibilities, in certain institutions at least, of very rapid promotion. Helju-Aulik Bennet, "The *Chin* System and the *Raznochintsy* in the Government of Alexander III, 1881-1894" (Ph.D. diss., University of California, Berkeley, 1971), 50-80, also overemphasizes obstacles to rapid promotion.

34. *Svod zakonov* (1857), 3, articles 664-669. It must be remembered that time-in-grade intervals differed according to social class and educational at-

tainment. The discussion here concerns only members of the highest *razriad*, that is, individuals who had completed institutions of higher education. Members of the *dvorianstvo* and others with only secondary or primary educations had theoretically to endure even longer time-in-grade levels.

35. It seems that even the full time-in-grade requirement would have placed Russian officials in high posts at ages equivalent to Armstrong's estimate of 43 to 52 years of age for European administrative elites. However, fulfilling the time-in-grade requirement did not automatically mean promotion— that is, there were, no doubt, many "unsuccessful" chinovniki who remained "eternal titular councilors." On the other hand, as the data reveal, there was an acute shortage of capable men at the top, and ministers could not afford to wait out time-in-grade intervals to raise men to responsible positions.

36. *Svod zakonov* (1857), vol. 3, article 665.

37. *Svod zakonov* (1857), vol. 3, articles 360-369, 556.

38. N. I. Lazarevskii, *Lektsii po russkomu gosudarstvennomu pravu*, vol. 2, *Administrativnoe pravo* (St. Petersburg, 1910), 65-137. Apparently the efficacy of the table of ranks was discussed in a number of commissions during the second half of the nineteenth century. The system was never altered, however,. See also Iu. B. Solov'ev, *Samoderzhavie i dvorianstvo v kontse XIX veka* (Leningrad, 1973).

39. *Svod zakonov* (1857), 3, articles 1154-1186. See also 1, book 6, articles 1-869.

40. Lazarevskii, *Lektsii*, 113-120; Torke, "Das russische Beamtentum," 173-222.

41. This does not mean, of course, that the dysfunctions peculiar to the MVD and the Russian bureaucracy as a whole disappeared. On the contrary, the MVD continued to have a great difficulty coping with its responsibilities after 1861 and was never able to solve certain endemic structural and procedural problems.

42. TsGIA SSSR F. 851 (Collection of A. V. Golovnin) op. 1 d. 8 ll. 9-16.

43. Insarskii, "Zapiski," 13-16; Shumakher, "Pozdnyia vospominaniia," 112-115; "Mezhdu strokami," 820-825. Insarskii's service record is found in TsGIA SSSR F. 1284 op. 50 d. 260.

44. In addition to Miliutin and Shumakher, F. L. Barykov, who directed the Zemskii otdel for a 13-year period (1869-1882), may be seen as an example of this type. See TsGIA SSSR F. 1284 op. 67 d. 186 ll. 19ob-38. Miliutin's biography is well known and need not be elaborated here. Shumakher was a classic organization man who worked quietly and loyally behind the scenes with great impact on ministry policy. See his defense of Timashev and ministry policies in A. D. Shumakher, "Neskol'ko slov o g.-a. Timasheve i otnoshenii ego k obshchestvennym uchrezdeniiam," *Vestnik evropy*, 6, no. 12 (1893): 846-857. For further details on the careers of these men, see Orlovsky, "Ministerial Power."

45. N. P. Mansurov served as director of the Department of General Affairs from 1866 to 1880. See TsGIA SSSR F. 1162 op. 6 d. 313 ll. 193-220. L. S. Makov (d. 309 ll. 40-67) and V. D. Zaika (F. 1284 op. 67 d. 174 ll. 122ob.-140) served as secretary of the minister's chancery and as director of the Depart-

ment of General Affairs, respectively. Noteworthy examples of assistant ministers are A. G. Troinitskii (F. 1162 op. 6 d. 555 ll. 51-80), who held the office from 1861 to 1867, and M. S. Kakhanov (d. 230 ll. 78-98ob), assistant minister during Loris-Melikov's brief tenure as minister. Troinitskii worked on statistical and censorship matters and wrote *Krepostnoe naselenie v Rossii po desiatoi narodnoi perepisei* (St. Petersburg, 1861). Kakhanov was one of Loris-Melikov's most trusted aides. He drafted many legislative proposals, including the abortive "constitutional" project of January 28, 1881.

46. The best example would be M. R. Shidlovskii (TsGIA SSSR F. 1284 op. 67 d. 132 ll. 46-61), one of the two assistant ministers appointed by his fellow general, Timashev, in 1871. Shidlovskii held this post for five years to the incredulity of men like Valuev, who viewed it as just one more sign of the decline of the MVD under Timashev. Valuev, *Dnevnik*, 2:303.

47. See Charles Ruud, "The Russian Empire's New Censorship Law of 1865," *Canadian-Slavic Studies*, 3, no. 2 (Summer 1969): 235-245.

48. When Valuev left the MVD in 1868, he included the censorship problem among the four most important issues the government had to deal with. Valuev, *Dnevnik*, 2:496-499.

49. Two exceptions were A. G. Lazarevskii, who served as vice-director of the Department of General Affairs (1863-1866), and M. N. Pokhvisnev, who served as director of the Department of Executive Police (1863-1866). On the former, see TsGIA SSSR F. 776 op. 4 d. 419 ll. 1-36; on the latter, F. 1284 op. 76 d. 47 ll. 5ob.-34.

50. Possible exceptions might be D. I. Kamenskii, who served early in his career as a censor in Kiev (TsGIA SSSR F. 776 op. 4 d. 213 ll. 92-101); V. V. Grigor'ev, professor of eastern languages at St. Petersburg University (op. 11 d. 105 ll. 5ob.-32); and N. V. Varadinov, who wrote the official history of the MVD (op. 2 d. 134 ll. 39-56).

51. Many, like E. M. Feoktistov and F. P. Elenev, remained in office into the 1880s and 1890s. See E. M. Feoktistov, *Za kulisami politiki i literatury 1848-1896, vospominaniia* (Leningrad, 1923); for Elenev, TsGIA SSSR F. 776 op. 4 d. 209 ll. 106-108 and F. 777 (St. Petersburg Censorship Committee) op. 2 d. 134 ll. 39-56.

52. Typical of the censorship appointments made by Valuev and Timashev were V. I. Fuks, appointed in 1865, and D. P. Skuratov, appointed in 1878. (P. D. Stremoukhov and M. R. Shidlovskii could also be included here, since both served as censors. Because of their careers prior to becoming censors, however, I have placed them in other categories.) Fuks worked with Valuev in the Ministry of State Domains until 1861, when Valuev brought him into the MVD as an official of special missions. Fuks was Valuev's trusted lieutenant on the commission that prepared the 1865 censorship law and was named an original member of the Main Directorate of Press Affairs. During his long service in the ministry he also worked on questions involving the state peasantry, reform of the table of organization and finances, supervision and reform of the St. Petersburg police and prisons, and the introduction of a censorship system in Poland. In 1883 he set forth the pro-administration view of separation of powers and the conflict between the police and the post-1864

judicial system. See V. I. Fuks, *Sud i politsiia*, 2 vols. (Moscow, 1889). The close relationship between censorship appointments and the political views of Valuev and Timashev was also apparent during Loris-Melikov's brief ministry. He tried to alter the policies of his predecessors and use the censorship to conciliate society and to aid in the reform process. To this end in 1880 he appointed N. S. Abaza (TsGIA SSSR F. 1162 op. 6 d. 2 ll. 70-80) first as member of the Supreme Executive Commission and then as chief of the Main Directorate of Press Affairs. Abaza was a man of proven administrative skill and progressive political views, and he was a relative of one of Loris-Melikov's group of "liberal" ministers, A. A. Abaza, the minister of finance. On Loris-Melikov's use of censorship and the hostile reaction of high officials to his censorship policies, see P. A. Zaionchkovskii, *Krizis samoderzhaviia*, 262-269; Valuev, *Dnevnik 1877-1884*, 146-147.

53. Although Valuev appointed many socially prominent men of proven loyalty and little talent, he also brought several talented individuals of this category into the ministry. The best examples are B. P. Obukhov (TsGIA SSSR F. 1284 op. 67 d. 72 ll. 5ob.-25) and P. D. Stremoukhov (F. 776 op. 4 d. 224 ll. 119-133), who served under both Valuev and Timashev (Obukhov as governor of Pskov and assistant minister of internal affairs and Stremoukhov as a member of the Council of the Minister and the Main Directorate of Press Affairs). Both left behind published evidence of their statist ideology held while serving in the government. See, for example, Obukhov, *Russkii administrator*; P. D. Stremoukhov, "Iz vospominaniia o grafe P. A. Valueve," *Russkaia starina*, 116 (November 1903): 273-293.

54. The five police directors during Alexander's reign prior to August 1880 were S. R. Zhdanov (1855-1861), TsGIA SSSR F. 1349 op. 3 d. 786 ll. 77-86 and F. 1405 op. 63 d. 5733 ll. 23ob. -40; D. N. Tolstoi (1861-1863), Tolstoi "Zapiski," 5-33; M. N. Pokhvisnev (1863-1866), TsGIA SSSR F. 1284 op. 76 d. 47; Baron I. O. Velio (1866-1868 and 1800-1881), F. 1162 op. 6 d. 77 ll. 55ob. - 80; and P. P. Kosagovskii (1868-1880), F. 1284 op. 67 d. 139 ll. 101 ob. 8 116. Another key figure of this period was the ministry's first jurisconsult, P. T. Kititsyn (1867-1880), F. 1291 op. 123 d. 102 ll. 42-59. Appointed by Valuev, Kititsyn served as jurisconsult until Loris-Melikov came to power in 1880. He worked on many legislative matters and wrote significant memoranda and projects on administrative and police reform. He also chaired several small commissions which tried to ameliorate the growing conflict between the courts and the administration (especially the police). Kititsyn was unflinching in his support of administrative power as a principle and of the interests of the ministry as well as the government as a whole. On Kititsyn's reform projects of the late 1860s, see Korf, *Administrativnaia iustitsiia*, 1:312-321. See also "Kratkii soobrazheniia po proektu ob ustroistve uezdnoi politsii," in TsGIA SSSR F. 908 op. 1 d. 277, and the projects and materials in dd. 274, 371, 375.

55. Tolstoi's appointment resulted from his personal relationship to Valuev, who knew Tolstoi's capabilities well from periods of prior service together.

56. Plehve's service record is in TsGIA SSSR F. 1162 op. 6 d. 419 ll. 163-

167ff; Durnovo's in F. 1284 op. 51 d. 261 ll. 110ob.-122, 188ob.-189.

57. These attitudes were carried forward into their initial MVD appointments in 1881, Plehve as the director of the enlarged Department of State Police, and Durnovo as the head of the newly formed Judicial Section (a combination of the old Jurisconsult Section of the MVD and the Corps of Gendarmes).

58. See, for example, V. I. Gurko, *Features and Figures of the Past: Government and Opinion in the Reign of Nicholas II* (Stanford, 1939), 107-249, 438-458; Howard D. Mehlinger and John M. Thompson, *Count Witte and the Tsarist Government in the 1905 Revolution* (Bloomington, 1972); Wayne S. Santoni, "P. N. Durnovo as Minister of Internal Affairs in the Witte Cabinet: A Study in Suppression" (Ph.D. diss., University of Kansas, 1968).

59. There is evidence that after Loris-Melikov's fall from power in 1881, the new minister of internal affairs, Ignat'ev, purged the ministry of some middle-level officials regarded as politically unreliable. Zaionchkovskii, *Krizis samoderzhaviia*, 300-378.

5. Policies of the Guardians

1. No modern comprehensive analysis of the reign of Alexander II exists. The most valuable general treatment remains that of S. S. Tatishchev, *Imperator Aleksandr II. Ego zhizn' i tsarstvovanie*, 2 vols. (St. Petersburg, 1911). See also G. A. Dzhanshiev, *Iz epokhi velikikh reform*, 5th ed. (Moscow, 1894); A. A. Golovachev, *Desiat' let reform 1861-1871 gg.* (St. Petersburg, 1872); A. A. Kornilov, *Obshchestvennoe dvizhenie pri Aleksandre II (1855-1881). Istoricheskie ocherki* (Moscow, 1909); and W. E. Mosse, *Alexander II and the Modernization of Russia* (New York, 1962). M. E. Almedingen, *The Emperor Alexander II: A Study* (London, 1962), and S. Graham, *Tsar of Freedom: The Life and Reign of Alexander II* (New Haven, 1935), are superficial biographies.

2. See the discussions of the historiography of the decision to reform from above in Alfred J. Rieber, ed., *The Politics of Autocracy: Letters of Alexander II to Prince A. I. Bariatinskii, 1857-1864* (Paris, 1966), 15-58; Terence Emmons, *Russian Landed Gentry*, 47-52; and Field, *End of Serfdom*, 50-64.

3. See, for example, Valuev's scathing indictment which Grand Duke Konstantin Nikolaevich gave widespread publicity within the government: Valuev, "Duma russkago," 349-360. Valuev emphasized the excessive centralization, formalism, and lack of adequate control that fostered a system of official lies and reduced the government to powerlessness.

4. This is the point of view expressed in the works cited in note 1. In a recent article, Alfred J. Rieber moves away from the traditional view and argues that throughout the reign Alexander worked to secure his own supremacy over the bureaucracy. He also argues that the basic continuity of the reign is found in Alexander's and the government's quest to fulfill the state's fiscal and military needs. See Alfred J. Rieber, "Alexander II: A Revisionist View," *Journal of Modern History*, 43, no. 1 (March 1971): 42-58. On the Karakozov assassination attempt and its aftermath, see Tatishchev, *Imperator Aleksandr II*, 2:4-11; Mosse, *Alexander II*, 113-117; Orzhekhovskii, *Iz istorii*, 7-25. See

also Iu. I. Gerasimova, "Krizis pravitel'stvennoi politiki v gody revoliutsion-noi situatsii i Aleksandr II," in M. V. Nechkina, ed., *Revoliutsionnaia situat-siia v Rossii v 1859-1861gg.* 2 (Moscow, 1962): 93-106.

5. For a discussion of the different groupings within Alexander II's autoc-racy, see A. E. Presniakov, "Samoderzhavie Aleksandra II," *Russkoe prosh-loe*, 1, 4 (1923): 3-20.

6. Field, *End of Serfdom*, 354-358, 362-367.

7. It is generally accepted that Alexander forced Lanskoi and Miliutin out of the MVD to placate landowners and their conservative supporters in the government. Zaionchkovskii, "Valuev," 1:28.

8. The former view was commonly held by liberal public opinion, the latter by the more enlightened members of the bureaucracy itself. Kornilov, *Obshchestvennoe dvizhenie*, 107, 178-182, 188-189.

9. Hutton, "Reform of City Government." On the 1874 military reform, see Miller, *Dmitrii Miliutin*, 182-230; Zaionchkovskii, *Voennye reformy*, 254-339.

10. See especially Chernukha, *Vnutrenniaia politika* and *Krestianskii vopros*; Orzhekhovskii, *Administratsiia i pechat'* and *Iz istorii*; N. A. Troit-skii, *Tsarskie sudy protiv revoliutsionnoi Rossii: Politicheskie protsessy 1871-1880gg.* (Saratov, 1976) and *Bezumstvo khrabrykh: Russkie revoliutsionery i karatel'naia politika tsarizma 1866-1822 gg.* (Moscow, 1978); V. A. Tvardov-skaia, *Ideologiia poreformennogo samoderzhaviia (M. N. Katkov i ego izda-niia)* (Moscow, 1978); M. V. Nechkina ed., *Revoliutsionnaia situatsiia v Rossii v seredine XIX veka: Kollektivnaia monografiia* (Moscow, 1978); N. M. Druzhinin, *Russkaia derevnia na perelome 1861-1880 gg.* (Moscow, 1978); John G. Gantvoort, "Relations between Government and Zemstvos under Valuev and Timashev, 1864-1876" (Ph.D. diss., University of Illinois, 1971); and E. V. Vilenskii, *Sudebnaia reforma i kontrreforma v Rossii* (Saratov, 1969). See also the discussion by Daniel Field in "The Reforms of the 1860's," in S. N. Baron and N. W. Heer, eds., *Windows on the Russian Past: Essays on Soviet Historiography since Stalin* (Columbus, Ohio, 1977), 89-104.

11. Recent scholarship has shown in great detail the connections between the government programs of the Witte and Stolypin eras and the programs that were partially or never consummated during Alexander II's reign. See, for example, V. S. Diakin, "Stolypin i dvorianstvo (Proval mestnoi reformy)," Akademiia Nauk SSSR, *Problemy krest'ianskogo zemlevladeniia*, 231-274; *Samoderzhavie, burzhuaziia i dvorianstvo v 1907-1911 gg.* (Leningrad, 1978). Also, Gilbert S. Doctorow, "The Introduction of Parliamentary Institutions in Russia during the Revolution of 1905-1907" (Ph.D. diss., Columbia Univer-sity, 1975); Mehlinger and Thompson, *Count Witte and the Tsarist Govern-ment*; A. Ia. Avrekh, *Stolypin i tret'ia duma* (Moscow, 1968); Macey, "Rus-sian Bureaucracy."

12. Chernukha, *Vnutrenniaia politika*.

13. Orzhekhovskii, *Iz istorii*.

14. Tvardovskaia, *Ideologiia poreforemennogo samoderzhaviia*.

15. In writing about the MVD and emancipation, some scholars stress the contributions of key MVD officials and ignore the ministry's institutional con-

tribution, while others oversimplify the ministry's "leadership" in the complex legislative process. See Field, *End of Serfdom*; Emmons, *Russian Landed Gentry*; Zaionchkovskii, *Otmena*; L. G. Zakharova, "Dvorianstvo i pravitel'stvennaia programma otmeny krepostnogo prava v Rossii," *Voprosy istorii*, 9 (1973): 32-51; "Pravitel'stvennaia programma otmeny krepostnogo prava v Rossii," *Istoriia SSSR*, 2 (1975): 22-47; "Programma otmeny krepostnogo prava redaktsionnykh komissii i dvorianstvo (Iz istorii krest'ianskoi reformy 1861 g. v Rossii)," *Vestnik moskovskogo universiteta*, historical series 8, no. 2 (1979): 22-37.

16. A. I. Levshin, "Dostopamiatnye minuty v moei zhizni: Zapiska Alekseia Irakleevicha Levshina," *Russkii arkhiv*, 8 (1885): 475-557; Field, *End of Serfdom*, 50-64, 76-77, 92-98. Much of my analysis of the MVD's role in emancipation is based on Field's remarkably thorough reconstruction of the reform process.

17. Emmons argues that the MVD maintained full initiative and implies that it dominated the secret committee: Emmons, *Russian Landed Gentry*, 51-52, 61-62. See also Druzhinin, *Russkaia derevnia*, 25-28.

18. Levshin, "Dostopamiatnye minuty," 535, 539n, 544-545.

19. Zakharova, "Pravitel'stvennaia programma," 25-27.

20. Here I have in mind the similarities in form and function between the political struggles in Russia and those surrounding the relations between parliamentary institutions and the regimes in France and Prussia.

21. Field, *End of Serfdom*, 133, 140-141.

22. Field, *End of Serfdom*, 150-152; Lincoln, "Tsar's Most Loyal Servitors," 379-428.

23. Field, *End of Serfdom*, 233-358; Zakharova, "Pravitel'stvennaia programma," 27-47; Zaionchkovskii, *Otmena*, 108-124.

24. Field, *End of Serfdom*, 324-358; Zaionchkovskii, *Otmena*, 125-151. See also Macey, "Russian Bureaucracy," 14-30.

25. TsGIA SSSR F. 1284 op. 66 d. 49; F. 1275 op. 1 d. 102; F. 1275 op. 93 d. 22. See especially F. 1284 op. 66 d. 11 ll. 1-508.

26. Valuev, *Dnevnik*, 1:330.

27. Valuev and other MVD officials repeatedly made this point. See, for example, Valuev's 1861 report to the Council of Ministers on MVD activities, TsGIA SSSR F. 1275 op. 93 d. 22 ll. 5-41, and the 1860 Lanskoi report, op. 1 d. 102.

28. See "Doklad Tovarishcha Tikhomirova—Ob organizatsii apparata mestnogo administrativnogo upravleniia (otdely upravlenii)," *Vestnik NKVD*, nos. 21-22 (September 26, 1918), 17-19.

29. The name of the Kakhanov commission was the Special Commission for the Preparation of Projects for Local Administration. On the founding of the commission, see TsGIA SSSR F. 1284 op. 241 ll. 211-213, 275-277. Most commission materials were published in 1884: *Materialy vysochaishei uchrezhdennoi Osoboi Komissii stats sekretaria Kakhanova dlia sostavleniia proektov mestnogo upravleniia* (St. Petersburg, 1884). The original manuscripts in TsGIA SSSR F. 1317 offer some added details and the tsar's handwritten commentary.

30. Starr, *Decentralization*, 3-184.

31. Ibid., 185-241; Garmiza, *Podgotovka*, 130-155.

32. P. A. Valuev, "O preobrazovanii gubernskikh uchrezhdenii MVD," TsGIA SSSR, F. 1286 op. 24 d. 834.

33. In tracing the MVD's relationship to its provincial administration, I examined a little-used source—the bound volumes of MVD departmental circulars to the provincial governors for the 1860s and 1870s. Though for most years (those of the Turkish War are an exception) the ministry produced substantial annual volumes of these circulars, I was struck by the triviality of many of the communications and, in general, the lack of overall direction from the center on the interpretation of important points of law that had broad political implications. The circulars reflect the preoccupation of the provincial directorates with rather unimportant administrative matters quite apart from the activities of the provincial hierarchies of other ministries. When important edicts were issued in St. Petersburg, such as the 1866 law strengthening the office of governor and the 1874 reform of the peasant administration, the ministry did try to explicate the meaning of these changes for administrators, but the central ministry point of view emphasized the control and police functions of the local administrators. These simply reflected the general central ministry policy of "containment" of independent activity in the provinces. See, for example, *Sbornik tsirkuliarov MVD za 1874* (St. Petersburg, 1875).

34. *PSZ* II, no. 42,180. For the State Council discussions, see TsGIA SSSR F. 1286 op. 24 d. 834 ll. 132-32ob.

35. See the revealing reports from provincial governors on the failure of the temporary changes in TsGIA SSR F. 1286 op. 24 d. 834 ll. 143ff. and op. 31 d. 2 ll. 19-31. More materials on reform of the provincial chanceries is located in op. 24 d. 835, "O preobrazovanii gubernskikh pravlenii i gubernatorskikh kantseliarii."

36. TsGIA SSSR F. 908 op. 1 d. 297 ll. 1-19ob. Valuev, "Zapiska o polozhenii gubernskogo upravleniia."

37. Ibid., ll. 1ob.-2.

38. Ibid., l. 19.

39. Orzhekhovskii, *Iz istorii*, 69-74.

40. Ibid., 77.

41. Ibid., 66.

42. TsGIA SSSR F. 1286 op. 24 d. 835.

43. *Vestnik evropy*, no. 5 (May 1870), 374-381.

44. *Vestnik evropy*, no. 10 (October 1874), 819-833.

45. See, for example, John Keep, *The Russian Revolution: A Study in Mass Mobilization* (New York, 1976); Marc Ferro, *La révolution de 1917: Octobre naissance d'une société* (Paris, 1976).

46. *Vestnik evropy*, no. 4 (April 1873), 844-850; no. 6 (June 1873), 812-813.

47. My discussion of the *Vyt'* is based mainly on Peter Czap, Jr., "P. A. Valuyev's Proposal for a *Vyt'* Administration, 1864," *Slavonic and East European Review*, 45, no. 105 (July 1967): 391-410.

48. One might even trace this back to the 1859 Murav'ev plan for a *volost' popechitel'*, though this official would have been an official of the nobility rather than of the MVD.

49. Ibid., 403-404.

50. Robert P. Browder and Alexander F. Kerensky, *The Russian Provisional Government, 1917*, 3 vols. (Stanford, 1961), 1:282-291.

51. *Vestnik evropy*, no. 9 (September 1876), 341-351; no. 11 (November 1876), 423-429.

52. Orzhekhovskii, *Iz istorii*, 78-82.

53. Ibid., 78-82; Zaionchkovskii, *Pravitel'stvennyi apparat*, 143, 178.

54. One must keep in mind, of course, that the lower officeholders in the MVD provincial hierarchy exhibited markedly inferior levels of education and competence.

55. During the ministry's post-1905 onslaught on the provincial administrative problem, one of Stolypin's MVD co-workers prepared a first-rate summary of the 20 volumes of Kakhanov commission materials. See M. V. Ispavin, *Obzor trudov Vysochaishei utverzhdennoi, pod predsedatel'stvom Stats-Sekretaria Kakhanova, Osoboi Komissii*, 2 parts (St. Petersburg, 1908).

56. TsGIA SSSR F. 1317 (Kakhanov Commission), op. 1 d. 3 ll. 1-3ob., 6-8; F. 1317 op. 1 d. 18 ll. 2-2ob, 18 ob.; F. 1317 op. 1 d. 7 ll. 231-249.

57. Ispavin, *Obzor*, 1:189-217.

58. *Vestnik NKVD*, nos. 21-22 (September 26, 1918), 17-19.

59. Ispavin, *Obzor*, 1:136-162, 195-217.

60. For the best discussion of Tolstoi in the 1880s, see Taranovskii, "Politics of Counter-Reform," 373-574.

61. Ispavin, *Obzor*, 1:204-206.

62. Ibid., 44-79, 84-116, 189-197.

63. Abbott, "Police Reform," 42-60.

64. Ibid., 61-72.

65. TsGIA SSSR F. 1286 op. 53 d. 271; L. S. Makov, *Kratkii ocherk deiatel'nosti Ministerstva Vnutrennikh Del za dvadtsatipiatiletie 1855-1880 g.* (St. Petersburg, 1880), 73; Zaionchkovskii, *Krizis samoderzhaviia*, 68.

66. Abbott, "Police Reform," 68-72, 76-81.

67. Ibid., 88. For the intermediary Solov'ev program adopted by the Main Committee on May 16, 1858, see *PSZ* II, no. 33,166a.

68. Abbott, "Police Reform," 104-109.

69. Ibid., 110-113; *PSZ* II, nos. 35,890, 35,891, and 35,892.

70. Abbott, "Police Reform," 117-178.

71. Ibid., 119, 129-143. See also Tolstoi, "Zapiska"; *PSZ* II, no. 39,087.

72. Abbott, "Police Reform," 182-185.

73. Orzhekhovskii, *Iz istorii*, 57-87; TsGIA SSSR F. 908 op. 1 d. 310 ll. 215-220.

74. Abbott, "Police Reform," 230-233. See also the materials in TsGIA SSSR F. 1286 op. 53 d. 271.

75. Orzhekhovskii, *Iz istorii*, 83-107; B. B. Veselovskii, *Istoriia zemstva za sorok let*, 4 vols. (St. Petersburg, 1911), esp. vol. 3; Starr, *Decentralization*, 185-354; Gantvoort, "Relations between Government and Zemstvos";

Garmiza, *Podgotovka*, V. Iu. Skalon, *Zemskie voprosy* (Moscow, 1882).

76. Veselovskii, *Istoriia zemstva za sorok let*, 3:1-2.

77. Garmiza, *Podgotovka*, 139-144.

78. Valuev, "O vnutrennem sostoianii Rossii 26 iiunia 1862 g."; Garmiza, "Predpolozheniia i proekty," 143.

79. TsGIA SSSR F. 908 op. 1 d. 175 l. 130.

80. Korkunov, *Russkoe gosudarstvennoe pravo*, 2:533-535; Lazarevskii, *Lektsii*, 50-52; B. B. Veselovskii, "Detsentralizatsiia upravleniia i zadachi zemstva," in B. B. Veselovskii and Z. G. Frenkel, eds., *Iubileinyi zemskii sbornik 1864-1914* (St. Petersburg, 1914), 77-85.

81. Gantvoort, "Relations between Government and Zemstvos," 28-102, 116-128, 174.

82. N. M. Pirumova, *Zemskoe liberal'noe dvizhenie: Sotsial'nye korni i evoliutsiia do nachala XX veka* (Moscow, 1977), 44-52. For the debates dealing with the 1889 and 1890 legislation relating to the zemstvos, see L. G. Zakharova, *Zemskaia kontrreforma 1890 g.* (Moscow, 1968), 91-165; Taranovski, "Politics of Counter-Reform," 371-574.

83. Veselovskii, *Istoriia zemstva za sorok let*, 3:47-140.

84. Valuev's ambivalent attitude toward the zemstvos—his genuine desire to reform them while keeping them politically contained—is seen in his January 1867 memorandum to Alexander II, "Essay on the Present Situation of the Matter of the Introduction of Zemstvo Institutions and the Activities of Those Institutions in the Provinces Where They Have Been Created," TsGIA SSSR F. 908 op. 1 d. 283 ll. 2-35. The memorandum was recently published in *Sovetskii arkhiv*, no. 4 (1971), 79-87. See also James A. Malloy, Jr., "A Police Assessment of Local Self-Government in Russia: The Third Section Reports on the Early Zemstvo," *Jahrbücher für Geschichte Osteuropas*, Band 24, Heft 4 (1976), 499-511, and "Russian Liberalism and the Closing of the 1867 St. Petersburg zemstvo," *Canadian Slavic Studies*, 4, no. 4 (1970): 635-670.

85. Gantvoort, "Relations between Government and Zemstvos," 120-150; V. G. Chernukha, "Vsepoddanneishii doklad komissii P. A. Valueva ot 2 aprelia 1872 g. kak istochnik po istorii podatnoi reformy v Rossii," Akademiia Nauk SSSR, *Vspomogatel'nye istoricheskie distsipliny*, 3 (Leningrad 1969): 262-269, and *Vnutrenniaia politika*, 211-225.

86. Makov, *Kratkii ocherk*, 63-66.

87. Zaionchkovskii, *Krizis samoderzhaviia*, 58-148; Zakharova, *Zemskaia kontrreforma*, 55-62.

88. Zakharova, *Zemskaia kontrreforma*, 56; Serodonin, *Istoricheskii obzor*, 3, part 1, 148.

89. Hutton, "Reform of City Government"; *Materialy otnosiashchiesia do novago obshchestvennago ustroistva v gorodakh imperii*, 4 vols. (St. Petersburg, 1877).

90. *Gorodskie poseleniia v Rossiiskoi Imperii*, 7 vols. (St. Petersburg, 1860-1865); *Ekonomicheskoe sostoianie gorodskikh poselenii Evropeiskoi Rossii v 1861-1862 gg.*, 2 vols. (St. Petersburg, 1863).

91. *Materialy*, 1:1-2; Hutton, "Reform of City Government," 15-17.

92. *Materialy*, 1:3-30. The committees demanded an end to arbitrary and

stifling central government interference and the establishment of all-class representation.

93. Ibid., 1:306-310.

94. Lincoln, "Tsar's Most Loyal Servitors," 534-538.

95. Starr, *Decentralization*, 279-289.

96. *Materialy*, 1:469-494.

97. Hutton, "Reform of City Government," 46-65; *Materialy*, 1:273-280, 2:1-20, 3:5-58.

98. *Materialy*, 2:387-459, 3:11-40, 328-515. The last special commission forwarded the draft legislation to the State Council on March 21, 1870. Alexander approved it on June 16.

99. MVD proposals were attacked by Western-oriented liberals for being too bureaucratic. For example, in September 1870 the *European Messenger* published a fine commentary on the municipal reforms. Giving the government and the MVD generally high marks for passing the legislation, the journal voiced several major criticisms. First, the legislation was introduced in only 45 cities, not at all in the western provinces. Second, the powers of the provincial governors and administration were still intolerably and ominously vague in relation to the new self-government organs. The MVD retained too much control and police power. Third, the new provincial boards for municipal affairs, mixed-composition collegial organs meant to mediate between administration and self-government, were unproven in this role, though they provided some hope for improvements. Fourth, the government had neglected tax reform in the cities and had not taken measures to update outmoded social structures. Finally, the electoral laws governing the city dumas favored the property-owning members of the nobility and others in the cities at the expense of the apartment-renting educated and cultured elements (professionals and intellectuals). *Vestnik evropy*, no. 9 (September 1870), 370-374.

100. Zelnik, *Labor and society*; V. Ia. Laverychev, *Tsarizm i rabochii vopros v Rossii (1861-1917 gg.)*. (Moscow, 1972), 12-54.

101. See especially Gregory L. Freeze, "Caste and Emancipation: The Changing Status of Clerical Families in the Great Reforms," in David L. Ransel, ed., *The Family in Imperial Russia: New Lines of Historical Research* (Urbana, 1978), 124-150; "P. A. Valuyev and the Politics of Church Reform (1861-1862)," *Slavonic and East European Review*, 56, no. 1 (1978): 68-87; V. Ia. Laverychev, *Krupnaia burzhuaziia v poreformennoi Rossii 1861-1900* (Moscow, 1974), 13-108. P. G. Ryndziundskii, *Utverzhdenie kapitalizma v Rossii 1850-1880 gg.* (Moscow, 1978), 229-283.

102. Zelnik, *Labor and Society*, 69-118.

103. Ibid., 21-43, 80-118; Laverychev, *Tsarizm*, 16-18.

104. The following discussion is based on Zelnik, *Labor and Society*, 123-199, 330-336; and on Laverychev, *Tsarizm*, 18-38.

105. In 1870, for example, in response to the Nevsky strike, provincial governors were given the right to exile workers administratively. Zelnik correctly portrays this as a blow to the "integrity of the judicial reforms." It was yet another manifestation of the resurgence of ministerial power and police authority in the MVD of the 1870s. Zelnik, *Labor and Society*, 352-369.

106. Ibid., 363-385.

107. Ibid., 58-171. See also Walter Sablinsky, *The Road to Bloody Sunday: Father Gapon and the St. Petersburg Massacre of 1905* (Princeton, 1976), 3-33; Jeremiah Schneiderman, *Sergei Zubatov and Revolutionary Marxism: The Struggle for the Working Class in Tsarist Russia* (Ithaca, 1976), 15-68.

108. Chernukha, *Krest'ianskii vopros*, 25-69; Macey, "Russian Bureaucracy," 14-80.

109. Chernukha, *Krest'ianskii vopros*, 147-191.

110. Chernukha presents Timashev's and the ministry's agrarian and fiscal policies from 1868 to 1878 in considerable detail. *Krest'ianskii vopros*, 61-204. See also Macey, "Russian Bureaucracy," 29-36.

111. Orzhekhovskii, *Administratsiia i pechat'*; Charles Ruud, "The Russian Empire's New Censorship Law of 1865," *Canadian Slavic Studies*, 3, no. 2 (1969): 235-245; Lincoln, "Tsar's Most Loyal Servitors," 523-558.

112. *PSZ* II, no. 41,988.

113. Ruud, "Censorship Law of 1865," 241-244; Orzhekhovskii, *Administratsiia i pechat'*, 29-33, 46-52; Tvardovskaia, *Ideologiia poreformennogo samoderzhaviia*, 60-70.

114. Valuev, *Dnevnik*, 2:253-254; Orzhekhovskii, *Administratsiia i pechat'*, 57-58; Feoktistov, *Za kulisami*, 350.

115. Orzhekhovskii, *Administratsiia i pechat'*, 69-79, presents the various laws and administrative edicts for both the Timashev and Valuev ministries in detail.

116. The laws of May 19, 1871 (*PSZ* II, no. 49, 615); June 7, 1872 (*PSZ* II, no. 50,956); September 1, 1878 (not in the *PSZ*); August 9, 1878 (*PSZ* II, no. 58,778). Vilenskii, *Sudebnaia reforma*, 308-310, 322-323; Zaionchkovskii, *Krizis samoderzhaviia*, 76-79. See also N. A. Troitskii, *Tsarskie sudy protiv revoliutsionnoi Rossii: Politicheskie protsessy 1871-1880 gg.* (Saratov, 1976).

117. On the joint stock company policy, see L. E. Shepelev, *Aktsionernye kompanii v Rossii* (Leningrad, 1973), 58-133.

118. Field, *End of Serfdom*, 265-323; Zakharova, "Pravitel'stvennaia programma," 22-47.

119. Garmiza, *Podgotovka*, 155-163; Bermanskii, "Konstitutsionnye proekty," 229-230; Zakharova, *Zemskaia kontrreforma*, 46-47; Valuev, *Dnevnik*, 1:148, 189.

120. P. A. Valuev, "O vnutrennem sostoianii Rossii 26 iiunia 1862 g."; Garmiza, "Predpolozheniia i proekty," 143.

121. Zakharova, *Zemskaia kontrreforma*, 48-50; Valuev, *Dnevnik*, 2:219.

122. Zakharova, *Zemskaia kontrreforma*, 52-54.

123. "Perepiska ministra vnutrennikh del P. A. Valueva i gosudarstvennogo sekretaria S. N. Urosova v 1866 g.," *Istoriia SSSR*, no. 2 (March-April 1973), 115-127.

124. The following discussion is based largely on V. G. Chernukha, "Problema politicheskoi reformy v pravitel'stvennykh krugakh Rossii v nachale 70-x godov XIX v.," in Akademiia Nauk SSSR, *Problemy krest'ianskogo zemlevladeniia i vnutrennei politiki Rossii dooktiabr'skii period* (Leningrad, 1972), 138-191, and on Chernukha, *Vnutrenniaia politika*, 96-135.

6. The "Dictatorship of the Heart"

1. "Vsepoddanneishii otchet o svoei deiatel'nosti v dolzhnosti vremennago Kharkovskago general-gubernatora za apr. 1879 po ianv. 1880," TsGIA SSSR F. 908 op. 1 d. 402 l. 26. Major works on the Loris-Melikov era include P. A. Zaionchkovskii, *Krizis samoderzhaviia*; and M. I Kheifets, *Vtoraia revoliutsionnaia situatsiia v Rossii (konets 70-x—nachalo 80-x godov XIX veka): Krizis pravitel'stvennoi politiki* (Moscow, 1963). The latter work is worthwhile but suffers from the author's attempts to fit data into a crude Marxist framework. Hans Heilbronner, "The Administrations of Loris-Melikov and Ignatiev 1880-1882" (Ph.D. diss., University of Michigan, 1954), summarizes the large body of published materials on the subject.

2. *RBS*, 10:696. Archival materials on Loris-Melikov's administration of the Terek *oblast'* may be found in TsGIA SSSR F. 866 op. 1 d. 32, 34, 41, 140.

3. Hans Heilbronner, "The Russian Plague of 1878-79," *Slavic Review*, 21, no. 1 (March 1962): 89-112.

4. Zaionchkovskii, *Krizis samoderzhaviia*, 85-91, 96-98, 147.

5. On Loris-Melikov's activities as governor-general of Kharkov, see Zaionchkovskii, *Krizis samoderzhaviia*, 96-98. Loris' views on education policy were discussed in St. Petersburg at one of the special conferences chaired by Valuev. See the report of this conference, dated July 28, 1879, in TsGIA SSSR F. 908 op. 1 d. 395 l. 37. The Loris-Melikov appointment was urged upon Alexander by Miliutin, according to A. F. Koni, *Na zhiznennom puti* (Revel'-Berlin, n.d.), 3:5. See also Valuev, *Dnevnik 1877-1884*, 59-63. In his diary, however, Miliutin expressed surprise about the creation of the Supreme Executive Commission and the appointment of Loris. Miliutin, *Dnevnik 1878-1880*, 216-217. The idea for the commission apparently came from the future Alexander III, who had picked it up from Katkov. Valuev worked out the actual form and functions of the commission. Zaionchkovskii, *Krizis samoderzhaviia*, 154.

6. Loris-Melikov, "Vsepoddanneishii otchet o svoei deiatel'nosti." TsGIA SSSR F. 908 op. 1 d. 402 ll. 1-7.

7. Ibid., ll. 10-14. There was not a single execution during Loris-Melikov's term as governor-general of Kharkov. He made use of military courts in 15 cases, and exercised power of administrative exile in 67 cases, 37 of which were political.

8. Ibid., ll. 24-25. Here Alexander penciled in *"soobrazit'."*

9. Ibid., l. 26. Here the tsar wrote *"da."*

10. Ibid., ll. 24-29.

11. Ibid., ll. 31-32.

12. Ibid., l. 35.

13. See note 5 above. Valuev to Alexander II, February 11, 1880, in TsGIA SSSR F. 908 op. 1 d. 395 ll. 46-47ob.

14. *PSZ* II, no. 60,492. A copy of the Senate *ukaz* is found in TsGIA SSSR F. 569 op. 1 d. 31 ll. 1-5. The remaining governors-general were retained, but made subordinate to the main chief.

15. Miliutin, *Dnevnik 1878-1880*, 217; Valuev, *Dnevnik 1877-1884*, 67.

16. Zaionchkovskii, *Krizis samoderzhaviia*, 156. Zaionchkovskii portrays

the dictatorship as a centralization of power after the unsuccessful decentralization represented by the governors-general. On the official and public reaction to the creation of the Supreme Executive Commission and the Loris-Melikov appointment. see 157-164. The Commission apparently had only five plenary sessions during the six months of its existence. The journals of the first three meetings (March 4, 11, and 24, 1880) have been published in *Russkii arkhiv*, book 12 (1915), 220-238. The journals of the fourth and fifth sessions (April 15 and May 1) are found in TsGAOR F. 569 op. 1 d. 37 ll. 29-33 and F. 569 op. 1 d. 36 ll. 68-69. The activities of the Supreme Executive Commission are discussed in Zaionchkovskii, *Krizis samoderzhaviia*, 165-189.

17. *Pravitel'stvennyi vestnik*, February 15, 1880.

18. TsGAOR F. 569 op. 1 d. 33 ll. 1-4. A law of March 3, 1880, temporarily subordinated the Third Section to the main chief of the Supreme Executive Commission. *PSZ* II, no. 60,609.

19. Journals of the Supreme Executive Commission, *Russkii arkhiv*, book 12 (1915), 220-238.

20. Ibid., 238-248; N. V. Golitsyn, "Konstitutsiia grafa Loris-Melikova: Materialy dlia ee istorii," *Byloe*, nos. 4-5 (1918), 154-161.

21. Valuev, *Dnevnik 1877-1884*, 83-87; Miliutin, *Dnevnik 1878-1880*, 243; Feoktistov, *Za kulisami*, 185-189.

22. Materials showing the relationship between Loris-Melikov and the principal provincial and city officials nominally under the jurisdiction of Makov and the MVD are to be found in the collection of the chancery of the MVD, TsGIA SSSR F. 1282 op. 1 dd. 640, 647. Loris attempted to coordinate the activities of officials in the area of political crimes according to the policies he established in the Supreme Executive Commission. For the Loris-Melikov project on zemstvo activities, see TsGAOR F. 569 op. 1 d. 54 ll. 1-12. In effect, he forced Makov and the MVD to follow his lead in easing the legacy of MVD/government restriction of zemstvo activities. See also Zaionchkovskii, *Krizis samoderzhaviia*, 221.

23. Valuev, *Dnevnik 1877-1884*, 104-107; Zaionchkovskii, *Krizis samoderzhaviia*, 226-227.

24. *PSZ* II, no. 61,279. This was only the first step in the unification of the police organs. The actual structural changes that resulted in the Department of State Police did not take place until November 15.

25. Valuev, *Dnevnik 1877-1884*, 109; Zaionchkovskii, *Krizis samoderzhaviia*, 226-227; Kheifets, *Vtoraia revoliutsionnaia situatsiia*, 138; *Vestnik evropy*, no. 3 (1880), 388.

26. TsGAOR F. 569 op. 1 d. 64 ll. 2-14. Valuev (*Dnevnik 1877-1884*, 107) argued that Makov's unexpected initiatives in the areas of zemstvo and press law reform precipitated Loris-Melikov's move in late July.

27. "Dokladnaia zapiska o preobrazovanii politsii, 1 Avg. 1880," TsGAOR F. 569 op. 1 d. 65 ll. 6-8. In this report Loris argued for the integration of all police and gendarmes down to the provincial level. He wanted to make the provincial gendarme commanders second vice-governors to educate them as to their proper civil-government role as well as to improve government control of police activities.

28. The August 11 report is "Vsepoddanneishii doklad ministra vnutrennikh del 11-go avgusta 1880 goda," *Russkii arkhiv*, no. 11 (1912), 417-419 (handwritten copy is in TsGAOR F. 569 op. 1 d. 87 ll. 1-6.) On the history of senatorial revisions, see E. S. Paina, "Senatorskie revizii i ikh arkhivnye materialy (XIX-nachalo XX v.)," in Glavnoe Arkhivnoe Upravlenie SSSR, *Nekotorye voprosy izucheniia istoricheskikh dokumentov XIX-nachala XX v. Sbornik statei* (Leningrad, 1967), 147-175; *Istoriia pravitel'stvuiushchago senata za dvesti let 1711-1911*, 4 vols. (St. Petersburg, 1911), 4:180-214; N. M. Druzhinin, "Senatorskie revizii 1860-1870-x godov (K voprosu o realizatsii reformy 1861 g.)," *Istoricheskie zapiski*, 79 (1966): 139-175. From 1863 to 1865 Valuev thwarted several attempts of the Ministry of Finance to initiate revisions of Orel Province, where there was evidence of repeated siphoning of tax money to the pockets of the police. See *Istoriia pravitel'stvuiushchago senata*, 4:187-188. Also, the laws governing senatorial revisions were removed from the 1876 edition of the Digest of Laws.

29. "Osoboe nastavlenie senatoram, naznachennym po Vysochaishemu poveleniiu dlia proizvodstva obshchei revizii v guberniiakh: Kazanskoi, Kostromskoi, Voronezhskoi, Tambovskoi, Kievskoi, Chernigovskoi, Saratovskoi, i Samarskoi," *Russkii arkhiv*, no. 11 (1912), 419-429.

30. "Vsepoddanneishii doklad ministra vnutrennikh del 1 Avg. 1880," *Russkii arkhiv*, no. 11 (1912), 417-418.

31. "Osoboe nastavlenie senatoram," *Russkii arkhiv*, no. 11 (1912), 419-424.

32. See, for example, "Osobyi zhurnal Komiteta ministrov 20 okt. 1881 po vnesennym Ministrom vnutrennikh del vsepoddanneishim zapiskam Senatora Shamshina o proizvedennoi im revizii Saratovskoi i Samarskoi gubernii," TsGIA SSSR F. 1263 op. 1 d. 4189 ll. 298-307.

33. Zaionchkovskii, *Krizis samoderzhaviia*, 235-236.

34. Loris-Melikov's words were reported in *Otechestvennye zapiski* (September 1880), 140-142.

35. Zaionchkovskii, *Krizis samoderzhaviia*, 236.

36. See the opinion of S. A. Muromtsev, quoted ibid., 237.

37. The November 15 law, published in *Sobranie uzakonenii Rossiiskoi Imperii 1880 g.*, no. 112, 802, represented the enactment of a lengthy report submitted by Loris-Melikov to Alexander on November 10: "O polnom sliianii vysshego zavedovaniia politsiei v odno uchrezhdenii-Ministerstvo vnutrennikh del," TsGIA SSSR F. 1284 op. 241 d. 81 ll. 414-430, 543-549.

38. The director would receive 10,000 rubles as opposed to 7,000 for other departmental directors, the vice-director would receive 5,000 instead of 4,000, and so on. Loris requested a total of 104,200 rubles for the Department of State Police, a saving of 40,370 over the combined budgets of the Third Section (91,699) and the MVD Department of Executive Police (52,871). The large sum of 558,957 rubles, formerly allotted to the Third Section for secret expenses, was to accrue to the MVD. The first director of the Department of State Police was Baron I. O. Velio, director of the Department of Post and Telegraph and former director (1866-1868) of the Department of Executive Police. The first vice-director was V. M. Iuzefovich.

39. TsGIA SSSR F. 1284 op. 241 d. 81 ll. 425-430.

40. Loris wanted the work of the Supreme Executive Commission relating to state crimes continued in the new Judicial Section. The directorship was to be a *Klass* IV position with a salary of 6,000 rubles. In addition, the section was to have two *deloproizvoditeli* (3,000 rubles each) and two assistants (1,500 rubles each). The total outlay was projected at 18,600 rubles.

41. These requests were presented in a separate report on November 10, which was also approved by Alexander. Depending on the province, governors could make up to 9,900 rubles as of January 1, 1881.

42. Zaionchkovskii, *Krizis samoderzhaviia*, 247-249.

43. Loris-Melikov's economic policies are treated in Zaionchkovskii, *Krizis samoderzhaviia*, 249-258; Kheifets, *Vtoraia revoliutsionnaia situatsiia*, 142-151. On the conflict between the MVD and the Ministry of Finance, see Yaney, *Systematization*, 308-317; "Some Aspects of the Imperial Russian Government on the Eve of the First World War," *Slavonic and East European Review*, 43 (December 1964): 68-90.

44. *PSZ* II, no. 61,578.

45. Peretts, *Dnevnik*, 11-12. See also Valuev, *Dnevnik 1877-1884*, 129.

46. Zaionchkovskii, *Krizis samoderzhaviia*, 254-258. Loris went to the Committee of Ministers and organized a special conference on the question of famine relief and various forms of economic aid to the villages. Ten years later, these problems would pose enormous difficulties for the MVD. See Richard Robbins, *Famine in Russia, 1891-1892* (New York, 1975).

47. Zaionchkovskii, *Krizis samoderzhaviia*, 256; Peretts, *Dnevnik*, 9.

48. Zaionchkovskii, *Krizis samoderzhaviia*, 252-253.

49. See the project outlined in Loris-Melikov's letter of May 1880 to Makov, in TsGAOR F. 569 op. 1 d. 54 ll. 1-12.

50. Zaionchkovskii, *Krizis samoderzhaviia*, 259. See also Kakhanov's letter to Loris-Melikov on July 27, 1880, on permitting such discussions within the boundaries of the June 27, 1874, law that created the local boards on peasant affairs: TsGAOR F. 569 op. 1 d. 63 ll. 1-5.

51. On the Kherson affair, see Zaionchkovskii, *Krizis samoderzhaviia*, 260-261. On Loris-Melikov's thoughts concerning a consultative body based on the zemstvos, see A. I. Koshelev, *Zapiski Aleksandra Ivanovicha Kosheleva (1812-1883 gody)* (Berlin, 1884), 253.

52. Zaionchkovskii, *Krizis samoderzhaviia*, 269-283.

53. I. V. Orzhekhovskii, *Administratsiia i pechat' mezhdu dvumia revoliutsionnymi situatsiiami* (Gor'kii, 1973).

54. Zaionchkovskii, *Krizis samoderzhaviia*, 262-269; Valuev, *Dnevnik 1877-1884*, 122-125, 146-147.

55. Valuev to Chief N. S. Abaza of the Main Directorate of Press Affairs, December 8, 1880, quoted in Zaionchkovskii, *Krizis samoderzhaviia*, 264-265.

56. Later it was wrongly called a constitutional project by critics of the extreme left and right. The notion that it was a constitution was spread by Alexander III and conservatives who feared any weakening of the autocratic principle. Several variants of the project are found in TsGAOR F. 569 op. 1 d. 96 ll. 1-30. The different redactions reveal minor word changes, most likely in an

attempt to make the project more acceptable to Alexander. For example, the word "deputies" is crossed out and replaced with the Russian words *vybornye* and *izbrannye*, etc. The final project was also published in Golitsyn, "Materialy," 162-166.

57. "Vsepoddanneishii doklad ministra vnutrennikh del grafa M. T. Loris-Melikova, ot 28 ianvaria 1881 g.," in Golitsyn, "Materialy," 162-166.

58. Loris-Melikov to D. M. Sol'skii, February 5, 1881, in Golitsyn, *Materialy*, 167. See also Valuev, *Dnevnik 1877-1884*, 142-143.

59. "Zhurnal osobago soveshchaniia sozvannago dlia obsuzhdeniia dokladnoi zapiski ministra vnutrennikh del," Golitsyn, *Materialy*, 167-173; see also "Proekt pravitel'stvennago soobshcheniia," ibid., 173-177.

60. On the original January 28 project, Alexander placed a question mark in the margin at the mention of calling 10-15 representatives to participate in the State Council. It is therefore likely that this aspect of the project was eliminated to help insure the tsar's acceptance of the project as a whole. See also Valuev, *Dnevnik 1877-1884*, 144-147.

61. On the aftermath of the assassination, see Zaionchkovskii, *Krizis samoderzhaviia*, 300-378. The fateful March 8 session of the Council of Ministers, at which adoption of the Loris-Melikov project was postponed, signaling a major reversal in his political fortunes, is treated in Hans Heilbronner, "Alexander III and the Reform Plan of Loris-Melikov," *Journal of Modern History*, 33, no. 4 (December 1961): 384-397. The memoir of the session, based on conversations between Loris-Melikov and V. A. Bil'basov (an editor of the liberal newspaper *Golos*), is in Golitsyn, "Materialy," 188-193. See also Peretts, *Dnevnik*, 24-27; Valuev, *Dnevnik 1877-1884*, 150-154.

62. The liberal response is epitomized by the *European Messenger*'s Domestic Survey section for the period February 1880-June 1881: the journal supported Loris-Melikov's policies in general, but was circumspect in its discussion of specifics. The public had limited access to information; the journal understood that the policies of Loris-Melikov were interrelated, that they constituted a system, that they were meant to transform politics, and that from the very beginning they were intimately connected to pressing economic (particularly agrarian) problems, as well as to society's quest for a voice in political life. The journal was skeptical. For example, though it praised Loris-Melikov's abolition of the Third Section in August 1880, it expressed fears that the MVD might continue the Third Section's functions under another guise. Also, in the summer of 1880, it gave restrained approval to the announcement of senatorial revisions because of the failures, by such grandiose commissions as Valuev's Agricultural Commission in the early 1870s, to produce results. The *European Messenger* understood well, however, that the manifesto of April 29, 1881, and the subsequent retirement of Loris and his closest advisers signaled a reversal of policies and a threat to hard-won liberal gains.

63. For example, in "Chronicle of Internal Life," a section of *Russkoe bogatstvo*, nos. 1-2 (1881), liberalism was lambasted for emphasizing formalistic, personal freedoms while ignoring the massive economic misery of the people.

64. See especially Diakin, *Samoderzhavie*; Avrekh, *Stolypin i tret'ia duma*; Hosking, *The Russian Constitutional Experiment*; Mehlinger and

Thompson, *Count Witte and the Tsarist Government*; and Doctorow, "The Introduction of Parliamentary Institutions."

65. For example, Khiefets, *Vtoraia revoliutsionnaia situatsiia*.

66. Though it should be added, however, that the political struggle continued even behind those walls, within the bureaucracy. Taranovski, "Politics of Counter-Reform," 303-574.

7. Conclusion

1. For a recent attempt to compare Russian and European absolutism, see Anderson, *Lineages*, 15-59, 195-235, 328-360.

2. Ibid., 361-394, 435-461. See also the works of H. D. Harootunian, *Toward Restoration: The Growth of Political Consciousness in Tokugawa, Japan* (Berkeley, 1970); Roderic H. Davison, *Reform in the Ottoman Empire, 1856-1876* (New York, 1973); Stanford J. Shaw, *Between Old and New: The Ottoman Empire under Sultan Selim III, 1789-1807* (Cambridge, Mass., 1971); Mary C. Wright, *The Last Stand of Chinese Conservatism: The T'ung Chih Restoration, 1862-1874* (Stanford, 1967); Carter V. Findley, *Bureaucratic Reform in the Ottoman Empire: The Sublime Porte, 1789-1922* (Princeton, 1980).

3. E. J. Hobsbawm, *The Age of Capital, 1848-1875* (New York, 1975), 1, 61.

4. See, in particular, Joseph Pittau, S.J., *Political Thought in Early Meiji Japan, 1868-1889* (Cambridge, Mass., 1967), 131-195.

5. On the problems of periodization in comparative social science, see Armstrong, *European Administrative Elite*, 27-45. Armstrong argues forcefully for asynchronic comparison of administrative elites according to stages of economic growth in their respective countries and their attitudes toward economic development. Here, I uphold the primacy of political and institutional renovation in a synchronic comparison.

6. On Bonapartism, a concept frequently misunderstood, see Manfred Hagen, "Der russische 'Bonapartismus' nach 1906," *Jahrbücher für Geschichte Osteuropas*, Band 24, Heft 3 (1976), 368-393; Allan Mitchell, "Bonapartism as a Model for Bismarckian Politics," *Journal of Modern History*, 49 (June 1977): 181-209; Michael Stürmer, *Regierung und Reichstag im Bismarckstaat 1871-1880* (Düsseldorf, 1974); Hans-Ulrich Wehler, *Bismarck und der Imperialismus* (Cologne, 1969); Theodore Zeldin, *France, 1848-1945*, 1 (Oxford, 1973): 504-569, and *The Political System of Napoleon III* (New York, 1971). See, in particular, V. S. Diakin's superb history of the Stolypin era, *Samoderzhavie*. Diakin develops Bonapartism as an analytic category derived from and applied to Stolypin's politics and programs. Diakin quite successfully raised the level of debate with his explanatory model and his synthetic skills. Yet I would quarrel with his choice of the term "Bonapartism" for the phenomenon he describes because of the many misleading connotations of that term. For a fuller discussion, see my forthcoming article "Late Imperial Russian Government and the Bonapartist Model."

7. Michael Stürmer, "Konservatismus und Revolution in Bismarcks Politik," in *Das kaiserliche Deutschland: Politik und Gesellschaft, 1870-1918* (Düsseldorf, 1974), 143-167.

Bibliography

Primary Sources

ARCHIVAL COLLECTIONS

TsGIA SSSR (Tsentral'nyi gosudarstvennyi istoricheskii arkhiv: Central State Historical Archive of the Soviet Union, Leningrad)

F. 565 Ministry of Finance, Department of the State Treasury
F. 776 St. Petersburg Censorship Committee
F. 777 Main Directorate of Press Affairs
F. 821 Department of Religious Affairs of Foreign Faiths, MVD
F. 851 A. V. Golovnin
F. 866 M. T. Loris-Melikov
F. 908 P. A. Valuev
F. 982 S. S. Lanskoi
F. 1149 State Council, Department of Laws
F. 1152 State Council, Department of the Economy
F. 1162 Imperial State Chancery
F. 1261 Second Section of His Majesty's Own Chancery
F. 1263 Committee of Ministers
F. 1275 Council of Ministers
F. 1282 Chancery of the MVD
F. 1284 Department of General Affairs, MVD
F. 1286 Department of Executive Police, MVD
F. 1287 Economic Department, MVD
F. 1291 *Zemskii otdel*, MVD
F. 1317 Kakhanov Commission
F. 1349 Senate, Special Collection of Personnel Records
F. 1405 Ministry of Justice
F. 1687 A. E. Timashev

GPB OR (Gosudarstvennaia publichnaia biblioteka imeni Saltykova-

Shchedrina, otdel rukopisei: State Public Library, Saltykov-Shchedrin, Manuscript Division, Leningrad)

F. 531   A. S. Norov

F. 126   P. A. Valuev

TsGAOR (Tsentral'nyi gosudarstvennyi arkhiv oktiabr'skoi revoliutsii: Central State Archive of the October Revolution, Moscow)

f. 569   M. T. Loris Melikov

PUBLISHED LAWS, DOCUMENTS, GOVERNMENT COMMISSION MATERIALS

Adres kalendar obshchaia rospis' nachal'stvuiushchikh i prochikh dolzhnostnykh lits po vsem upravleniem Rossiiskoi Imperii. St. Petersburg, 1765-1916.

Bermanskii, K. L. "Konstitutsionnye proekty tsarstvovaniia Aleksandra II." *Vestnik prava*, 35, no. 9 (November 1905): 223-291.

"Biurokraticheskaia voina 1839-ogo g." *Russkaia starina*, 32 (1881): 890-895.

"Bumagi Komiteta 6 Dekabria 1826 goda, otnosiashchiiasia do preobrazovaniia gubernskago upravleniia." *Sbornik Imperatorskago Russkago Istoricheskago Obshchestva*, 90:212-358. St. Petersburg, 1894.

Garmiza, V. V., ed. "Predpolozheniia i proekty P. A. Valueva po voprosam vnutrennei politiki (1862-1866 gg.)." *Istoricheskii arkhiv*, 3 (January-February 1958): 138-153.

Golitsyn, N. V. "Konstitutsiia grafa Loris-Melikova: Materialy dlia ee istorii." *Byloe*, nos. 4-5 (1918), 125-186.

"Gr. Loris-Melikov i imp. Aleksandr II o polozhenii Rossii v sentiabre 1880 g." *Byloe*, no. 4 (1917), 34-38.

Ivanova, L. M., ed. *Krest'ianskoe dvizhenie v Rossii v 1861-1869 gg. Sbornik dokumentov.* Moscow, 1964.

Kavelin, K. D. "Pis'mo K. D. Kavelina k grafu M. T. Loris-Melikovu: 19'go fevralia 1880 goda. (c predisloviem i primechaniiami professora D. A. Korsakova)." *Russkaia mysl'*, 27, no. 5 (March 1906), 27-37.

Loris-Melikov, M. T. "Ispoved' grafa Loris-Melikova," *Katorga i ssylka*, book 2, no. 15 (1925), 118-125.

Materialy dlia istorii uprazdeniia krepostnogo sostoianiia pomeshchich'ikh krest'ian v Rossii v Tsarstvovanii Imperatora Aleksandra II. Comp. D. P. Khrushchov. 3 vols. Berlin, 1860-1862.

Materialy otnosiashchiesia do novago obshchestvennago ustroistva v gorodakh imperii. 4 vols. St. Petersburg, 1877.

Materialy sobrannye dlia vysochaishei uchrezhdennoi kommissii o preobrazovanii gubernskikh i uezdnykh uchrezhdenii. Part 1, *Materialy istoricheskie i zakonodatel'nye.* St. Petersburg, 1870.

Materialy vysochaishei uchrezhdennoi Osoboi Komissii stats sekretaria Kakhanova dlia sostavleniia proektov mestnogo upravleniia. St. Petersburg, 1884.

Obshchii sostav ministerstva vnutrennikh del, n.p., 1858, 1861, 1869.

Obukhov, B. *Russkii administrator noveishei shkoly: zapiska pskovskago gubernatora i otvet na nee.* Berlin, 1868.

"Perepiska Aleksandra III s. gr. M. T. Loris-Melikovym (1880-1881 gg.)." *Krasnyi arkhiv,* 1, no. 8 (1925), 101-131.

"Perepiska ministra vnutrennikh del P. A. Valueva i gosudarstvennogo sekretaria S. N. Urusova v 1866 godu." *Istoriia SSSR,* no. 2 (March-April 1973), 115-127.

Pobedonostsev, K. P. *K. P. Pobedonostsev i ego korrespondenty, pis'ma i zapiski s predisloviem M. N. Pokrovskogo, Tom I. novum regnum, polutom l-i.* Moscow-Petrograd, 1923.

———— *Pis'ma Pobedonostseva k Aleksandru III: Tom I s predisloviem M. N. Pokrovskogo.* Moscow, 1925.

Polnoe Sobranie Zakonov Rossiiskoi Imperii s 1649 g. First series (Sobranie pervoe), 1649-1825, 45 vols. Second series, 1825-1881, 55 vols. St. Petersburg, 1830 ff.

Predtechenskii, A. V., ed. *Krest'ianskoe dvizhenie v Rossii v 1825-1849 gg. Sbornik dokumentov.* Moscow, 1961.

Sbornik tsirkuliarov i instruktsii ministerstva vnutrennykh del s uchrezhdeniia ministerstva po 1-e okt. 1853. St. Petersburg, 1854.

Sbornik tsirkuliarov i instruktsii ministerstva vnutrennikh del za 1858-1861 gg. Ed. D. Chukovskii. St. Petersburg, 1873. *1862-1864,* 1873. *1865-1866,* 1873. *1867-1868,* 1874. *1872-1873,* 1874. *1874,* 1875. *1875,* 1877. *1876,* 1877. *1877,* 1880. *1878,* 1880. *1879,* 1880.

Sbornik tsirkuliarov ministerstva vnutrennikh del za 1880-1884 gg. Ed. D. V. Chichinadze. St. Petersburg, 1886.

"Senatorskie revizii 1880 goda." *Russkii arkhiv,* no. 11 (1912), 417-429.

Spisok grazhdanskim chinam pervykh chetyrekh klassov. St. Petersburg, 1842-1916.

Spisok grazhdanskim chinam pervykh trekh klassov. St. Petersburg, 1855-1916.

Spisok vysshim chinam gosudarstvennago, gubernskago i eparkhial'nago upravleniia. St. Petersburg, 1834-1916.

Svod Zakonov Rossiiskoi Imperii, izdaniia 1857. St. Petersburg, 1857.

Troinitskii, G. A., ed. "P. A. Valuev i A. G. Troinitskii." *Russkaia starina* (July-October 1899), 99:467-480, 697-706; 100:231-239.

Troshchinskii, D. P. "Zapiska Dmitriia Prokof'evicha Troshchinskago o ministerstvakh." *Sbornik Imperatorskago Russkago Istoricheskago Obshchestva*, 3:1-162. St. Petersburg, 1868.

Valuev, P. A. "Duma russkago (vo vtoroi polovine 1855 goda)." *Russkaia starina*, 49 (March 1891): 349-360.

—— "Graf P. A. Valuev o polozhenii Rossii v 1882 godu." *Minuvshie gody*, 1, no. 9 (September 1908): 25-31.

Vorontsov, S. F. "O vnutrennem upravlenii v Rossii; zapiska grafa S. R. Vorontsova, 1803." *Russkii arkhiv*, book 2 (1881), 155-162.

Voskresenskii, N. A. *Zakonodatel'nye akty Petra I- Akty o vysshikh gosudarstvennykh ustanovleniiakh*. Vol. 1. Moscow-Leningrad, 1945.

"Vsepoddanneishii doklad gr. P. A. Valueva i dokumenty k Verkhovnoi Rasporiaditel'noi Kommissii 1880 g. kasatel'nye." *Russkii arkhiv*, nos. 11-12 (1915), 216-248.

"Vsepoddanneishii doklad 11 aprelia 1880 g." *Russkii arkhiv*, nos. 11-12 (1915), 238-248.

"Zapiska Imperatora Pavla I ob ustroistve raznykh chastei gosudarstvennago upravleniia." *Sbornik Imperatorskago Russkago Istoricheskago Obshchestva*, 90 (St. Petersburg, 1894): 1-4.

"Zapiska neizvestnago litsa o gosudarstvennom ustroistve 5 Ianv. 1880." *Russkii arkhiv*, 3 (1909): 443-461.

"Zapiska P. A. Valueva Aleksandru II o zemskikh uchrezhdeniiakh (ianvar' 1867 goda)." *Sovetskii arkhiv*, no. 4 (1971), 79-87.

DIARIES AND MEMOIRS

Arsen'ev, K. K. "Vospominaniia K. K. Arsen'eva ob Uchilishche Pravovedeniia 1849-1855." *Russkaia starina*, 50 (April 1886): 199-220.

Artem'ev, A. I. "Iz Dnevnika 1856-1857 godov." In *M. E. Saltykov-Shchedrin v vospominaniiakh sovremennikov*, pp. 427-440. Moscow, 1957.

Belogolovyi, N. A. "Graf Mikhail Tarielovich Loris-Melikov, 1878-1888." In *Vospominaniia i drugie stat'i*, pp. 156-193. 3rd ed. Moscow, 1898.

Bogdanovich, A. B. *Tri poslednykh samoderzhtsa: Dnevnik*. Moscow-Leningrad, 1924.

Chicherin, B. N. *Vospominaniia Borisa Nikolaevicha Chicherina: puteshestvie za granitsu*. Moscow, 1932.

—— *Vospominaniia Borisa Nikolaevicha Chicherina: zemstvo i moskovskaia duma*. Moscow, 1934.

Derzhavin, G. R. *Zapiski Gavriila Romanovicha Derzhavina, 1743-1812*. Moscow, 1860.

Faresov, A. "Dve vstrechi s Grafom M. T. Loris-Melikovym." *Istori-*

cheskii vestnik, 99 (February 1905): 490-500.

Feoktistov, E. M. *Za kulisami politiki i literatury 1848-1896: vospominaniia*. Leningrad, 1929.

Insarskii, V. A. "Zapiski Vasiliia Antonovicha Insarskago," *Russkaia starina* (January 1894-September 1895), 81 (January 1894); 1-61, (February 1894): 1-45, (March 1894): 1-38, (April 1894): 36-59, (May 1894): 1-28, (June 1894): 33-62; 82 (November 1894): 27-57, (December 1894): 28-52; 83 (January 1895): 92-124, (February 1895): 53-91, (March 1895): 29-74, (April 1895): 3-42, (June 1895): 3-38; 84 (July 1895): 3-56, (August 1895): 3-39, (September 1895): 3-40.

Jelavich, Charles and Barbara, eds. *The Education of a Russian Statesman: The Memoirs of Nicholas Karlovich Giers*. Berkeley and Los Angeles, 1962.

Kizevetter, A. A. *Na rubezhe dvukh stoletii (vospominaniia 1881-1914)*. Prague, 1929.

Koni, A. F. "Graf M. T. Loris-Melikov," In *Sobranie sochinenii*, 5: 184-216. Moscow, 1968.

Koshelev, A. I. *Zapiski Aleksandra Ivanovicha Kosheleva (1812-1883 gody)*. Berlin, 1884.

Levshin, A. I. "Dostopamiatnye minuty v moei zhizni: Zapiska Alekseia Irakleevicha Levshina." *Russkii arkhiv*, 23, no. 8 (1885): 475-557.

Lutskii, V. K. "Iz zapisok V. K. Lutskago." *Russkaia starina*, (February-March 1904), 117:303-323, 557-575; 118:137-150, 321-336.

Mel'nikov, P. I. "vospominaniia o V. I. Dale." *Russkii vestnik*, 104 (1873): 275-340.

"Mezhdu strokami odnogo formuliarnago spiska 1823-1881." *Russkaia starina*, 32 (1881): 817-855.

Meshcherskii, Kniaz' V. P. *Moi vospominaniia*. 2 vols. St. Petersburg, 1897-1898.

Miliutin, D. A. *Dnevnik D. A. Miliutina 1878-1880*. Vol. 3. Moscow, 1950.

—— *Dnevnik D. A. Miliutina 1881-1882*. Vol. 4. Moscow, 1950.

Miliutina, Mariia A. "Iz zapisok Marii Agleevny Miliutinoi." *Russkaia starina* (January-April 1899), 97:39-65, 265-288, 575-601; 98:105-127.

Nikitenko, A. V. *Dnevnik A. V. Nikitenko*. 3 vols. Moscow-Leningrad, 1955.

Panteleev, L. "Moi vstrechi s gr. M. T. Loris-Melikovym." *Golos minuvshego*, no. 8 (1914), 97-109.

Peretts, E. A. *Dnevnik E. A. Perettsa, gosudarstvennogo sekretaria (1880-1883)*. Moscow-Leningrad, 1927.

Polovtsov, A. A. *Dnevnik gosudarstvennogo sekretaria A. A. Polovtsova v dvukh tomakh.* Vol. 1, 1883-1886. Vol. 2, 1887-1892. Moscow, 1966.

Semenov-Tian-Shanskii, P. P. *Epokha osvobozhdeniia krest'ian v Rossii (1857-1861) v vospominaniakh P. P. Semenov-Tian-Shanskago.* 2 vols. St. Petersburg, 1911-1916.

Shumakher, A. D. "Neskol'ko slov o g.-a. Timasheve i otnoshenii ego k obshchestvennym uchrezhdeniiam." *Vestnik evropy,* 6, no. 12 (1893): 846-857.

――― "Pozdnyia vospominaniia o davno minuvshikh vremenakh." *Vestnik evropy,* 196, no. 3 (1899): 89-128.

Solov'ev, Ia. S. "Krest'ianskoe delo v 1856-59 gg.: Otryvok iz zapisok senatora, tainogo sovetnika Ia. A. Solov'eva." *Russkaia starina,* 27 (February 1880): 347-360.

――― "Zapiski senatora Iakova Aleksandrovicha Solov'eva: Krest'ianskoe delo v tsarstvovanii Aleksandra II." *Russkaia starina* (February 1881-March 1884); 30:213-246, 721-756; 31:1-32; 33: 227-258, 561-596; 34:105-154, 389-426; 36:131-154, 221-252; 38: 259-290, 579-614; 41:241-276, 575-608.

Stasov, V. V. "Uchilishche pravovedeniia sorok let tomu nazad, 1836-1842." *Russkaia starina,* 29 (1880): 1015-1042; 30 (1881): 393-422, 573-602; 31 (1881): 247-282.

Stremoukhov, P. D. "Iz vospominanii o grafe P. A. Valueve." *Russkaia starina,* 116 (November 1903): 273-293.

――― "Zametka odnogo iz deputatov pervago prizyva." *Russkaia starina,* 102, no. 4 (1900): 139-144.

Tiutchev, I. A. "V uchilishche pravovedeniia v 1847-1852 gg. Vospominaniia po povodu 50-letnego iubileia uchilishcha." *Russkaia starina,* 48 (1885): 436-452, 663-678; 49 (1886): 361-376.

Tolstoi, D. N. "Zapiski grafa Dmitriia Nikolaevicha Tolstago." *Russkii arkhiv,* 23, no. 2 (1885): 5-33.

"V pribaltiiskom krae: Iz zapisok russkago chinovnika 1856-1866." *Russkaia starina,* 35 (1882): 59-90.

Valuev, P. A. *Dnevnik P. A. Valueva ministra vnutrennikh del.* Ed. P. A. Zaionchkovskii. Vol. 1, 1861-1864. Vol. 2, 1865-1876. Moscow, 1961.

――― *Dnevnik 1877-1884.* Ed. V. Ia. Iakovlev-Bogucharskii and P. E. Shchegolev. Petrograd, 1919.

――― "Dnevnik za 1847-1860 gg." *Russkaia starina* (April-November 1891); 70:167-182, 339-349, 603-616; 71:71-82, 265-278, 547-602; 72:139-154.

Vigel', F. F. *Zapiski.* Ed. S. Ia. Shtreikh. 2 vols. Moscow, 1928.

De Vogüé, Eugène Melchior. "Le Général Loris-Mélikof, derniers mois du règne de L'Empereur Alexandre II." In *Spectacles Contemporains*. Paris, 1891.

OFFICIAL MVD NEWSPAPERS AND JOURNALS AND OTHER JOURNALS
Zhurnal ministerstva vnutrennikh del
Pravitel'stvennyi vestnik
Russkoe bogatstvo
Severnaia pochta
Vestnik evropy

Secondary Sources

Abbott, Robert James. "Police Reform in Russia, 1858-1878." Ph.D. dissertation, Princeton University, 1971.

Adrianov, S. A. *Ministerstvo Vnutrennikh Del. Istoricheskii Ocherk.* 3 vols. St. Petersburg, 1901.

Aleksandrov, M. S. *Gosudarstvo, biurokratiia, i absoliutizm v istorii Rossii.* St. Petersburg, 1910.

Almedingen, M. E. *The Emperor Alexander II: A Study.* London, 1962.

Ambler, Effie. *Russian Journalism and Politics, 1861-1881: The Career of Aleksei S. Suvorin.* Detroit, 1972.

Amburger, Erik. *Geschichte der Behördenorganisation Russlands von Peter den Grossen bis 1917.* Leiden, 1966.

Anderson, Perry. *Lineages of the Absolutist State.* London, 1974.

Andreev, M. "Samoderzhavie i zakonnost'." *Russkoe bogatstvo*, nos. 11-12 (November-December 1905): 127-147.

Andreevskii, I. E. *Politseiskoe pravo.* 2 vols. St. Petersburg, 1874.

Armstrong, John A. *The European Administrative Elite.* Princeton, 1973.

———— "Old Regime Governors: Bureaucratic and Patrimonial Attributes." *Comparative Studies in Society and History*, 14 (1972): 2-29.

———— "Tsarist and Soviet Elite Administrators." *Slavic Review*, 31, no. 1 (March 1972): 1-28.

Artsimovich, V. A. *Viktor Antonovich Artsimovich-vospominaniia-kharakteristika.* St. Petersburg, 1904.

Avineri, Shlomo. *Hegel's Theory of the Modern State.* Cambridge, England, 1972.

Avrekh, A. Ia. *Stolypin i tret'ia duma.* Moscow, 1968.

Balazs, Etienne. *Chinese Civilization and Bureaucracy: Variations on a Theme.* Trans. H. M. Wright, ed. Arthur F. Wright. New Haven and London, 1964.

Barker, Ernest. *The Development of Public Services in Western Eu-*

rope, 1660-1930. London, 1944.

Baron, Samuel H., and Heer, Nancy W., eds. *Windows on the Russian Past—Essays on Soviet Historiography since Stalin.* Columbus, Ohio, 1977.

Bays, Daniel H. *China Enters the Twentieth Century: Chang Chih-tung and the Issues of a New Age, 1895-1909.* Ann Arbor, 1978.

Beasley, W. G. *The Meiji Restoration.* Stanford, Calif., 1972.

Bendix, Reinhard. "Bureaucracy." In *International Encyclopedia of the Social Sciences,* 2:206-219. New York, 1968.

Bennet, Helju Aulik. "The *Chin* System and the *Raznochintsy* in the Government of Alexander III, 1881-1894." Ph.D. dissertation, University of California, Berkeley, 1973.

Benson, Sumner. "Boris Chicherin and the Dilemma of Russian Liberalism." Ph.D. dissertation, Harvard University, 1968.

Black, Cyril. *The Dynamics of Modernization: A Study in Comparative History.* New York, Evanston, London, 1966.

Black, Cyril E., et al. *The Modernization of Japan and Russia: A Comparative Study.* New York, London, 1975.

Blackwell, William T. *The Beginnings of Russian Industrialization, 1800-1860.* Princeton, 1968.

Blinov, I. *Gubernatory: istoriko-iuridicheskii ocherk.* St. Petersburg, 1904.

Bliokh, I. C. *Finansy Rossii XIX stoletie: Istoriia-statistika.* 2 vols. St. Petersburg, 1882.

Blum, Jerome. *The End of the Old Order in Rural Europe.* Princeton, 1978.

Bogoslovskii, M. *Oblastnaia reforma Petra Velikago: Provintsiia 1719-27 gg.* Moscow, 1902.

Bogucharskii, V. Ia. (Iakovlev). *Iz istorii politicheskoi bor'by v 70-x i 80-x gg. XIX veka.* Moscow, 1912.

Von Borch, Herbert. *Obrigkeit und Widerstand, zur politischen Soziologie des Beamtentums.* Tübingen, 1954.

Bowen, Ralph H. *German Theories of the Corporative State with Special Reference to the Period 1870-1919.* New York, London, 1947.

Butler, Nancy. "*Vol'noe Slovo* and the *Zemstvo* Union: Was Russian Liberalism Dead in 1881?" *Canadian Slavonic Papers,* 16, no. 1 (1974): 14-37.

Byrnes, Robert F. *Pobedonostsev, His Life and Thought.* Bloomington, 1968.

Chermenskii, E. D. *Burzhuaziia i tsarizm v pervoe russkoi revoliutsii.* 2nd ed. Moscow, 1970.

Chernukha, V. G. *Krest'ianskii vopros v pravitel'stvennoi politike*

Rossii (60-70 gody XIX v.). Leningrad, 1972.

—— "Programmnaia zapiska ministra vnutrennikh del P. A. Valueva ot 22 sentiabria 1861g." Akademiia Nauk SSSR, Otdelenie Istorii, Arkhiograficheskaia Komissiia, Leningradskoe Otdelenie, *Vspomogatel'nye istoricheskie distsipliny,* 7:210-220. Leningrad, 1976.

—— "Problema politicheskoi reformy v pravitel'stvennykh krugakh Rossii v nachale 70-x godov XIX v." In Akademiia Nauk SSSR, Institut Istorii SSSR, Leningradskoe Otdelenie, *Problemy krest'ianskogo zemlevladeniia i vnutrennei politiki Rossi: dooktiabr'skii period,* pp. 138-191. Leningrad, 1972.

—— "Sovet Ministrov v 1857-1861 gg." In Akademiia Nauk SSSR, Otdelenie Istorii, Arkhiograficheskaia Komissiia, Leningradskoe Otdelenie, *Vspomogatel'nye istoricheskie distsipliny,* 5:120-136. Leningrad, 1973.

—— *Vnutrenniaia politika tsarizma c serediny 50-x do nachala 80-x gg. XIX v.* Leningrad, 1978.

—— "Vsepoddanneishii doklad komissii P. A. Valueva ot 2 aprelia 1872 g. kak istochnik po istorii podatnoi reformy v Rossii." In Akademiia Nauk SSSR, Otdelenie Istorii, Arkhiograficheskaia Komissiia, Leningradskoe Otdelenie, *Vspomogatel'nye istoricheskie distsipliny,* 2:262-269. Leningrad, 1969.

Chizhevskii, D. I. *Gegel' v Rossii.* Paris, 1939.

Christian, David. "The 'Senatorial Party' and the Theory of Collegial Government, 1801-1803." *Russian Review,* 38, no. 3 (July 1979): 298-322.

Christoff, Peter K. *An Introduction to Nineteenth-Century Russian Slavophilism. A Study in Ideas, Volume I: A. S. Xomjakov.* The Hague, 1961.

—— *An Introduction to Nineteenth-Century Russian Slavophilism. A Study in Ideas, Volume II: I. V. Kireevskij.* The Hague, 1972.

Cohen, Emmeline W. *The Growth of the British Civil Service, 1780-1939.* London and Hamden, Conn., 1965.

Cohen, Paul A., and Schrecker, John E., eds. *Reform in Nineteenth-Century China.* Cambridge, London, 1976.

Crozier, Michel. *The Bureaucratic Phenomenon.* Chicago, 1967.

Crummey, Robert O. "Peter and the Boiar Aristocracy." *Canadian-American Slavic Studies,* 8, no. 2 (Summer 1974): 274-287.

—— "The Reconstitution of the Boiar Aristocracy, 1613-45." *Forschungen zur osteuropäischen Geschichte,* 18 (1973): 187-220.

Czap, Peter, Jr. "P. A. Valuyev's Proposal for a *Vyt'* Administration, 1864." *The Slavonic and East European Review,* 45, no. 105 (July

1967): 391-410.

Dashkevich, Leonid. *Nashe ministerstvo vnutrennikh del.* Berlin, 1895.

Davidovich, A. M. *Samoderzhavie v epokhu imperializma: klassovaia sushchnost' i evoliutsiia absoliutizma v Rossii.* Moscow, 1975.

Davison, Roderic H. *Reform in the Ottoman Empire, 1856-1876.* New York, 1973.

Demidova, N. F. "Biurokratizatsiia gosudarstvennogo apparata absoliutizma v XVII-XVIII vv." In *Absoliutizm v Rossii, XVII-XVIII vv.: Sbornik statei*, pp. 206-242. Moscow, 1964.

———— "Prikaznye liudi XVII v. (Sotsial'nyi sostav i istochniki formirovaniia)." *Istoricheskie zapiski*, 90 (1972): 332-354.

Deutscher, Isaac. "Roots of Bureaucracy." *Canadian Slavic Studies*, 3, no. 3 (Fall 1969): 453-472.

Diakin, V. S. *Samoderzhavie, burzhuaziia i dvorianstvo v 1970-1911gg.* Leningrad, 1978.

———— "Stolypin i dvorianstvo (Proval mestnoi reformy)." Akademiia Nauk, Institut Istorii SSSR, Leningradskoe Otdelenie, *Problemy krest'ianskogo zemlevladeniia i vnutrennei politiki Rossii; dooktiabrskii period*, pp. 231-274. Leningrad, 1972.

Diatlova, N. P. "Otchety gubernatorov kak istoricheskii istochnik." In Glavnoe Arkhivnoe Upravlenie, *Problemy arkhivovedeniia i istochnikovedeniia*, pp. 227-246. Leningrad, 1964.

Doctorow, Gilbert S. "The Fundamental State Laws of 23 April 1906." *Russian Review*, 35, no. 1 (January 1976): 33-52.

———— "The Government Program of 17 October 1905." *Russian Review*, 34, no. 2 (April 1975): 123-136.

———— "The Introduction of Parliamentary Institutions in Russia during the Revolution of 1905-1907." Ph.D. dissertation, Columbia University, 1975.

Druzhinin, N. M. *Gosudarstvennye krest'iane i reforma P.D. Kiseleva.* 2 vols. Moscow-Leningrad, 1946-1958.

———— *Russkaia derevnia na perelome 1861-1880 gg.* Moscow, 1978.

———— "Senatorskie revizii 1860-1870-x godov (K voprosu o realizatsii reformy 1861 g.)." *Istoricheskie zapiski*, 79 (1966): 139-175.

Ducroq, Théophile. *Cours de droit administratif et de législation française des finances, avec introduction de droit constitutionnel et les principes du droit public.* 7th ed. 7 vols. Paris, 1897-1905.

Duguit, Léon. *Manuel de droit constitutionnel.* 3rd ed. Paris, 1918.

Dzhanshiev, G. A. *Iz epokhi velikikh reform.* 5th ed. Moscow, 1894.

Edeen, Alf. "The Civil Service: Its Composition and Status." In C. E. Black, ed., *The Transformation of Russian Society: Aspects of*

Social Change since 1861, pp. 274-292. Cambridge, 1960.

Eisenstadt, S. N. *The Political Systems of Empires: The Rise and Fall of the Historical Bureaucratic Societies*. New York, 1969.

—— *Revolution and the Transformation of Societies: A Comparative Study of Civilizations*. New York, London, 1978.

Elwitt, Sanford. *The Making of the Third Republic: Class and Politics in France, 1868-1884*. Baton Rouge, La., 1975.

Emmons, Terence. *The Russian Landed Gentry and the Peasant Emancipation of 1861*. Cambridge, England, 1968.

Engelberg, Ernst. "Zur Entstehung und historischen Stellung des Preussisch-Deutschen Bonapartismus." In F. Klein and J. Streisand, eds., *Beiträge zum neuen Geschichtsbild*, pp. 236-251. Berlin, 1956.

Entsiklopedicheskii slovar'. Ed. F. A. Brokgauz and I. A. Efron. 82 vols. and 2 supplementary vols. St. Petersburg, 1891-1907.

Eroshkin, N. P. *Istoriia gosudarstvennykh uchrezhdenii dorevoliutsionnoi Rossii*. Moscow, 1968.

—— "Samoderzhavie pervoi poloviny XIX veka i ego politicheskie instituty (k voprosu o klassovoi sushchnosti absoliutizma)." *Istoriia SSSR*, 1 (January-February 1975): 37-59.

Evreinov, V. A. *Grazhdanskoe chinoproizvodstvo v Rossii*. St. Petersburg, 1898.

Eyck, Erich. *Bismarck and the German Empire*. New York, 1958.

Field, Daniel. *The End of Serfdom: Nobility and Bureaucracy in Russia, 1855-61*. Cambridge, 1976.

—— "Kavelin and Russian Liberalism." *Slavic Review*, 32, no. 1 (March 1973): 59-78.

—— "The Reforms of the 1860's." In S. N. Baron and N. W. Heer, eds., *Windows on the Russian Past: Essays on Soviet Historiography since Stalin*, pp. 89-104. Columbus, Ohio, 1977.

Filippov, A. N. "Istoricheskii ocherk obrazovaniia ministerstv v Rossii." *Zhurnal ministerstva iustitsii*, no. 9 (November 1902), 39-73; no. 10 (December 1902), 1-26.

Findley, Carter V. *Bureaucratic Reform in the Ottoman Empire: The Sublime Porte, 1789-1922*. Princeton, 1980.

Fischer, George. *Russian Liberalism: From Gentry to Intelligentsia*. Cambridge, 1958.

Flynn, James. "The Universities, the Gentry and the Russian Imperial Services, 1815-1825." *Canadian Slavic Studies*, 2 (Winter 1968): 486-503.

Freeze, Gregory L. "Caste and Emancipation: The Changing Status of Clerical Families in the Great Reforms." In David L. Ransel, ed., *The Family in Imperial Russia: New Lines of Historical Research*, pp. 124-150. Urbana, 1978.

———— "P. A. Valuyev and the Politics of Church Reform (1861-62)." *The Slavonic and East European Review*, 56, no. 1 (January 1978): 68-87.

Fuks, V. I. *Sud i politsiia*. 2 vols. Moscow, 1889.

Gantvoort, John G. "Relations between Government and Zemstvos under Valuev and Timashev, 1864-1876." Ph.D. dissertation, University of Illinois, 1971.

Garmiza, V. V. *Podgotovka zemskoi reformy 1864 goda*. Moscow, 1957.

Geertz, Clifford. "Ideology as a Cultural System." In *The Interpretation of Cultures: Selected Essays*, pp. 193-233. New York, 1973.

Gernet, M. N. *Istoriia tsarskoi tiurmy*. 2nd ed. 5 vols. Moscow, 1952.

Gerschenkron, Alexander. *Europe in the Russian Mirror: Four Lectures in Economic History*. Cambridge, England, 1970.

———— "Soviet Marxism and Absolutism." *Slavic Review*, 30 (December 1971): 853-869.

Gerstein, Linda. *Nikolai Strakhov*. Cambridge, 1971.

Gerth, H. H., and Mills, C. Wright, eds. *From Max Weber: Essays in Sociology*. New York, 1958.

Gierke, Otto. *Natural Law and the Theory of Society, 1500-1800*. Trans. Ernest Barker. 2 vols. Cambridge, England, 1934.

Gindin, I. F. *Gosudarstvennyi Bank i ekonomicheskaia politika Tsarskogo pravitel'stva (1861-1892 gody)*. Moscow, 1960.

Gleason, Abbott. *European and Muscovite: Ivan Kireevsky and the Origins of Slavophilism*. Cambridge, 1972.

Golovachev, A. A. *Desiat' let reform, 1861-1871 gg*. St. Petersburg, 1872.

Gorfein, G. M. "Osnovnye istochniki po istorii vysshikh i tsentral'- nykh uchrezhdenii XIX-nachala XX v." Glavnoe Arkhivnoe Upravlenie SSSR, *Nekotorye voprosy izucheniia istoricheskikh dokumentov XIX-nachala XX v.: Sbornik statei*, pp. 73-110. Leningrad, 1967.

Got'e, Iu. V. *Istoriia oblastnogo upravleniia v Rossii ot Petra I do Ekateriny II*. 2 vols. Moscow, 1913, 1941.

Gradovskii, A. D. *Nachala russkago gosudarstvennago prava*. In *Sobranie sochinenii A. D. Gradovskago*. Vol. 8. St. Petersburg, 1907.

———— *Trudnye gody 1876-1880: Ocherki i opyti*. St. Petersburg, 1880.

———— *Vysshaia administratsiia Rossii XVIII st. i general prokurory*. In *Sobranie sochinenii A. D. Gradovskago*, 1:37-297. St. Petersburg, 1899.

Graham, S. *Tsar of Freedom: The Life and Reign of Alexander II*. New Haven, 1935.

Gribowski, Wiatscheslav. *Das Staatsrecht des russischen Reiches*. Tübingen, 1912.

Grothusen, Klaus-Detlev. *Die historische Rechtsschule Russlands: Ein Beitrag zur russischen Geistegeschichte in der zweiten Hälfte des 19. Jahrhunderts*. In *Giessener Abhandlungen zur Agrar und Wirtschaftsforschung des europäischen Ostens*. Vol. 18. Giessen. 1962.

Gurko, V. I. *Features and Figures of the Past: Government and Opinion in the Reign of Nicholas II*. Trans. L. Matveev. Stanford, London, 1939.

Hagen, Manfred. "Der russische 'Bonapartismus' nach 1906." *Jahrbücher für Geschichte Osteuropas*, 24 (1976): 369-393.

Haimson, Leopold H. "The Parties and the State: The Evolution of Political Attitudes." In Michael Cherniavsky, ed., *The Structure of Russian History: Interpretive Essays*, pp. 309-340. New York, 1970.

Haltzel, Michael H. "The Reaction of the Baltic Germans to Russification during the Nineteenth Century." Ph.D. dissertation, Harvard University, 1971.

Harootunian, H. D. *Toward Restoration: The Growth of Political Consciousness in Tokugawa Japan*. Berkeley, Los Angeles, London, 1970.

Hassell, James. "Implementation of the Table of Ranks during the Eighteenth Century." *Slavic Review*, 29, no. 2 (June 1970): 283-295.

———— "The Vicissitudes of Russian Administrative Reform, 1762-1801." Ph.D. dissertation, Cornell University, 1967.

Heilbronner, Hans. "The Administrations of Loris-Melikov and Ignatiev 1880-1882." Ph.D. dissertation, University of Michigan, 1954.

———— "Alexander III and the Reform Plan of Loris-Melikov." *Journal of Modern History*, 33, no. 4 (December 1961): 384-397.

———— "The Russian Plague of 1878-79." *Slavic Review*, 21, no. 1 (March 1962): 89-112.

Hellie, Richard. *Enserfment and Military Change in Muscovy*. Chicago, 1971.

Hintze, Otto. "Die Entstehung der modernen Staatsministerien." In *Staat und Verfassung*, ed. F. Hartung, pp. 265-310. Leipzig, 1941.

Hobsbawm, E. J. *The Age of Capital, 1848-1875*. New York, 1975.

Hosking, Geoffrey, A. *The Russian Constitutional Experiment: Government and Duma, 1907-1914*. Cambridge, England, 1973.

Hough, Jerry F. "The Bureaucratic Model and the Nature of the Soviet System." *Journal of Comparative Administration*, 5, no. 2 (August 1973): 134-167.

—— "The Party *Apparatchiki*." In H. Gordon Skilling and Franklyn Griffiths, eds., *Interest Groups in Soviet Politics*, pp. 47-92. Princeton, 1971.

Hue de Grais (Graf). *Handbuch der Verfassung und Verwaltung in Preussen und dem Deutschen Reiche*. Berlin, 1906.

Hutton, Lester Thomas. "The Reform of City Government in Russia, 1860-1870." *Ph.D. dissertation*, University of Illinois, 1972.

Ispavin, M. V. *Obzor trudov Vysochaishei utverzhdennoi, pod predsedatel'stvom Stats-Sekretaria Kakhanova, Osoboi Komissii*. 2 parts. St. Petersburg, 1908.

Istoriia pravitel'stvuiushchago senata za dvesti let 1711-1911 gg. 4 vols. St. Petersburg, 1911.

Ivanovskii, V. V. "Biurokratia, kak samostoiatel'nyi obshchestvennyi klass." *Russkaia mysl'*, book 8 (1903), 1-23.

—— "Kollegial'noe nachalo v ministerskoi organizatsii." *Zhurnal iuridicheskogo obshchestva pri Imperatorskom Sankt Peterburgskom universitete*, book 7 (1895), 1-28.

James, Herman G. *Principles of Prussian Administration*. New York, 1913.

Jones, Robert E. *The Emancipation of the Russian Nobility, 1762-1785*. Princeton, 1973.

Kann, Robert A. *The Multinational Empire: Nationalism and National Reform in the Habsburg Monarchy, 1848-1918*. Vol. 2. New York, 1950.

—— *The Problem of Restoration: A Study in Comparative Political History*. Berkeley, Los Angeles, 1968.

Kaiser, Friedhelm Barthold. *Die russische Justizreform von 1864: zur Geschichte der russischen Justiz von Katharina II bis 1917*. Studien zur Geschichte Osteuropas. Vol. 14. Leiden, 1972.

Karnovich, E. *Russkoe chinovnichestvo v byloe i nastoiashchee vremia*. St. Petersburg, 1897.

Karpovich, Michael. "Two Types of Russian Liberalism: Maklakov and Miliukov." In E. J. Simmons, ed., *Continuity and Change in Russian and Soviet Thought*, pp. 129-143. Cambridge, 1955.

Katz, Martin. *Mikhail N. Katkov: A Political Biography, 1818-1887*. The Hague, 1966.

Keep, John. "Light and Shade in the History of the Russian Administration." *Canadian-American Slavic Studies*, 6, no. 1 (Spring 1972): 1-9.

———— "The Muscovite Elite and the Approach to Pluralism." *Slavonic and East European Review*, 48, no. 111 (April 1970): 201-231.

———— "Paul I and the Militarization of Government." *Canadian-American Slavic Studies*, 7, no. 1 (Spring 1973): 1-14.

———— "Programming the Past: Imperial Russian Bureaucracy and Society under the Scrutiny of Mr. George Yaney." *Canadian-American Slavic Studies*, 8, no. 2 (Winter 1974): 569-580.

Kennan, George. *Siberia and the Exile System*. 2 vols. London, 1891.

Kheifets, M. I. *Vtoraia revoliutsionnaia situatsiia v rossii (konets 70-x —nachalo 80-x godov XIX veka): Krizis pravitel'stvennoi politiki*. Moscow, 1963.

Kiniapina, N. S. *Politika russkogo samoderzhaviia v oblasti promyshlennosti*. Moscow, 1968.

Kipp, Jacob Walter. "The Grand Duke Konstantin Nikolaevich and the Epoch of the Great Reforms, 1855-1866." Ph.D. dissertation, Pennsylvania State University, 1970.

———— "M. Kh. Reutern on the Russian State and Economy: A Liberal Bureaucrat during the Crimean Era, 1845-1860." *Journal of Modern History*, 47 (September 1975): 437-459.

Kirchheimer, Otto. *Political Justice: The Use of Legal Procedure for Political Ends*. Princeton, 1961.

Kistiakovskii, B. *Stranitsy proshlago: K istorii konstitutsionnago dvizheniia v Rossii*. Moscow, 1912.

Kitaev, V. A. *Ot frondy k okhranitel'stvu: Iz istorii russkoi liberal'noi mysli 50-60x godov XIX veka*. Moscow, 1972.

Kliuchevskii, V. O. *Sochineniia*. 8 vols. Moscow, 1958.

Klochkov, M. V. *Ocherki pravitel'stvennoi deiatel'nosti vremeni Pavla I*. Petrograd, 1916.

Knutson, Gordon Dale. "Peter Valuev: A Conservative's Approach and Reactions to the Reforms of Alexander II." Ph.D. dissertation, University of Kansas, 1970.

Korelin, A. D. "Dvorianstvo v poreformennoi Rossii, 1861-1904." *Istoricheskie zapiski*, no. 87 (1971): 91-173.

———— "Institut predvoditelei dvorianstvo; o sotsial'nom i politicheskom polozhenii dvorian." *Istoriia SSSR*, 3 (1978): 31-48.

Korf, Baron S. A. *Administrativnaia iustitsiia v Rossii*. 2 vols. St. Petersburg, 1910.

Korkunov, N. M. *Russkoe gosudarstvennoe pravo*. 2 vols. 6th ed. St. Petersburg, 1909.

———— *Ukaz i zakon*. St. Petersburg, 1894.

Kornilov, A. A. *Obshchestvennoe dvizhenie pri Aleksandre II (1855-*

1881). Istoricheskie ocherki. Moscow, 1909.

Kovalevskii, M. M. *Konstitutsiia grafa Loris-Melikova.* London, 1893.

Krieger, Leonard. *An Essay on the Theory of Enlightened Despotism.* Chicago, 1975.

―――― *The Politics of Discretion: Pufendorf and the Acceptance of Natural Law.* Chicago, 1965.

Kucherov, Samuel. *Courts, Lawyers and Trials under the Last Three Tsars.* New York, 1953.

LaPalombara, Joseph G., ed. *Bureaucracy and Political Development.* Princeton, 1963.

Latkin, V.N. *Uchebnik istorii Russkago prava perioda imperii XVIII-XIX st.* St. Petersburg, 1909.

Laverychev, V. Ia. *Krupnaia burzhuaziia v poreformennoi Rossii (1861-1900 gg).* Moscow, 1974.

―――― *Tsarizm i rabochii vopros v Rossii (1861-1917 gg.).* Moscow, 1972.

Lazarevskii, N. I. *Lektsii po russkomu gosudarstvennomu pravu.* Vol. 2, *Administrativnoe pravo.* St. Petersburg, 1910.

Leikina-Svirskaia, V. R. *Intelligentsiia v Rossii vo vtoroi polovine XIX veka.* Moscow, 1971.

Lenin, V. I. "Goniteli zemstva i annibaly liberalizma." In V. I. Lenin, *Polnoe sobranie sochinenii,* pp. 25-72. 5th ed. Moscow, 1959.

Leontovitsch, Victor. *Geschichte des Liberalismus in Russland.* Frankfurt am Main, 1957.

Leroy-Beaulieu, A. *The Empire of the Tsars and the Russians.* Trans. Z. Ragozin. 3 vols. New York, 1898.

―――― *Un homme d'état Russe (Nicolas Milutine): D' après sa correspondance inedité.* Paris, 1884.

Leslie, R. F. *Reform and Insurrection in Russian Poland, 1856-1865.* Westport, Conn., 1969.

Levin, Sh. M. *Obshchestvennoe dvizhenie v Rossii v 60-70-e gody XIX veka.* Moscow, 1958.

Lewis, Bernard. *The Emergence of Modern Turkey.* 2nd ed. London, 1969.

Liashchenko, P. I. *History of the National Economy of Russia to the 1917 Revolution.* New York, 1949.

Lincoln, W. Bruce. "The Circle of the Grand Duchess Yelena Pavlovna, 1847-1861." *The Slavonic and East European Review,* 48, no. 112 (July 1970): 373-387.

―――― "The Daily Life of St. Petersburg Officials in the Mid-Nineteenth Century." *Oxford Slavonic Papers,* n.s., 8 (Oxford, 1975): 82-100.

——— "The Genesis of an 'Enlightened' Bureaucracy in Russia, 1825-1856." *Jahrbücher für Geschichte Osteuropas*, Band 20, Heft 3 (September 1972): 321-330.

——— "The Makings of a New Polish Policy: N. A. Milyutin and the Polish Question, 1861-1863." *The Polish Review*, 15, no. 1 (Winter 1970): 54-66.

——— "The Ministers of Alexander II." *Cahiers du monde russe et soviétique*, 17, no. 4 (1976): 467-484.

——— "The Ministers of Nicholas I: A Brief Inquiry into Their Backgrounds and Service Careers." *Russian Review*, 34, no. 3 (July 1975): 308-323.

——— "N. A. Miliutin and the St. Petersburg Municipal Act of 1846: A Study in Reform under Nicholas I." *Slavic Review*, 33, no. 1 (March 1974): 55-68.

——— *Nicholas I, Emperor and Autocrat of All the Russias*. London, 1978.

——— "A Profile of the Russian Bureaucracy on the Eve of the Great Reforms." *Jahrbücher für Geschichte Osteuropas*, Band 27, Heft 2 (1979), 181-196.

——— "Russia's 'Enlightened' Bureaucrats and the Problem of State Reform 1848-1856." *Cahiers du monde russe et soviétique*, 12, no. 4 (October-December 1971): 410-421.

——— "The Tsar's Most Loyal Servitors: Russia's Enlightened Bureaucracy (1825-1881)." Unpublished manuscript.

Lokhvitskii, A. V. *Guberniia eia zemskiia i pravitel'stvenniia uchrezhdeniia*. St. Petersburg, 1864.

Luig, Lucie. *Zur Geschichte des russischen Innenministeriums unter Nikolaus I*. Wiesbaden, 1968.

Macartney, C. A. *The Hapsburg Empire, 1790-1918*. New York, 1969.

Macey, David Anthony James. "The Russian Bureaucracy and the 'Peasant Problem': The Pre-history of the Stolypin Reforms, 1861-1907." Ph.D. dissertation, Columbia University, 1976.

McFarlin, Harold A. "The Extension of the Imperial Russian Civil Service to the Lowest Office Workers: The Creation of the Chancery Clerkship, 1827-1833." *Russian History* 1, no. 1 (1974): 1-17.

——— "Recruitment Norms for the Russian Civil Service in 1833: The Chancery Clerkship." *Societias: A Review of Social History*, Summer 1973, pp. 61-73.

McGrew, Roderick E. *Russia and the Cholera, 1823-1832*. Madison, Milwaukee, 1965.

MacMaster, Robert E. *Danilevsky: A Russian Totalitarian Philosopher*. Cambridge, 1967.

Makashin, S. *Saltykov-Shchedrin na rubezhe 1850-1860 godov: Bio-*

grafiia. Moscow, 1972.

Makov, L. S. *Kratkii ocherk deiatel'nosti Ministerstva Vnutrennikh Del za dvadtsatipiatiletie 1855-1880 g.* St. Petersburg, 1880.

Malkova, Z. I., and Pliukhina, M. A. "Dokumenty vysshikh i tsentral'nykh uchrezhdenii XIX—nachala XX v. kak istochnik biograficheskikh svedenii." In Glavnoe Arkhivnoe Upravlenie SSSR, *Nekotorye voprosy izucheniia istoricheskikh dokumentov XIX-nachala XX v.: Sbornik statei*, pp. 204-228. Leningrad, 1967.

Malloy, James A., Jr. "A Police Assessment of Local Self-Government in Russia: The Third Section Reports on the Early Zemstvo," *Jahrbücher für Geschichte Osteuropas*, Band 24, Heft 4 (1976), 499-511.

——— "Russian Liberalism and the Closing of the 1867 St. Petersburg zemstvo." *Canadian Slavic Studies*, 4, no. 4 (1970): 653-670.

Mannheim, Karl. "Conservative Thought." In Kurt Wolff, ed., *From Karl Mannheim*, pp. 132-222. New York, 1971.

——— *Ideology and Utopia: An Introduction to the Sociology of Knowledge.* Trans. L. Wirth and E. Shils. New York, 1966.

Mazour, Anatole G. *The First Russian Revolution, 1825: The Decembrist Movement, Its Origins, Development, and Significance.* Stanford, 1961.

Matskina, R. Iu. "Ministerskie otchety i ikh osobennosti kak istoricheskii istochnik." In Glavnoe Arkhivnoe Upravlenie SSSR, *Problemy arkhivovedeniia i istochnikovedeniia*, pp. 209-226. Leningrad, 1964.

Meehan-Waters, Brenda. "The Muscovite Noble Origins of the Russians in the Generalitet of 1730." *Cahiers du monde russe et soviétique*, 12, nos. 1-2 (January-June 1971): 28-75.

——— "The Russian Aristocracy and the Reforms of Peter the Great." *Canadian-American Slavic Studies*, 8, no. 2 (Summer 1974): 288-302.

Mehlinger, Howard D., and Thompson, John M. *Count Witte and the Tsarist Government in the 1905 Revolution.* Bloomington, 1972.

Mel'nikov, P. I. *Polnoe sobranie sochinenii P. I. Mel'nikova (Andreia Pecherskago).* 10 vols. St. Petersburg and Moscow, 1897.

Merguerian, Barbara. "Political Ideas in Russia during the Time of Peter the Great, 1682-1730." Ph.D. dissertation, Harvard University, 1970.

Merton, Robert, ed. *Reader in Bureaucracy.* Glencoe, 1952.

Miller, Forrestt A. *Dmitrii Miliutin and the Reform Era in Russia.* Nashville, 1968.

Mitchell, Allan. "Bonapartism as a Model for Bismarckian Politics." *Journal of Modern History*, 49 (June 1977): 181-209.

Mommsen, Wolfgang J. *The Age of Bureaucracy: Perspectives on the Political Sociology of Max Weber*. New York, 1974.

Monas, Sidney. "Bureaucracy in Russia under Nicholas I." In Michael Cherniavsky, ed., *The Structure of Russian History: Interpretive Essays*, pp. 269-281. New York, 1970.

—— *The Third Section: Police and Society in Russia under Nicholas I*. Cambridge, 1961.

Mosse, W. E. *Alexander II and the Modernization of Russia*. New York, 1962.

—— "Aspects of Tsarist Bureaucracy: Recruitment to the Imperial State Council 1855-1914." *Slavonic and East European Review*, 57, no. 2 (1979): 240-254.

Nechkina, M. V., ed. *Revoliutsionnaia situatsiia v Rossii v seredine XIX veka: Kollektivnaia monografiia*. Moscow, 1978.

Neumann, Franz. *The Democratic and the Authoritarian State: Essays in Political and Legal History*. Glencoe, 1957.

Neupokoev, V. I. "Podatnyi vopros v khode reformy 1861g." In M. V. Nechkina, ed., *Epokha chernyshevskogo: Revoliutsionnaia situatsiia v Rossii v 1859-1861 gg*, 7:212-229. Moscow, 1978.

Nikolai Mikhailovich (velikii kniaz'). *Graf Pavel' Aleksandrovich Stroganov (1774-1817): Istoricheskoe izsledovanie epokhi Imperatora Aleksandra I*. 3 vols. St. Petersburg, 1903.

Orzhekhovskii, I. V. *Administratsiia i pechat' mezhdu dvumia revoliutsionnymi situatsiiami (1866-1878)*. Gor'kii, 1973.

—— *Iz istorii vnutrennei politiki samoderzhaviia v 60-70-kh godakh XIX veka*. Gor'kii, 1974.

—— "Komitet 'obshchestvennogo spaseniia' 1866g." *Obshchestvenno-politicheskaia mysl' i klassovaia bor'ba v Rossii v XVIII XX vv.*, pp. 53-68. Gor'kii, 1973.

——"Reorganizatsiia zhandarmskogo upravleniia v sviazy c pravitel'stvennoi reaktsii 60-70-x gg XIX veka." *Voprosy istorii obshchestvenno-politicheskoi mysli i vnutrennei politiki Rossii v XIX v.*, pp. 42-88. Gor'kii, 1971.

—— "Tret'e otdelenie." *Voprosy istorii*, no. 2 (1972), 109-22.

Pavlenko, N. I. "Petr I (k izucheniiu sotsial'no-politicheskikh vzgliadov)." In N. I. Pavlenko, L. A. Nikiforov, and M. Ia. Valkov, eds., *Rossiia v period reform Petra I*, pp. 40-102. Moscow, 1973.

Payne, Howard C. *The Police State of Louis Napoleon Bonaparte, 1851-1869*. Seattle, 1966.

Pelczynski, Z. A., ed. *Hegel's Political Philosophy, Problems and Perspectives: A Collection of New Essays*. Cambridge, England, 1971.

Pflanze, Otto. *Bismarck and the Development of Germany*. Princeton, 1963.

Pintner, Walter M. *Russian Economic Policy under Nicholas I.* Ithaca, 1967.

—— "The Social Characteristics of the Early Nineteenth Century Russian Bureaucracy." *Slavic Review,* 29, no. 3 (September 1970): 429-443.

Pintner, Walter M., and Rowney, Don Karl, eds. *Russian Officialdom from the Seventeenth through the Twentieth Centuries: The Bureaucratization of Russian Society.* Chapel Hill, 1980.

Pipes, Richard. *Karamzin's Memoir on Ancient and Modern Russia: A Translation and Analysis.* New York, 1966.

—— "Russian Conservatism in the Second Half of the Nineteenth Century." *Slavic Review,* 30 (March 1971): 121-128.

—— *Russia under the Old Regime.* New York, 1974.

Pirumova, N. M. *Zemskoe liberal'noe dvizhenie: sotsial'nye korni i evoliutsiia do nachala xx veka.* Moscow, 1977.

Pittau, Joseph. *Political Thought in Early Meiji Japan, 1868-1889.* Cambridge, 1967.

Pobedonostsev, K. P. *Reflections of a Russian Statesman.* Trans. Robert C. Long. Ann Arbor, 1968.

Pocock, J. G. A. "Languages and Their Implications: The Transformation of the Study of Political Thought." In *Politics, Language and Time: Essays on Political Thought and History,* pp. 3-41. New York, 1973.

Pokrovskii, S. P. *Ministerskaia vlast' v Rossii: istoriko-iuridicheskoe izsledovanie.* Iaroslavl', 1906.

Polievktov, M. *Nikolai I: Biografiia i obzor tsarstvovaniia.* Moscow, 1918.

Predtechenskii, A. V. *Ocherki obshchestvenno-politicheskoi istorii Rossii v pervoi chetverti XIX veka.* Moscow-Leningrad, 1957.

Presniakov, A. "Samoderzhavie Aleksandra II." In *Russkoe proshloe,* 1, no. 4 (1923): 3-20.

—— *Apogei samoderzhaviia: Nikolai I.* Leningrad, 1925.

Przeworski, Adam, and Teune, Henry. *The Logic of Comparative Social Inquiry.* New York, London, Toronto, Sidney, 1970.

Pye, Lucian W., and Verba, Sidney, eds. *Political Culture and Political Development.* Princeton, 1965.

Pypin, A. *Obshchestvennoe dvizhenie v Rossii pri Aleksandre I.* Petrograd, 1918.

—— *Russkoe masonstvo.* Petrograd, 1916.

Raeff, Marc. "The Bureaucratic Phenomena of Imperial Russia, 1700-1905." *American Historical Review,* 84, no. 2 (1979): 399-411.

—— "L'etat, le gouvernement et la tradition politique en Russie impériale avant 1861" *Revue d'histoire moderne et contemporaine*, 9 (October-December): 295-307.

———— *Michael Speransky, Statesman of Imperial Russia, 1772-1839.* The Hague, 1957.

———— *Origins of the Russian Intelligentsia: The Eighteenth Century Nobility.* New York, 1966.

———— *Plans for Political Reform in Imperial Russia, 1730-1905.* Englewood Cliffs, N.J., 1966.

———— "The Russian Autocracy and Its Officials." In H. McLean, M. E. Malia, and G. Fisher, eds., *Russian Thought and Politics*, Harvard Slavic Studies, 4:77-91. Cambridge, 1957.

———— "Some Reflections on Russian Liberalism." *The Russian Review*, 18, no. 3 (July 1959): 218-230.

———— "The Well-Ordered Police State and the Development of Modernity in Seventeenth and Eighteenth-Century Europe: An Attempt at a Comparative Approach." *American Historical Review*, 80, no. 5 (December 1975): 1221-1243.

Ransel, David L. *The Politics of Catherinian Russia: The Panin Party.* New Haven, London, 1975.

Rheinstein, Max, ed. *Max Weber on Law in Economy and Society.* Cambridge, 1954.

Riasanovsky, Nicholas V. *Nicholas I and Official Nationality in Russia, 1825-1855.* Berkeley, Los Angeles, 1969.

———— *A Parting of the Ways: Government and the Educated Public in Russia, 1801-1855.* Oxford, 1976.

Rieber, Alfred J. "Alexander II: A Revisionist View." *Journal of Modern History*, 43, no. 1 (March 1971): 42-58.

———— *The Politics of Autocracy: Letters of Alexander II to Prince A.I. Bariatinskii, 1857-1864.* Paris, The Hague, 1966.

Robbins, Richard, Jr. *Famine in Russia, 1891-1892: The Imperial Government Responds to a Crisis.* New York, London, 1975.

Rosenblum, Nancy L. *Bentham's Theory of the Modern State.* Cambridge, 1978.

Romanovich-Slavatinskii, V. E. *Dvorianstvo v Rossii s XVIII v. do otmeny krepostnogo prava.* St. Petersburg, 1870.

Rosenberg, Hans. *Bureaucracy, Aristocracy and Autocracy: The Prussian Experience, 1660-1815.* Cambridge, 1958.

———— "Political and Social Consequences of the Great Depression of 1873-1896 in Central Europe." In *Imperial Germany*, ed. James J. Sheehan. New York, London, 1976.

Rowney, Don Karl. "Higher Civil Servants in the Russian Ministry of Internal Affairs: Some Demographic and Career Characteristics, 1905-1916." *Slavic Review*, 31, no. 1 (March 1972): 101-110.

———— "Study of the Imperial Ministry of Internal Affairs in the Light of Organizational Theory." In Roger E. Kanet, ed., *The Behavior Revolution and Communist Studies*, pp. 209-231. New York, 1971.

Rubinshtein, N. L. *Russkaia istoriografiia*. Moscow, 1941.

Russkii biograficheskii slovar'. 25 vols. (incomplete). Moscow-St. Petersburg-Petrograd, 1896-1918.

Ruud, Charles A. "A. V. Golovnin and Liberal Russian Censorship, January-June 1862." *The Slavonic and East European Review*, 50, no. 119 (April 1972): 199-219.

———— "The Russian Empire's New Censorship Law of 1865." *Canadian Slavic Studies*, 3, no. 2 (Summer 1969): 235-245.

Saltykov-Schedrin, M. *Tchinovnicks: Sketches of Provincial Life*. Trans. Frederick Aston. London, 1861.

Santoni, Wayne S. "P. N. Durnovo as Minister of Internal Affairs in the Witte Cabinet: A Study in Suppression." Ph.D. dissertation, University of Kansas, 1968.

Schapiro, Leonard. *Rationalism and Nationalism in Russian Nineteenth Century Political Thought*. New Haven, London, 1967.

Scheibert, Peter. "Marginelien zu einer neuen Speranskii-Biographie." *Jahrbücher für Geschichte Osteuropas*, Band 6, Heft 4 (1958), 449-467.

———— "Uber den Liberalismus in Russland," *Jahrbücher für Geschichte Osteuropas*, Band 7, Heft 1 (1959), 34-48.

Seredonin, S. M. *Istoricheskii obzor deiatel'nosti komiteta ministrov*. 3 vols. St. Petersburg, 1902.

Sergeevich, V. *Lektsii i izsledovaniia po drevnei istorii russkago prava*. St. Petersburg, 1910.

Service, Elman R. *Primitive Social Organization: An Evolutionary Perspective*. New York, 1971.

Shaw, Stanford. *Between Old and New: The Ottoman Empire under Sultan Selim III, 1789-1807*. Cambridge, 1971.

Sheehan, James J., ed. *Imperial Germany*. New York, London, 1976.

Shepelev, L. E. *Aktsionernye kompanii v Rossii*. Leningrad, 1973.

———— *Otmenennye istoriei chiny, zvaniia i tituly v Rossiiskoi imperii*. Leningrad, 1977.

Silberman, Bernard S. *Ministers of Modernization: Elite Mobility in the Meiji Restoration, 1863-1873*. Tucson, 1964.

Silberman, Bernard S., and Harry Harootunian, eds. *Modern Japanese Leadership: Transition and Change*. Tucson, 1966.

Sinel, Allen. *The Classroom and the Chancellery: State Educational Reform in Russia under Count Dmitry Tolstoi*. Cambridge, 1973.

Skal'kovskii, K. A., ed. *Nashi gosudarstvennye i obshchestvennye deiateli*. St. Petersburg, 1890.

Skocpol, Theda. *States and Social Revolutions: A Comparative Analysis of France, Russia and China*. Cambridge, England, 1979.

Sladkevich, N. G. *Ocherki istorii obshchestvennoi mysli Rossii v kontse 50-x—nachale 60-x godov XIX veka (Bor'ba obshchestvennykh techenii v gody pervoi revoliutsionnoi situatsii)*. Leningrad, 1962.

Sliozberg, G. B. *Dorevoliutsionnyi stroi Rossii*. Paris, 1933.

Solov'ev, Iu. B. *Samoderzhavie i dvorianstvo v kontse XIX veka*. Leningrad, 1973.

Solov'ev, S. M. *Istoriia Rossii s drevneishikh vremen*. 15 vols. Moscow, 1960-1966.

Speranskii, M. M. *Proekty i zapiski*. Ed. S. N. Valk. Moscow-Leningrad, 1961.

Squire, P. S. *The Third Department: The Establishment and Practice of the Political Police in the Russia of Nicholas I*. Cambridge, England, 1968.

Starr, S. Frederick. *Decentralization and Self-Government in Russia, 1830-1870*. Princeton, 1972.

Stern, Fritz. *Gold and Iron: Bismarck, Bleichröder and the Building of the German Empire*. New York, 1977.

Sternheimer, Stephen. "Administering Development and Developing Administration: Organizational Conflict in Tsarist Bureaucracy, 1906-1914." *Canadian-American Slavic Studies*, 9, no. 3 (October 1975): 277-301.

——— "Administration and Political Development: An Inquiry into the Tsarist and Soviet Experiences." Ph.D. dissertation, University of Chicago, 1974.

Steward, Julian H. *Theory of Culture Change—The Methodology of Multilinear Evolution*. Urbana, Chicago, London, 1955.

Stites, Richard. *The Women's Liberation Movement in Russia, Feminism, Nihilism, and Bolshevism, 1860-1930*. Princeton, 1978.

Stroev, V. N. *Stoletie Sobstvennoi Ego Imperatorskago Velichestva Kantseliarii*. St. Petersburg, 1912.

Stürmer, Michael, ed. *Das kaiserliche Deutschland: Politik und Gesellschaft, 1870-1918*. Düsseldorf, 1970.

——— *Regierung und Reichstag im Bismarck-Staat 1871-1880: Cäsarismus oder Parlamentarismus*. Düsseldorf, 1974.

Sumner, B. H. *Peter the Great and the Emergence of Russia*. New York, 1962.

Szeftel, Marc. "The Form of Government of the Russian Empire Prior to the Constitutional Reforms of 1905-06." In John Shelton Curtiss, ed., *Essays in Russian and Soviet History in Honor of Geroid*

Tanquary Robinson, pp. 105-119. New York, 1963.

Taranovski, Theodore. "The Politics of Counter-Reform: Autocracy and Bureaucracy in the Reign of Alexander III, 1881-1894." Ph.D. dissertation, Harvard University, 1976.

Tatishchev, S. S. *Imperator Aleksandr II. Ego zhizn' i tsarstvovanie.* 2 vols. St. Petersburg, 1911.

Taylor, Jackson, Jr. "D. A. Tolstoi and the Ministry of Internal Affairs 1882-1889." Ph.D. dissertation, New York University, 1970.

Thaden, Edward C. *Conservative Nationalism in Nineteenth Century Russia.* Seattle, 1964.

Thompson, J. M. *Louis Napoleon and the Second Empire.* New York, 1955.

Torke, Hans-Joachim. "Die Entwicklung des Absolutismus-Problems in der sowjetischen Historiographie seit 1917." *Jahrbücher für Geschichte Osteuropas*, Band 21, Heft 4 (1973), 113-133.

———— "Continuity and Change in the Relations between Bureaucracy and Society in Russia, 1613-1861." *Canadian Slavic Studies*, 5, no. 4 (Winter 1971): 457-476.

———— "Die neuere Sowjethistoriographie zum Problem der russischen Absolutismus." *Forschungen zur osteuropäischen Geschichte*, 20 (1973): 113-133.

———— "Das russische Beamtentum in der ersten Hälfte des 19. Jahrhunderts." *Forschungen zur osteuropäischen Geschichte*, 13 (1967): 7-345.

———— *Die staatsbedingte Gesellschaft in Moskauer Reich: Zar und Zemlja in der altrussischen Herschaftsverfassung, 1613-1689.* Leiden, 1974.

Troinitskii, A. *Krepostnoe naselenie v Rossii po desiatoi narodnoi perepisi: statisticheskoe issledovanie.* St. Petersburg, 1861.

Troitskii, N. A. *Bezumstvo khrabrykh: Russkie revoliutsionery i karatel'naia politika tsarizma 1866-1882 gg.* Moscow, 1978.

———— *Tsarskie sudy protiv revoliutsionnoi Rossii: Politicheskie protsessy 1871-1880 gg.* Saratov, 1976.

Troitskii, S. M. *Finansovaia politika russkogo absoliutizma v XVIII veke.* Moscow, 1966.

———— *Russkii absoliutizm i dvorianstvo v XVIII v. Formirovanie biurokratii.* Moscow, 1974.

Tvardovskaia, V. A. "Ideolog Samoderzhaviia v period krizisa'verkhov' na rubezhe 70-80-x godov XIX v." *Istoricheskie zapiski*, 91 (1973): 217-266.

———— *Ideologiia poreformennogo samoderzhaviia (M. N. Katkov i ego izdaniia).* Moscow, 1978.

Twitchett, Denis, and Fairbank, John K., eds. *The Cambridge History of China.* Vol. 10. Cambridge, England, 1978.

Unger, Roberto Mangabeira. *Law in Modern Society: Toward a Criticism of Social Theory.* New York, 1976.

Ustiugov, N. V. "Evoliutsiia prikaznogo stroia russkogo gosudarstva v XVII v." In *Absoliutizm v Rossii XVII-XVIII vv.: Sbornik statei,* pp. 134-167. Moscow, 1964.

Val'denberg, V. *Drevnerusskiia ucheniia o predelakh tsarskoi vlasti.* Petrograd, 1916.

Varadinov, N. V. *Istoriia ministerstva vnutrennikh del.* 8 parts in 3 vols. St. Petersburg, 1858-1863.

Venturi, Franco. *Roots of Revolution: A History of the Populist and Socialist Movements in Nineteenth Century Russia.* Trans. Francis Haskell. New York, 1966.

Veselovskii, B. B. *Istoriia zemstva za sorok let.* 4 vols. St. Petersburg, 1909-1911.

Vilenskaia, E. S. "Tsar' osvoboditel' i ego zapadnye biografi." *Istoriia SSSR,* no. 1 (1966), 221-228.

Vilenskii, B. V. *Sudebnaia reforma i kontrreforma v Rossii.* Saratov, 1969.

Vinogradova, L. V. "Osnovnye vidy dokumentov senata i organizatsiia ego deloproizvodstva." Glavnoe Arkhivnoe Upravlenie SSSR, *Nekotorye voprosy izucheniia istoricheskikh dokumentov XIX nachala XXv.: Sbornik statei,* pp. 111-133. Leningrad, 1967.

Von Laue, Theodore H. *Sergei Witte and the Industrialization of Russia.* New York, 1969.

Walicki, Andrzej. *The Slavophile Controversy: History of a Conservative Utopia in Nineteenth-Century Russian Thought.* Trans. Hilda Andrews-Rusiecka. Oxford, 1975.

Walkin, Jacob. *The Rise of Democracy in Pre-Revolutionary Russia: Political and Social Institutions under the Last Three Tsars.* New York, 1962.

Ward, Robert E., and Rustow, Dankwart A., eds. *Political Modernization in Japan and Turkey.* Princeton, 1964.

Weber, Max. *The Theory of Social and Economic Organization.* Trans. Talcott Parsons. New York, 1947.

Wehler, Hans-Ulrich. *Bismarck und der Imperialismus.* Cologne, 1969.

——— *Das Deutsche Kaiserreich 1871-1918.* Göttingen, 1973.

Witte, S. Iu. *Samoderzhavie i zemstvo.* 2nd ed. Stuttgart, 1903.

Wittram, Reinhard. *Peter I: Czar und Kaiser.* 2 vols. Göttingen, 1964.

Wortman, Richard S. *The Development of a Russian Legal Consciousness.* Chicago, London, 1976.

——— "Judicial Personnel and the Court Reform of 1864." *Canadian*

Slavic Studies, 111, no. 2 (Summer 1969): 224-234.

—— "Koshelev, Samarin, and Cherkassky and the Fate of Liberal Slavophilism." *Slavic Review*, 21 (June 1962): 261-279.

Yaney, George L. "Bureaucracy and Freedom: N. M. Korkunov's Theory of the State." *American Historical Review*, 71 (January 1966): 468-486.

—— "Law, Society and the Domestic Regime in Russia in Historical Perspective." *American Political Science Review*, 59 (June 1965): 379-390.

—— "Some Aspects of the Imperial Russian Government on the Eve of the First World War." *Slavonic and East European Review*, 43 (December 1964): 68-90.

—— *The Systematization of Russian government: Social Evolution and the Domestic Administration of Imperial Russia, 1711-1905.* Urbana, 1973.

Wright, Mary Clabaugh. *The Last Stand of Chinese Conservatism, The T'ung-Chih Restoration, 1862-1864.* Stanford, Calif., 1957.

Zablotskii-Desiatovskii, A. P. *Graf P. D. Kiselev i ego vremia.* 4 vols. St. Petersburg, 1882.

Zaionchkovskii, P. A. "Gubernskaia administratsiia nakanune krymskoi voiny." *Voprosy istorii*, no. 9 (September 1975), 33-51.

—— *Krizis samoderzhaviia na rubezhe 1870-1880-x godov.* Moscow, 1964.

—— *Otmena krepostnogo prava v Rossii.* Moscow, 1954.

—— "P. A. Valuev (Biograficheskii ocherk)." In P. A. Valuev, *Dnevnik*, 1:17-54. Moscow, 1961.

—— "Podgotovka i priniatie zakona 24 noiabria 1866 g. o gosudarstvennykh krest'ianakh." *Istoriia SSSR*, no. 4 (July-August 1958), 103-113.

—— *Pravitel'stvennyi apparat samoderzhavnoi Rossii v XIX v.* Moscow, 1978.

—— *Provedenie v zhizn' krest'ianskoi reformy 1861 g.* Moscow, 1958.

—— *Rossiiskoe samoderzhavie v kontse XIX stoletiia.* Moscow, 1970.

—— ed. *Spravochnik po istorii dorevoliutsionnoi Rossii: Bibliografiia.* Moscow, 1971.

—— *Voennye reformy 1860-1870 gg. v Rossii.* Moscow, 1952.

—— "Vysshaia biurokratiia nakanune krymskoi voiny." *Istoriia SSSR*, no. 4 (July-August 1974), 154-164.

Zakharova, L. G. "Dvorianstvo i pravitel'stvennaia programma otmeny krepostnogo prava v Rossii." *Voprosy istorii*, 1973, no. 9, 32-51.

——— "Pravitel'stvennaia programma otmeny krepostnogo prava v Rossii." *Istoriia SSSR*, 1975, no. 2, 22-47.

——— "Programma otmeny krepostnogo prava redaktsionnykh komissii i dvorianstvo (Iz istorii krest'ianskoi reformy 1861 g. v Rossii)." *Vestnik moskovskogo universiteta*, historical series (8), no. 2 (1979), 22-37.

——— *Zemskaia kontrreforma 1890 g.* Moscow, 1968.

Zeldin, Theodore. *France, 1848-1945: Ambition, Love and Politics.* Vol. 1, Oxford, 1973.

——— *The Political System of Napoleon III.* New York, 1958.

Zelnik, Reginald. *Labor and Society in Tsarist Russia: The Factory Workers of St. Petersburg, 1855-1870.* Stanford, 1971.

Index